Adjustment to Severe Physical Disability

A Metamorphosis

McGraw-Hill Series in Special Education

ROBERT M. SMITH, *Consulting Editor*

Adjustment to Severe Physical Disability

A Metamorphosis

Charlene DeLoach
Bobby G. Greer

Professors of Special Education and Rehabilitation
Memphis State University

McGraw-Hill Book Company

New York St. Louis San Francisco Auckland Bogotá Hamburg
Johannesburg London Madrid Mexico Montreal New Delhi
Panama Paris São Paulo Singapore Sydney Tokyo Toronto

ADJUSTMENT TO SEVERE PHYSICAL DISABILITY
A Metamorphosis

1 2 3 4 5 6 7 8 9 0   DODO   8 9 8 7 6 5 4 3 2 1

This book was set in Times Roman by Automated Composition Service, Inc.
The editors were Phillip A. Butcher, Kaye Pace, and Barry Benjamin;
the production supervisor was John Mancia.
The cover was designed by John Hite.
R. R. Donnelley & Sons Company was printer and binder.

Library of Congress Cataloging in Publication Data

DeLoach, Charlene.
   Adjustment to severe physical disability.

   (McGraw-Hill series in special education)
   Includes index.
   1.   Physically handicapped—Psychology.
2.   Adjustment (Psychology) 3.   Physically
handicapped—Rehabilitation. I.   Greer, Bobby G.,
joint author. II. Title. [DNLM: 1.   Handicapped
—Psychology. 2.   Adaptation, Psychological.
3.   Social adjustment. 4.   Attitude to health.
HV3011 D361a]
RD798.D4   362.4′01′9   80-17612
ISBN 0-07-016281-6

ACKNOWLEDGMENTS
Excerpt from *The Presentation of Self in Everyday Life* by Erving Goffman.
   Copyright © 1959 by Erving Goffman. Used by permission of Doubleday
   & Company, Inc.
Excerpts reprinted from *Psychology Today Magazine:* "Our Failing Reverence
   for Life" by Elizabeth Hall and Paul Cameron, copyright © 1976 by
   Ziff-Davis Publishing Company, and "Reactions to the Handicapped—Sweaty Palms
   and Saccharine Words" by Jack Horn, copyright © 1975 by Ziff-Davis
   Publishing Company.

Contents

Preface

In searching for material for graduate and undergraduate courses in the psychosocial aspects of disability, the authors could not find a suitable book, one specific enough to cover the essential cognitive information and yet comprehensive enough to include the affective dimensions of rehabilitation-related work: the issues, the attitudes, the barriers, the debates. Since the ultimate goal of such work is rehabilitation of the total person, our courses were designed to give students (1) a firm grounding in theory and an overview of pertinent research, (2) a chance to explore and reassess their own attitudes toward disability and disabled persons, and (3) the opportunity to meet and interact with a variety of disabled persons, parents of disabled children, and practicing professionals.

The courses, once established, were successful. Students found them both interesting and of practical use in working with disabled clients or students. Originally designed for those working on degrees in rehabilitation counseling and special education, the courses began to attract students and practitioners in physical therapy, occupational therapy, recreational therapy, social work, guidance and counseling, and optometry.

In addition to using sections of several texts, innumerable journal articles, and the resources listed in the Appendixes, we found ourselves developing a great deal of original material not otherwise available in print. To reduce the need for volumnious note taking, we decided to write a book that would increase students' knowledge of the area, allow them to be more comfortable in face-to-face interactions with disabled persons, and enhance their ability to identify with and empathetically understand disabled individuals.

The students in these courses already are—or will soon become—the key people whose professional skills can spell the difference between failure and fulfillment in the lives of their disabled clients. But the "professional skills" needed to help humans are more than those required to repair automobiles. While future professionals are still students, therefore, they must be made aware of how their success as teachers or counselors can be profoundly affected by their personal values and attitudes. Too many persons still subscribe to the belief that effective education or rehabilitation stems from a trained professional's doing something *to* or *for* rather than *with*, those in need of his or her* services. Disabled children and adults are thinking, reacting human beings whose motivations, self-confidence, and self-esteem have been proven to be related to rehabilitation/education outcomes. In addition, future professionals must be made aware of the need for advocacy, new legislation, better public attitudes, and an improved physical environment to make desired rehabilitation/education outcomes attainable. Working with the total person means more than physical restoration, psychological adjustment, and educational services. Working with the total person involves helping that person make the transition from a medical or educational setting to one's community, and supporting legislation and barrier-removal that will allow the person to move freely within and contribute to that community.

Adjustment to Severe Physical Disability: A Metamorphosis, then, is designed for professionals-in-training, practicing professionals, and parents or families of disabled persons. The book deals with (1) the societal misconceptions that impede the physical, psychological, and social adjustment of disabled persons; (2) the effects these misconceptions have on the attitudes and effectiveness of those who work with disabled persons; and (3) existing services, laws, environmental changes, and technological advances that affect both the efforts of professionals and the lives of disabled persons. In keeping with the goals of this book, the content ranges from hard science to advocacy, from objective data to personal experiences. Case illustrations are designed to stimulate discussion and self-exploration, as well as to illuminate the factual basis for author opinions with no printed sources. Ideally, these illustrations will serve a heuristic function, leading students to conduct needed research into the psychosocial aspects of disability.

The authors wish to express their deep appreciation to the two persons whose contributions were invaluable to the completion of this book: Joyce Greer and William DeLoach. Joyce read and reviewed the books found in Appendix A, edited the final draft, and typed innumerable drafts and revisions with an un-

---

*For an explanation of the use of masculine and feminine pronouns in this book, see Chapter 2, page 15.

paralleled cheerfulness and forbearance. Bill edited the second-to-last draft, contributed to the Preface, Chapter 1, and the Conclusion, and diplomatically guided the writing efforts of Charlene. In addition the authors would like to express their appreciation to Anthony Segal, M.D., and Graves Enck, Ph.D., for the medical and sociological information they provided.

Most of Chapter 1 and all of Chapters 2, 9, 10, 12, and 13 were written by Bobby Greer. Chapters 3, 4, 5, 6, 7, 8, and 11 were written by Charlene DeLoach.

Charlene DeLoach
Bobby G. Greer

Adjustment to Severe Physical Disability

A Metamorphosis

Introduction and Overview

It is estimated that at present, 29 million Americans have some type of disabling condition.* Of this group, approximately 15 million have severe and permanent disabilities (National Center for Health Statistics, 1977). Some are born with such conditions, while others acquire them sometime during their lives. How does the presence of such severe and permanent conditions affect the lives of such persons? What has society done and what remains to be done to enhance life's opportunities to the fullest for these members of our population who find themselves faced with severe and permanent impairments? This book attempts to address these questions from both a scholarly and a personalized viewpoint.

Many works currently available have presented the problems of the disabled from what might be termed the "science of rehabilitation" perspective. In working with hundreds of students in the field of special education and rehabilitation, we have found such works often to be dry and boring for our students. A more personalized, "human interest," view appears to be more appealing. While we recognize that concepts taught should be documented by research and/or valid

---

*Throughout this text reference will be made to prevalence figures of the number of disabled persons in the United States. These figures will differ and the discrepancy will be a function of the source being quoted. The above figure (29 million) is probably the most conservative: the White House Conference on Handicapped Individuals estimates 36 million, and an article in *Newsweek* often quoted throughout this book reports 35 million.

observations, we also believe that material from which one learns about a field does not have to be bland and erudite.

In this chapter we will discuss:

   1   The background of the authors in order for the reader to fully appreciate our perspective
   2   The central thesis of this text
   3   The process of adjustment to severe physical disability, which we term *metamorphosis*

ABOUT THE AUTHORS

To comprehend the frame of reference of this text, the reader needs to know about its authors. Some say we are uniquely qualified to write this book. We work as professors teaching full time in the department of special education and rehabilitation at Memphis State University. Dr. DeLoach had polio during the epidemic of 1952, when she was beginning her senior year of high school in Wausau, Wisconsin. Dr. Greer was born with cerebral palsy in Waxahachie, Texas, a small town south of Dallas. It is our intimate experience with physical disability—not just our own disabilities but also those of the friends and clients we have worked with over the years—that makes this book special. The direct experiences we have had cannot be compared to doing course work and reading professional and scientific works *about* the disabled. Here, in brief, is a summary of our "professional" preparation.

Charlene Poch DeLoach contracted both spinal and bulbar polio. She spent three months in an iron lung, followed by nine months on a rocking bed (which provides a milder degree of respiratory assistance than an iron lung). Today, she remains totally paralyzed in the trunk, in both legs, and in all but the middle and ring fingers of her right hand, which she can close but not open. She has partial use of both arms and her left hand. She does not have to use a respirator; and after more than twenty years of pushing a manual wheelchair, she now uses an electric one.

Charlene's early rehabilitation was complicated by the fact that there were no medical rehabilitation services available to her in the beginning. Moreover, because of the severity of her disability and her gender (her Division of Vocational Rehabilitation counselor believed that college was a waste of time for women), she was denied the services of the DVR from 1953 until 1959. In 1958, however, she was sent by the March of Dimes (Polio Foundation) to Warm Springs, Georgia. There, a psychologist became very interested in Charlene's potential and lent her support to Charlene's parents in their fight to secure the services of the DVR. Eventually, Charlene's DVR counselor permitted her to take a correspondence course in freshman composition. After successfully completing that and several other courses, she was allowed to enroll in the University of Illinois at Champaign-Urbana in 1962. During a nine-year sojourn at the University of Illinois, she completed a B.S. degree in medical journalism, a master's degree in rehabilitation counseling, and by working as a research assistant, a Ph.D. degree in counseling psychology.

In 1967, Charlene married William DeLoach. Bill was paralyzed in 1957 in a diving accident and is a quadriplegic. He is currently associate professor of English at Memphis State University. The DeLoaches live in their own home without outside assistance or attendants. They travel cross-country in their custom-built Roycemobile, a modified van which they both drive from their wheelchairs.

After Bill joined the faculty at Memphis State, Charlene was a counseling psychologist at the Veterans Administration Hospital in Memphis, where she worked on the spinal cord injury ward. In 1974 she joined the faculty of the department of special education and rehabilitation, where she teaches in the rehabilitation counselor training program. She is an active participant in many organizations and was a delegate to the 1977 White House Conference on Handicapped Individuals. Among the other organizations with which she is affiliated are the American Personnel and Guidance Association, the National Rehabilitation Association, the Tennessee Governor's Committee on Employment of the Handicapped, and the Mayor's Advisory Committee on Disability and Rehabilitation Planning.

Bobby Greer was born after a very difficult labor and was initially diagnosed brain-damaged. Later his parents were informed that Bobby had spastic paralysis (cerebral palsy). He began school in a regular class and attended regular classes through the fifth grade. In the sixth grade he transferred to a special school for orthopedically handicapped children. After three years he went to and completed his public school education at a regular high school in San Antonio, Texas. Throughout adolescence, his disability, according to both professional and lay opinion, appeared to become less severe. Presently he walks with a shuffling gait, speaks with a slight slurring of words, and has some difficulty with tasks requiring a considerable degree of eye-hand coordination.

In 1960, Bobby completed a B.S. in psychology at North Texas State University. He then attended the University of Arkansas at Fayetteville, where he received his master's degree in vocational rehabilitation counseling. For one year he worked as a rehabilitation counselor at a private workshop in Dallas, Texas. He was awarded a fellowship by the United Cerebral Palsy Research Foundation to work on his doctorate at the University of Texas at Austin. It was while he attended UT that he met and married Joyce Estess. She was a business major and has no physical disability. After receiving a Ph.D. in educational psychology from the University of Texas, Bobby worked in New York and Washington, D.C., before moving to Memphis in 1967, to accept a teaching position at Memphis State University. He is currently professor of special education and rehabilitation. The Greers have two adopted children, David and Judy. Judy was born with a cleft palate and is currently receiving therapeutic procedures to minimize her speech and cosmetic defects.

Dr. Greer has received many awards, among them the Tennessee Governor's Trophy for the Handicapped Citizen of the Year and the Gallantry Award of the National Easter Seal Society. He is a member of the American Psychological Association, the National Rehabilitation Association, and the Council for Exceptional Children, and has served for nine years as a member of the Board of Directors of Sheltered Occupational Shop, a sheltered workshop for the mentally retarded. His avocation is giving lectures on nonverbal communications, and he is a member of the Institute for Nonverbal Communications Research.

It is readily apparent from this brief summary of the authors' experiences and backgrounds that they represent some similarities and contrasts. Both are physically disabled, yet one has been disabled from birth, the other from adolescence. Both are professionals in rehabilitation, yet one is male and the other female. Both are married, one to a nondisabled spouse, the other to a disabled spouse. The "blend" of experiences of the two authors, then, provides some breadth to the "disabled" perspective. We hope this work will reflect this perspective.

ABOUT THIS BOOK

The central thesis of this book is that, if certain opportunities exist, physical disablement does not spell maladjustment and tragedy. On the contrary, it can be the beginning of a new and different experience. For this to take place, however, both the individual who is disabled and persons around him must deal with certain issues as well as make certain modifications in their value systems and life styles. The organization of this book is designed to describe such modifications in the approximate sequence in which they usually occur. First we examine the intangible barriers to successful adjustment. Next we examine the implications these intangible barriers have had on various aspects of the lives of physically handicapped persons. The third section of this book deals with some of the tangible barriers which must be confronted in the form of legislation, rehabilitation programs, and community modifications. The final portion of this book discusses the processes involved in learning to live with a disability.

This book is addressed to a multiplicity of audiences. First, for students of special education or rehabilitation, it is hoped that an "inside" perspective will increase their effectiveness as teachers or counselors. Professionals in the field of helping the disabled adjust will also profit. The disabled, their family members, and their friends will benefit as well from the concepts and issues discussed here, which will assure them that they are not alone in their feelings concerning their circumstances or those of a handicapped friend or family member.

METAMORPHOSIS: THE ULTIMATE GOAL

In grappling with the barriers, problems, and processes involved in coming to terms with a physical disability, the authors found that the term *metamorphosis* came to mind.

Metamorphosis is a term borrowed from the biological sciences and refers to a transformation of form. In nature, this is often a transformation from an unattractive creature (caterpillar) to a most attractive one (butterfly). Transposing this concept to the process of adjusting to physical disability—or "stigma incorporation," as we term it—makes the process a little less simple and obvious. The metamorphosis undergone by a person with a disability is primarily an internal process, involving a transformation in how the individual sees himself or herself. Only secondarily do those on the outside have a chance to gain glimpses of this process through a changed presence on the part of the disabled individual. Such outward changes may be evidenced in a pleasant smile, a more assured posture, a brighter outlook for the future—and, in many cases, a sincere concern for others instead of, previously evidenced, a totally egocentric orientation.

In its biological framework, metamorphosis is a set, predetermined process. Some may not see this as analogous to the psychological processes involved in adjustment to disability, since such processes are not predetermined. However, the "blueprints" of nature are not always followed. Caterpillars do *not* always become butterflies and tadpoles are not always transformed to frogs! Though the process is completed more often than not, many external factors such as insecticides, predators, and the like must be considered. Analogous to this, there are external factors to be considered in adjustment to disability: what a teacher, counselor, or medical rehabilitator does or does not do can abet the metamorphosis of disabled persons, or thwart it.

The process of metamorphosis for the disabled individual is a *gradual* transformation of the individual's self-state. He or she has worked through the disabling myths to a certain degree, has learned to discriminate in evaluating the advice offered by professionals, and has begun to perceive assets, as well as liabilities, in a changed identity. As the disabled individual learns to focus upon and strengthen assets, she finds that liabilities can be safely relegated, most of the time, to the backstage areas of her world. Most of all, she discovers that life's agenda still beckons: somewhere in the flux of places to go, people to meet, things to see or hear or buy, parties to plan, careers to develop—there is an ever-evolving *raison d'être.*

This process is, despite the media stereotype to the contrary, common to the great majority of those who grow up disabled or become disabled later in life. But, more importantly, its full fruition is *not* customarily realized in the form of a Franklin Roosevelt or a Helen Keller. Such truly remarkable persons are to be admired, but should not be established as a yardstick by which the achievements of other disabled persons are judged. Metamorphosis is a beautiful aspect of man's nature; and the most beautiful of its forms are the less dramatic, quiet resolutions of ordinary Jane or John Does who, finding themselves disabled, rise above all, or most, of the barriers to be discussed in this book to take their rightful places in life in the ordinary roles of wage earner, wife or husband, coworker, customer, citizen, and taxpayer. Only the few persons known to such Jane or John Does are aware of this process. No bands play, no movies are made with them in starring roles. They merely go about their daily routines as some of the marvelous monuments to the resilience of human nature.

We, the authors, sincerely hope that the reader, be you a professional in training, a practicing professional, a disabled individual, or a friend of the disabled, will acquire a finer-tuned appreciation for the process of metamorphosis. Whether you take professional pride in observing it unfold in a client, personal pride in feeling it unfold in yourself, or an admiring pride in seeing it take place in a loved one, you will be in a better position to fully appreciate the traumas and triumphs involved.

Chapter 2

Words Related to Disability: How and How Not to Use Them

Words are the basic units of speech by which we communicate ideas and thoughts. We use them with such regularity that we rarely give thought to their origins and more subtle meanings. The study of word origins is termed "etymology." Through etymology, we are able to trace the original meanings of words and from this discover some of the more subtle implications which such words convey. We begin this book with a discussion of words so that the reader may grasp the origins and nuances of terms used frequently in reference to disabling conditions. The very words utilized in discussing such conditions are the foundations of society's perception, through time, of the status of the disabled individual.

This chapter will discuss:

1   The cognitive and affective (emotional) connotations of words
2   The origins of many commonly used terms in reference to persons with disabilities
3   The rules one should observe in using such words

WORDS: COGNITIVE AND AFFECTIVE CONSIDERATIONS

For a person embarking on a field of study, it is imperative to be familiar with the field's unique language. Even for the longtime veteran of a field, sometimes it is refreshing to examine words used every day in a new or different light. It is also important that anyone working in a field understand not only the technical meanings of certain commonly used terms, but their value-laden aspects as well. Here, we will attempt to examine the nature of words frequently used in reference to work with the severely physically handicapped individual.

As they are used in day-to-day routine, words assume one of two characteristics. First, terms (words) are used to convey certain cognitive (technical) concepts. In this cognitive mode, words, in and of themselves, have no inherent emotional overtones. For example, if a physician states that an individual is a "C6 quad," he is describing a disabling condition possessed by that individual. There are no particular indications as to the physician's personal emotional regard for the individual being described. However, there are terms, words, and phrases which connote very definite emotional overtones. Many words used to refer to the physically disabled have certain negative and/or derogatory affects (emotions) attached to them. Such terms are rarely, if ever, emotionally loaded when they are first used. Only after a period of usage do they come to acquire such value-laden meanings. Burgdorf (1980) describes this change in word usage as follows:

> The development of terminology applied to handicaps has tended to follow an evolutionary pattern. New terms are selected, generally from medical or social science, to describe a particular condition; the innovative terminology is often acclaimed as the ultimate, precise, scientific name for the condition. The new term is introduced into the vocabulary of leading professionals and gradually is absorbed into general usage. Over the course of many years, the term becomes associated with social stereotypes and acquires derogatory connotations. Eventually, it is replaced by a new term, which does not yet have any negative implications, and the process begins all over again. (p. 46)

At one time, according to Burgdorf (1980), "cripple" was acceptable medical parlance. Today it has been replaced by such terms as "orthopedically handicapped" or "mobility-impaired." Therefore, one should be cautious that terms or words one uses are current and up to date.

An example of such a connotative transition in meaning is the term "affliction" or its derivatives, such as "afflicted." According to the *Oxford English Dictionary* (*OED*), "affliction" is derived from "afflight," meaning "to dash against; to throw down; to stress" (vol. I, p. 159). The entry pertinent here defines this term as "The state of being afflicted; sore pain of body or trouble of mind; misery, distress." None of these meanings is very flattering; and in the latter definition one can glean possible origins of the "twisted body, twisted mind" concept. Of course, affliction is a term of considerable antiquity and is rarely used in present-day professional rehabilitation settings, but it still has dire connotations regarding the person of reference, and one still finds it being used by many of the uninitiated. The point here is that physically disabled individuals, upon hearing another refer to their "afflictions," will tend to disregard anything else of value the speaker may have to say because of the speaker's obvious ignorance of appropriate terminology.

Unlike the term "affliction," with its noted antiquity, many terms that come into use in the field of rehabilitation become derogatory very quickly, and therefore outdated. One such example is the term "spastic." According to Cardwell (1956), this term was once used in a generic sense to describe or refer to the neuromotor condition now known as cerebral palsy. Although this term now is reserved to refer to a specific type of cerebral palsy, for many persons the term spastic still refers generically to all such conditions, particularly in Great Britain, which today has the Spastic's Society. In current American slang, however, the term spastic has come to refer to an erratic, unpredictable, and deviant type of behavior. This term, once used to describe a specific medical syndrome, is used by contemporary young people to "put down" a deviant peer.

The person working in, or just entering, the field of rehabilitation should be aware of such finer nuances of terms. While such a person might think he is using a certain term in a technical, non-value-laden sense, he may be innocently using terms with very derogatory connotations for the person whom he is trying to help.

ORIGINS OF GENERAL TERMS

Certain terms in the field of rehabilitation are used so frequently and routinely that few persons give much thought to their origins. Yet, by examining the origins of such terms, an individual may be in a better position to evaluate the finer nuances of such terms, which extend beyond their strict technical meaning.

Older Terms

Three terms which were used in earlier times in reference to the physically disabled were "halt," "lame," and "blind." The term "halt" comes from the Old English verb *haltian*. According to the *Oxford English Dictionary,* it means "to be lame, walk lame, limp" (vol. V, p. 46). Weekly (1967) indicates that "lame" refers to the origin of a general weakness of limb, paralysis (vol. II). According to this same source (Weekly, vol. I), the term "blind" has a rather complex origin. In the oldest usage, this term is French (*blinde*) and is used in a military sense of an obstruction. Another root is the German term *blende* meaning "to make blind."

Another older term referring to the physically disabled is "cripple." As will be shown later in this chapter, this term has acquired highly emotional, derogatory overtones. The *Oxford English Dictionary* indicates this term to have part of its origins from "creep" and the Scottish phrase, *cruppen together,* meaning "contracted in body and limb" (vol. II, pp. 1177–1178). An early version of the Bible makes reference to "A creeple from his mother's wombe" (Acts XIV, 8). A more recent edition (King James Version) of this passage reads: ". . . being a cripple from his mother's womb, who never had walked" (*OED*). Burgdorf (1980) states: "And modern formulations have discarded the logic underlying the word *cripple*, which has its derivation from the root "to creep"; with its demise went the image of a helpless individual crawling and dragging himself or herself along the ground" (p. 47).

Words of More Recent Usage

All terms referring to physical and/or mental deviations assume a standard by which such deviations are measured. Most frequently, such deviations are compared to the "normal." What, then, is the origin of this term? Weekly (1967, vol. II) states that "normal" derives from the Latin *normalis*, literally meaning "carpenter's square." In the *Merriam-Webster Book of Word Histories*, the derivation of this term is traced from its Latin form to its earliest use in English, where it meant "perpendicular." Later it was used to literally mean "according to rule." The old term for a college of education, "normal school," derived from the French *école normale*, meaning "model or standard school" (p. 161). It is interesting that originally the term normal denoted "square," "straight," or "perpendicular." Some popular references within subcultures of contemporary America still reflect this—e.g., nonhomosexuals are "straight" for homosexuals, and "square" has, at one time or another, been used by many subgroups to refer to one who behaves by the rule.

Another term encountered in reference to physical disability is "ability," with its many variants. In tracing the origins of this term, one discovers its derivation from the term "able." Able has as its origin the Latin word *habilis*, meaning "fit, apt," from *habere*, meaning "to have, to hold." Related terms are "capable" and the Modern French *habilete*, which transformed into the English form "hability" in the sixteenth and seventeenth centuries (Weekly, 1967, vol. I, pp. 4–5). When "ability" is combined with the prefix "dis-," the term "disability" is formed. Funk and Wagnalls (1977) indicates that one meaning of the prefix "dis-" is "deprivation of some quality, power, rank, etc.," and that the term disable is one example of this particular meaning (p. 377). This same source defines disability as ". . . that which disables; lack of ability, inability; legal incapacity or inability to act" (p. 377). Many of the terms we use currently—e.g., ability, disability, able, habilitate, rehabilitate—all go back to the terms *habilis* (fit) and *habere* (to have). "Disability," as a term referring to the state of a person, then, denotes one who is unfit or a "have-not." Other terms we use, like "rehabilitate," then refer to an attempt to make fit or provide something lacking.

The terms "handicap" or "handicapped" came into use in this field in the late 1800s or early 1900s. Prior to that time, their usage was from a totally different realm. According to the *Oxford English Dictionary* (vol. V, pp. 62–63), the term "handicap" was ". . . of obscure origin. . . . it appears to have originated in the phrase 'hand i' cap' or 'hand in the cap'. . . ." *The Merriam-Webster Book of Word Histories* elaborates upon the history of this term by citing its use by Samuel Pepys in 1660 to denote a type of betting sport. Later, according to this source, a bartering ritual was devised in which two barterers (traders) placed a certain amount of forfeit money in a cap. A third party to this ritual (the umpire) also placed money in the cap as well as setting the additional amount the party with the less desirable goods had to pay if the trade was agreed to, thus, "hand in cap." A further elaboration on this procedure is described in this source (p. 102); here, it is our intention to illuminate the origin of the term. Also, the *Oxford English Dictionary* indicates that later on, in the sport of horse racing, weights were placed on the faster horses to give the slower ones a better chance of winning. The term only later came to be used in the sense of ". . . to place anyone at a disadvantage of any embarrassment, impediment, or disability; to weight unduly" (*OED*, p. 63). It is somewhat unclear when and who developed the use of the term "handicapped" as a synonym for physical or mental impairment. Oberman (1965), in his text on the history of the vocational rehabilitation system, states that the Red Cross first established a Bureau for the Handicapped in St. Louis after World War I.

The term "stigma" (past participle, "stigmatized") has come into usage recently primarily due to the writings of Erving Goffman (1963). Stigma, according to the *Oxford English Dictionary*, originates from the Greek for a "mark made by a pointed instrument, brand"; thus, the English derivative "stick." One definition of stigma proffered by the *Oxford English Dictionary* is "A mark of disgrace or infamy; a sign of severe censure or condemnation; regarded as impressed on a person or thing; a brand." Despite these rather dire, ominous definitions, Goffman's use of the term has recently come into vogue, and this term, along with the concepts postulated through Goffman's treatise on this subject, will be referred to frequently in the present text. In this book, the term will refer to the social connotation brought about by possessing a physical disability.

The terms handicapped and disabled are widely used in the current field dealing with the rehabilitation of the severely physically impaired. Some authorities, such as Wright (1960), state that disabled, or disability, is the preferred term. Wright's reasoning is that disability denotes a physical condition, whereas handicap, or handicapped, denotes social and other types of encumbrances placed upon the person as the result of the physical condition. In a sense, Wright is correct: disability as traced here seems to imply a physical condition, while handicap is of a social origin. Burgdorf (1980), on the other hand, traces the origin of these two terms from semantic, social, and legal viewpoints and appears to prefer the term handicap. It should be noted that the impetus to use handicapped is partly sanctioned by organizations established by the American public, such as the White House Conference on Handicapped Individuals. The two authors of this textbook disagree to some extent with one another on which is *the* preferred term! To resolve this situation they have decided for the purposes of the total book that disability (disabled) and handicap (handicapped) will be used interchangeably. We are not alone or arbitrary in making such a decision. Burgdorf (1980) states:

> In an attempt to find a path out of what one author has called "the semantic morass of what constitutes impairment, disability, or handicap" the approach in the remainder of this book reflects a decision to not shy away from the use of the word *handicapped* in referring to persons with physical and mental impairments. Furthermore, if the term *disabled* is used, it will be considered as interchangeable with *handicapped*. This approach is, as statutes and court decisions on subsequent pages demonstrate, fully consistent with the choices of terminology employed by lawmakers and courts. (p. 10)

In this section we have explored the origins of several of the more general terms used in reference to the physically handicapped. This does not begin to exhaust the number of terms whose origins might be equally as interesting. Terms such as "infirmity," "impediment," and "impairment," to mention a few, could have been explored. However, the terms explored here are those which (1) are used frequently in the literature and (2) will be used throughout this text. The reader is encouraged to pursue the origins of other terms for his own enlightenment. The primary objective here is to make the reader aware that the words one uses are frequently taken for granted and that in-depth exploration of their origins can improve one's perspective on the affective dimensions of such terms.

WORD USAGE: GUIDELINES FOR EFFECTIVE COMMUNICATION

The ultimate purpose of this discussion of words, their origins and current connotations is to assist the reader in communicating effectively with physically disabled persons. In the present section, an attempt is made to formulate some general guidelines for persons who, professionally and/or socially, interact with the disabled. These guidelines cannot be documented through citation of authoritative references. Rather, they constitute some general rules which the authors feel, through their personal and professional experiences, will help facilitate better relations between the physically disabled and individuals who desire to interact with them. To accomplish this task and to highlight the importance of such rules, it is necessary to discuss several concepts postulated by Goffman (1963) in his work *Stigma: Notes on the Management of Spoiled Identity.*

Goffman first postulates the concepts of the "own" and the "wise." In his frame of reference, the term "own" constitutes a group of individuals who share the same or similar stigmata, here referring to a physical disability. The "wise," on the other hand, are individuals who do not possess such stigmata, but who are viewed by the stigmatized group (the "own") as possessing knowledge, empathy, etc., which set them apart from other nonstigmatized persons. The "wise" may be spouses of stigmatized persons, parents, friends, close social acquaintances, or professionals who have developed rapport with the stigmatized group through their day-to-day work with them. It is critical to note that the status of being "wise" is *bestowed* on selected individuals by the stigmatized group. This status is to be earned by such individuals through the quality of their interaction with the group.

How this happens entails the understanding of two other concepts postulated by Goffman. When any two individuals interact, they are, according to Goffman, executing performances, much like actors in a drama. A good actor (interactant) executes a believable performance. Translated into day-to-day interaction, this means that one individual is perceived as sincere or "real" by the other. A poor actor (interactant) executes a less than believable performance. In day-to-day interaction, this translates into such an individual's coming across as insincere or "phony." The sincere impression is termed by Goffman "creditable." The phony impression is termed "discreditable." Individuals giving sincere ("crediting") impressions will earn the status of the "wise." Individuals being perceived as insincere ("discrediting") are considered not "wise," thus, not to be trusted. The rules to follow concerning terminology are designed to reduce the chances of individuals' being perceived as discreditable by the physically disabled with whom they seek to interact. Word usage is, in this sense, one critical aspect of achieving "wise" status.

1 *Do not be overly sensitive regarding the inappropriateness of everyday expressions.* When interacting with the disabled, many persons feel they are committing *faux pas* (social "no–no's") if they "slip" and use expressions such as "See what I mean" with someone who may be blind. Another example would be, "Let's run over and get something to eat" when speaking to someone who is in a wheelchair. To the naive person, that would on the surface be extremely insensitive. In certain cases, within specific contexts, it may be. But in the majority of instances where expressions such as these are used, they pass for everyday expressions with no belittling intent on the part of the speaker. In actuality, if no such intent is present, the use of these expressions by a nondisabled person speaking with a disabled person is quite a compliment to the latter! It indicates that the speaker feels quite comfortable with the individual and does not consider her first and foremost a disabled person. In a less healthy interaction the speaker may consider the disabled interactant highly fragile, with feelings which are easily hurt and may feel compelled to be highly vigilant in censoring statements that may indirectly refer to an ability which is impaired or lacking in the disabled person. In very close relationships between nondisabled and disabled persons or in friendships between individuals with different types of disabilities, such *faux pas* become humorous and are taken to be indicators of close, warm friendships. One of the authors, who has cerebral palsy, kids his nondisabled spouse when she says, "Don't shake the bed!" when he is dressing and she is still attempting to sleep. The critical factor here is a feeling of close, friendly feelings, even in casual relations. If the everyday expression is used innocently and with no other intent, the speaker should feel no guilt. Even if the disabled person becomes ruffled or upset by the remark, the cause may be more the disabled person's oversensitivity and thus *his* problem to resolve.

2   *Be aware of what terms are "in," as well as what terms are considered antiquated or demeaning by the disabled, but be very cautious when using them.* Like all subgroups, the disabled frequently use "in" terms for efficient communication and/or building group identity. Some naive persons prematurely assume they have achieved a "wise" status and use certain "in" terms too freely. If these persons are not really considered to be "wise," such usage can be counterproductive, i.e., the speakers are discredited.

What are some examples of such "in" terms? They vary from locale to locale, and change in usage from one period of time to another. Currently, some physically disabled persons on crutches or in wheelchairs refer to themselves or others as "gimps," meaning impaired in ambulation. In isolation, "gimp" or "gimpie" is very belittling. As an "in" term it is highly acceptable with certain groups. For a nondisabled person to use this term is grossly inappropriate unless he or she has been awarded a high status within the disabled group in question. The same will be true of a "normie" (the "in" term meaning a nondisabled person) using any of the terms to follow. Most disabled individuals dislike the term cripple; however, another "in" term with similar meaning to "gimp" would be "crip," a contraction of cripple. In recent years, the term "spas" or "spazz" (sic) is an "in" term with persons having certain neuromotor problems. Within groups comprising largely the severely visually limited (the blind), members often refer to one another as "blinks." Persons who use crutches to ambulate often refer to the crutches as "sticks." Many disabled persons have varying terms for referring to the nondisabled. "Normie," "A.B." (meaning able-bodied), and "walkie" (specifically used by persons in wheelchairs) all make reference to the nondisabled.

For specific groups in specific locales there are a myriad of other similar terms. It is the responsibility of anyone desiring close interaction with disabled persons in general, or with a distinct disability group, to ascertain the local "in" terminology in their locale. It is also imperative for such an individual to keep up with changes in terms and the finer nuances within the group of interest, for such terms rarely remain static, changing as the group sees the need for retaining their "own" vocabulary.

An individual should not only be judicious in the use of "in" terms but should also exercise discretion in using outdated, antiquated terminology. Terms and phrases such as "crippled," "deaf and dumb," "defective," "maimed," and "fits" (referring to convulsive seizures) are all to one extent or another out of date. As such, these terms are perceived by the disabled as "inflammatory put-downs." Cochran (1977) lists several pejorative (negative) terms along with some more preferred terms. Those which he classifies as pejorative in connotation are: "unfortunate," "victim," "afflicted," "sufferer," "wheelchair-bound," "confined," "restricted," and "normal," which implies that the disabled are abnormal. Terms more preferred in usage, according to this source, are: "able-bodied" as opposed to "normal," "crutch user," and "wheelchair-ambulator." Cochran emphasizes that crutches *free* persons, they do not restrict; and that wheelchairs afford mobility. In general, the users of such pejorative terms are labeled un-"wise" unless they clearly indicate awareness of the terms' derogatory connotations.

Despite these cautions, however, the person desiring the achievement of a "wise" status with the physically disabled should be cognizant of all such "in" terms as well as antiquated terminology. Such knowledge serves two purposes. First, the person will know what handicapped individuals are saying when they use these terms in conversation. For example, individuals in wheelchairs who drive will often make reference to being "parked in." The phrase means that someone in another automobile has parked so close to their car that they do not have room enough to enter their own vehicle and must wait for the other person to move the blocking car. Second, such knowledge affords the person the opportunity to use such terms in appropriate context and thus give a creditable knowledge of the lingo.

3   *Be extremely careful in using any reference to "normal" people.* The main thrust of this text is that, other than experiencing certain unique inconveniences accompanying physical impairment, persons with physical handicaps lead *normal* lives. Any references comparing them to "normal" people negates this concept. "You do that just like a normal person!" may be intended as a compliment, but really implies, "You are not normal." "How do you think normal people react to . . . ?" is another discrediting use of the term normal. It would be much better to refer to the "nondisabled" or even "normies" if the speaker is relatively certain of his "wise" status. With specific disability groups, terms more specific than nondisabled may be more appropriate. For example, the terms "seeing" with the visually impaired, "hearing" with the deaf, and "walkie" with the wheelchair-bound in most contexts would be more appropriate than "normal."

4   *Attempt to stay away from "zoo keeper" phraseology.* In the chapter on the "omniscience of the experts," the concept of "zoo keeper" thinking is detailed. Here, it is intended to refer to un-"wise" persons attempting to convince a physically disabled person of their expertise on the "trials and tribulations" of being handicapped through their close association with other persons who are disabled. "A lot of my friends in wheelchairs . . . ," "A good buddy of mine who is deaf . . . ,"

"Many of my clients who are . . . ," and "My mother who teaches cerebral palsied children . . ." are all such references. To the disabled person, such references are not impressive, to say the least! These references are the racial equivalent to "A lot of my best friends are black (or Jewish, or Chicano, *ad infinitum*)." Individuals are individuals. The disabled person frequently cannot identify with another person merely because they both have similar physical impairments. This is not intended to discourage a person from making known the fact that he has some knowledge of the social situation of a physically handicapped individual. It is the manner in which such knowledge is conveyed that is the focal point of this guideline. The major offense of such references is the fact that the individual is trying to document his authority on a subject based merely on social acquaintance or, more unjustifiably, on the fact that the individual has had a "vast" amount of personal and/or professional experience with individuals who have experienced some physical impediment. Such expertise can be conveyed more appropriately by asking specific questions on topics, problems, etc. not ordinarily recognized by "normies." For example, "What has been your experience in handling . . . type of problems?" The blank is filled in with a specific problem common to individuals with certain disabilities.

5 *Don't be afraid to admit ignorance on a topic or subject when it seems necessary to understand the gist of a conversation.* Too often, individuals feign knowledge of topics that they do not possess. In such instances, an individual can actually give a more creditable impression by stating a lack of knowledge. This, of course, is not always the case. For instance, one individual with a spinal cord injury returning to the spinal cord ward of the hospital in which he was confined attempted to convince his buddies on the ward that a particular psychologist did not know a "damn thing" because the psychologist was ignorant of what a Davol bag* was! However, most times the general rule is: when in doubt of one's knowledge, inquire about the subject. Sometimes you may be taken as a fool, but the majority of times you will be perceived as "real." There is a psychological principle operating here that is critical to a healthy interaction. Too often, the physically handicapped are on the taking end of an exchange. By asking such questions, the other person is affording the physically impaired individual an opportunity to be helpful, i.e., to give or provide information—a more active and sometimes desirable role.

6 *When in doubt, use everyday language.* Nothing is so discreditable as using special terminology erroneously. If a person has doubts concerning the exact meaning of a word or phrase, he shouldn't attempt to use it. In a somewhat similar vein, one should not try to dazzle others with his terminological prowess. Once again, the reader is cautioned not to use outdated terms as everyday language. "Disabled" is currently more desirable than "crippled," "handicap" is currently more desirable than "affliction," etc. Within these general boundaries, however, it is better to be simple and clear rather than technical and unclear.

Another reason for using simpler language when in doubt is that linguistic revisionism is an ongoing phenomenon. "Linguistic revisionism" is a phrase denoting the tendency within specialized fields to constantly change terms, from a

---

*A type of device for disposing of waste material for individuals with bladder incontinence.

once acceptable form to a new, more acceptable one. The force behind such change is often some organization which feels that the older term has become stigmatized within society as a whole, so that a newer, less stigmatizing one is desirable. For example, in the area of mental retardation, what was once referred to as "mongolism" is now termed "Down's syndrome." Various persons working with people who have seizure-type disabilities now prefer the term "episodic convulsive disorder" to the term "epilepsy." Persons working in the area of visual disorders are now beginning to use the term "sightless" in some instances in place of "blind." With such ongoing trends in term usage, it is best to stick to simple language.

WORD USAGE WITHIN THIS BOOK

As in any specialized area, the study of the psychosocial aspects of severe physical disability has a language all its own. This language consists of conventional terms as well as a unique code system of acronyms, a type of linguistic shorthand used for efficiency. For example, instead of having to state the concept "activities of daily living" or, even more cumbersome, the activities involved in dressing one's self, grooming one's self, household maintenance tasks, meal preparation, etc., all this is conveyed in the acronym "ADL." Since these conventional terms and acronyms are used frequently throughout this text as well in as the profession itself, any serious student should acquire familiarity with their special meanings. For this purpose, Appendix A provides a listing of such terms and acronyms with their definitions for easy reference.

Terminological Conventions in This Book: A Disclaimer

Two conventions of word usage followed in this book should be mentioned. First, in reference to equality between the sexes, thought was given to the "he vs. she" convention in regard to its usage here. The authors considered using he/she, him/her type references. However, in other documents, such a convention made for awkward reading. Therefore, when a specific individual is not concerned, we have decided to randomly alternate between such usages. Therefore, "he" will be used in one place and the next such usage may be either "he" or "she." In certain passages, however, the authors will make specific references to themselves. It should be remembered that one is female, the other male. Therefore, one such reference using "she" may be followed by another using "he."

Another convention used in this text deals with references to those about whom the book is written: individuals with disabilities. There is a definite semantic difference between the phrase "individual with a disability" and "disabled individual." In the former, the object of reference is an individual first and only secondarily does he have a disability. In the latter, the individual is first disabled, then an individual. Despite the philosophic and semantic chasm between these two phrases, the sheer frequency of references in this book dictates that "disabled (handicapped) individual" be used for convenience. The authors are well aware of the difference in meaning and in their oral communications attempt to use the former phrase. Similarly, in places we use "the disabled" or "the handicapped" for ease of reference, but again, we are not insensitive to the not-so-subtle nuances of this usage.

Chapter 3

The First Disabling Myth: The Deification of Normality

Several myths surrounding the severely physically disabled pervade the fabric of our society, affecting the way nondisabled persons view, relate to, and treat persons with physical limitations. These myths also affect the way disabled persons view their own disabilities, impeding their adjustment and ability to assume cherished social roles and enjoy life to the fullest. Because these myths, these false *ideas*, can be more debilitating than *physical limitations* they are best described as the "disabling myths."

The most pervasive myth, the "deification of normality," contends that one must be physically normal to lead a productive and self-fulfilling life. Adherents of this myth would be amazed to learn that a totally blind woman, like Susan S., can manage a household and raise children, or that a man with cerebral palsy, like Clarence M., can marry an attractive, nondisabled woman and successfully practice law.

What differentiates Clarence and Susan from similarly disabled persons who are dependent, depressed, and withdrawn from society is their highly developed self-care, home management, and interpersonal coping skills. Clarence and Susan face their limitations realistically without becoming overwhelmed by the changes these limitations bring about.

This chapter will:

1 Explore the roots of the "deification of normality" myth and the effect this myth has on the adjustment of disabled persons
2 Trace how this myth influences the attitudes and behaviors of persons in rehabilitation-related professions
3 Introduce coping techniques and strategies which will be discussed in detail in Chapter 13

DISABLING SOCIETAL ATTITUDES

A society's interpretations of the differences among its members can influence the growth of the individual within that society. In 1925 the British *Cripples Journal* conducted a historical analysis of disabled personages such as Byron, Pope, Milton, and Beethoven, and concluded that the implications of a disability depend on society's response to disability. Long before the days of antibiotics, computerized reading devices, and battery-powered hearing aids, restrictions imposed by societal attitudes were recognized as more "disabling" than any loss of physical capabilities.

This is why the lives of disabled persons have varied from society to society and from period to period within the same society. One clue to how a society treats its disabled members is how its dominant religion translates disability into spiritual terms. Disability is a momentous event, and persons with nonscientific mentalities feel compelled to assign it some spiritual *raison d'être*, as they do the other major events of birth, marriage, parenthood, and death. In such religions' interpretations, a disabled person may be seen as someone possessed, bearing the stigma of committed or referred sin—or as someone blessed, bearing the sign of God's grace.

Apart from religious influences are a society's secular interpretations of the differences among its members. Do these differences reveal strength or weakness of will, desirable or undesirable character traits? In our present society, surveys of attitudes toward disabled persons indicate that while verbalized attitudes are positive, unverbalized attitudes remain influenced by hostile prejudice.

AVERSION TO THE DISABLED: IS IT NATURAL?

The common rationale for aversive feelings and repressive behaviors toward those with discernible physical differences is that these are instinctive responses to disability, that only our being civilized prevents us from eliminating our defective fellows as do primitive peoples and wild animals. Animal psychologists and cultural anthropologists, however, deny the existence of instinctive hostile attitudes toward those who deviate physically. For example, paralyzed hens maintain their position in the pecking order and wolves neither attack nor avoid other pack members with physical abnormalities (Wright, 1960). Among the primitive tribes studied by Maisel are several which neither destroy nor ostracize disabled members: the Palaung, who believe that persons born with certain birth defects, i.e., extra fingers or a harelip, are extremely lucky; the Semang of the Malay Peninsula, whose chief relied on a long stick to move about; and the Ponape of the Eastern Carolines, who treat disabled and emotionally disturbed children no differently than other children (Maisel, 1953).

Linguist Peter Farb (1975) describes an outstanding example of a primitive people's accommodation and assimilation of persons with one particular disability. While studying tribes in the Amazon River Valley, Farb discovered one tribe which uses both speech and a linguistically complex sign language, so that hearing members can communicate with those who cannot hear. As Farb observed, when hearing members are talking and a deaf member joins them, everyone uses the communal sign language, according the deaf full social inclusion.

THE PHENOMENON OF HUMAN ADAPTABILITY

Another factor contributing to the myth that disabled individuals are incapable of leading productive, self-satisfying lives is the link which once existed between physical normality and the ability to survive. Cavemen with crushed or amputated limbs who did not succumb to infection or shock became easy game for the predators of their time. If they protected themselves by not venturing out for food, they could expect little assistance from their fellows who themselves struggled to survive.

But the world has changed. With advances in technology and medicine, the average life span has increased from 20 years at the time of Christ to more than 70 today. These advances have affected the lives of the disabled and nondisabled alike. Innumerable persons with hypertension, diabetes, emphysema, or kidney failure are alive today because of some drug or medical treatment that would have been considered extraordinary twenty-five years ago. With reduced infant and geriatric mortality rates, the person with no disability is becoming a rarity. No longer must one have four limbs, good vision, keen hearing, and well-coordinated movements to establish a satisfying life.

The active, well-adjusted, severely disabled person of the late twentieth century is a living example of the phenomenon of human adaptability. Within the span of ancient to recent history, their innate coping skills, coupled with the efforts of helping professionals, family, and friends, have made it increasingly possible for the disabled to reenter society successfully. Today, while physical normality makes survival easier, it is not necessary to be physically normal in order to survive.

PHYSICAL SURVIVAL OF THE SEVERELY DISABLED

Physical survival of the severely disabled depends on two abilities: the ability to overcome life-threatening aspects of disabling conditions and the ability to perform routine tasks of everyday life. Surviving the acute stage of accident or illness to live as a healthy, though permanently disabled, person is not difficult for someone who obtains appropriate medical care. Successful surgical techniques range from putting in bypasses for persons with occluded coronary arteries to installing shunts to control the cerebral spinal fluid in children born with spina bifida. Antibiotics prevent, eliminate, or control urinary infections in persons paralyzed with polio, or respiratory infections in persons with advanced muscular dystrophy. The severely disabled, if taught medical self-management and if given adequate treatment in health-crisis situations, can live long, healthy lives.

Physical survival in terms of environmental coping skills is also within the capabilities of all but the most severely disabled. Chapter 11 covers adaptive devices and accessibility standards that allow persons with some strength in their arms or with full use of their legs and feet to live independently or with a modicum of help. Government publications describe, and the Chicago Museum of Science and Industry has on display, kitchens convenient for persons with severe cardiac conditions. The Job Development Laboratory at George Washington University designs modifications and equipment that permit persons functioning as quadriplegics, i.e., with rheumatoid arthritis, cerebral palsy, multiple sclerosis, Friedreich's ataxia, poliomyelitis, etc., to function in many competitive jobs once closed to them. Parents who are blind tie bells on their infants' shoes to keep track of where their children are, and parents who are deaf use voice-activated flashing lights to alert them to their children's cries. The ways in which persons survive and survive well are limited only by their own imaginations and the imaginations of professionals who work to solve the practical living problems of the disabled.

Fortunately, in today's world, few persons hunt for or raise their own food, make their own garments, or build and repair their own homes. In a society which is specialized better to meet the survival needs of its members, it is less important to be able to perform basic survival tasks than to be able to purchase the talents of persons who perform those tasks for others.

Our concrete urban jungles, bewailed by Toffler in *Future Shock* (1971), come close to being the promised land for the severely disabled, while unspoiled, natural settings can be a treacherous Eden for those who cannot see, walk, or hear. Given a ramped or street-level home and an accessible community (see Chapter 11), persons with mobility problems can live, love, and labor with little inconvenience from their physical limitations. Even fewer adaptations are necessary for those with slight incoordination or sensory problems.

Unfortunately, physical well-being and a suitable occupation are not enough to fulfill disabled persons any more than they are enough to fulfill anyone else. As Maslow (1970) points out, human beings require social recognition, esteem, and a sense of belonging to prosper psychologically. If they are to live fulfilling lives, the severely disabled must have the opportunity to socialize to the extent they wish, to engage in pastimes that are within their capabilities, and to feel good about themselves as persons. This process of psychological adjustment can be difficult when the disabled individuals live among people who find it more difficult to adjust to the disability than the disabled themselves.

PSYCHOLOGICAL ADJUSTMENT OF THE SEVERELY PHYSICALLY DISABLED

Many nondisabled people find it difficult to understand how a disabled person can be fully aware of the ramifications of the loss of normal appearance and/or functioning and still be well-adjusted emotionally. In their survey of the extensive literature on psychological adjustment of the disabled, Roessler and Bolton (1978) concluded, as did authors of similar surveys before (Barker, Wright, Meyerson, and Gonick, 1953; Pringle, 1964; Wright, 1960; Shontz, 1975; and McDaniel, 1976), that: (1) there are no specific personality traits associated with specific disabilities, i.e., the deaf are not significantly more paranoid than hearing people; (2) there is no proven relationship between severity of disability and psychological adjustment, i.e., the partially sighted are not more well-adjusted than the blind; and (3) there is no uniform degree to which similarly disabled persons adjust. In short, the relationship between disability and personality is inconsistent, because what a disability means to a person depends on how he interprets that disability, not on how severe the disability is.

In Chapter 12, stigma incorporation is offered as a theory which enhances understanding of the adjustment process. In this section, the multitude of individual reactions to disabling conditions will be discussed in terms of stress theory.

Disability and Stress

Stress is defined as a situation which places an adjustive demand on an individual. When situations are weighted to indicate the relative strength of their adjustive demands, the death of a spouse equals 100 and Christmas equals 12 (Dohrenwend and Dohrenwend, 1974), but these weights vary for each individual. Therefore, in assessing the stress of any one situation for any one individual we must consider those factors which affect severity of stress: (1) how long the situation lasts, (2) the individual's tolerance for stress, (3) multiplicity of stressful situations, (4) the individual's perception of the situation, and (5) whether stress is combined with threat.

1   The longer a situation persists, the greater the stress. Death of a loved spouse is more stressful because the void created by his loss takes a longer time to fill. Christmas is less stressful because it is a season which passes quickly.

2   Individuals vary in their tolerance for stress, as has been observed in newborns. One child may react violently to a loud sound or sudden loss of support, while another barely reacts to the same stimulus.

3   The greater the number of stressful situations, the greater the stress. If one loses one's spouse, one's job, and one's home in a fire, the stress will be greater than if any of these events occurred in isolation.

4   How a person interprets a situation is a major factor in severity of stress. A woman who feels indifferent to her husband may experience little stress upon his death, while a woman having a close relationship with her husband may suffer stress severe enough to precipitate suicide.

5   Finally, if stress is combined with threat, the severity of the perceived stress will be greater than in a nonthreatening situation. A flat tire on the way to an important appointment can create stress. But the stress is compounded if the flat tire occurs in an undesirable neighborhood at night.

Any disability creates stress because it places many adjustive demands on an individual. Take for example the adjustive demands placed on an individual who loses his sight. These demands are physical—learning Braille or how to use a white cane or guide dog; psychological—altering assumptions of reality to incorporate the fact of a permanent disability; and social—developing new interests involving friends, because going to foreign films with subtitles is no longer satisfying. However, the severity of the stress experienced by a blind individual will vary in terms of the five factors mentioned above. Disability-related stress might be greater for someone who is told that his blindness is permanent, caused by a malignant tumor, and whose fiancée breaks their engagement than for someone who is told that he might recover some vision and whose fiancée is supportive. Nevertheless, it is impossible to predict any individual's reaction with total accuracy. The first person may have wanted to end his engagement and may believe that whatever happens is God's will, while the second person might be unable to tolerate even one week without being able to see.

Sources of Stress

The three major sources of stress are frustrations, conflicts, and pressures. Frustrations are obstacles which block a person's attempts to go where he wants to go and do what he wants to do. In general, frustrations are either environmental or social. Environmental frustrations can be major, as when floods or tornadoes destroy accustomed sources of food and shelter, or minor, as when the television stops working during the last game of the World Series. For the disabled, architectural barriers are common environmental frustrations (see Chapter 11). For example, shortly after the DeLoaches moved to Memphis, they discovered that the wheelchair repair shop where they went to have a flat tire fixed was not accessible—a situation not without a certain irony. After asking for help into and out of the shop, they decided to stop somewhere to eat, but didn't know which restaurants were accessible. As they drove along a main thoroughfare, they came to one restaurant with no curb cut, another with steps at the entrance, and a seafood restaurant with no parking suitable for a wheelchair van. Finally, six miles farther and half an hour later, they found a steak house with a ramp and ample parking. Had they not used wheelchairs or driven a special vehicle, the DeLoaches could have eaten and returned home long before they actually found a restaurant they could enter.

    Social frustrations are subtle obstacles imposed by society which prevent an individual's full participation within that society. For the disabled, social exclusion is the most stressful social frustration because it is based on covert understandings and not on overt social regulations, which could be altered by legislation, or on mastery of certain rules of behavior (Goffman, 1963).

    The second source of stress arises from conflict situations. A disabled person may be forced to choose between two equally desirable goals—taking a job she wants or retaining her disability pension—or between two equally undesirable goals—accepting a job she doesn't want or having no job at all. The stress in conflict situations arises from the need to make a decision between two choices, neither of which is completely satisfactory.

    The final source of stress comes from internal and external pressures which shape behaviors. Internal pressures arise from a person's own expectations, while external pressures arise from the expectations of others. A permanently disabled person who is surrounded by those who believe he can walk, see, or hear again will experience a great deal of stress, especially if he, too, believes his disability could be overcome if only he tried hard enough.

Stress for the severely disabled varies from stress for the nondisabled in several ways. First, the disabled encounter more potential sources of stress (Chapter 11). Second, the disabled encounter stressful situations more frequently. Since, according to stress theorists, excessive stress leads to emotional maladjustment, why is there no proven relationship between disability and psychopathology? The answer lies in the ability of human beings to utilize psychological defenses in stressful situations until they develop the competencies to deal with those situations.

Psychological Mechanisms for Dealing with Disability-Related Stress

To help simplify a complex area of human behavior, the psychological mechanisms used to deal with stress are typically divided into two categories: the ego defense mechanisms and the task-oriented mechanisms (Coleman, 1964).

The Ego Defense Mechanisms When a person encounters an extremely stressful situation, his unconscious response is to protect his self-concept by distorting reality. Ego defense mechanisms ward off facts which, if comprehended in their entirety, might be too overwhelming to integrate easily. Although lists of these mechanisms sometimes conflict, in all of them ego defense mechanisms share several common characteristics: (1) they operate on an unconscious level; (2) they protect an individual's emotional integration by distorting reality; (3) they are used by everyone and are, therefore, standard ways of reacting to stress; and (4) because they operate on an unconscious level and distort reality, they are not effective in removing or reducing sources of stress permanentiy, or in allowing a person to modify his self-concept to incorporate immutable facts.

Immediately after the onset of disability, the ego defenses are essential to beginning the adjustment process. These mechanisms allow persons to incorporate the fact of disability gradually without becoming overwhelmed by an immediate grasp of the ramifications of their altered physical conditions.

Cobb (1973) describes ten mechanisms which she contends disabled persons use in the process of coming to terms psychologically with a severe physical disability. Although Cobb describes these ten mechanisms in a certain order, she cautions that not every person utilizes each mechanism or progresses in an orderly fashion through the hierarchy. During the course of any one day a person may bring each of these mechanisms into play, but as she becomes more accepting of her disability, overreliance on mechanisms toward the beginning of the hierarchy diminishes and reliance on those toward the end increases. According to Cobb, the sequence of mechanisms used in the process of metamorphosis is as follows.

Denial Like one who is told that he has a terminal illness or that someone he loves has died, a person acquiring a disability reduces the impact of his situation by simply denying its reality. Usually a newly disabled person believes that he is dreaming, that not being able to see, hear, or move is a nightmare from which he will awaken. As days pass, however, and the disability persists, he will pass into the second stage of denial—denying that the disability is permanent. This second stage can last for years, causing a person to concentrate on seeking a cure, rather than on learning how to live with a disability. As Cobb points out, if a person continues to deny that the disability exists and is permanent, rehabilitation cannot be totally successful. For example, Neil K. lost his sight in a car accident while he was drunk. Neil believed God was punishing him and argued that there was no need for therapy because when God was through, God would restore his sight. In working with someone like Neil, one possible approach is to convince him that the skills learned in therapy might be useful until God decides to act.

Withdrawal   To shut out information that might contradict the belief that a disability is not permanent, people often withdraw from those around them, becoming ever more egocentric in their concerns. Sometimes withdrawal allows a person to begin assessing her situation, to begin healing psychologically. Other times withdrawal may presage a deep depression.

Regression   Regression is the mechanism whereby a person begins to behave as she did at an earlier age. A man or woman with economic and familial responsibilities, after acquiring a disability, may abandon mature behaviors, thus shedding the burdens of adulthood. Once some of the more overwhelming problems are at least partially overcome, the newly disabled person may regain enough confidence to again act responsibly.

Repression   Repression is the mechanism whereby unacceptable thoughts are shut out of a person's awareness. This mechanism may be necessary for the adjustment of some disabled persons. Unless an individual who once harbored negative attitudes toward disabled persons can selectively forget his own previous reactions, he may be unable to accept himself as a worthwhile person with a disability.

Reaction Formation   In reaction formation an individual is unable to accept his feelings and desires, and so behaves in ways that are directly opposite to the way he wants to behave. A reaction formation is revealed by the fervor with which an idea or belief is expressed: e.g., oversolicitousness toward a disabled child may mask an unconscious rejection of that child.

Fantasy   Fantasy is the mechanism whereby persons gain, through imagination, satisfactions denied in real life. According to Cobb, fantasy, especially role playing, can reduce the psychological stress stemming from a disability. For example, most persons are afraid to appear in public after they become disabled, but through role playing they can both desensitize themselves and develop a repertoire of behaviors to deal with any unpleasant situations they may encounter. When social anxieties cause a disabled person to resist leaving the shelter of hospital or home, it is often helpful to have that person imagine the worst thing that could happen to him. Typically when a person verbalizes his worst fears, he discovers that he can survive the situation, whatever it entails, and his reluctance to appear in public may be reduced.

Rationalization   Rationalization is the mechanism which provides justifiable reasons for thinking what we think and behaving the way we do. Cobb describes four types of rationalization. The first type operates by blaming incidential causes, as when a workman blames his tools for his lack of skill or a disabled person blames her disability for her failures. Some persons believe they are unpopular because they are disabled. That may of course be true, but it is also true that certain persons, disabled or not, are not likable. The second type of rationalization operates by devaluing unobtainable goals, i.e., by the "sour grapes" rationalization where, for example, a person convinces himself that he doesn't mind losing a job because the salary was too low. Hank K., a patient in a VA hospital, came from a family in which males typically died from heart disease before they reached 40. Hank devalued his relatives' physical attributes, believing that their involvement in sports and physically demanding occupations was the sole factor in their early deaths from heart disease. The third type operates by finding something desirable in an otherwise undesirable situation. Cobb believes this "sweet lemon" rationalization is indispensable to adjustment to disability. In support of Cobbs' belief are autobiographies of disabled persons which reveal "sweet lemon" rationalizations. In one, the author says being blind has made him a better person because he no longer judges others by external characteristics, such as color of skin or style of clothing. The fourth type of rationalization operates by mentally balancing positive and negative traits. This "doctrine of balances" holds that pretty women are dumb and disabled persons are more understanding because of their disabilities.

Projection   Projection is the mechanism which assigns to others one's own unacceptable thoughts and feelings. A thief who believes everyone else steals uses projection. According to Cobb, when a person believes people are repelled by her disability, she may be projecting her own tendencies to be repelled by the disabilities of others.

Identification   Identification is the mechanism whereby a person achieves personal satisfaction through the successes of those with whom he identifies. A former football player may experience a sense of personal accomplishment through the successes of his former team. Identification, according to Cobb, is essential to adjustment. By identifying with others, the person decreases his egocentric orientation and begins to rebuild his self-esteem through the accomplishments of persons with whom he feels a special link.

Compensation   Compensation is the mechanism whereby persons make up a deficit in one area of their lives by capitalizing on their strengths in other areas. Well-directed compensatory efforts contribute to adjustment because they allow one to experience success. Learning to drive has compensatory effects for those who move slowly or with difficulty. A turning point in the adjustment process often occurs when persons who have been dependent on others discover they can help someone else.

These ego defense mechanisms are invaluable in a situation which overtaxes existing competencies because they prevent excessive stress. But when an individual has experienced success and is more confident of her ability to cope, ego defense mechanisms give way to a task-oriented approach to stress-producing situations. For the disabled, the realization that they can survive despite the fact that they are disabled can reduce their reliance on mechanisms which distort reality in favor of mechanisms which alter reality.

Task-Oriented Mechanisms   Task-oriented mechanisms differ from ego defense mechanisms in several ways. Task-oriented mechanisms, instead of distorting reality, entail a realistic appraisal of stress-producing situations. For the disabled, a task-oriented approach means analyzing a problem to discover a method of solving it.

In order to competently handle the adjustive demands created by a disability, a person needs practical information as to how he can manage day-to-day living problems. An ongoing association with similarly disabled persons can provide not only an opportunity to identify with their successes, but also access to survival lore, which is otherwise difficult to acquire. From simple problems such as how a blind person can identify clothing to avoid wearing mismatched outfits, to complex questions such as which method of translating the written word—Braille, Opticon, or computerized reading machine—would be best to meet the demands of business and/or personal life, the range of solutions depends on the creativity of individuals and their communications with persons who have faced similar problems.

It would be impossible to apply a task-oriented approach to every situation encountered during a day. The ego defense mechanisms provide an efficient method of dealing with inconsequential sources of stress. If Neil depends on a friend to help him buy groceries and one afternoon that friend is unable to go shopping, rather than appraising the situation, developing possible solutions, trying one out, and then evaluating its success, Neil would probably use a "sweet lemon" rationalization—he'd rather eat beans than steak tonight because steak is too expensive. An important milestone in the adjustment process is the ability to use the task-oriented approach effectively, because a disability is no longer so overwhelming that its ramifications cannot be faced without depression, withdrawal, or hostility. The key to metamorphosis is confidence in one's ability ultimately to cope.

Why don't the disabled, as a group, exhibit a greater degree of psychopathology than the nondisabled, who are less subject to stress from frustrations, conflicts, and pressures? To a degree the answer lies in the ability of the disabled to redefine potentially stressful situations. Someone who is nondisabled may be overwhelmed by the time it takes a cerebral-palsied child to tie her shoelaces. The child, however, may be operating by a different set of standards. Instead of thinking, "I'm wasting ten minutes tying my shoelaces," she may reason, "I'm glad I don't have arthritis because Jimmy can't even reach his shoes." If that child were allowed to utilize a task-oriented approach and to make her goal fastening her shoes and not developing eye-hand coordination, she could eliminate the problem by wearing zippered boots.

In addition to taking a problem-solving approach to the concrete tasks of everyday life, another external sign of internal adjustment is a person's development of interests which replace those no longer available to him. In the early stages of metamorphosis, a newly disabled person benefits from the attempts of others to include him in activities he previously enjoyed. If a disability is minimal, many persons can again participate in former leisure-time pursuits. If, however, a disability is severe enough to relegate a person to a spectator's role, eventually his self-respect and confidence will make him no longer content to spend his spare time "tagging along."

Eventually he will reach the stage where he will not only admit he is bored, he will realize he has better things to do than watch others enjoy themselves. If he had been active in athletics, he may develop an interest in wheelchair sports, in which even those who seldom use wheelchairs—amputees or persons with stiff ankle or knee joints—play basketball or football, race, fence and do archery. If his disability is severe, he may undertake the more cerebral challenges of bridge or chess.

In either case, a disabled person who is adjusting to his physical changes begins to feel restricted by associating solely with persons who are more physically active. Developing new interests does not mean that he ceases to cherish the companionship of nondisabled friends, old or new, but rather that he has discovered in himself the wherewithal to abandon his nostalgia for old pursuits, that he no longer needs the acceptance of those who were his friends before he became disabled to affirm his self-worth.

SOCIAL SURVIVAL OF THE SEVERELY PHYSICALLY DISABLED

Unlike physical survival, which depends less on normal physical functioning, or psychological survival, which stems from a resurgence of self-confidence and stigma incorporation (see Chapter 12), social survival is difficult for those who lack normal appearance or behaviors. To enhance social survival, the Civil Rights Act of 1964 made it illegal to discriminate against most minority groups, and what the Civil Rights Act did for women, racial minorities, and ethnic groups, the Rehabilitation Act of 1973 extended to the disabled. But while personal access to jobs, education, or public establishments can be legislated, personal acceptance by one's colleagues or acquaintances cannot. Therefore, the most stressful of the social frustrations are those stemming from unwritten rules of social acceptance which cannot be attacked directly. Often a person is unaware that he has violated an unwritten standard, and so has little chance of gaining the acceptance he seeks. For the disabled, the violation may be clear, but the means to avoid continuing violations may be lacking. Specific techniques which help enhance chances of social acceptance are discussed in Chapter 13.

But even with training in special techniques, the severely disabled may be unable to adhere to accepted modes of behavior. Irving Goffman, in his theory of "impression management," explains why personal appearance and demeanor are important in determining whether one is accepted socially. According to Goffman, appearance is important in face-to-face interactions with strangers because the way a person looks and behaves provides the only clues we have as to who she is, what she does, and, most important, what degree of consideration she has the right to expect from us. These external clues are of paramount importance because each of us must behave in an appropriate manner to make the best possible social impression. If someone will not or cannot give us the requisite clue as to what is appropriate on our part, we may be trapped into what Goffman defines as the cardinal social sin—giving a discreditable interpersonal performance. Therefore, we tend to ostracize persons whom we do not trust to give us reliable clues.

Where does that leave us in regard to the social survival of the physically disabled? Let us examine some behaviors that Goffman cites as socially discrediting:

> . . . a performer may accidentlly convey incapacity, impropriety or disrespect by momentarily losing muscular control of himself. He may trip, stumble, fall; he may belch, yawn, make a slip of the tongue, scratch himself or be flatulent; he may accidentally impinge upon the body of another participant . . . may act in such a way as to give the impression that he is too much or too little concerned with the interaction. He may stutter, forget his lines, appear nervous, or guilty, or self-conscious; he may give way to inappropriate outbursts of laughter, anger or other kinds of affect which momentarily incapacitate him as an interactant; he may show too much serious involvement and interest or too little. . . ." (1959, p. 52.)

In short, Goffman's list of discrediting behaviors contains behaviors that may result from neurological, muscular, or sensory disabilities. Some persons with cerebral palsy have a permanent loss of "muscular control" and so may "trip, stumble, fall," or give vent to "inappropriate outbursts of laughter." Similarly, a deaf person, trying to keep track of a conversation, may "show too much serious involvement or too little." Perhaps Goffman has unintentionally explained the research which indicates that persons with cerebral palsy or hearing problems rank lower on social preference scales than persons from other disability groups (Horn, 1975).

Passing as Nondisabled

Many disabled persons, such as epileptics who cannot get jobs if they admit their epilepsy on job applications, pass themselves off as nondisabled whenever possible. Passing allows disabled persons to get past the initial stage of social encounters to where less obvious, but more essential, personal traits influence a relationship. For an amputee this might mean wearing a cosmetic hand for social occasions, reserving use of the more functional hook for work situations. If, however, an amputee cannot afford more than one prosthesis, she will have to decide which is more important, appearing normal or functioning efficiently.

The Disadvantages of Passing   Although for the visibly disabled passing as nondisabled is impossible, for those who can pass, the price, in social terms, may be high. As Goffman points out, in social encounters the major problem facing a visibly disabled person is tension management, i.e., how he can reduce the discomfort his disability creates in others. A person with a less discernible disability has a twofold problem: information management and tension management. Such a person must try to prevent any discrediting information from being revealed. But if others eventually discover his disability, he must then deal with the resulting tension. Often when a previously unsuspecting person discovers that she has been relating to a disabled person, her discomfort is greater than if she had known from the outset.

Example 3A   Joan E.: Disguising a Disability Can Backfire

Joan had had polio when she was 5 and had been left with completely paralyzed arms and unimpaired trunk and legs. She had some function in the thumb of her left hand. On both hands the fingers were curled in toward the palms and could not be straightened out. While still a child, Joan had had her left arm fused at about a 65-degree angle to allow her some use of that arm and hand.

Unfortunately, Joan was the only child of parents who were very much ashamed of her disability and who insisted that she behave as though she were not disabled. She was taught to respond to questions about her disability with comments such as, "There's nothing wrong with me. I just have a little difficulty with my arms." And with Joan's ability to walk and her tendency to wear garments with long sleeves, she did, at a casual glance, appear to be nondisabled.

But that mirage was too often shattered, with devastating effects on Joan's emotional adjustment. One evening in a theater lobby, Joan was buying a box of popcorn to carry into the darkened theater where she could eat it with her tongue. The vendor who was waiting on Joan had evidently noticed nothing unusual about her and was, therefore, totally unprepared when Joan, clutching a fifty-cent piece between her thumb and forefinger, hiked her arm up on the counter, bringing her tiny fist directly in front of the vendor's eyes. The vendor, startled, burst into tears, and, humiliated beyond reason, so did Joan before she rushed out of the theater.

In other instances passing can be as detrimental to one's physical well-being as to one's social survival.

Example 3B   Frank P.: Hidden Disability Dilemma
(Damned If You Hide It, Dead If You Don't)

Frank P. was a 6-foot 4-inch, huskily built teenager who had had rheumatic fever as a child and whose heart was damaged as a result. Before entering high school, Frank had few problems restricting his activities in keeping with the decreased tolerance of his heart. He watched his diet, took penicillin shots regularly, got plenty of rest, and avoided strenuous activities, all without his friends realizing that he was limited in a way they were not.

But once Frank entered high school, his friends began to pressure him to play football and basketball. Because he had the build of an athlete and seemed to be bursting with good health, they couldn't understand why he wouldn't join the teams which needed good players.

Frank was in a dilemma. He could reveal a disability which he had spent years learning to conceal, risking the pity of his classmates; or he could join the teams, risking his physical well-being. What he did do was withdraw socially. Frank immersed himself in his studies, alienating many who couldn't understand the reason for his behavior.

Eventually high school became such an interpersonal nightmare that Frank sought help from his counselor. By the time he reached college, Frank had come to accept himself and no longer made excuses if he was asked to join in activities which could endanger his health. Married now, with three children and an engineering job in California, Frank is no longer concerned about his disability, except for working to maintain his health.

Advantages of Passing   In certain social situations, however, a minimally disabled person might have sound reasons for passing. He may have discovered that people fear the type of disability he has. For example, many still believe epilepsy creates violence or cerebral palsy is contagious. In some cases passing allows a person to become securely established in a job or relationship before his disability becomes known. The stigma associated with his condition may then be reduced because others are already aware of what a reliable worker or an enjoyable companion he is.

Example 3C   Mike: When a Disguise Works Surprisingly Well

Mike was a socially skilled psychology intern in a Southern VA Hospital. One day the chief of the service mentioned to several staff members how well Mike handled his disability. The staff members had to agree because none had realized Mike was disabled. The chief then related the following incident:

Mike's dissertation director was puzzled by Mike's clumsiness in his psychodiagnostic course. Such awkwardness did not fit in with his overall impression of Mike's competence. When he asked Mike why he was having difficulty handling the testing materials, Mike thrust his right hand forward. It was, of course, artificial.

As Wright (1960) points out, hands tend to be in the area of visual presence, not in the area of visual concern. A cosmetic prosthesis will often be "seen" as a flesh-and-blood hand, simply because the viewer expects it to be a flesh-and-blood hand. A fellow amputee has no such expectation and so spots prostheses quickly. It is, however, the difference between what exists and what is assumed to exist that makes artificial hands, eyes, and limbs so effective in casual social encounters.

Some Techniques of Passing   In order to pass successfully, approximating normal body parts or normal body behaviors is not enough. To complete the illusion of physical normality, a person must be adept in techniques of distraction, i.e., social behaviors which serve to keep a disability out of the limelight.

Take Mike, for example. Like Joan, he wore garments with sleeves that came well over his wrist line. He wore a large signet ring on his left (normal) hand and not even a watch on his right. A reserved person, he spoke with restrained gestures of both arms, his left gesturing more widely. During lunch and coffee breaks he positioned his right hand around his cup or water glass or kept it beneath the table. When using his right hand, in cutting meat, for example, he talked animatedly, maintaining eye contact with his listeners or with whomever else was speaking. Mike's method of coping included his choosing a largely verbal occupation.

Similarly, blind persons often escape notice when they turn their eyes toward whomever is speaking, as sighted people do. Deaf persons learn to nod in noncommittal fashion when they lose track of a conversation, and persons with canes or crutches automatically lay them on the floor rather than propping them against a wall where they would be more obvious. Every disability group develops techniques which, if not concealing a disability completely, tend to minimize its importance.

Whether passing is disadvantageous or advantageous depends largely on the reason why a person wants to pass. If passing serves a practical purpose and does not merely reflect a negative self-concept, then it can be a sign of adjustment and of concern for the comfort of others. If, however, a person passes because he is ashamed of being disabled, then passing indicates a lack of self-respect and self-esteem. Since a disability is an immutable characteristic of a person, its recognition and incorporation into an overall positive concept of self are indispensable to psychological adjustment (Wright, 1960). To attain optimum adjustment, the severely physically disabled person must become a social maverick because he can never conform totally to his peer group. If he tries to act and look the same as his nondisabled contemporaries, he will only approximate their standards. This may sacrifice his potential for their approval, for often behaving "normally" means being unable to function as fully as possible.

Social Pressure Encouraging Passing or Voluntary Social Withdrawal

Social expectations for a person with discreditable behavior often can affect the individual more adversely than the behavior itself. For example, the fear many have of epileptics has no basis in fact. Evidence indicates that epilepsy endangers neither the epileptic nor her associates. Even during grand mal seizures, few epileptics sustain injuries other than an occasional dislocated shoulder or bump on the head, and they create no threat to anyone in their vicinity. Instead of physical injury, the greatest damage created by a seizure is to the psychological equilibrium of those who witness it.

Example 3D   Old Charlie: Strange Behaviors Only Disturb Those Who Don't Know the Routine

A counselor stopped in an unfamiliar bar for an after-work drink. As he was relaxing at the bar, the man next to him, who was evidently a regular customer, went into a grand mal seizure. The counselor, who had no experience with epileptics whose sei-zures were not controlled, was aghast when none of the other customers paid attention to the plight of someone whom they had treated as a valued friend only seconds before. In his fall the man had grazed his head and the blood trickling from his forehead added an unnecessary touch of drama to the scene. The counselor, distraught, had risen to offer his—he wasn't certain what—aid, when the bartender laid a reassuring hand on his arm and said, "Don't pay old Charlie any mind. He does that all the time. He'll be right as rain in a couple of minutes." "Old Charlie" was, and promptly celebrated his recovery with a band-aid and a beer. Old Charlie was fortunate. He had found social acceptance of a rare and intelligent sort.

Obviously, the purpose of the above example is not to imply that persons having seizures should not be given special consideration so that the possibility of their sustaining even a minor injury is minimized. Nor is it meant to suggest that epileptics should drink alcohol. The point is that too often an epileptic is over-medicated or isolated from social situations not for his own benefit but rather for the benefit of those who might be made uncomfortable by a seizure.

The same rationale operates in situations where cerebral palsied persons who have limbs which jerk uncontrollably, unclear speech, and saliva dripping from the corners of their mouths, but who are, nonetheless, able to live by themselves and move freely within their communities, are made unwelcome in public places and are encouraged to withhold themselves from social situations.

Ostensibly, passing is encouraged when persons can pass and voluntary withdrawal is encouraged if they cannot pass, because of a desire to protect them from social rejection. But who really benefits from these expectations and where do these expectations lead?

The above question is not as rhetorical as it sounds. In one afternoon during the 1976 American Personnel and Guidance Association (APGA) convention in Chicago, two women participants in wheelchairs were barred from a clothing store and a restaurant in the Loop. The clothing store had a policy of not allowing baby strollers on the premises and this policy was extended to customers in wheel-chairs. Although there were empty tables in the restaurant, the manager insisted the women would be more comfortable eating elsewhere.

The Effect of Passing or Social Withdrawal on Adjustment   Passing as nondisabled or withdrawing from potentially embarassing social situations does reduce the stress stemming from overt interpersonal rejection, but it does nothing to change the attitudes resulting in such rejection. When a person succeeds in appearing as nondisabled or simply does not go out in public, the sensibilities of the nondisabled may be protected but their attitudes are neither changed nor chal-lenged. Moreover, self-effacement does nothing to encourage the development of alternative social behaviors which might lead to inclusion rather than exclusion. If the disabled are to enhance their social survival, they must be helped to learn social skills that may win them acceptance even though they are disabled and, according to English (1971), should not be denied the contact with the nondisabled which is necessary to combat prejudice and discrimination.

Coping Techniques Which Can Enhance Social Survival

To achieve metamorphosis, a person must learn to adjust to a nondisabled world. There are, of course, limits to the degree of adjustment which can be expected of the disabled; but adjust they must if they are to share in the rewards enjoyed by others.

Some techniques which aid social adjustment are those which ease face-to-face interactions with others. According to Gellman (1959), some disabled persons provoke discrimination by their behaviors. Both Siller (1976) and English (1971) believe it is the responsibility of the disabled to improve their relationships with other persons. Roessler and Bolton (1978) offer a training model to improve the interpersonal skills of disabled persons.

Nevertheless, to expect a newly disabled person, who is struggling to adjust and to survive physically and psychologically, to assume the sole responsibility for her social adjustment, too, is expecting a lot. While it is impossible to remove the burden of social adjustment entirely from the shoulders of the disabled, it is possible to lighten it. For example, social behaviors which put the nondisabled at ease are important, for without some of these behaviors, movement into subsequent stages of adjustment is inhibited. But what begin as coping behaviors can easily deteriorate into placating behaviors which do nothing to increase the self-esteem or the perceived status of disabled persons. Two such behaviors are the use of humor and the skillful introduction of the topic of one's disability into an ongoing conversation. Judiciously used, these behaviors can reduce social tension (Wright, 1960). But a person who relies heavily on humor may find himself trapped in the role of resident court jester and discover that his acceptance is conditional, i.e., based on his ability to make others laugh. Similarly, a person who habitually talks about her disability to put others at ease may find herself a social isolate, not because she is disabled but because she has become a bore.

WHAT IS GOOD ADJUSTMENT?

The goals and implications of any behavioral training models should be subjected to careful analysis before such training is implemented. Sometimes the goals are (1) acceptance of one's disability and (2) the ability to merge into society, thereby losing one's identity as a disabled human being. These goals may be too one-sided. The conditions necessary for metamorphosis result from changes within the person, along with changes within his physical and social environment. Society must also adjust to its disabled members; and today changes are occurring in legislation, education, and architecture which are designed to incorporate the disabled into society as disabled persons living normal lives and not as pseudonormal people leading pseudonormal lives (see Chapters 9, 10, and 11).

Adjustment, then, means more than self-acceptance and responsible behaviors. The severely physically disabled must also develop social techniques and psychological mechanisms to cope with the behaviors of others. Even the most socially adept disabled person will experience more rejection than his nondisabled counterparts. Therefore, professionals and paraprofessionals who work with the disabled must do more than teach the disabled how to behave toward others. They must also help the disabled strengthen their self-concepts, so that instead of being annihilated, they will be able to function in spite of negative social experiences.

CONSEQUENCES OF DEIFYING NORMALITY

In preceding sections the physical, psychological, and social adjustment of severely physically disabled persons have been presented as separate aspects of the process of metamorphosis, but they are not separate. It is difficult, if not impossible, for a disabled person to feel good about herself if she has no control over her physical environment or if she is discounted in social relationships. Therefore, helping a person to become physically independent and socially competent should enhance that person's psychological adjustment. And as her psychological adjustment improves, her competence in solving physical and interpersonal problems should also improve. Unfortunately, reverence for normal appearance and behaviors can alter the conditions necessary for a natural unfolding of the adjustment process by adversely affecting (1) the attitudes of the disabled themselves and (2) the attitudes of those professionals important to the adjustment of disabled persons.

Rejection of the Disabled by the Disabled

As members of the same society as the nondisabled, the disabled internalize the same standards for desirable physical attributes. The discomfort a nondisabled person experiences while talking to a disabled person (Horn, 1975) also occurs when a not-yet-adjusted disabled person encounters someone else who is disabled. In face-to-face encounters with the disabled, nondisabled persons subjectively report positive reactions, but their physiological responses indicate high anxiety and their nonverbal behaviors radiate avoidance and rejection. According to Horn, if you are the nondisabled participant, "Your palms sweat. Your face feels tight. You smile and nod agreeably, trying hard to look interested in the conversation, but you'd really rather be somewhere else. The occasion could be a job interview, a particularly disastrous blind date—or perhaps you are talking to an amputee, a paraplegic or a victim of cerebral palsy" (p. 122).

The same reactions seem to occur when disabled persons encounter someone with a different disability or someone with a more severe disability. According to Safilios-Rothschild (1970), those who have succeeded in reentering the world divorce themselves from those who have not. Even with the recent increase in cohesiveness among the disabled (see Chapter 8), many still deny kinship with those who share similar environmental and social problems.

A Case of Compartmentalization by a Disabled Professional

A participant in the 1975 national convention of the National Rehabilitation Association (NRA) was an example of the psychological compartmentalization of persons who, successful in business, politics, or a profession, deny that they are disabled, too. The convention organizers had provided a wheelchair-accessible van to transport disabled conference participants to and from the airport. This participant, who used a wheelchair, was evidently not averse to special accommodations, for he quickly installed himself and his luggage in the modified vehicle. On the way to the hotel, another passenger asked him if he planned to attend a special meeting of the Consumer Division the next day. In response, he turned red in the face and snapped, "No, I am not! *I* am a professional, *not* a consumer." After that he sat silently in his wheelchair on his way to a hotel where he had, undoubtedly, reserved a wheelchair-accessible room.

The refusal to associate oneself with other disabled persons does nothing to improve the situation of all who share the same social stigma. But the reasons for this refusal are easy to understand. Many persons fear that the tendency of the general public to see and treat all disabled persons alike will lead to the further segregation rather than integration of all disabled persons. Already, accessible communities have been designed in which disabled persons are expected to live apart from those who are not disabled. Most disabled persons, however, do not want to live together in enclaves of their own because, as Laurie (1978) and Riel (1977) point out, disabled persons have nothing in common except the fact of and the problems engendered by their disabilities.

In the feasibility study conducted for Independence Hall, a housing unit adapted for the severely disabled in Houston, opposition to the project came from those disabled professionals and businessmen who could acquire or build private modified housing. This lack of support stemmed partly from their not wanting to be classed with other disabled persons and partly from their concern that, under the guise of special consideration, disabled persons might someday be forced to live in ghettos for the elderly and disabled.

This is no idle fear, because precedents for this type of forced containment already exist in other countries. Holland has Het Dorp, a model village for disabled persons. In concept, Het Dorp and similar communities are both practical and humane. In practice, however, Het Dorp has as many qualities of a prison as of a sanctuary. Not only was the village built on such hilly land that over half of the residents' power wheelchairs are in need of repair at any one time (Wolfensberger, 1978), but villagers must sacrifice their autonomy in order to live there.

Once institutionalized, the disabled, unlike criminals, are often incarcerated for life. They cannot leave unless they are released through some administrative decision which is beyond their control to initiate. The ever-present possibility of being effectively and totally removed from society, due to society's tendency to regard the disabled as a homogeneous entity, causes many disabled persons to avoid association with other disabled persons.

Influence on Professional Attitudes and Behaviors

Rehabilitation professionals, as members of the wider society, are not immune to the generally negative attitudes toward persons with discernible physical differences. Many students who are also practicing rehabilitation counselors prefer not to work with persons with particular disabilities or with the severely disabled. Some of their reasons are practical. For example, they may work in a system which imposes a quota of successful rehabilitations each year to qualify for merit raises or promotions. Having too many severely disabled persons in their caseload can jeopardize those raises and promotions because the severely disabled usually require more time and effort to rehabilitate. In studies, commonly referred to as "unpopularity contests," subjects rank disabling conditions according to their perceived social desirability. Typically, amputees are more acceptable than paraplegics, arthritics more acceptable than the cerebral palsied, and persons with so-called character weaknesses—ex-convicts and ex-mental patients—are least acceptable of all (Horn, 1975).

The cause of a disabling condition can also affect both the attitudes and the behaviors of those persons who are expected to serve the disabled impartially. If a person becomes disabled through some wrongdoing of his own—driving while intoxicated or robbing a bank—he will seldom receive the support or understanding he would have had as the victim of a germ or genetic accident.

The tendency to judge the morality of those who require professional services has been documented by Stanton (1970). In *Clients Come Last*, Stanton points out how difficult it is to garner public support and monies for community mental health centers, as opposed to organizations concerned with treating disabling diseases or birth defects. Stanton concludes that the emotionally disturbed are seen as undeserving, as deliberately choosing not to follow society's dictates, while those with adventitious or congenital disabilities are viewed as unfortunates who are deserving of any help that can be given them.

Influence on Rehabilitation Practices

Since the deification of normality in our society defines any variation from accepted social standards as undesirable, this myth influences rehabilitation practices and retards the adjustment of the severely disabled. For example, one social standard holds that it is most desirable to move about unassisted in an upright position, not as desirable to use crutches, braces or canes, and least desirable to use a wheelchair. Professionals must realize that what is important is not *how* one accomplishes the activities of daily living (ADL), but rather *how successful* one's methods are.

When medical treatment cannot completely restore a person's physical function, evaluating rehabilitation success by how closely the posttrauma patient resembles his pretrauma self can impede his full utilization of remaining physical abilities. When the ability to move about is valued more if one moves about in an upright position, one may be discouraged or actively prevented from using a faster, safer, and less tiring mode of movement, such as a gurney (wheeled stretcher) or a wheelchair. Unquestionably, definite advantages accrue from standing or walking upright, i.e., prevention of mineral depletion of the bones, facilitation of urinary drainage, and improvement of the overall efficiency of the circulatory system. But these same physiological benefits may be gained by maintaining an upright position on a standing board or on braces and crutches for several hours each day. More important, standing exercises conserve the most precious commodity a disabled person has—his time. Standing or being stood facing a workbench or kitchen counter means a person can read, prepare a meal, or repair a radio while he is upright. Moreover, standing by a solid piece of furniture often reduces the fear of falling, thus encouraging a person to continue a therapeutic regimen he might otherwise resist.

In addition to losing time he needs for other activities, the person who engages in nonfunctional walking depletes his energies in an essentially useless activity. While a nondisabled person burns up 3.6 calories per minute walking, a person using braces and crutches efficiently burns up 8.0 calories per minute (Trigiano, 1974). A paraplegic may require approximately six times as much energy to walk as does a nondisabled person. When such persons are trained to approximate normal ambulation, it is done not for their benefit as much as for the self-gratification of those persons who equate professional competence with a patient's ability to move in an upright position.

Example 3E   Leo R.: What Price Pseudonormal Walking?

In 1958 at the Georgia Warm Springs Foundation, Leo R., an outpatient severely paralyzed with polio, was brought in to demonstrate what he had learned in therapy to a group of visiting experts in poliomyelitis. Leo's therapist lifted Leo to his feet and locked his long-leg braces. Then Leo laboriously dragged himself around the room by repeatedly pulling his inert legs toward his extended crutches. Once he had completed a circle, he carefully positioned himself in front of his wheelchair and then dropped into it, his legs sticking straight out in front of him.

According to his therapist, Leo would not increase his speed, his strength or his skill in ambulating; he would never be able to get up on his braces without help; and he would never be able to change directions, so that circling was his only means of returning to his starting point. Not only was Leo unable to perform any useful function while he was on his feet, he was running a risk of losing what function remained in his partially enervated muscles by overworking them in these daily walkabouts (Bennett, 1965). The only benefit accruing from his efforts appeared to be his therapist's pleasure in getting him to parody normal stance and locomotion. From a psychological standpoint, Leo, although compliant, later expressed humiliation at his awkwardness and helplessness in getting in and out of his wheelchair.

In more recent years, less emphasis has been placed on purposeless activities that approximate but do not replicate the physiological functioning of nondisabled persons. The fact has been recognized that the disabled, too, have a limited amount of adaptive energy available to meet the routine demands of life. Everyone's energy level is governed to some extent by genetic factors, but it can be modified somewhat by drugs, changes in one's living situation, and certain disease processes. For example, fatigue is a side effect of multiple sclerosis and lethargy results from a deficiency of a hormone from the thyroid gland.

Even if particular disabilities do not directly decrease a person's energy, they may reduce the amount he has available for work or leisure-time activities, because an inordinate amount must be expended on self-care activities. The more severe the disability, the more energy that must be diverted to nonnegotiable activities of daily living and the less energy that is available for nonessential tasks (Strauss, 1975).

Nontherapeutic Therapy

If severely physically disabled persons are to cope with energy-depleting aspects of their lives, they must husband their energy expenditures to meet the unavoidable demands of living. In certain cases, a 20-year-old severely disabled person will be carrying out his daily routine with the energy level of a 70-year-old, whose only disability is the enervation accompanying age. When viewed in this context, one can understand why exercising for exercising's sake can bankrupt the resources a person must husband to live in a nondisabled world.

That is why traditional therapy programs, especially those carried out on an outpatient basis, can impede a permanently disabled person's ability to cope. When disabled persons begin therapy after the onset of a disease or accident, there is no substitute for treatment from a qualified therapist, but once they learn the purpose and the safety limits of muscle strengthening or maintaining routines, those same exercises should be incorporated into activities which can be performed within the home. How much more practicable it would be to strengthen one's arm and shoulder muscles at home, lifting wet clothes in and out of the washer, instead of pulling weights in a therapy room far removed from the dirty laundry. Too often, routine tasks of living and prescribed therapy programs are viewed as separate and distinct undertakings, when a merging of the two could reduce the demands on persons who have no time or energy to spare.

Many professionals have difficulty accepting that the severely disabled can, with the necessary modifications of equipment and technique, care for themselves and hold jobs commensurate with their interests and abilities. Unless a person is confined to bed for medical reasons—such as advanced congestive heart failure or extensive paralysis—he should be capable of some degree of physical independence within his living situation. Many who spend years warehoused in nursing homes do not require twenty-four-hour care. Many nursing home residents only require help getting out of bed in the morning and back into bed at night. Dressing and toileting needs can be met with clothing modifications or provision of urinals and specially designed wheelchairs with zipper backs or toilet-seat cushions. If suitable housing were available, these people could manage their own affairs throughout the day, with help for a short period in the morning, in the evening, and in emergency situations.

Some severely physically disabled persons, however, can live independently without any attendant care. These persons have been taught to dress themselves, manage their personal hygiene, and with modified public or private transportation, work in competitive employment. They can live in apartments or in homes of their own and require only minor environmental modifications—wide bathroom doors, ramped entrances, and perhaps cooking areas with electric pots, toaster ovens, or frypans instead of large appliances. Only when they fall, become ill, or break their adaptive devices do they require outside assistance.

Ideally, such persons would have community resources available for the times when they require special assistance. Micro-Alert is a commercially available device which is designed to provide help in emergencies. When help is required, the person triggers the device, thus signaling a central answering service which then alerts persons on a prearranged list to come to his aid.

Many, however, have established ad hoc support systems, within which they function with a minimum of danger or personal anxiety. In some communities police departments respond quickly to emergencies involving disabled persons. In some cases, the person has an informal network of friends and neighbors who help when the need arises. In return, the disabled may provide services of their own, such as typing or small appliance repairs, to prevent their relationships from becoming too one-sided. A few have the financial resources to hire someone to check in on them periodically. Unfortunately, not many can afford to pay for such services, and it is a rare community that has volunteer groups willing to provide them.

Promoting Dependent Behaviors: The Submyth of Fragility

To no group of persons does the deification of normality do more damage than to the severely physically disabled. Cerebral palsied persons with gross motor incoordination or persons with advanced muscular dystrophy can neither look nor function like "other people," but their differences in appearance and functioning do not preclude many from thinking, feeling, and living the same type of lives as do nondisabled persons. Persons who appear incompetent on the surface may own their own homes, work in sheltered or competitive employment, and attend to their own daily needs.

On the other hand, there is a danger that stressing the potentials of such persons will create a countermyth to the deification of normality, a myth that all a severely disabled person requires to live independently and be gainfully employed is sufficient motivation. This is not true. A severely disabled person requires more than motivation, information, and modifications to live the same type of life as do her nondisabled counterparts. To live in the world of the nondisabled without continual assistance and financial support from others requires a willingness to sacrifice some of the time, effort, and monies others expend on leisure-time pursuits or on nonessential items (see Chapter 6).

Because of these sacrifices, these expenditures of time and energy, many believe that severely disabled persons should not try to control and manage their own lives. They find it difficult to reconcile the time and effort required by a disabled person to accomplish a routine task with the time and effort other people require. A physical therapist who gets up, showers, dresses, eats a hearty breakfast, feeds the dog, washes the dishes, and empties the trash within fifty-five minutes can't comprehend how a person who requires two and one-half hours just to get up, wash, and dress can be pleased with her accomplishments.

But while the time and energy the disabled expend to remain independent could be reduced considerably if someone else were to clean their homes, cook their meals, and take care of their personal needs, the disabled can only conserve with the help of other people and will still lose time of their own. Whoever assists her, a disabled person cannot disengage herself completely, since it is her body which is being cared for or transported about. Moreover, increased independence increases personal security, for parents will die, spouses may leave, and friends can lose interest in relationships where they give too much and the other person gives too little.

Unfortunately, at the present time, rehabilitation policies promote dependent rather than independent behaviors, and rehabilitation personnel tend to overprotect those with whom they work. Overprotection, which arises from a commendable concern for a disabled person's welfare, can dampen her physical and psychological well-being more than the stresses of independent living. As the quadriplegic wife of another quadriplegic put it, "Why should we be dependent on others just because if we struggle along on our own, we may burn ourselves out and no longer be able to live alone? Those outsiders who think we should rely on attendant care so we don't overdo are asking too much. They want us to live as though we were helpless long before we actually are. If George [her husband] and I should have to enter a nursing home tomorrow, we will have had the satisfaction of living by ourselves for fourteen precious years."

The decision whether to live as independently as possible or to let others assume the responsibility of directing and managing one's life should be left to the individual, after she has been given all available information regarding what options remain open to her, what skills she can acquire, and what assistive devices will be provided should she choose to live on her own.

DESTROYING THE MYTH THROUGH ATTITUDE CHANGE

If the impact of the deification of normality myth is to be reduced, an impetus toward change must come from either professionals or the disabled themselves. Severely physically disabled persons who lead "normal" lives go farther toward changing attitudes than any amount of rhetoric. But in order to set an example, the disabled must be visibly successful, and this will not occur until all who can be are restored to full social participation.

Promoting Responsible Nonconformity

Unless a disabled person adopts certain nonconforming behaviors, he may never become fully rehabilitated. For example, when one person is attempting to put himself on an equal footing with another, he might say, "He puts his pants on the same way I do," but if that person is disabled, the statement might not apply. In order to function to the best of his remaining abilities, a disabled person must accept that, although he cannot put "his pants on the same way" others do, the important thing is that he can put them on. As far as the activities of daily living are concerned, effective rehabilitation methods teach persons that it is the goal that is all-important, not the way in which one reaches it.

In too many rehabilitation settings independence in bathing, for example, is equated with the ability to transfer in and out of a tub—a formidable task for young paraplegics with the arms of an athlete, but even more so for elderly hemiplegics. The normal hazards of tub baths are compounded when a person has lost some use of body muscles.

Rehabilitators who are goal-oriented will impress upon their patients that what is important is meeting the two goals of bathing: maintaining health and eliminating odor. Bathing in tubs, or even showering, is not the only way to keep the body germ- and odor-free. Medical rehabilitators must work to convince patients that if they can keep their feet clean and free from sores, it doesn't matter how they do it—whether by soaking them in a tub or in a toilet bowl filled with clean, soapy water.

Care should be taken, however, not to force patients to use methods which are so unorthodox that the patients' physical adjustment is fostered at the expense of their psychological adjustment. For example, for some elderly persons who have taken tub baths all their lives, the psychological benefits of continuing a lifelong habit might outweigh the physical risks. Or immersion in warm water may have secondary benefits, such as relief of arthritic joint pain, or reduced spasticity in the cerebral palsied, which cannot be obtained in shower, sink, or bed baths. Although each case must be considered individually, those who teach practical living skills must make certain that their personal values do not adversely limit the living potentials of those with whom they work.

Flexibility versus Rigidity in Evaluating Physical Competencies

Professionals can combat the influence of the deification of normality on their patients by changing the methods by which they determine how well a person can cope with his physical limitations. Most functional evaluation techniques equate full functioning with the ability to perform a task without using any adaptive devices. According to this standard, a below-the-knee amputee, who uses a prosthesis to walk or climb, is not fully functional. If similar standards of physical functioning were applied to all individuals, persons who fly to meetings or drive to work would be classified as not fully functional because they used a plane or car to get to their destination.

Fortunately, the deficiencies of equating full function with the absence of assistive devices are beginning to be recognized. A better means of evaluating physical capabilities is to determine whether or not a task can be completed in a reasonable amount of time. Using this standard, the ability to walk upstairs would be evaluated by the time required to get from the bottom of a flight of stairs to the top, thereby incorporating energy requirements and safety considerations into the overall evaluation.

Although time-function evaluations are a step in the direction of redefining normality, they are subject to the same relative distortions as assistive-device-function evaluations. It is difficult for someone who has never lived with a disability to determine whether an activity is too time consuming to be practicable within a particular living situation. Is it unfeasible for a man with poliomyelitis to dress himself if he takes forty-five minutes to pull on his trousers or for a woman with multiple sclerosis to clean her own home if she spends three hours just vacuuming the rugs?

To determine functionality, one must consider the context of a person's daily routine. What other demands are there on his time? How patient is he? Has he much tolerance for frustration? How strong is his drive for independence? What is the possibility that he may require less time by practicing, by using a different method, or by being equipped with a particular assistive device? And, finally, will those with whom he lives allow him to complete the task without interfering?

How optimistic a newly disabled person is about his potential is largely based on the flexibility and optimism of those who foster and guide his efforts during the early stages of his adjustment. If his mentors are overwhelmed by the time and effort he requires, it will be difficult for him to refrain from constantly comparing how he does things now to how he did them before. Until he stops making such comparisons, his adjustment will be stymied.

Success as a Catalyst for Success

A newly disabled person is often overcome by the difficulty of regaining her self-care skills. But once she has proved to herself that she can live independently, she will usually fight to retain whatever independence she has, for she quickly learns the hidden implications of a dependent status. Unless a person has strong dependency needs, she will find that despite the reliability or good will of those upon whom one depends, dependency always entails sacrifice on the part of the person who is dependent. When accommodations are made in a relationship where one person is dependent on another, the one who is dependent is expected to make them. In families where the husband is physically dependent, the wife makes the important decisions (Carpenter, 1974). Dependency entails a loss of control over one's own affairs and in one's relationships. The ever-present possibility of needed help being withheld if one does not comply with the demands of others leaves the dependent person with two choices: resorting to passive-aggressive behaviors in the attempt to regain some control in a relationship, or withdrawing into totally submissive behaviors.

For these reasons, disabled persons, if they believe they have a choice, prefer to live independently for as long as they can. Any successful experience strengthens a person's self-confidence and encourages her to develop more self-care skills until she reaches the limits of her ability to live independently, free from reliance on others.

TWO EXAMPLES: ONE WHO DEIFIED AND ONE WHO DEFIED

Deifying normality guarantees the failure of disabled persons because it imposes unrealistic conditions for leading a productive and self-fulfilling life. Instead of reassessing the importance of "normal" appearance and behavior, many severely physically disabled persons become living caricatures who attempt to appear as normal as possible. For them it is not the disability which limits their life chances but rather their compulsion to be what they are not—nondisabled.

Example 3F   Tom: What Price the Male Model Look?

Tom, a polio quadriplegic, lost his chance for a college education because he wanted to appear less disabled than he was. Tom's paralysis was extensive. He had no movement in his legs and little in his arms and hands. Tom could, however, have wheeled himself to his classes by riding a wheelchair-accessible bus to and from his classroom buildings. But since Tom couldn't grip his wheel rims, he needed to have pegs attached to them so he could push the pegs with his wrists. However, Tom didn't like the way the pegs looked and detested getting his wrists and shirtsleeves dirty—inevitable when one pushes a wheelchair, especially through rain or snow. He therefore chose to sit immobile but immaculate and wait for a passing student to push him wherever he needed to go. Consequently, Tom missed too many classes and flunked out of college. Well-groomed, he lives at home with his aged parents.

Example 3G   Larry W.: Quadriplegic, Psychologist, Husband, Professor

For Tom, looking "normal" was more important than a college degree with the chance for a secure and financially independent future. Sequestered at home, a living monument to normality, Tom forms a vivid contrast to Larry, a spinal-cord-injured quadriplegic who is now a psychology professor. When he was in college, Larry pushed himself from one end of his campus to the other, too impatient to regulate his activities according to the schedules of the wheelchair-accessible buses. His hands were constantly dirty and chapped from pushing through slush in winter and rain-swept streets in summer, and his jacket cuffs were ragged from the constant friction of his wrists against his wheels.

Larry was gregarious and hated to eat alone. His usual routine at mealtime was to fill his tray in the dormitory cafeteria, find a table where a group of girls was sitting, introduce himself, and settle in. That was how he met Georgia, the homecoming queen contestant he eventually married.

Larry is living proof that how a person feels about himself and how he presents himself to others have more to do with his personal and social success than does his physical ability or comeliness. Unfortunately, if a peson is unaware of the possibilities open to him, his disability cannot help having a more catastrophic effect on his physical, psychological, and social survival than if he were aware of and confident enough to explore those possibilities. If he learns what options are open to him as a disabled human being, and if he receives appropriate training and services from knowledgeable professionals, the effects of his disability on his life may be reduced to a manageable inconvenience in this age of concrete and mechanical marvels.

Chapter 4

The Second Disabling Myth:
The Omniscience of
the Experts

Living a satisfying, productive life as a severely physically disabled person requires complex adjustments in both goals set and techniques used to reach them. Those who are "successful" spend years developing the expertise which allows them to live like other people. Whether a disabled person fulfills his potential or is unnecessarily dependent on others depends to a large degree on the attitudes and competencies of those rehabilitators who work with him during the intensive stage of his rehabilitation.

What types of attitudes predominate in rehabilitation-related fields? How knowledgeable are professionals in these fields concerning the lives successfully rehabilitated persons lead? According to existing research (Dembo, 1970; Goffman, 1963; Kerr, 1970; Ort, Ford, and Liske, 1964; Ramsey, 1978; Safilios-Rothschild, 1970; and Shontz, 1975), helping professionals share general misconceptions about and negative attitudes toward disability. Like laymen, professionals deify normality, and this hinders their ability to differentiate between what is desirable and what is necessary in human appearance and behavior.

What is most detrimental, however, is not that professionals are subject to human error, but that others expect experts to be infallible, to be aware of all existing knowledge in the area of their expertise, and to use their knowledge in the best interests of their clients. Because these expectations are unfounded, we call this belief in the omniscience of the experts the second disabling myth.

This chapter will:

1 Discuss the effect of professional attitudes on physical and psychological adjustment

2 Explain why professionals have a hard time predicting the living potentials of disabled persons outside institutional settings

3 Compare and contrast the two sometimes compatible, sometimes disparate goals of rehabilitation—physical restoration and role resumption

4 Suggest ways professionals could improve their knowledge of and services to severely disabled persons

Foundation of the Myth

There is a social paradigm which holds that when one encounters a problem one cannot solve oneself, one can obtain the solution from a person who wears the appropriate uniform or who has the proper certificate on his or her wall. This paradigm presents no difficulty when problems are clearly defined and require an expertise obtainable through academic training or professional experience. For a toothache, one seeks the assistance of a dentist who may, in turn, refer one to an expert in root canals. For a stalled car, one first turns to a mechanic at a local service station but may end up with someone who only repairs transmissions.

Severe disability, however, is more complex than an abscessed tooth or stripped gears. What those who become severely and permanently disabled need is not simply a concrete solution to a distinct physiological problem—fusion of a shattered spinal column or an exercise regimen for partially deenervated muscles— but rather an entire reshaping of their life-styles, their skills, and their expectations (Wright, 1960; Roessler and Bolton, 1978). Some of the necessary reshaping can be achieved through the combined efforts of competent specialists on rehabilitation teams, but much can be worked out only by the disabled themselves over a long period of time. There are many small details of living which must be mastered but which cannot be incorporated into a structured rehabilitation/education program: Where does one shop if one cannot walk; how does one shop if one cannot see; which foods are easier to prepare if one has cerebral palsy?

An expert who believes he has the answers to all the problems facing persons with diverse disabilities usually does not know all the questions. Yet many professionals judge every day such questions as which persons will be able to live independently, which should be institutionalized, which could succeed in competitive employment, or which would be a good spouse or parent. If lack of knowledge or aversive reactions cause a professional to view severe disability as a catastrophic event which destroys one's chance for a happy, fulfilling life, it will be difficult for her clients/patients/students to ever grow beyond her definition of their situation. If, however, the disabled are surrounded by professionals who react as did a young amputee's father when he heard his son had lost a leg, "Lost a leg, has he? What's so bad about that? Rest of him's in good shape, hain't it?" (Viscardi, 1952, p. 143), they may find it much easier to adopt the matter-of-fact view toward their disabilities that will optimize their eventual adjustment.

THE DIVERSITY OF PROFESSIONAL ATTITUDES TO DISABILITY

There is much diversity in the attitudes of professionals toward the disabled, just as there is in those of the general public (Barker et al., 1953; Gellman, 1959; Siller, 1976). Few see the disabled simply as human beings with human strengths and human frailties; rather, the disabled are assigned to a different class of being altogether, either superhuman or more commonly, subhuman. For example, L. D., who worked for HEW, believed disabled persons were "simply wonderful." In 1977 when a controversy arose over the issuance of the regulations of Section 504 of the Rehabilitation Act of 1973, persons working in regional HEW offices were warned that disabled persons might try to bomb their offices. L. D. was affronted that anyone could think a disabled person would consider engaging in terrorist activities. She was unaware of incidents like the one in Illinois in the late 1960s, when a wheelchair-using University of Illinois student threw a firebomb through a police station window, seriously injuring an officer. Unfortunately, when those who idealize disabled persons discover that the disabled display the entire range of human behaviors from saintly to satanical, they often become so disillusioned that their unrealistically positive attitudes give way to equally unrealistic negative ones.

More common, however, are professionals who express consistently low opinions of their clients' motives and behaviors: "All my clients are lower class and lazy"; "All they want is something for nothing"; or "What good does it do for me to get them a job? I can't do their work for them." Armed with innumerable excuses, such professionals ward off any fears they might otherwise have that a client's failure might stem from something they have or have not done. But whether the qualities they assign are superhuman or subhuman, the results are the same. By stripping the disabled of their humanness, these professionals have absolved themselves of any guilt or doubts concerning their own attitudes and behaviors.

Many factors contribute to the difficulty professionals have with viewing disabled persons as more than perpetual clients or patients. First, rehabilitation-related professions are stigmatized professions. By working with persons who are devalued in society, those in such professions reflect some of the stigma associated with disabled persons. Both their status and their salaries are lower than those of comparable persons working with other types of clientele. Second, such professions are highly dependent on public and private funding but seldom receive the amount of money needed to finance the services necessary for severely disabled persons to resume their accustomed social roles. Finally, such professions tend to be exhausting psychologically, causing many a dedicated professional to experience what Emner (1979) describes as "professional burnout." Government regulations and bureaucratic policies, designed to improve services, often merely increase the amount of necessary paperwork, leaving the professional even less time and energy for working with individuals. And as the disabled and their families become aware of the discrepancy between services supposedly available and services actually received, they tend to attack the more accessible professional, rather than the system itself or the decisions of behind-the-scenes policy makers.

Although professionals work under many constraints which limit the services they can provide, these constraints do not justify their often harmful attitudes toward their clients/patients/students. When a professional harbors negative attitudes toward those with whom he works, his attitudes can do more to impede adjustment than the attitudes of any other group of persons except the family.

Within any rehabilitation setting the prevalence of positive or negative attitudes can greatly influence the effectiveness of the setting as a whole. When disabled persons or family members become aware of deleterious attitudes among the personnel, they may attempt to transfer to an institution or agency where staff attitudes are generally positive. Unfortunately, outstanding rehabilitation centers and hospitals typically have long waiting lists. With a scarcity of good rehabilitation settings, few families are as fortunate as one Mid-South family, which finally succeeded in transferring their son to the Texas Institute for Rehabilitation and Research (TIRR) after an unfavorable experience with a rehabilitation center in their home town. According to Ronnie's parents, "The worst insult was that the nurses, attendants, doctors and therapists all tried to break Ronnie's spirit. The doctors said he might be able to feed himself. The physical therapists were going to quit because he would never walk anyway. The nurses made fun of spinal cord patients' inability to control their bladders. The management of the hospital was indifferent . . . they said he was a hopeless cripple; at TIRR they will train him to be independent. . . ."

Ort, Ford, Liske, and Pattishall (1965), in a study of medical students' and practicing physicians' attitudes toward chronically ill and permanently disabled persons, discovered that their subjects had a deep aversion toward working with these kinds of patients. Some researchers believe these attitudes stem partly from the fact that rehabilitation medicine, as taught in most medical schools, is dull and unmotivating. Others believe these attitudes stem from the orientation to the "cause, result, cure, closure" course of a physician-patient encounter (Gee, 1960; Ort et al., 1964) that medical students receive during training. Promulgated as the ideal relationship, this sequence allows a physician to exercise his expertise, achieve success, and maintain a sense of superiority, which is enhanced by the reactions of grateful patients. But when a physician works with the permanently disabled, he is denied the satisfaction of a successful closure and the sense of omnipotence which results when a patient is cured. Compounding this lack of closure is the continuing sense of personal failure which assails many who work with permanently disabled persons. This sense of personal failure may be particularly acute if a physician who knows little about life as a disabled person equates disability with tragedy.

BEHAVIORAL INDICATIONS OF UNDERLYING DEVALUATING ATTITUDES

Much of the evidence which indicates professionals have devaluating attitudes toward disabled persons is found by examining professional behavior patterns. Common behavioral tendencies among professionals take the form of: (1) over-emphasizing the effects of disability on adjustment; (2) interpreting as abnormal behaviors considered normal in nondisabled persons; (3) treating the disabled in terms of their disabilities instead of their other characteristics; and (4) consistently underestimating potentials of those with whom they work. If behaviors can be assumed to reflect underlying attitudes, then the tendency of professionals toward the above behaviors reveals the existence of widespread devaluating attitudes. Roessler and Bolton (1978) conclude that the expression of devaluating attitudes toward the disabled impedes their personal adjustment and that such attitudes will be especially deleterious when expressed by professionals.

Overemphasizing the Effects of Disability on Psychological Adjustment

One indication of the type of attitudes experts hold toward the physically disabled is the fact that the most researched area in rehabilitation, according to Roessler and Bolton (1978), is the effect of disability on psychological adjustment. Although surveys have consistently concluded that the psychological adjustment of the disabled population does not differ from that of the nondisabled, researchers persist. When they discover no significant difference between the adjustment of disabled and nondisabled subjects, they suggest that the findings may be due to imprecise measures, nonrepresentative subjects, tendency of self-report inventories to elicit socially desirable responses, or an undiscovered variable linking disability and psychopathology. Few entertain the possibility that when disabled persons are considered as a group, there may be little correlation between severity or type of disability and personal adjustment.

Misinterpreting "Normal" Behavior of the Disabled

Supporting the expectation that disability entails some degree of personal maladjustment is the tendency to interpret certain behaviors differently in the disabled than in the nondisabled. Many specific behaviors can be described by two terms with vastly different connotations. Someone who is extroverted could also be described as other-directed, but while the label "extrovert" positively implies that she is gregarious and interested in people, the label "other-directed" negatively implies that she has a paucity of inner resources and is utterly dependent on others for her emotional stability.

So it is with the disabled. When a person has become used to living with a disability, unless faced with an unexpected barrier or a query from the curious, he often tends to be oblivious to his physical limitations. This obliviousness may seem to be a denial of the disability to an outsider for whom the disability is glaringly evident and overwhelming in its implications. It is difficult for those who do not share a particular disability to comprehend, both cognitively and affectively, that ambulating in a wheelchair, communicating by reading lips, or traveling about with the aid of a guide dog eventually require neither analytic interpretation nor emotional suppression. For an old-time amputee, putting on an artificial leg is no more emotion-provoking than for a nonamputee to pull on his socks.

In adjusting psychologically, a disabled person has been typically described as going through four stages of adjustment: (1) *denial*, when he rejects the fact or the permanency of his disability; (2) *depression*, when he begins to realize he is in truth disabled and sees himself in an apparently hopeless situation; (3) *hostility*, when he stops wondering "Why me?" and begins to think "Why not you?"; and finally, (4) *acceptance*, which ranges from passive resignation to the coping behaviors described in Chapter 3. But the universality of these stages is called into question by persons like Hohmann (1975), Wright (1960), Mueller (1962), Cook (1976), and Rubin and Roessler (1978). In describing her concept "requirement of mourning," Wright says that the nondisabled's expectation that the disabled must be depressed over loss of physical functioning may stem from a need to have the disabled mourn the loss of what the nondisabled themselves value highly, thereby confirming their personal values. The role of so-called hostile behaviors in the adjustment process also requires further investigation and, perhaps, reinterpretation. Evaluating certain behaviors as hostile may arise more from the disruptiveness of such behaviors than from what they reveal about a person's adjustment.

If a newly disabled person is depressed, those working with her find it easy to tolerate behaviors with which they can empathize. But if she tries to assume some control of her own affairs, tolerance is replaced by anger and empathetic understanding by behaviors designed to keep her under control. In a rehabilitation setting, rewards go to the cooperative (passive) person who does not disrupt routine or challenge staff policies. Aggressive behaviors are countered with behavior modification techniques, and if such techniques are successful, routine is restored at the expense of the person's psychological growth through independence-enhancing behaviors.

Research has shown that hostility may be as much an indication of increased adjustment as a manifestation of a neurotic defense (Siller, 1976; Vineberg and Willems, 1971). As an example, consider a situation where someone finds himself in a hospital or rehabilitation setting. At first, overwhelmed by the apparently catastrophic consequences of his condition, fearful that he might die, the newly disabled person looks to the staff, hoping that somewhere, somehow, they can administer a medicine or treatment that will effect a cure. Overlooking no possible source of help, he may turn to his minister, priest, or rabbi to seek God's intervention in a situation which seems beyond human control. Reinforcing his growing egocentrism is the fact that he lives in a setting where everyone around him is concerned with his bodily needs, functions, and incapacities. Attendants bathe him, nurses bring him medication, and physicians, often appearing with a retinue of students, nurses, and interns, discuss his most intimate physical functions as though he were incapable of either understanding or embarrassment.

But the newly disabled person has not always been disabled. A short time ago he may have characterized himself primarily as a husband, a father, a certified public accountant, and a Catholic. And, inevitably, as the impact of his disability lessens through familiarity, he begins to think of himself again in terms of his former social roles. The newly acquired aspect of himself slowly is incorporated into a new concept of self (Wright, 1960). Longer and longer periods of time occur when matters unrelated to his disability occupy his attention.

As the disability becomes incorporated into his self-concept, he begins to experience a renewed sense of self-worth, giving him the confidence to assert himself as a self-governing adult. But it is hard for those around him to assess the amount of psychological adjustment taking place. Because his disability and its ramifications still predominate in their concerns, those working with him continue to see and treat him as a child-adult. They assume that their previously unchallenged authority over him is still acceptable at a time when he, like an adolescent who has savored the adult status which is sometimes imposed on him and sometimes denied him, has begun to flex his psychological muscles.

Suddenly the staff is faced with a need to convince their patient of the desirability of any therapeutic regimen they prescribe. When he refuses to go to therapy, they usually don't interpret his refusal as an attempt to exercise his right to say yes or no, but rather as a regression to irrational or dependent behaviors. In an environment which places a high value on submissive behaviors, where staff authority is believed indispensable to rehabilitation success, self-assertive behaviors are diagnosed as potentially dangerous changes in behavior.

Why isn't patient assertiveness viewed as a positive sign? Why isn't a movement toward self-determination hailed as proof that a person is progressing psychologically to where he feels safe defying those on whom he once was dependent for approval and, hence, for his physical well-being? The assertiveness of a recently disabled person indicates that he is freeing himself from dependence on others to clarify what *his* disability means in the living of *his* life.

Stereotyping the Disabled

The tendency to treat the disabled primarily in terms of their disability often leads to their being stereotyped. When students ask, "What is it like to be disabled?" they expect answers pertaining to (1) physical feeling, i.e., "Does it hurt?" or (2) physical ability, i.e., "Isn't it depressing not being able to dance?" But the essential meaning of a disability does not lie in changed physical sensations or lost physical skills. To the person well past the initial stages of her adjustment, the major impact of her disability is her loss of control in social situations. Disabled adults, according to Goffman, are not treated as their nondisability-related characteristics would otherwise lead them to be treated. The disabled must constantly struggle to maintain the mastery over their own affairs that the nondisabled are granted automatically.

Nancy Kerr, a Ph.D. who uses a wheelchair, recounts her experiences when she has entered rehabilitation hospitals not as a patient but as a professional:

Example 4A   Treated as a Stereotype, Not as a Person

"On countless occasions, I have been wheeling along in treatment settings in various parts of the country, tending to my business, when an attendant or nurse would hustle alongside and challengingly or sarcastically say, 'Hey, where do you think you're going?' or sometimes 'You're not supposed to be out here—go to your room.' On one occasion, solely on the basis of my occupancy of a wheelchair, a nurse tried physically to put me to bed! More than once my wheelchair has been hijacked by an attendant who, without comment, wheeled me to the dining room of his institution."

Dr. Kerr points out that once she explains who she is, the staff member, realizing that his or her behavior was inappropriate, responds, "Oh, I'm sorry. I thought you were a patient!", unaware that the behavior would be inappropriate even if she were a patient (Kerr, 1970, p. 845).

This tendency to stereotype the disabled often means that they are denied ordinary social consideration taken for granted by the general public. Being visibly disabled in any manner may mean that librarians as you wait to check out books, clerks as you wait to try on shoes, or receptionists as you wait to make a dental appointment ignore you because they don't think an unaccompanied disabled person could possibly be a patron, customer, or patient and so assume that you are waiting for your keeper to arrive.

Underestimating Potentials of the Disabled

A final indication of devaluating attitudes on the part of professionals is their tendency to underestimate the capabilities and potentials of their clients/patients/ students. Before her discharge, a newly disabled patient may realize that experts can err in predicting the life she will lead in the world outside. Mrs. Linda P. describes her experience as follows:

Example 4B   The Pessimism of Medical "Experts" versus the Realism of Those with Experience

"At first everything seemed hopeless. My doctor said I would be able to feed myself, but anything more would be gravy. I wanted to marry, to have a home of my own, but I'd get so depressed, especially watching TV commercials. I'd see a wife drive up in her car, get out, take groceries out of the trunk and, after running up the kitchen steps, put her groceries on the table. Such a simple thing, buying and bringing home groceries, but I thought I couldn't even do that. I was wrong. Some disabled persons I met in the hospital told me that even if I was in a wheelchair, as long as I could use my arms, I could drive a car with hand controls. By using ramps in place of steps, I now bring home all the groceries I need on my lap."

One factor which may militate against helping professionals' understanding how disabled clients/patients can function outside of treatment settings is their inability to identify, in a positive sense, with severely disabled persons. This can be as true for disabled professionals as it is for nondisabled; a blind rehabilitation counselor may know little of the problems or potentials of the totally deaf. And because those who work with disabled persons are more aware than most of how easy it is to acquire a disability, they often fear the effects of disability more than a layman who may not know anyone who has become permanently disabled.

Some professionals, however, justify their consistent underrating of clients' potentials as fostering realistic as opposed to unrealistic expectations. This rationale is expressed in staff meetings and at national conventions of rehabilitators. Monographs warn against sponsoring cerebral palsied persons for professional training because no one may hire them. When disabled persons with professional degrees remain unemployed, however, it is more often due to inadequate placement services than to unrealistic aspirations on the person's part. If someone has the ability to get a professional degree, he has the ability to work as a professional. If, as is sometimes the case, he cannot obtain a position, this does not prove his expectations were unreasonable. When one is severely disabled, nothing is easy, and finding a job is no exception. But if qualified disabled persons, with their supportive cadre of helping professionals, do not continually assault physical barriers at job sites or attitudinal barriers in employers' minds, they will never be employed in the wide range of jobs they are qualified to perform. If everyone assumes that blind persons cannot be computer programmers (which is not true) because there are no blind computer programmers, and as a result refuses to train them, then there will never be any programmers who are blind. "Accepting reality" may mean settling for an undesirable but remediable situation, as if Pasteur had stopped experimenting, saying, "Rabies! Why look for a cure? Everyone knows none exists."

Unfortunately, some persons do harbor unrealistic expectations concerning the kind of work they can do. But the greater danger lies in such persons' failing not because of their expansive goals but because of the limited vision of those who are in a position to offer or withhold necessary monies and services. Sometimes the best way to convince someone that he will not succeed in college is to allow him to enroll in a correspondence course, while he continues with the other phases of his rehabilitation. Few persons, regardless of their disabilities, are incapable of learning from experience. And there is always a chance that the person who was judged incapable of college work will do well in a correspondence course and all subsequent college courses.

THE NARROWING EFFECT OF PROFESSIONAL EXPERIENCE

The narrow experience rehabilitators have with disabled persons often prevents them from realizing the true potentials and limitations of the disabled. Rehabilitation professionals work only with persons who are in a state of crisis: medical rehabilitators with the newly disabled who have not yet accepted or learned to cope with an altered physical condition, vocational counselors with those in desperate need of employment, special educators with those who are struggling to master requisite social and educational skills. Conversely, the medical rehabilitator does not come in contact with healthy, fully functioning disabled persons, just as the counselor has no official contact with those who are gainfully employed or the educator with those able to assume the responsibilities of adulthood. The narrow experience of most professionals limits their perception, producing the general tendency to interpret attitudes and behaviors in terms of a disabling condition. This tendency can produce misconceptions such as the following one about people in wheelchairs.

Example 4C   Can Wheelchair People Throw a Party?

A graduate student in rehabilitation counseling roomed with a nurse, who exclaimed when she heard the student was going to a party at the DeLoaches', "How can people in wheelchairs give a party? They are always so depressed." The student, who had had a course on the psychosocial aspects of disability, was curious and asked the nurse why she believed people in wheelchairs were "always so depressed." The nurse, who worked on the surgical floor of a general medical hospital, said she had had one patient who used a wheelchair, and that person, who was scheduled to have a kidney removed, was extremely depressed. The nurse didn't consider major surgery, with its possible consequences of a need for dialysis, an adequate reason for depression, whether or not one was in a wheelchair.

When professionals generalize specific individuals' behaviors to disabled persons as a whole, they are much like a zoo keeper who, from the knowledge he has gleaned from his daily work with lions, thinks of himself as an expert. The zoo keeper may assume all lions are like Leo in a cage over there—lazy, not very aggressive, low in sex drive, and dependent on his keeper to keep his cage clean, his body healthy, and his stomach full. Similarly, the rehabilitator might believe all disabled persons are like those she works with in her clinic, hospital, school, or agency—lazy, passive, sexually inactive, and dependent. The rehabilitator may not realize the extent to which her work setting is inconvenient for severely disabled persons who, when they control their environment, may not be, using Wright's (1960) definition, "handicapped."

What happens to a person, totally independent in her own milieu, when she checks into a hospital? If she uses a wheelchair, after she transfers into bed, her chair is moved into a corner of the room or out into the hall. Without her wheelchair, she cannot go to the bathroom, into the day room, to the window, or out into the hall unless someone helps her. Consequently, staff members assume she is as dependent at home as she is forced to be in a restricted setting.

Example 4D   Wheelchair as Grab Bar

A physical therapist who teaches in a Western medical school has Bart F., a polio quadriplegic, speak to his students to illustrate the difficulty therapists often have in understanding how patients function at home. The therapist has Bart, who has little strength in his trunk and upper extremities, relate an experience that happened to him when he was learning to turn over and sit up. After several sessions during which Bart had futilely strained and twisted trying to turn himself over and come to a sitting position, he finally reached over and, grabbing the rim of his wheelchair, pulled himself over and up. Bart's sense of triumph was short-lived, however, because his therapist said that using his wheelchair as a grab bar wouldn't work, since Bart wouldn't have his chair available when he was in bed. The therapist was correct as far as Bart's hospital stay was concerned, because his chair was automatically taken out of his room as soon as he was in bed and wasn't returned until he was ready to get out of bed. But the therapist was wrong as far as Bart's home life was concerned. When he returned home, Bart kept his chair by his bed until he transferred into it and wheeled away. Normal living conditions for Bart and others like him mean a wheelchair is always available—unless someone interferes and takes it away.

The Effects of Professional Training

This therapy instructor was trying to make his students aware of their need to visualize as accurately as possible their patients' actual living situations, so that their preconceptions would not hinder patients' progress unnecessarily. Many schools associated with rehabilitation centers do commendable jobs of training professionals who have both the flexible attitudes and the practical knowledge required to rehabilitate persons to the greatest possible degree.

Rehabilitation medicine, however, is a fast-growing field in which new techniques and assistive devices are developed every day, and an informational and attitudinal lag exists between what disabled persons can do and what many rehabilitators believe they can. Those who are aware of the problems and achievements of spinal-cord-injured (SCI) quadriplegics who were trained in centers like the University of Illinois's Rehabilitation-Education Center are especially discouraged when they read textbooks or hear professional presentations concerning such quadriplegics' physical and occupational potentials. They know that many quadriplegics routinely accomplish what many experts say they cannot. Many of these persons bathe and dress themselves, take care of their toileting needs, cook, clean their homes—some with occasional help, some with no help at all— drive cars or modified vans with hand controls, and, if they do not have full-time jobs, engage in a wide range of activities, from going fishing to doing volunteer work within their communities. Those who work full time hold jobs that range from selling magazines over the telephone to programming computers for IBM (Laurie, 1977).

It is difficult to reconcile what quadriplegics accomplish every day with what students in various professional fields are being taught concerning quadriplegics' functional abilities. Perpetuating outdated expectations which influence client/ patient progress are charts which incorrectly describe quadriplegics' functional potentials, which hang in numerous therapy units, and which are reproduced in current textbooks. The following is an example (see Glossary for explanation of abbreviated Spinal Cord Injury Code):

> C6   Permits activities of C5 (dependent for dressing and hygiene activities) as well as transferring to and from wheelchair, able to propel wheelchair for short distance on level, able to manage feeding with specially adapted utensils as well as handwriting or electric typewriter with more ease and with simpler adaptive devices. Wrist motion provides a grasping mechanism to hold larger objects.
>
> C7   Manages transfer, dressing and hygiene activities with minimal assistance. Able to write and use electric typewriter without adaptive apparatus.
>
> T1   Able to accomplish all manual activities. Requires only minimal, if any, help in transfer, dressing and hygiene activities. May manage automobile with hand controls. (Freed, 1965, pp. 272-273.)

Freed claims that "knowledge of the level of cord involvement permits, in the absence of complications and given a well-motivated individual," a prediction of functional potential. He continues by saying what the experiences of countless persons prove is untrue: "The quadriplegic patient will always require some attendant care."

More recent textbooks, such as *Rehabilitation* (1976) and *Introduction to Rehabilitation* (1979), are no more up to date concerning the potentials of this particular disability group than Freed's chapter which continues to be cited to identify critical levels of spinal cord functioning (Bitter, 1979). Dr. DeLoach's husband, for example, is diagnosed as a quadriplegic with a complete cervical lesion of the spinal cord, resulting from a diving accident which crushed his fifth and sixth cervical vertebrae. To date, he has pushed a manual wheelchair two miles back and forth to the author's apartment when they were dating (so much for "short distances"); driven an automobile with hand controls on a 4000-mile trip (proving you don't have to be a T1 paraplegic to be able to "manage automobile with hand controls"); driven a modified van round trip from Memphis to Boston, with side trips to Manhattan, Niagara Falls, and Washington, D.C.; proved his capabilities "for dressing and hygiene activities"; and works as an English professor who corrects hundreds of student papers each semester (well "able to manage handwriting" by attaching pen to hand with a wide rubber band).

Lack of Necessary Manpower and Monies

Why do inaccurate prognoses of future functioning persist when many rehabilitators admit in private that their clients/patients could do more than the goals set for them imply? The answer, in part, may be a lack of manpower and monies.

Excessive workloads and inadequate budgets restrict the effectiveness of many who work in rehabilitation. Most agencies and institutions depend on grant monies for continued operation. This dependency not only fosters insecurity among staff members who do not know from year to year if their positions will be funded, but it also channels inordinate amounts of time and energy into writing and resubmitting grants. What time and effort go into securing and maintaining needed monies must be subtracted from the time and effort which otherwise would be spent on the services essential to successful rehabilitation outcomes.

In addition to the ongoing struggle for funds is the irrefutable fact that, given the same degree of intelligence and motivation, someone with a minor disability is more easily and quickly rehabilitated than someone with a severe disability. On the average, it requires five hours for a below-the-elbow amputee to learn to use his artificial limb, while it requires twelve hours for an above-the-elbow amputee to master his. Similarly, teaching a quadriplegic independent living skills may take twice as long as teaching a paraplegic the same skills. Therefore, in inadequately staffed and inadequately funded rehabilitation settings, decisions may be made to rehabilitate ten paraplegics in the same length of time it would take to rehabilitate five quadriplegics.

Then, too, the more severe the disability, the more costly any assistive devices needed to increase functioning. A paraplegic may require a manual wheelchair and automobile hand controls in order to return to his home and community. His wheelchair could be a secondhand or inexpensive model because he could repair the chair himself, if he had a supply of parts and the necessary tools. A quadriplegic, however, often requires an electric wheelchair, which is expensive to purchase and maintain. Moreover, if his chair is transistorized, he cannot repair it himself and may have to have an extra chair to avoid being immobilized whenever a module must go back to the factory for repair or replacement.

In short, when a professional sets treatment goals for a severely disabled person, it may not be the *impossibility* but the *unfeasibility* of attaining functional independence that elicits a negative prognosis. If a greater proportion of time and equipment monies were devoted to those with complex problems, the rehabilitation of those with more easily resolved problems might suffer. But practical reasons for not providing services do not justify prognoses which foster the conviction that severely disabled persons lack the potential to do more. In the case mentioned above, why was the prognosis in one rehabilitation setting that Ronnie was to be "a hopeless cripple," while in another, that he would learn "to be independent"? Were staff members in one setting less competent than staff members in the other, or was it their policy to present a negative prognosis, hoping that their definition of potential would be accepted, allowing them to concentrate their efforts on persons who could easily be helped?

RESULTS OF THE MYTH AND THE ATTITUDES IT FOSTERS

One result of experts' belief in their own omniscience and of the behaviors and attitudes which their belief fosters is the tendency of disabled persons to regard rehabilitation professionals and professional organizations with increasing suspicion. The rise of consumerism among the disabled will be treated in Chapter 8, but the taproots of consumerism will be discussed in the following two sections.

Self-Fulfilling Prophecies: When Prognosis Is Poisonous

If Ronnie and his family had accepted the more negative prognosis, he might have lived as a "hopeless cripple" for the rest of his life. When one becomes or is born disabled, he depends totally on the assessments of experts to determine his future potential and to prescribe the best course of treatment. Rarely do newly disabled adults have any previous experience with what living with a disability entails, and rarely are children born into families of similarly disabled persons. The disabled must therefore rely completely on those who specialize in some disability-related area. But if these "experts" have little practical experience with how disabled persons manage, if they rely on what they've learned in clinics or classrooms, they may hinder more than they help the necessary transition from "hopeless cripple" to competent, albeit disabled, human being. Most disruptive to the otherwise orderly process of metamorphosis are experts who believe in the infallibility of their judgments. By instilling others with their pessimistic attitudes and assessments, such professionals shape the behaviors of the disabled in a manner that ensures that those attitudes and assessments will be validated.

Jim is a severely disabled person who once believed the prognosis that he would never live alone or obtain a job. After he came in contact with a group of physically and economically independent persons with similar disabilities, he proved the prognosis was inaccurate. Aware that only a fortunate set of circumstances separates him from persons who remain dependent on the largess of others, Jim worries:

> What about the plight of the newly disabled person? He knows that he has become suddenly and mysteriously "*different*." The world at large does not understand him; his own family feels uneasy and looks sideways at him; and with his future (he fears) made

obsolete, his past seemingly irrelevant and his body disobedient or even dangerous, he doesn't even understand himself. The self-esteem, indeed the whole psychological identity of the newly disabled person, is exceedingly vulnerable at this point. Into this vacuum of understanding come the "experts." Lord help the patient whose "experts" act less like professionals than like undertakers, as if their only task were to get the corpse decently out of the way and to pacify the survivors.

What vulnerable patient, faced with degree-laden, high-ranking experts who regard him as something less than human, can resist the onslaught or challenge their verdicts? . . . He sincerely believes that they know more about him than he knows about himself. And believing their verdicts, he makes them come true. Thus the experts are vindicated for their negative expectations have been fulfilled.

It is inconsistent to expect the disabled to resume their responsibilities, to be physically and economically independent, when at the same time they are expected to be psychologically dependent, to accede to the authority of others. In settings where the disabled are expected to learn as many independent living skills as possible, institutional routine often mitigates against their practicing the skills they struggled to acquire. Severely disabled persons require long periods of time to carry out the simplest tasks, and their time requirements will conflict with the schedules necessary in an efficiently run rehabilitation program. Therefore, skills practiced in therapy are seldom practiced in a living situation. A patient who has difficulty feeding himself will practice eating skills in therapy, but will be fed on the ward because it is faster. He will strengthen his arms lifting weights in therapy, but someone else will push him back and forth to his therapy sessions so he will get there in time.

Such dependency-enhancing environments eventually extinguish independent behaviors by reinforcing dependent behaviors, and the severely physically disabled person, through conditioning, will end up enjoying her dependent status. Encouraged to be dependent first by professionals who dictate treatment goals on the basis that the severely disabled are incapable of living independently and second by living situations structured so they cannot function autonomously, the disabled often find it impossible to free themselves of the need and eventually the desire for assistance. Consequently, pessimistic prognoses will have been fulfilled, with more individuals being discharged unnecessarily into the care of families or custodial institutions.

Those rehabilitators who do believe severely disabled persons can thrive outside of their bedroom or institutional walls often encounter resistance from fellow professionals. When Trigiano and Mitchell published an article on the successful training of C6 quadriplegics in independent living skills (1970), other physicians called their statements into question (Stoler, 1971). The varying successes of similarly disabled persons may be explained in terms of the self-fulfilling prophecy. Perhaps Trigiano and Mitchell expected the quadriplegics they worked with to become completely independent, and so they learned to function independently. Perhaps Stoler did not believe his patients could achieve total independence, and so they did not. As Kerr (1974) points out, staff expectations play a major role in eventual patient performance.

Although the number of profoundly disabled persons who are contributing members of society continues to increase, it is still less than the number of similarly disabled persons who have the same potential but lack the resources to develop it. Disabled individuals like Bill L., a corporation lawyer with cerebral palsy and unintelligible speech, or Marilyn O., a social worker in a chest disease hospital whose multiple sclerosis has progressed to where she has difficulty operating her power chair, are exceptional, not because of their accomplishments, but because they received the best rehabilitation services available.

Inappropriate Treatment and Advice

Whatever the reasons underlying professionals' misconceptions concerning the living competencies of the physically disabled, these misconceptions have far-reaching effects on the eventual adjustment of their clients/patients. Many conditions, such as orthopedic or neurological disorders, can create life-threatening, secondary disabilities unless proper, long-term medical care is available. Therefore, persons with a variety of physical disabilities are forced to rely on those medical rehabilitators and other medical specialists who will accept disabled persons as patients and who will adjust their treatment methods to the special needs of these patients. Unfortunately, many otherwise competent physicians fail to respond to the special needs of the disabled and discount these patients' expertise regarding their own disabilities.

Example 4E Blurred, Useless X-Rays

Sandra Diamond, a counseling psychologist with cerebral palsy, discusses the problems she has had in trying to obtain medical care: "If, God forbid, I'm sick . . . that's the biggest problem. . . . I've had surgery . . . where . . . you've got to be x-rayed. Well, there's no way in this world that you're going to x-ray me. You can take pictures but you'll have blurs—there's nothing. And the last time I explained that there's no way you can x-ray me in this hospital, I had some minor surgery, unrelated to CP, again. At first, they tie you down and, of course, the ties break. There you are, you're upset, because your straps have broken and then four marine-types come and hold you down. It sounds funny, but it's really quite humiliating. Here I am, a 33-year-old professional woman, saying, 'You cannot x-ray me. There is no way. If you give me anesthesia, I'm sure you will get a few good pictures, but awake, there is no way.' There is no way to take blood from me. They tell me, 'Put your arm out so we can take some blood.' 'Okay, here's the arm.' The next thing you know, the blood is gushing all over the place. You can't do that. What I'm trying to say in essence is that the medical and paramedical fields don't know about the CP. They know there is brain damage and they know that I'm retarded—that they know—and I should be drooling and they can't figure out why I don't drool, but they don't know that they can treat me medically in a special way. You can still patch me up but it takes a little thinking.

". . . If I was to walk into your office and you were about to give me an injection and you say to me, 'Sandra, it will hurt much less if I give it to you in the butt' and I tell you, 'Doctor, it will hurt me three times as much in the butt,' I know that your experience tells you one thing, but my experience tells me that I've got to sit eighteen hours a day and it's going to hurt me more than if you give it to me in the arm which is used very little. Now, I know this about me. Now I'm going to tell you to give me a pill instead of a liquid; but you tell me, 'Sandra, a liquid will work much quicker, it will be more soothing.' Okay, then it's not going to stay down. So it's if I tell you how to treat me, I'm not a doctor. I'm not saying give me penicillin instead of lincocin. I'm just saying: listen to me and my experience, because I know me." (Richardson, 1972, pp. 534–535)

The above case illustrates the lack of credibility disabled persons have in the eyes of some medical and paramedical professionals. In part their lack of credibility is due to the tendency of physicians to underestimate the medical knowledge of patients in general (Pratt, Seligmann, and Reader, 1958; McKinlay, 1975). In part it is due to the nature of the ideal physician-patient relationship as described by physicians themselves. According to a study of physicians' attitudes by Ort, Ford, and Liske (1964), the ideal physician-patient relationship is one where the physician controls the relationship, his authority goes unquestioned, and the patient eagerly submits to that authority. Since the key ingredient of medical success is seen as the physician's authority over his patient, loss of authority is equated with loss of professional effectiveness. Therefore, not only are patients' viewpoints deemed inconsequential, but any patient influence on treatment procedures may be seen as a threat to desired treatment outcomes.

The Informed Patient: Alternatives to Total Submissiveness

Although the dominant physician–submissive patient relationship is often appropriate for acute medical care, it is often inappropriate for treating the chronically ill or physically disabled. Once the acute stage of his disabling disease or accident is past, a severely physically disabled person will have to obtain medical care outside a rehabilitation setting, from physicians who may not be familiar with the special needs and complications his condition creates. If he is to survive in these circumstances, he must control some phases of his medical treatment.

A minority of disabled persons have served in the armed forces, and therefore most are ineligible for the specialized medical services available in VA hospitals. According to testimony in the continuing oversight hearings on the Rehabilitation Act of 1973, "there are approximately 200,000 spinal cord injury victims presently living in the United States. Approximately 10,000 to 12,000 new injuries occur every year." Yet only about 10 percent of the spinal-cord-injured are veterans, and the same ratio exists for most adventitious disabilities (Lancaster, 1976, p. 32).

Therefore, the majority of disabled persons are patients of physicians with little or no rehabilitation expertise. Even physicians who specialize in disability-related areas, such as urology or dermatology, are not likely to have much experience with the overall complications of the wide variety of disabling conditions. Simply not enough persons with any one disability seek care from any one physician to allow her to become familiar with their special requirements. Therefore, in order to avoid unnecessary health hazards, disabled persons must oversee, to some degree, the medical treatment they receive, including prescribed drugs or procedures. For example, persons with paralyzed lower limbs, whatever the cause, are subject to chronic or recurrent urinary infections which could damage their kidneys. Many drugs routinely prescribed for disorders which do not involve the urinary tract have nephrotoxic (kidney-damaging) side effects and are therefore contraindicated for persons with already impaired kidneys. As part of their self-care training, disabled persons should be taught to consult a Physician's Desk Reference (PDR) whenever drugs are prescribed for them. A PDR lists the primary and secondary effects of most medications currently in use.

Doctor as Gatekeeper: No Access to Medicine—without an M.D.'s Prescription/Evaluation

More than their physical well-being may be endangered by the difficulty the disabled have getting appropriate medical care. Their entire rehabilitation process is affected by the prognoses and treatments prescribed by the physicians who consult for or head most rehabilitation teams. Before a physical therapist can begin a functional training program or a rehabilitation counselor can provide job training and placement services, a physician must prescribe the type of therapeutic training or evaluate the person as being able to profit from rehabilitation services. Upon the evaluation of one physician, who, being human, is subject to error, depend not only what services are offered but whether any services are offered at all. The impact of physicians on the futures of disabled persons is sobering in light of the evidence that physicians, in general, are inaccurate in estimating both the degree of physical restoration possible and the quality of life a severely disabled person can live (Conner and Leitner, 1971). According to Margolin (1971), "The severity of the physical limitation is not even a good indicator of the patient's vocational potential."

It is difficult for physicians, whose lives are devoted to healing, to view those who cannot be healed as anything other than unfortunate. Their pessimism causes further complications when it spreads not only to their patients but to their patients' families as well.

The Disabled Family Member: Source of Stress, Source of Joy

Autobiographies and parents' biographies of disabled persons reveal the experts' inability to estimate a disabled person's ability to cope or his family's ability to incorporate him into family life (see Appendix B). Disability does create stress in a family. Marriages may end, brothers and sisters may feel neglected, and individuals may not be able to deal with the continual drain on financial and emotional resources. One problem a family faces in adjusting to a member's disability is that while the other members go through the same early stages of denial, depression, and hostility/assertion, they have greater difficulty finally adjusting than do the disabled themselves. A disabled person, who cannot escape his disability, often has little choice but to adjust to whatever degree he is capable. Other family members, however, may feel trapped by someone else's problems. Nondisabled family members may be all too aware that if the disabled person were gone, family life could return to normal; or that if they left, they could leave behind disability-related problems as well. Nevertheless, although a disabled child or adult creates stress within a family group, many professionals are excessively pessimistic and underestimate families' abilities to eventually adjust to and cope with disability-related stress.

Professional pessimism stems from the fact that families in difficulty are highly visible, because they are the families which seek professional help. Thus, when a rehabilitation professional considers the effect of disability on significant others, his reference group consists of those who are most distressed. Families that are coping successfully are invisible within the community as far as social service agencies or helping professionals are concerned. Moreover, when the effects of disabled family members on family structure are studied, the subjects usually consist of those who, having sought professional help, are known to potential researchers.

The result is a negative bias which reflects the skewed experience of most professionals. S. I. Hayakawa in his series of articles "The Experience of a Retarded Child in the Family" states, "Professional advice . . . was to put him into an institution at once because 'it would not be fair to the other children' to have such a handicapped child at home" (Hayakawa, 1976, p. 6).

Hayakawa's son, who was kept at home against professional advice and who proved to be a joy and an asset to his family, was born in the 1950s. But instead of a growing optimism in the intervening decades, professional pessimism is increasing (Ramsey, 1978). Parents of mentally retarded and physically disabled children born today receive similar advice, if they are not outrightly denied access to medical treatment which would save their children's lives (Ramsey, 1978; Patrick, 1978).

Example 4F   A Routine Question That Saved a Child

Mrs. Audrey K., whose daughter has spina bifida, was instrumental in forming a support organization for parents with disabled newborns in the Boston area. When Audrey's physician revealed her baby had a congenital defect, he said, "Of course, you'll want to have her institutionalized." Because Audrey and her husband Paulo knew nothing about spina bifida, they assumed they had no other choice, although they did not want to give up their child, disabled or not.

But everyone they consulted supported the idea of institutionalization. A neurologist friend assured them such children grew up to be vegetables.* Other friends related tales of marriages destroyed and brothers and sisters with emotional problems resulting from a disabled child in the family. While Audrey and Paulo were not resigned to placing their baby in an institution, they finally believed they had no alternative. Then the day they were to sign the final papers, a secretary at the institution asked a question that altered their future: "Why do you want to put your child in here?" It was the first indication they had that there was any other choice.

Four years later Audrey and Paulo are the parents of a bright, loving daughter who lives at home, walks with braces, and is the reason her parents have founded a group for parents in similar circumstances.

The alleged "omniscience of the experts" has proved to be a destructive myth. Eradication of that myth provides a challenge which must be met both by society—

---

*About 70 percent of children with spina bifida have some degree of retardation.

which needs its experts—and by the experts—who must live in society. Eradication would be easier if laymen were less ignorant about their own bodies—if they studied human anatomy and physiology in school along with flowers and frogs; if experts were less jealous of their prerogatives—if they could sometimes say "I don't know" and even listen to their patients; and if medical schools trained more physiatrists the only M.D.'s specifically trained in medical rehabilitation.

The final section of this chapter will concentrate on one proposed method of countering the disabling effects of the myth that experts are omniscient. How well a severely physically disabled person eventually adjusts depends on that all-important stage when the person has been discharged from a rehabilitation center or program and begins to put his newly developed skills to work. During this stage the severely physically disabled person is in dire need of ongoing support services to help him make the transition to the outside world without falling into unnecessarily dependent behaviors. During this stage, his rehabilitators need immediate and constant feedback concerning his progress and any problems he encounters so that they can revamp their treatment program to better meet the needs of disabled persons in the future.

THE NEED FOR A NEW MODEL FOR REHABILITATION OF THE SEVERELY DISABLED

Rehabilitation professionals, within their area of specialization, are generally hard-working and competent. Most physicians who work in disability-related areas keep their medical knowledge up to date and spend extra time with patients who are frightened or depressed.

What is true for physicians is equally true for the majority of professionals in rehabilitation—therapists, social workers, psychologists, vocational evaluators, counselors, and teachers. Their dedication is all the more outstanding when one considers that their salaries are lower, their work more challenging, and their total success rate lower than those of professionals who work outside disability-related fields.

Away from the Medical Model

If malicious mismanagement or willful ignorance is not the issue, what is the problem concerning the quality of services received by disabled persons? The problem is that the medical model of rehabilitation is inadequate to optimally rehabilitate the severely disabled. Moreover, a continuing adherence to the medical model is largely responsible for the devaluating attitudes with which many professionals view the capabilities of their clients/patients/students.

The medical model of rehabilitation has as its goal the physical restoration of disabled persons. After the acute stage is past, physical restoration begins. Surgery is performed, muscles are exercised, joints are made more flexible, motor skills are practiced. After as much physiological functioning as possible has been restored, techniques will be taught to reduce the effects of whatever physical limitations remain. All possible sources of financial aid will be ferreted out to maintain the family until the disabled person can return to her old job or be retrained for a new one. To overcome her fears of returning to the outside world, she will be exposed to it gradually: a weekend at home, an occasional shopping trip or social event in the safe company of other patients.

Although this description of the medical model is not complete and does not begin to represent the efforts of medical rehabilitators in their true complexity, many disabled persons, especially those born with a disability, experience even less than what is described above. Even for those who are fully immersed in medical rehabilitation, this model does not meet all their needs. The medical model is based on the premises that when a person has a disability, something can be done to reduce or eliminate the effects of that disability, and that when physical restoration is successful, role restoration will occur automatically.

Severely physically disabled persons, however, by definition will never be physically restored. The assumption which too often follows is that they can never again resume their prior social roles. Under the medical model they often do not, at least while they are actively engaged in rehabilitation. Therefore, medical rehabilitators mistake incomplete rehabilitation for an inability to be fully rehabilitated. Believing it is either too difficult or impossible for the severely disabled to live independently, they instill their patients with their preconceptions and so their patients do not attain maximum independence.

The inappropriateness of the medical model for all persons, regardless of the severity of their disabilities, wasn't obvious when such persons only lived a short time, before architectural barriers began to fall, or before rehabilitation technology advanced to where it is today. By the early 1970s the inappropriateness of the medical model began to become openly acknowledged. Kutner's 1971 editorial entitled "Rehabilitation: Whose Goals? Whose Priorities?" highlighted the conflict between physical restoration and role resumption. Kutner questions the practice of channeling the bulk of rehabilitation monies into physical restoration efforts, with little being earmarked for services to the millions of permanently disabled who could, nevertheless, resume their social roles.

No one could deny that physical restoration should be the primary goal of rehabilitation, but when physical restoration is impossible, what then? Children with spina bifida no longer die before reaching 14. Adults with spinal cord injury now live normal or near-normal lifespans. At the same time, nursing homes have extensive waiting lists; parents grow elderly and die. Where will the severely disabled live? What are they going to do with their lives? Who will take care of them?

Some persons, of course, are so profoundly disabled that they require attendant or custodial care. But what about the severely disabled who have the potential to live in and contribute to society? Some, with the support of family and with survival skills learned from similarly disabled persons, are living independently. But rehabilitation for them is a lifelong task. Relying on the chance help of family and other disabled individuals is an inefficient mode of rehabilitation when there is already an existing rehabilitation bureaucracy which could be modified to meet their needs.

Beyond the Medical Model

If independent living as a rehabilitation goal is to receive the high priority intended by the 1978 amendments to the 1973 Rehabilitation Act, there must be some lifelong support services offered to severely disabled persons when they first reenter their communities. These support services should not promote the physical or psychological dependency of such persons but should rather provide hands-on emergency services in crisis situations when the disabled cannot help themselves.

Several successful prototypes for such services already exist and can be modified to meet the needs of a specific urban or rural area. In Arkansas, the Spinal Cord Injury Commission provides long-term services to SCI clients of the Arkansas Division of Vocational Rehabilitation. Commission counselors offer services ranging from job placement to moving a client's household from one town to another. Independent living centers, such as Berkeley's Center for Independent Living, provide listings of accessible apartments and available attendants, training for attendants, wheelchair repair, accessible transportation, and personal counseling. Such ongoing support services optimize the abilities of the most severely disabled to control and manage their own lives. Independent living as it is usually defined means the ability to care for oneself, maintain one's own home, and be mobile within one's community. But independent living, in the legal sense of the term, is defined as maximum independence within the capacities of persons having some physical limitations but who, nevertheless, can manage their own lives and choose the style of living they prefer. The Arkansas Spinal Cord Injury Commission and the Berkeley Center for Independent Living provide such persons with the resources necessary to attain maximum independence.

The Community Reentry Specialist   In rural areas or in areas with no independent living centers, a need exists for a new breed of counselor—a community reentry specialist (CRES). A CRES would be someone who specialized in recognizing and devising solutions to problems faced by severely disabled persons moving back into their communities after medical rehabilitation or long-term institutionalization. Not just a coordinator of existing services or a provider of information, the CRES would act as an on-the-spot troubleshooter. In setting up such a specialization, great care must be taken to keep such specialists from becoming just one more link in the chain of service organizations which refer persons with problems requiring immediate attention from one organization to another without anyone's ever leaving the office to offer concrete help.

In order to prevent the position of CRES from deteriorating into an office-based, paper-shuffling job, the following requirements would have to be met:

1   The CRES would be thoroughly familiar with the community in which she works. She would know which services are already available, which services are lacking, and which existing services could be expanded to meet the needs of her clients.

2   The CRES would not write grants to establish or continue services, or provide global services himself. For example, if there were no accessible public transportation, he would not provide transportation himself, except in crisis situations, such as when the regular driver for a blind person becomes ill.

3 The CRES would be hired by and directly responsible to the commissioner of rehabilitation in her state. In this way she could communicate gaps in services directly to the person in the best position to fill those gaps.

4 The CRES would have no quota to meet and would have a staff to handle his paperwork. Periodically the commissioner would evaluate his performance by on-site visits and by randomly interviewing persons comprising his caseload.

5 The CRES would be flexible and enjoy the challenge of nonroutine work.

6 The CRES would have at least minimal manual skills, so she could construct a temporary ramp at a vital location until a permanent one could be installed.

7 The CRES would have the counseling skills necessary to recognize when clients need in-depth therapy and the personal skills necessary to correct inappropriate client behaviors without alienating the client.

8 The CRES's primary goal would be to help clients develop independent problem-solving skills to where they could make their own decisions and learn to live with the consequences of those decisions.

9 With these general guidelines, the CRES would develop his own duties, according to what resources were available in his community, his clients' readiness for independent behaviors, and the need for providing varying degrees of emotional support for individual clients.

In summary, the intermediate goal of the CRES would be to provide the information, coordination, and hands-on services severely physically disabled persons require immediately after they reenter their communities. The ultimate goal of such a specialist would be to wean his clients, physically and psychologically, until they reach their maximum potential for independent living. For medical rehabilitators as well as for the severely disabled, the CRES would provide that long-absent bridge between hospital and home.

Chapter 5

The Third Disabling Myth: The Asexuality of the Disabled

After their pain has lessened and their fear of dying receded, newly disabled persons begin to reassess their lives and their relationships. Physical concerns give way to social concerns. Will members of the opposite sex still find them attractive? Will they be able to continue current relationships as friends, lovers, or spouses.

The sexual uncertainties of newly disabled men and women are exacerbated by two types of attitudes: (1) those revealed by many helping professionals and (2) their own predisability feelings about disabled persons as sexual beings. Professionals are often reluctant to address these concerns of the disabled, signaling disabled seekers of information that matters are as bad as they feared, or worse. The newly disabled's own predisability attitudes will make them aware that others now view them as tragically neutered, incapable of gratifying sexual activity.

Through experience, the disabled find the picture is not quite so bleak. They may see others, some more disabled than they, marry. If those they find attractive are not attracted to them, they realize the nondisabled have identical problems. Evidence shows that if they are typical, they will marry eventually and their marriages will be more stable than those of the general population.

This chapter will:

1 Explore the outmoded laws and attitudes which perpetuate the myth of asexuality of the disabled

2 Discuss sexual drives, activities, and relationships of persons with various disabilities

3 Discuss the special sexual problems of childhood, adolescence, and adulthood

4 Describe social pressures which dissuade nondisabled persons from making public commitments to disabled persons

5 Offer guidelines for sexual counseling with disabled persons

OUTMODED LAWS AND ATTITUDES

Example 5A   June M.   A Housewife Who Was Sterilized against Her Will

June M., an attractive housewife in her early twenties, has been married for four years to Leo, a foreman in a northern Wisconsin lumber mill. Both June, who is said to be a better-than-average homemaker by her neighbors, and Leo, who has been employed at the mill for sixteen years, would like to have children of their own. June, however, is classified as mentally retarded and was sterilized in early puberty by a physician who was acceding to her mother's wishes. June's mother feared June would become pregnant and did not want the responsibility of raising her daughter's children. She removed June from the institution in which June was living and, against the resident physician's advice, took June elsewhere for a tubal ligation. At that time no one—not June, her parents or the institution's staff—believed June could live outside an institutional environment, would marry someone able to act as a buffer for her against the complexities of life in our society, and would be capable of caring for children of her own—if she were physically able to have them.

June is one of thousands who have been affected by the outmoded laws and attitudes society maintains concerning the sex drives, sexual capabilities, and sexuality of persons with a wide range of disabilities. The disabled, especially epileptics or the mentally retarded, face the possibility of being sterilized without their knowledge or consent. Sexual activities which are condoned in others are often begrudged or denied the disabled, especially if they live in custodial institutions (Heslinga, Shellen, and Verkuyl, 1974). Many are refused the right to marry within religions which doubt their sexual potency and which hold there can be no church marriage if the husband "is unable to carry the marital act to termination." Until August 1977, a Catholic who had a vasectomy or who was sterile but capable of coitus could have his marriage nullified because the Vatican's Pontifical Tribunal had previously annulled marriages when the husband could not "ejaculate semen produced in the testicles" (*Commercial Appeal*, August 6, 1977, p. 14). Those who have children fear a meddling neighbor or relative will complain to some social agency, resulting in their children's being taken from them. Finally, those who are unable to have children find it nearly impossible to adopt unless a child has a physical defect or racial characteristic which makes him difficult to place (Heslinga et al., 1974). One couple who had a son of their own decided to adopt the other children they wanted, but found they could only adopt severely disabled children. Since they both used wheelchairs, they feared such children might require more care than they could consistently give, and they questioned a system which reasoned they were incapable of caring for normal children, but able to care for children with special needs.

MISCONCEPTIONS PERPETUATED BY MEDIA IMAGES

Many of the legal and quasi-legal proscriptions against disabled persons' exercising their sexual rights arise from widespread misconceptions regarding their sexual capacities and incapacities. Best-selling books, long-running plays, and popular movies distort and magnify any problems they might have. For centuries the communications media have perpetuated three representations of the sexuality of the disabled: (1) the disabled as uninterested, i.e., asexual; (2) the disabled as interested but incapable, i.e., sexually frustrated; and (3) the disabled as interested and capable but behaving abnormally, i.e., sexually perverted (Heslinga et al., 1974; Wright, 1960).

Although all disabled persons suffer from sexual miscasting, dwarfs are most often portrayed as asexual. Victor Hugo's Quasimodo in *The Hunchback of Notre Dame* worshipped La Esmeralda but harbored no expectation that a relationship with her was possible. Therefore, in Hugo's portrayal, Quasimodo, despite his heroic efforts on her behalf, accepts the fact that La Esmeralda's physical passion is reserved for her stalwart soldier lover. Although Hugo's tale may arouse a reader's sympathy, it does nothing to increase a reader's understanding or acceptance of physical liaisons between the nondisabled and the disabled.

From early childhood attitudes are thus molded: different is ugly; deformed is evil; those who are physically different deviate in all other aspects of their lives also. In *The Wizard of Oz* the wicked witch is bent and ugly, while the good witch stands straight and lovely. How inoffensive is a children's story in which a young girl lives with seven adult males who are not related to her. If "Snow White and the Seven Dwarfs" became "Snow White and the Seven Huntsmen," however, the story would no longer be for children. Little harm is done when fairy tales give the impression that living "happily ever after" describes the married life of adults, but too many adults fail to outgrow the related childhood illusion that living "happily ever after" is reserved for "perfect specimens" like princes and princesses—never for anyone dwarfed, deformed, or disabled. Even lives of disabled persons from history are distorted in media presentations. Wright (1960) describes how the movie *Moulin Rouge* depicts Toulouse-Lautrec as twisted and embittered by his unrequited passion for a prostitute, when in reality he was well known for his successes with women, despite his short stature. Often the desire for dramatic effect causes half-truths to replace plebeian facts, strengthening public misconceptions about disabled persons.

Equally as damaging as being portrayed as asexual is being portrayed as sexually impotent. D. H. Lawrence's *Lady Chatterley's Lover*, as far as disabled males are concerned, is more of a literary emasculator than a literary masterpiece. In lieu of enlightening the reader about their sexual abilities, *Lady Chatterley's Lover* strengthens existing stereotypes of men in wheelchairs as unable to satisfy women's sexual needs. As Hohmann (*Rehabilitating the Person with Spinal Cord*

Injury, 1972) points out, more disabled men are rendered impotent by the sexual mythology that justifies a liaison between Lady Chatterley and her gardener than by the physiological effects of their disabilities.

Some strides have been made recently in portraying more realistically the sexuality of the disabled. After seeing the sexuality of cerebral-palsied persons discussed in the film *Like Other People*, an undergraduate student realized she had been treating a 35-year-old cerebral-palsied patient of hers as a child, not as an adult male. The movie *Coming Home* (1978) made a media breakthrough with its frank and accurate portrayal of the sexual functioning of paraplegic males.

ROOTS OF THE MYTH

In part, present-day misconceptions about the sexuality of the disabled are based on facts which are no longer true. When the life expectancy of most disabled persons was short, when the onset of a disability resulted in discomfort and continual ill health, sexual concerns gave way to comfort and survival concerns. Today, the life expectancy of all disabled persons has increased dramatically, but in the 1940s a child born with spina bifida had a life expectancy of approximately 14 years as did children born with Down's syndrome. Sexual matters were not very relevant when few reached the age of puberty.

Those whose disabilities were not life-threatening—the blind, the deaf, the cerebral palsied—spent most of their lives sequestered at home or in institutions, emerging only on rare and closely supervised occasions. They had few chances to meet anyone with whom they might establish an intimate relationship. Those who escaped the life of a shut-in tended to be unobtrusive. Before sexual freedom and equal rights for the handicapped became social movements, the sexual relationships of disabled individuals were private affairs, without influence on public attitudes or policies. Thirty years ago one might see a legless man selling pencils on a street corner or pass a blind man playing an accordion for coins in some large city, but one seldom saw disabled people engaged in everyday activities. Because most did not mingle with persons outside of their families or institutional settings, they had little opportunity to meet, court, and marry. Therefore, with little opportunity to be sexually active, such persons were considered incapable of sexual activity.

THE ROLE OF THE VETERANS IN ERODING THE MYTH

The rise in sexual consciousness among the disabled began with the medical advances of World War II and reached fruition in the general sexual revolution that influenced those disabled in the Vietnam war.

Late Forties: The World War II Vets

Thousands of servicemen who were severely disabled during World War II survived despite the probability of having shortened life expectancies. They returned to their communities and, being young and active, refused to spend their lives sitting at home, looking at the world from their bedroom windows. Stanley Kramer's movie *The Men* portrays the rehabilitation advances that allowed these veterans to move back into their communities. Folding wheelchairs, hand controls for automobiles, government-financed modified homes, and continuous specialized medical services helped smooth the transition from shut-in to active community participant. Disability pensions for those with service-connected injuries allowed such vets to marry and support families, regardless of whether they were able to find employment in the postwar economy.

But although the World War II veteran was assertive in attacking the barriers preventing him from full community participation, he was the product of a sexually conservative age, which held that a person's sexual preferences and activities were as sacrosanct as his bank account. Therefore, while the post-World War II era brought about a major attack on educational and attitudinal barriers facing disabled persons, it wasn't until the Vietnam war that sexual barriers began to crumble.

Late Sixties: The Vietnam Vets

The Vietnam vets were not only as young and active as their predecessors, they were also products of a generation more comfortable with sexuality and more vocal about sexual concerns. Before the 1960s it was assumed that a loss of sensation and paralysis of the lower limbs produced a loss of sexual functioning as well. But while the sexual reticence of the World War II veterans helped perpetuate this misconception, Vietnam vets did not worry silently about the effect of their disabilities on their sexual activities. They wanted, and some demanded, answers to their sexual questions. At first the answers they received mirrored popular myths concerning the disabled in general: (1) "Sex? Forget about it. It's all over," or (2) "Sex? Don't think about it and it won't bother you" (Hohmann, 1972).

The disabled, however, didn't forget about sex, and the matter of their own sexuality continued to plague them. Newly disabled vets, getting little satisfaction from professionals, were urged by those who had experienced some sexual successes to get out of the medical setting and see what they could do. Many on weekend passes bought the services of prostitutes to test their sexual functioning. Some, like Kovic, author of *Born on the Fourth of July,* waited until they were discharged, and then moved to enclaves of veterans in foreign countries where they experimented, unrestricted by the restraints of their own communities (Kovic, 1976).

Response of the Experts: The Beginnings of Research

Eventually the questions and experiences of the veterans had an effect. Investigators began to concentrate on the disability thought to have the most catastrophic effect on sexual functioning—spinal cord injury. Researchers like Cole, Comarr, and Hohmann began to add data to that already accumulated in hospitals and rehabilitation centers throughout the country. Cole discovered that paralyzed males were more concerned about their possible loss of sexual functioning than about not being able to walk (Mooney, Cole, and Chilgran, 1975).

Hohmann's research with thousands of SCI patients covered five aspects of sexual functioning: (1) sex resulting in physiological excitement culminating in orgasm; (2) sex for procreation; (3) sex to enhance one's ego; (4) sex to control another person; and (5) sex to establish a mutually satisfying relationship with another human being. Hohmann found that the majority of his subjects were able to engage in the last three types of sexual behavior, with a significant number being able to engage in all five (Hohmann, 1972). Comarr discovered that a majority of SCI men could successfully engage in intercourse. Separately, Cole, Hohmann, and Comarr concluded that even those few who were unable to have coitus did not lose their interest in sex or stop engaging in alternative sexual behaviors.

The Long Beach Conference

In the early 1970s a concerted effort was made to investigate the sexual concerns and capabilities of all disabled persons. In March of 1972 a workshop in Long Beach, California, touched on all aspects of the psychosocial rehabilitation of the spinal-cord-injured, including sex and marriage. Among those participating was Hohmann, then chief of psychology service at the Tucson VA Hospital. Himself an SCI paraplegic, Hohmann had worked with thousands of veterans. His articles on sex and the spinal-cord-injured are based upon both his professional and his personal experiences.

Another participant was A. Estin Comarr, chief of SCI service at the Long Beach VA Hospital. By the early 1970s Comarr had been conducting research on SCI patients for over thirty years. According to his report, "a substantial number, though not an overwhelming proportion of SCI patients, will have essentially normal sexual functioning. Another group will have an ability to perform sexually but will not experience orgasm or ejaculate. A third group will be unable to do anything as far as genital sexuality is concerned, but this does not mean that sex is a dead issue" (*Rehabilitating the Person with Spinal Cord Injury*, 1972, p. 15).

Unfortunately, as Hohmann points out, "the greatest problem is that more patients and staff members have read *Lady Chatterley's Lover* or know of or believe the portrayal of spinal-cord-injured patients that it sets forth, than have heard of Dr. Comarr's research. Too often, when an SCI patient visits his old hospital ward with a child on his knee, someone will joke about it—sometimes in front of him—that the child must be the milkman's. This is not only cruel, but very likely untrue" (*Rehabilitating the Person with Spinal Cord Injury*, 1972, p. 14).

The Civilian Sector: The Beginnings of Sex Education for M.D.'s

In addition to research conducted by the VA, by the early 1970s progress toward understanding the relationship between disability and sexual functioning was occurring in the civilian sector. Timothy D. Cole of the University of Minnesota Medical School was making public information originally designed to educate medical students in human sexuality and disability. Independently of Comarr, Cole had discovered that the majority of SCI men have erections, up to 70 percent with incomplete injuries ejaculate, and most of them successfully engage in intercourse. To correct existing misconceptions, Cole conducts workshops which are open to the disabled, their partners, and interested professionals. As part of the workshop, Cole shows many films, one of which has a quadriplegic and his wife, another a paraplegic and his wife, engaging in a variety of sexual activities. In collaboration with several other authors, Cole has published a book, *Sexual Options for Quadriplegics and Paraplegics* (Mooney, Cole, Chilgran, 1975), which uses photographs to demonstrate the ways SCI men and women can achieve sexual gratification.

SEX AND THE DISABLED: PHYSICAL COMPLICATIONS

Paralleling the growing acceptance that rehabilitation is incomplete if sexual rehabilitation is not part of an overall program is the proliferation of interest in the sexuality of all disabled persons, not only the spinal-cord-injured. During the 1970s, articles on sex and disability appeared in a variety of medical and other professional journals. The conclusion of many researchers during the last decade is that, while in terms of their sex drives disabled people do not differ from their nondisabled counterparts, physical disability, whatever the cause, has some effect on an individual's sexuality. Persons with physical disabilities have problems with sexual functioning that might not have arisen—or might have been less of a factor—had they not been disabled. The problems may be physiological, psychological, social, or a combination of all three.

The Limits of Common Sense

It is not always possible, however, to determine through common sense what problems beset persons with particular disabilities. One might believe that someone with a below-the-knee amputation from a gunshot wound would have no functional incapacities because his genitals are unaffected. Of course, if the amputation was caused by a vascular disorder which impeded normal blood flow, one might suspect that a similar interference with the blood supply to the penis would affect the ability to maintain an erection. But when an amputation is due to a traumatic injury, any problems with sexual functioning are thought to be psychological—impotency due to feeling less of a man—or social—potential partners' being repelled by the thought or sight of his stump. Whatever the cause of an amputation, however, physical problems can arise, such as impaired balance or phantom pain. The loss of one limb or two may require a change from a previously preferred position for intercourse to one in which balance can be maintained. Similarly, a position change may be necessary if a previously preferred position freed a now-absent hand for caressing one's partner. The phenomenon of phantom pain—usually a burning sensation in a missing limb—can be disruptive if it occurs immediately before orgasm.

Common sense might also lead one to the conclusion that persons confined to wheelchairs may be incapable of genitally based sexual activities, due to the area of their physical involvement. People, however, are paralyzed from a variety of causes, some of which, such as poliomyelitis, do not affect the ability to achieve an erection, ejaculate, or experience orgasm. Muscular dystrophy or multiple sclerosis may or may not have a debilitating effect on these mechanical aspects of sex. Spinal cord injury, unless it occurs in the second to fourth sacral segments of the spinal cord, usually does not affect the ability to have reflexogenic erections, which are initiated by nervous impulses entering the spinal cord directly from the periphery of the body (Weiss, 1972). Men with injuries above these segments may have erections that last longer than before they were disabled, because the damage to the cord prevents inhibiting impulses from the higher brain centers from reaching the cord below the injury. Approximately 10 percent of all men with cervical injuries are subject to priapism, a condition in which the penis remains erect. If priapism persists, muscle tissue will be replaced by fibrous tissue, causing a permanent erection, unless surgical measures are employed.

Finally, common sense leads one to err if one believes that physical disability results in a reduced sex drive. Only in cases where certain medications are used, such as in treating hypertension or in controlling epileptic seizures, is there a possible decrease in libido. Some disabled persons have naturally low sex drives, some naturally strong sex drives, but these are individual differences unrelated to a disabling condition. There is no proven relationship between type of disability and potency of one's sex drive.

The sexual abilities of persons with various disabilities have been compiled by Heslinga in *Not Made of Stone*. Heslinga explains how particular disabilities affect masturbation, coitus, fertility and, in the case of women, bearing and delivering children (Heslinga et al., 1974; see Table 5-1). Even when these sexual functions are intact, problems may arise with positioning, mobility, pain, spasms, or autonomic dysreflexia.

"Children of the Disabled—The Likelihood of Normality"?

According to Heslinga, disabled persons as a group have approximately the same chance of having a normal child as the general population. In determining whether a person with a particular disability is likely to have a normal child, one must know the concordance (linkage between heredity and disability) of the disability group. Concordance for persons with adventitious disabilities, such as spinal cord injury or poliomyelitis, is 0 percent. Concordance for persons with cerebral palsy is close to 0 percent, while for those with hemophilia it is 100 percent. Heslinga's findings may be explained by the fact that (1) approximately 5 percent of live-born children in the general population "either have major congenital malformations or develop severe mental retardation or both" (Omenn, 1978; Stein, 1978), and (2) persons with some hereditary defects, such as Tay-Sachs, do not live long enough to reproduce. A child born with Tay-Sachs appears normal at birth but within a few months begins to develop incoordination, seizures, blindness, and mental retardation, seldom living past his fourth year. Spina bifida, a neural tube defect in which the child is born with an open spine, follows Down's syndrome as the second most common birth defect, appearing in one out of 800 births. If parents have one child with this disorder, there is a 5 percent chance their next child will have the same defect. If one parent has spina bifida or any other neural tube defect, the chance increases to anywhere from 10 to 15 percent (Freeman, 1974).

If a disability is genetically linked, genetic counseling or prenatal tests such as amniocentesis (the procedure where a sample of the fluid surrounding the fetus is taken and tested for abnormal constituents) can often determine whether a fetus may be or is affected. Individual genetic counseling, although incapable of ensuring that any one child will be normal, can identify all chromosomal defects, such as Down's syndrome, and approximately seventy biochemical defects, such as Tay-Sachs (Omenn, 1978). If, as in some cases of spina bifida, a spinal defect is not large enough to allow fetal proteins to leak into the amniotic fluid, ultrasound can be used to detect the malformation of the spinal column. These procedures allow parents the option of choosing to abort a defective fetus or preparing for the birth of a disabled child. Today, much is known about the ability of disabled persons to engage in specific sexual behaviors and the possibility of a specific disability's being present in an unborn child.

Sex and the Disabled Woman

Less is known about the sexuality of disabled women than about their ability to carry out mechanical sexual functions. Until the late 1970s less research was done on the sexuality of disabled women than on that of disabled men. Most researchers, being male, may have been more interested in the sexual roles and function of men. Others, such as Safilios-Rothschild (1970), subscribe to the idea that, due to their traditional social roles, women's sexual identities are less affected by disability than are men's. According to Safilios-Rothschild, dependent women are more acceptable to potential partners than are men who need someone to care for them. This assumes, of course, that disability invariably involves dependency, which is not always true.

What is true, however, is that women are less affected by disability in their fertility and ability to engage in coitus than are men. Because a woman's reproductive functions are under hormonal control, not under both hormonal and neurological control, she can be totally paralyzed or unconscious and still ovulate, be impregnated, and bear and deliver a child. A disease or injury may cause a woman to miss her menstrual periods for a short period of time, but 50 percent of those who sustain spinal cord injuries do not miss a single period, although in rare cases menstruation may be absent for as long as two years. Moreover, the percentage of normal children born to disabled women is the same as that born to nondisabled women. Finally, childbirth is often easier for disabled women. While others must learn to or take drugs to relax their abdominal muscles, the muscles of women with flaccid paralysis lack innervation and are therefore naturally relaxed. For women with sensory losses, labor contractions are as pain-free as are their menstrual periods.

Although women's sexual functioning is less affected than men's, they do experience problems which are unique to or enhanced by their disabilities. For those with paralyzed abdominal muscles, there is less muscular support for their uteruses, and premature births or miscarriages must be closely guarded against. For those who lack sensation, premature births can also be a problem. Such women have had babies born in bedpans simply because they were unaware they were in labor. During labor, a woman's blood pressure may become dangerously

Table 5-1   Sexology of People with a Motor or a Condition Handicap

A. Those with a Motor Handicap

Brief indication of peculiarities and concrete medical therapy

	Coitus and masturbation*	
	Immediately before	**During**

1. Transverse lesion
  a. flaccid
    paralysis ⎤
 	
            ⎥ complete
 	
  b. spastic
    paralysis ⎦
	1. *a.* ♂ Usually no erection is possible
	  ♀ No reflex reaction to foreplay; no erection of the clitoris
	b. ♂ Definite erection, exclusively reflex; no sensation; often: erogenous zones above the level of the lesion
	♀ Sensation missing or only vegetative, with reflex erection of the clitoris; often erogenous zones above the level of the lesion
		1. *a.* ♂ Usually no erection is possible; no orgasm
		♀ No orgasm, quite often intellectual satisfaction; coitus is possible in a good, i.e., usually a supine position; sometimes an approach from behind is easier
		b. ♂ Sometimes a very short erection, sometimes a very long one; no orgasm, vegetative reactions as substitute; sometimes dangerous hypertension, to be treated with high dosage of atropine Infrequent ejaculation, urine is sometimes passed instead; sometimes abdominal spasms prevent coitus; often: woman must lie on man; possible catheter will hamper coitus
		♀ Sometimes contractions of the legs or adductor spasms (knees, legs *together*); valium 10 mg beforehand can help; sometimes hypertension

2. Spina bifida	2. ♂ Erections infrequent, but quite varied, sometimes reflex, sometimes psychogenic, sometimes both are possible, depending on which segments of the medulla have been injured	2. ♂ Usually impossible, sometimes possible; usually no orgasm, as the penis is insensitive; if ejaculation: orgasm too; mostly no ejaculation, fertility very slight to nil

	Special measures during	
Immediately after	**Pregnancy**	**Confinement**
1. *a.* ♂ Not applicable ♀ Some danger of re- flex hypertension *b.* ♂ Sometimes hyper- tension; sometimes excessive perspira- tion, headache ♀ As in the man	1. *a.* Fertility ± normal; very good control of kidney function essential *b.* Incontinence is a great problem *b.* Very good possibilities; good control of tension and kidney function; bladder training some- times difficult	1. *a.* Bearing down; usually possible but not reflex; first stage mostly painless; sup- port the perineum well during parturition; de- livery: in a clinic; where parturition is pro- tracted: pay attention to altering the position *b.* No pain during first stage; bearing down: sometimes quite possi- ble, sometimes diffi- cult; watch hyperten- sion during confine- ment and for spasms of the abdominal wall; frequent cramps at base of pelvis; always in hospital; sometimes forceps delivery, cae- sarian section or vacuum extraction
2. As before	2. Good urinological con- trol is essential; in the event of pregnancy in- continence is a great problem	2. First stage of labour usually not felt; usually possible to bear down; support perineum; not much is known exactly; the author has little experience of such patients

Table 5-1 Sexology of People with a Motor or a Condition Handicap (*Continued*)

A. Those with a Motor Handicap

		Coitus and masturbation*		
		Immediately before		During
		♀ usually no feeling; usually no erection of the clitoris, however this depends once more on the part of the medulla affected		♀ coitus perfectly possible; special positioning with care for paralysed legs; sometimes approach from behind
3. Infantile encephalopathy	3.	Agitation, uninhibited, worsening of spasms or athetotic movements	3.	Often premature ejaculation; heightened reflexes, sometimes unilateral sometimes bilateral; contractions (adductor spasms) can frustrate coitus; masturbation: often not possible manually due to spasms; all reflexes concerned can be retarded or accelerated; in people with athetosis coitus often unsuccessful, the same applies to self-administered masturbation
4. Hemiplegia	4.	Agitation, possibility of hypertension in both men and women	4.	Ditto, much effort required; mostly position is awkward; possibly premature ejaculation; usually impotence at the start of hemiplegia; later often: also look for hypertension and acute cardiac insufficiency; where there is angina pectoris: 0.25–0.5 mg glycerine trinitrate before coitus
5. Multiple sclerosis	5.	Agitation, increasing spasms; sensibility usually intact, often inconsiderate and exacting	5.	In ♂ all contingencies possible; impotence or strong erections; often premature ejaculation; worsen-

	Special measures during	
Immediately after	Pregnancy	Confinement
3. Probably tension and emotion subsides slowly	3. Quite good outlook in infantile encephalopathy; up to now: few pregnancies have occurred in the graver forms	3. Chance of retarded or exaggerated reflexes; abrupt labour pains; careful delivery; no pituitrin; possibly 5 mg valium several times; preferably in hospital
4. Prolonged excitement	4. Should be prevented; if present: very careful control of blood pressure and kidney function	4. Very good conditions required; watch for hypertension; anticipate bearing down; in hospital
5. Sometimes prolonged spasms; often great frustration	5. Definitely possible; uncertain whether the disease is aggravated by it, probably it is . . . ; 'pill' undesirable as	5. Few special remarks in slight cases; treat as spastic transverse lesions in more serious cases

Table 5-1 Sexology of People with a Motor or a Condition Handicap (*Continued*)

A. Those with a Motor Handicap

		Immediately before		Coitus and masturbation* During
				ing spasms; in ♀ adductor spasms may obstruct coitus (operation possible!); valium or other sedatives can help both sexes
6. Poliomyelitis	6.	Normal	6.	Normal but sometimes positioning difficult when paralysis is extensive
7. Rheumatism	7.	No special remarks	7.	Sometimes causes much pain to the affected partner; contractures sometimes demand special positioning; sometimes rules out normal delivery
8. Progressive muscular dystrophy	8.	No special remarks	8.	Sometimes poor heart function; *sometimes* special position necessary

B. Those with a Condition Handicap

		Immediately before		During
1. Hypertension	1.	Agitation can increase the tension	1.	Ditto; avoid great exertion; 'take it easy'
2. Heart trouble	2.	Quickened pulse rate and extra-systoles; in angina pectoris 0.5 mg glycerine trinitrate	2.	♂ Effort is rather *hard*, comparable to climbing rather steep stairs ♀ Effort not so hard; possibly with oxygen on hand (e.g., as a save-a-life unit); secluded if the internist so advises; coitus must sometimes be *prohibited* or coitus reservatus recommended

	Special measures during		
Immediately after		**Pregnancy**	**Confinement**
		contraceptive, therefore sterilization† as soon as possible, ♂ and ♀; pay close attention to passage of urine	
6. No special remarks	6.	Few special remarks; where abdominal muscles paralysed: corset support; ditto for weak back muscles	6. Few complications; in paralysis of abdominal muscles; bearing down impossible
7. No special remarks	7.	Undesirable when active; there is often an improvement during pregnancy and a relapse after the birth; preferably no cortisone	7. No complications; danger of exhaustion; watch the adrenal function if cortisone has been used
8. No special remarks	8.	Sometimes difficult; due to strong lordosis and muscular weakness	8. The muscular weakness can sometimes affect bearing down
1. No special remarks	1.	Undesirable in essential hypertension; the 'pill' decidedly not without danger; where pregnancy exists: *rigorous* control necessary	1. Avoid bearing down; admit to hospital
2. Increased pulse rate for a considerable period; extrasystoles	2.	Undesirable in decompensation; always consult the doctor; if present strict control	2. Avoid bearing down; admit to hospital

Table 5-1 Sexology of People with a Motor or a Condition Handicap (*Continued*)
B. Those with a Condition Handicap

		Coitus and masturbation*	
		Immediately before	**During**
3. Asthma	3.	Undesirable during an attack; when free from attack no special precautions	3. Sometimes initiates an attack; then anti-asthmatics *before* or during coitus
4. Patients under dialysis	4.	As in hypertension	4. As in hypertension
5. Diabetes	5.	No special precautions; occasionally local irritation	5. Quite often an inflamed glans and foreskin, or vaginitis present; can produce painful irritation: careful local hygiene; specialist's advice necessary before the 'pill' is used; impotence quite frequent

high, or conversely, drop drastically low. This is due to autonomic dysreflexia, a condition resulting from disruption of normal nerve pathways, causing inappropriate reflexes from normally innocuous stimuli, such as involuntary uterine contractions. Physicians who are familiar with the secondary complications of various disabilities can control autonomic dysreflexia and can prevent strokes from occurring during the birth process.

Less easily resolved, however, than ensuring safe deliveries, is the problem of unwanted pregnancies. Since a woman's fertility is unaffected by disability, and most methods of birth control pose unique dangers for disabled women, unwanted pregnancies often occur. For example, the most effective contraceptive, the birth control pill, is hazardous for those with paralyzed lower limbs or vascular disorders because of its bloodclotting propensities. Intrauterine devices are inappropriate for those with sensory impairments because the uterus may be perforated. Since there is no pain to warn of tissue damage, resulting infections could be far advanced before other symptoms indicated something was seriously wrong. Diaphragms are not only difficult for women with weak or paralyzed hands to insert, but may slip without being detected by those with sensory loss. If a couple is positive they do not want a child, a tubal ligation or vasectomy may be the answer,

		Special measures during		
	Immediately after	**Pregnancy**		**Confinement**
3.	Often prolonged breathlessness	3.	Asthma often improves during pregnancy; usual controls and medicines; before using cortisones consult specialists (internist and gynaecologist)	3.	Oxygen on hand; avoid bearing down hard
4.	No special precautions	4.	Undesirable; if present very strict control; before using contraceptives: consult gynaecologist and internist	4.	Not applicable
5.	As before	5.	Careful supervision of diabetes essential; in women there is less chance of pregnancy and greater chance of a heavy child and abortion	5.	No special problems; look out for heavy child and hydramnion

General remarks concerning masturbation: Masturbation is, of course, only possible if the hand function is relatively good and complete erection is possible (therefore *not* with low spina bifida, flaccid transverse lesion, sometimes not with M.S. etc.). The effort involved is slight, the excitement can be great, especially in spastic and athetotic subjects. (Source: Heslinga et al., 1974, p. 202A.)

†Unless a woman is in remission, being pregnant can exacerbate multiple sclerosis, as, for example, birth control pills. Therefore, in Scandinavia, women often choose to be sterilized in lieu of their other alternatives, i.e., being sexually inactive or risking an accelerated progression of their condition.

but such operations are difficult, often impossible, to reverse, while feelings about having a child are not. Contraceptive foam is the birth control method most often recommended for disabled women, but unfortunately, foam is also one of the least effective methods of birth control (Task Force on Concerns of Physically Disabled Women, 1978a, 1978b).

In addition to problems with birth control, disabled women who spend long hours sitting in wheelchairs or who must wear waterproof undergarments are subject to vaginal infections. When they are in contact with rubber or vinyl materials, the warm, moist environment surrounding their external genitalia provides an optimum medium for the various organisms that infect the vaginal area. Similar problems are reported by women with strong spasms that clamp their thighs tightly together, blocking air circulation to the genitals. More porous cushion covers, cloth fabrics for wheelchair seats, and devices to insert between the knees to keep the thighs slightly apart offer some relief, but do not eliminate the problem completely.

Sexual Problems of Disabled Males

Despite their difficulties with autonomic dysreflexia, birth control, and chronic infections, women are affected minimally by most disabilities, compared to men. Nevertheless, most men retain their sexual potency, i.e., their ability to attain and maintain an erection, and are able to engage in intercourse. To understand how men who have lost voluntary control and sensation in the genital area retain their potency, one must understand (1) upper and lower motor neuron sex, (2) the "law of the spinal cord," and (3) the two types of erections common to men with no physical impairments: psychogenic and reflexogenic.

Upper and Lower Motor Neurons   A motor neuron is a nerve cell which either (a) carries a signal to move a body part from the motor cortex of the brain to an area inside the spinal cord or (b) relays that signal to move a body part from the spinal cord to the muscle fiber, gland, etc., which carries out the intended movement. Put in its simplest terms, each body movement requires a chain of two motor neurons. The upper motor neuron, the first link in the chain, extends from the motor cortex of the brain to, for example, the second sacral spinal nerve (S2) of the spinal cord. In our example, the lower motor neuron, the second link in the chain, is part of the second sacral spinal nerve. It extends from the spinal cord to the genital area where it causes a muscle fiber to shorten or some other body micropart to respond. A desire to urinate, for example, would produce an impulse in the motor cortex, and that impulse would be carried by the upper motor neuron to the lower motor neuron. The lower motor neuron would pick up the impulse and carry it to the round muscle or sphincter surrounding the end of the urinary tract.

To reiterate, for the urinary sphincter to receive a stimulus causing it to react, a two-motor-neuron chain is required. The upper motor neuron extends from the motor cortex of the cerebral hemispheres to the area of the spinal cord in the small of the back. The lower motor neuron extends from the spinal cord to the urethral sphincter.

The Law of the Spinal Cord   The "law of the spinal cord" has two parts. The first states that following an injury to the spinal cord, there will be a period of spinal shock during which all reflex activity disappears within the cord at and below the point of injury. Reflex activity is movement that occurs without a person's consciously willing it. For example, when a physician hits a person's knee with a rubber hammer, the lower leg will jerk forward, no matter how hard the person tries to prevent the leg from moving. This knee-jerk reflex occurs when there is no impairment of the leg muscle, of the neuron carrying the impulse from the knee into the spinal cord (the sensory neuron), or of the lower motor neuron, which carries the impulse back out.

This is what happens in a simple reflex such as the patellar tendon reflex described above. The blow to the kneecap "fires" a sensory neuron which then carries the nervous impulse from the knee to the area just inside the back of the spinal cord. The impulse is then transmitted from the sensory neuron to the lower motor neuron which extends from the front (anterior horn) of the cord back to the knee where it causes the knee-jerk reaction one sees. If the sensory neuron is destroyed, no impulse can enter the cord, and since the motor neuron cannot relay an impulse that does not arrive, there will be no muscular response. If the sensory neuron is intact but the motor neuron is destroyed, the leg will remain motionless because the pathway from the cord back out to the muscle has been eliminated. In actual fact, the sensory and the motor neuron connect with many adjacent neurons—including the sensory tracts that ascend the cord—allowing one to "feel" the hammer blow. (For a more extensive treatment of the reflex arc, consult any introductory physiology text.)

The second portion of the "law of the spinal cord" states that once the period of spinal shock ends—a matter of days for a man—reflex activity will resume *below* the site of injury but will be gone permanently *at* the site of injury, due to the destruction of the lower motor neuron at that point (*Rehabilitating the Person with Spinal Cord Injury*, Comarr, 1972).

Psychogenic and Reflexogenic Erections   If one is to provide sexual counseling to men with spinal cord injuries, one must understand not only upper and lower motor neurons or "the law of the spinal cord," but also the two types of erections appearing in the nondisabled male: reflexogenic and psychogenic.

A psychogenic erection occurs in response to an excess of hormones in the bloodstream which eroticize the brain, or to an external mental stimulus, such as a picture or fragrance associated with a previous pleasurable sexual experience. The aroused brain sends impulses down the upper motor neuron to the erection center (S2-S4 segments) of the spinal cord, which then transmits that impulse, via the lower motor neuron and the autonomic nervous system, to the genitals.

Reflexogenic erections are those which occur in the absence of impulses coming from the brain. In reflexogenic erections, internal or external stimulation of the genital area causes the sensory neurons to carry impulses to the cord. Those sensory neurons then transmit the impulse via the lower motor neuron back to the genitalia, producing a penile erection. External stimuli which may cause a reflexogenic erection can range from massaging of the penis to compression of the scrotum. Internal stimuli can range from distention of the bladder to distention of the lower digestive tract. Reflexogenic erections, then, are those which occur in the absence of felt sexual desire, although for those who achieve both types of erections, the two overlap and are difficult to distinguish. A man may awaken with a reflexogenic erection and having the erection may create a desire for sexual intercourse, strengthening and maintaining the already existing erection.

For persons with complete damage of the spinal cord above the S2-S4 segments, psychogenic erections are rare. When they do occur, it is believed that the autonomic nervous system is still functioning. But for persons with complete lesions above the erection center, reflexogenic erections usually still take place. It is the low-level paraplegic, who was injured in the S2-S4 area, who will be impotent, unless he regains the ability to attain psychogenic erections. According to Comarr, the "law of the spinal cord" explains why 93 percent of his subjects with upper motor neuron injuries, although unable to attain psychogenic erections, had reflexogenic erections compared to 0 percent of his subjects with lower motor neuron injuries (*Rehabilitating the Person with Spinal Cord Injury*, 1972, p. 17).

Although 93 percent of Comarr's subjects had reflexogenic erections, only 73 percent successfully engaged in intercourse. In part, this discrepancy is due to some subjects' lacking sexual partners. In part, it is due to some having only spontaneous reflexogenic erections. For them, stimulation of the genitals produces no response, and so they must rely on internally stimulated erections to perform sexually. Such men find that when they are ready for sex, the time or place may be inconvenient or no partner may be available. Married couples in this situation usually rely on alternative methods of sexual expression in place of intercourse. Finally, some men with such erections are impotent because their erections are too weak or too fleeting. For them, too, alternative sexual activities are necessary.

Whether a man's reflexogenic erections can be initiated or are spontaneous, these reflexes will diminish with age. Therefore, men who rely on them should anticipate that their genitally based sexual activities may end sooner than those of men who are capable of having both types of erections.

Performance and/or Pleasure

Many men and women with sensory-motor impairments express great satisfaction with their sex lives. Many do not. Although some continue to enjoy sex, finding gratification in still being able to perform or give pleasure to their partner, they may feel their loss of orgiastic sensations is irreplaceable. Others, however, experience orgasms different than but equally as satisfying as those they experienced previously. Some develop a highly sensitive, secondary erogenous zone in the dermatone, or area of the body immediately above where their sensory loss begins. Those who have the most difficulty adjusting to their altered physical sensations tend to be persons for whom sex was largely a self-oriented activity, rather than one in which providing pleasure to someone else was a primary source of satisfaction.

Although there are certain guidelines, Comarr warns that it is impossible to predict how much sexual function any one individual will recover. Only the passage of time can reveal the eventual sexual functioning of a newly disabled person. There are some tests, however, which indicate whether a person should have normal sexual functioning. The two types of indicators of a person's functioning are: (1) rectal area indicators and (2) genital area indicators.

Normal sexual ability is indicated by a rectal examination in which the person has (a) tone (firmness and tension) in the external rectal sphincter, (b) the ability to voluntarily contract and relax the external sphincter, and (c) the presence of a positive bulbocavernosus reflex, where the anal sphincter tightens when pressure is applied to the glans penis. Normal sexual ability is also indicated by a genital area examination in which the person has pinprick sensation in the skin of the penis, the scrotum, and the saddle area of the thighs, i.e., the inner upper thighs adjacent to the genitals. If there is external sphincter tone and voluntary control, a positive bulbocavernosus reflex, and pinprick sensation in the penile, scrotal, and saddle area skin, sexual functioning should be normal. If it is not, the problem may be psychological rather than physiological (*Rehabilitating the Person with Spinal Cord Injury*, 1972).

Although it is impossible to predict the eventual functioning of any individual, it is possible to state that the majority of men with upper motor neuron injuries have reflexogenic erections, successfully engage in coitus, cannot ejaculate, cannot experience orgasms, and are infertile. There are, however, exceptions —persons who cannot function at all as well as persons with complete lesions who ejaculate, experience orgasms, and are fertile.

Male Fertility

Those who fall into the latter group, however, are rare. Most SCI men with complete lesions are infertile, even those who continue to ejaculate and have orgasms. Such men may produce sperm but their ejaculate either contains too few sperm to impregnate their partners or their sperm are dead, deformed, or immobile.

In the normal male a network of muscle fibers encases the scrotum and keeps the scrotal temperature within the optimum range for sperm survival. These fibers contract when the scrotal temperature begins to fall too low and pull the scrotum closer to the body, thereby elevating the temperature. Conversely, when the scrotal temperature rises, these fibers relax, dropping the scrotum away from the pelvic area. Since only living, motile sperm can fertilize an ovum, impairment of this homeostatic* mechanism means many men with neuromuscular disabilities are unable to sire children. Some SCI men have sperm counts as low as 2 million per cubic centimeter with mobility 10 percent and morphology (structure) 30 percent that of normal.

Declining Popularity of Parenthood

Fortunately, for those disabled persons who cannot have or are unable to care for children, the decline in the popularity of parenthood is a psychological boon. Several years ago, Heslinga et al. (1974) cautioned that marriages where one partner was disabled worked out well until the point in the relationship where, normally, a couple would begin a family. At that point, they felt, nondisabled partners sometimes become disenchanted with relationships that, besides having the normal stresses of marriage, seemed destined to remain childless.

More recently, many couples have been deciding to remain childless, for reasons partly social, partly economic. Career-oriented women are reluctant to spend their early adult years in child rearing. Moreover, children are not the economic asset they were in more agrarian times, when several strong sons meant the difference between subsistence farming and prosperity, or security for parents in their later years. Today, raising a child is a luxury, and with the change in cultural mores regarding children's obligations to care for aged or ailing parents, is often viewed as an unprofitable economic and emotional investment.

The increasing social acceptability of either limiting or not beginning a family is reflected in marriage ceremonies which now avoid any exhortations to be "fruitful and multiply" and in the official recognition of the Catholic Church that

---

*Relating to the state of equilibrium normally maintained among various body functions, e.g., temperature and blood pressure.

propagation is not the only valid reason for marriage. These changing expectations have important implications for marriages in which having children is impossible or infeasible. Nevertheless, it is important to remember that for most disabled women, including the spinal-cord-injured, as for most disabled men, excluding most of the spinal-cord-injured, conception is possible (Heslinga et al., 1974).

Special Sexual Problems of Some Disabled Individuals

Certain problems exist in making the sexual experience comfortable, convenient, and pleasurable for persons with certain types of disabilities and their partners. With consideration and forethought, most problems can be resolved without infringing on the enjoyment or performance of either partner.

Incontinence   One source of embarrassment and annoyance for some disabled persons is incontinence. Men and women who are catheter-free but who do not have full control of their urinary sphincters should empty their bladders before engaging in intercourse. Both men and women who use catheters and who find it difficult to remove the tubing prior to intercourse should secure it to the side of the penis or out of the way of the vaginal opening. Removing the tubing completely, however, helps avoid possible abrasions and irritations.

Reflexes   Reflexes often pose a considerable problem during sexual activities. The autonomic dysreflexia that complicates the birth process for SCI women can produce similar difficulties for both men and women during intercourse: headaches, dizziness, and other unpleasant and dangerous symptoms. In most instances, hypertensive or tranquilizing drugs can be taken to avert the effects of dysreflexia prior to and during intercourse (Woods, 1975). Less tractable are situations where hyperreflexia, i.e., excessive reflex activity, causes a woman's adductor muscles to pull her thighs tightly together. Unless muscle relaxants prove effective, the excitement and/or body contact of precoital activities can cause such strong spasms that intercourse, even with rear entry, may be impossible. For men, strong, uncontrolled leg spasms can prove hazardous to their partners. In one instance, a male patient requested a cordotomy—an operation which ends all peripheral reflex activity, including that allowing reflexogenic erections. Even though the operation would render him impotent, the patient and his wife were prepared to rely on other means of sexual gratification, because his spasms had caused him to bloody his wife's nose once too often.

Mobility and Pain   Pain and mobility problems sometimes beset persons whose mechanical ability to perform sexually is unimpaired. Severely paralyzed postpolios retain complete sexual functioning but their lack of mobility forces their partner into the active role, and their sensitivity to pain may mean their arms, legs, and pelvic area have to be supported carefully before they can proceed with sexual activity comfortably. The arthritic's stiffened joints may not only render him immobile, but may make a partner's most delicate touch unbearably painful (Heslinga et al., 1974).

Heart Disease   Although their mobility is unimpaired, persons with conges- tive heart failure or uncontrolled hypertension may find sex feasible only if they do not overexert themselves. Such persons may have to abandon their usual position for intercourse for a less demanding, though perhaps initially less satisfying, one, i.e., side by side facing the partner or lying in the spoon configuration. With severe disabilities, the nondisabled partner or more able partner may have to assume the top position, but unfortunately, the most feasible position physically is not always the most acceptable position psychologically. The mobility or general restrictions of a particular disability often conflict with the preferences or inhibitions of one or both partners. A man who associates the dominant position with masculinity may feel emasculated if his wife assumes that position. However, behaviors which to others may appear to stem from the limitations of a disability may actually be a couple's preferred mode of sexual expression. For example, a physician could not understand why a patient who had strong reflexogenic erections brought his wife to orgasm by manual stimulation, rather than through genital intercourse. The patient explained that his wife had always preferred clitoral stimulation to in- tercourse and, after her husband became disabled, her preference remained unchanged.

Alternative Methods

Alternative methods of sexual expression are as common among the disabled as among the nondisabled. For those without partners, masturbation serves to re- lieve tension and achieve sexual release. Some men who bring their wives to orgasm through genital intercourse cannot experience an orgasm themselves without masturbating manually or with a vibrator. A quadriplegic who fathered two children by artificially inseminating his wife with his ejaculate sometimes required four hours of stimulation before he climaxed.

Unfortunately, there are those with disorders such as muscular dystrophy or severe cerebral palsy who lack the necessary strength or control to masturbate. Others live in environments where any form of sexual activity is prohibited. Often- times, persons who are in a position to control the activities of severely disabled individuals regard masturbation as an abnormal rather than natural behavior. As a result, many disabled persons who do not know how to or who cannot mastur- bate suffer unrelieved sexual tension because any request for help or instruction is met with outrage or derision on the part of those who attend them (Heslinga et al., 1974). A different attitude prevails in European institutions, especially Scan- dinavian, where persons who cannot stimulate themselves are assisted by staff members.

Although genital-genital intercourse is the preferred mode of sexual behavior among disabled persons, even those with full sexual functioning sometimes prefer alternative sexual behaviors. Therefore, those who don't find these activities repugnant or a violation of their or their partner's religious beliefs engage, as do their nondisabled counterparts, in cunnilingus, fellatio, or any other behavior their ingenuity can devise. In fact, alternative methods of sexual expression may, if pain or mobility is a problem, be the only feasible sexual outlets. Moreover, it is important to remember, as Hohmann reminds us, that a substantial number of satisfactory marriages have lasted for more than a quarter of a century when a couple's sexual relationship consisted of deep regard, respect, and "understanding, combined with only the most casual petting, kissing or other expressions of tenderness." Hohmann warns those who teach, counsel, or advise the disabled that "those who presume to tell their clients that their sexual lives are over, that marriage is out of the question, that wives (or husbands) will soon be unfaithful or advise against establishing a permanent sexual liaison, not only show their gross ignorance of the facts, but they do serious harm . . ." (Hohmann, 1973).

SEXUALITY AND THE DISABLED

Whether they limit themselves to so-called "normal" behaviors, engage in alternative behaviors, or indulge only in casual expressions of tenderness, disabled persons partake of some form of sexual activity. While there have been an increased interest in the sexual aspects of disability and a marked improvement in disseminating sexual information, most available research concerns the mechanical aspects of sex. Sex, however, is a complex behavior, consisting of more than what one does in the privacy of one's bedroom or on the back seat of one's car. As Trieschmann (1975) points out, to discuss sex fully one must consider all of its components: (1) sex as a biological drive, (2) sex as learned behavior involving the genitals or the secondary erogenous zones, and (3) sex as the expression of both drive and learned behavior in a relationship with another human being. It is in the realm of sexual expression, i.e., sexuality, that the disabled face their greatest problems.

Sexuality, by definition, involves communicating and relating on many different levels—conversing, sharing interests, expressing feelings of attraction and warmth, as well as engaging in mutually satisfying sexual behaviors—not simply desiring sex or performing sexual activities. These other aspects of sexuality can pose problems for the severely physically disabled. For example, a discernible disability affects one's value in the sexual marketplace, to borrow a concept from Eric Fromm's *The Art of Love* (1956). A disabled man's deviation from what is considered normal often precludes potential partners from seeing him as sexually desirable. Disabled women rarely receive appreciative whistles, unless they are known to the whistler. One sexually active woman in a wheelchair, who works in the Chicago Loop, complains that when she eats lunch in a restaurant close to her office and men enter looking for someone with whom they might strike up an acquaintaince, their eyes pass over her as though she were a piece of restaurant furniture.

Fulfillment as a sexual being requires being seen and accepted by another as a worthwhile, desirable companion and having the other, in turn, relate to you, to share with you her joys, sorrows, and physical pleasures. Fortunately, many noninstitutionalized, non-homebound persons are able to forge this type of relationship. But according to research, they seem to search longer and work harder to establish relationships, and thus fulfill their sexual potential later in life than the nondisabled (Wright, 1960; Heslinga et al., 1974). The "late bloomer" syndrome of the disabled can be traced to several factors which contribute to their sexuality's developing differently from that of nondisabled peers.

PSYCHOLOGICAL ASPECTS OF A DISABLED CHILD'S DEVELOPMENT AS A SEXUAL BEING

All persons struggle for emotional and economic independence from their parents, but for those with severe disabilities the struggle is more difficult and lasts longer (Wright, 1960). The same is true for sexual maturity, which in our society is marked by marriage as the rite of passage. From childhood on, disabled persons are hampered in the development of their sexuality by the attitudes their disabilities provoke. For example, sex education for disabled children is a more volatile issue than sex education for nondisabled children. Many parents and professionals look on disabled children and adults as eternal innocents, as nonsexual beings. These persons see disabled children as not-quite-human beings who are—or should be—intrinsically pure, unsullied by sexual thoughts, desires, and questions. To teach these children about sex would be to open Pandora's box, since these children would then become aware of behaviors which their would-be benefactors erroneously believe will never be available to them as adults.

Eventually, these children are discovered not to be so innocent. When their bodies betray them by overt sexual responses, both their parents and professionals may be offended or frightened by situations they fear they can't control. A mother of a retarded, spastic teenage daughter may be repelled if, in the middle of a bath, her daughter asks to have her genital area rubbed harder because it "feels so good." Unprepared, the mother may suspect her daughter has homosexual or incestuous tendencies, when in fact her child simply lacks the social judgment of a nonretarded teenager, and so openly admits the pleasure she receives from stimulation of her erogenous zone.

Sex Education for the Blind Child

The reluctance of many persons to educate disabled children about sex is based on the real difficulties of teaching such children in a manner that is both effective and socially acceptable. How, for example, does one educate blind children about the anatomical differences between men and women? Sighted children learn this largely through visible differences in body shape, body size, clothing, and hair styles. But blind children experience their world through sound and touch. What sighted siblings learn about male and female anatomy automatically may remain a mystery to the blind child and, sometimes, even the blind adult. Parents who believe the human body is beautiful and wholesome are not averse to having their children see them nude. Nevertheless, these same parents may feel it is shameful somehow to allow a blind child to touch and explore their bodies. Therefore, a child who is blind may be retarded in terms of his early sex education. Outside the home this situation is compounded, for schools and institutions for the blind, like those for the retarded, usually have rigid restrictions prohibiting children's mutual exploration. Often such restrictions do not arise from the personal convictions of professional personnel or administrators, but rather from the attitudes of parents and the communities in which schools and institutions are located. Few institutions in the United States have begun to follow the example of those in European countries, where live nude models are used to teach blind children, through touch, the external differences between the sexes (Heslinga et al., 1974).

Restrictions That Impede Normal Modes of Sex Development

Like blind children who are limited by their sensory loss, other disabled children are limited by the restrictions on activities other children engage in naturally. Few severely disabled children experience the degree of personal privacy and autonomy accorded nondisabled children. Severely disabled children invariably have some-one—parent, brother, sister, or babysitter—who watches over them. While over-seeing these children's activities is necessary to prevent accidents or exploitation by other children and adults, it also prevents them from being free to participate in such sexually oriented activities as mutual exploration or sharing information garnered by other children.

As the disabled become older, they often attend schools where close super-vision and restrictions continue. In residential schools for the blind, the deaf, the orthopedically handicapped, or the mentally retarded, segregation of the sexes persists, as do set punishments for infractions of the rules.

Sex and the Retarded: Restriction or Education?

A male resident in an institution for the mentally retarded was confined to his living quarters for a week because he had a graduation-type photo of a girl in his wallet. Another resident in the same school (to show what the restriction on pictures was to prevent) was confined to his quarters for six weeks after he was found enjoying intercourse with another resident in a stairwell. The effectiveness of punishment in combating the intrinsic reward of a satisfying sexual encounter was exemplified by his response when, after his six weeks in solitary, he grinned and said, "It was worth it."

Denying information, imposing restrictions, and providing punishments have not prevented sexual interest, development, or experimentation. Instead, the absence of accurate information, social training, and sexual outlets channel other-wise normal sexual behaviors into seemingly deviant ones. Sex education adapted to the unique needs of each individual must therefore be provided. A consensus is growing among those who work with the severely and moderately retarded that sexual terms, sexual concepts, and impulse control must be taught to the retarded who, heretofore, were considered incapable of responsible sexual self-governance. If the attempt to teach them fails, at least an attempt will have been made to ameliorate a situation with no other ethically acceptable solutions. To date, re-ports from sex educators have been encouraging. Blue (1974), who specializes in sex education for the retarded, estimates 60 percent of his students benefit from sex education classes. He points out, however, that each class must be small, composed of persons with similar capacities to learn, designed to meet the unique goals of each group's members, and continued for an extended period of time, sometimes for more than a year.

Teaching techniques such as those developed by Blue are time-consuming and require ingenuity and personal dedication on the part of the educators. But as Blue points out, the alternative to sex education is inappropriate sexual behavior, unwanted children, increased drain of familial and community resources, and isolation from the community life to which the disabled are entitled.

One common conflict between retarded children and the adults around them arises from outmoded ideas concerning masturbation. Nearly all males and a majority of females are known to masturbate, an activity psychologists agree is a normal part of sexual development and useful, at all ages, to relieve stress and sexual tension, along with or in the absence of other sexual activities. However, continual and open masturbation in a classroom can be disturbing both to teachers and to any others present. In such situations, before confronting a child or attempting to modify her behavior, one should check for too-tight clothing or for rashes which may be precipitating the behavior. Only after all physical causes are eliminated should an issue be made of the fact that, while such behavior is not wrong, engaging in it during class is. Some children habitually masturbate while watching television by rocking back and forth over a foot drawn up beneath them. Parents have been successful in training such children by simply sending them to their room, allowing them to return after they have grown bored with their self-stimulating activity.

Because the disabled chid is already more restricted in her mobility and/or sensory abilities than other children, who have more opportunity to learn through normal childhood experiences, she must be carefully taught which sexual behaviors are acceptable and which are not. Supervised integration, not segregation, should be the rule in hospitals, schools, and developmental institutions. Not silence, but deliberate discussion of sexual terms, clinical and vernacular, and of sexual physiology should be routine with mentally retarded and physically disabled children. Terms and explanations must, of course, be tailored to each child's mental, social, and sexual development. Unfortunately, sex education is most often offered in the negative sense: "Thou shalt not. . . ." Since punishment is a less effective behavior modifier than reward, the "Thou shalt not" form of education has proved to be less effective than the physiological gratification which reinforces undesirable behaviors.

Pursuant to the argument that teaching such children about sex will provoke behaviors and expectations which would otherwise remain dormant is the argument that one cannot teach retarded children impulse control, or the ability to use their knowledge responsibly. This argument that the retarded are slaves to their impulses is a variation of the fear that retarded boys grow into uncontrollable sex maniacs. According to the families of retarded persons, however, too often the reverse is true. The mentally retarded are exploited sexually by those of normal intelligence, who use them in ways they do not use one another.

A final argument against sex education rests on the assumption that techniques or affordable materials are not available to teach those with mobility, sensory, or intellectual deficits. Today, a multitude of educational aids exist for use with physically disabled and mentally retarded children. Guides for the educator from educational publishing houses list available films, filmstrips, slides, and breakaway and tactile models of all kinds. Many materials are usable in the home as well, e.g., pictures in mail-order catalogs can be used to teach the profoundly retarded the difference between men and women, boys and girls. Some guides set behavioral objectives for children with different degrees of retardation.

For the profoundly retarded, successful sex education has three goals: learning that there is a difference between men and women, learning that men and women use different restrooms in public, and learning which public restroom to use. Sex education does not mean each child is taught sexual anatomy and physiology in detail. For some, sex education is successful when they use the right restroom away from home.

SPECIAL PROBLEMS OF THE DISABLED ADOLESCENT

Adolescence is the season of heightened sexual awareness, when one's personal worth is measured largely by one's ability to attract and establish relationships with attractive members of the opposite sex. Adolescence can pose seemingly insurmountable problems for a teenager who has been disabled from birth or early childhood, and who has had little experience with unsupervised boy-girl encounters. This lack of normal experiences in childhood tends to create a shyness and lack of self-confidence which exceeds that which is normal for any teenager. If disabled while in the teens, an adolescent may discover that behaviors which worked before are no longer possible or have lost their effectiveness.

Working Hard to Seem Casual

The disabled, to prosper in interpersonal relationships, have to at the same time be verbally assertive and be able to moderate their assertiveness so their behavior does not alienate others. For example, a blind student who is attracted to a student who sat next to him in a previous class can't just casually sit next to her when class reconvenes. If he wants to pursue the relationship, he must do more than hope that she will sit next to him again. To begin with, he must discover where she is—not an easy task when you can't see. He must have enough social skill to get her attention and enough social judgment not to embarrass her. If he has assessed her accurately, he will know which is the best approach—a direct "Hey, Sally. Give a yell so I know where you are. I want to sit next to you" or a more subtle "Sally, can I borrow last week's notes?" Similarly, someone using crutches or a wheelchair usually cannot maneuver adroitly enough to casually come up to a water fountain precisely when the person she is interested in stops for a drink. Therefore, a disabled person must spend a great deal of time and effort to arrange those seemingly coincidental encounters that are the beginnings of more lasting relationships.

Paradoxically, a disabled adolescent, who may have had little opportunity to practice social skills, faces a complex social task. He must be outgoing enough to establish and maintain social contacts. He must be emotionally resilient enough to recover from inevitable slights and rejections and not withdraw completely from early social mating rituals. And he must be socially astute enough to detect when his advances are well received and, if they are not, to modify his behavior to enhance his chance for success.

Need for Role Models

For those adolescents who lack social skills and judgment, there is need for interpersonal counseling and role models to help them develop their social abilities and their confidence in these abilities. Disabled adolescents need a great deal of support and understanding from those around them during this period of their lives. Torn with self-doubt and believing that they have little to hope for, they need to become acquainted with similarly, or more severely, disabled persons who are successful. Knowing those who are maritally and vocationally secure will not solve their immediate problem of how to get a date for Saturday night or how to enter-tain their date if they cannot dance, or see, or hear, but it may provide the en-couragement they need to keep from settling for less than they are capable of attaining. If disabled adolescents live where there are no similarly disabled persons or where the disabled still live as invalids, autobiographies, biographies, movies, or television shows, wisely chosen, can acquaint them with disabled persons who live full lives (see Appendix B). Superior to the usual stereotyped portrayals of permanently disabled persons are *The Other Side of the Mountain* and *The Other Side of the Mountain: Part II*, which trace Jill Kinmont's story from her days as a champion skier to her life as an SCI teacher and wife.

Even persons who are disabled later in life or who have highly developed social skills find it difficult to progress from mixed peer relationships to paired hetero-sexual relationships. In adolescence, physical appearance, both of oneself and of one's associates, is of paramount importance. In adolescence, one's friends greatly influence how one dresses, the opinions one prefers, and, more importantly, the kind of person one wants to be seen with. Autobiographies of disabled persons that cover their adolescent years (Eareckson, 1976; Valens, 1972; Kovic, 1976; and Kiser, 1974) reveal how hard it was for them to find someone who was willing to establish a sexual relationship with a person who, in addition to the usual mix of qualities and limitations, has a mental or physical handicap. While even those with profound disabilities (Brown, 1970) find an acceptance of sorts in cliques whose activities are undertaken as a group, problems arise when a disabled member tries to find someone who is willing to be identified as *the* girlfriend or *the* boyfriend of an obviously disabled person.

Example 5B   Should Jim Go Out with Elaine?

Often when a disabled adolescent begins to date, the boyfriend or girlfriend tries to encapsulate the relationship, striving to keep it secret. In public, he or she may suggest that they act as though they were just good friends, that they go where they are unlikely to run into anyone who knows them, or that they attend parties where it may be as-sumed they accidentally arrived or left together. Jim, a rehabilitation counselor, tells about Elaine, a girl he used to date. Elaine uses crutches, having had polio as a child. Jim enjoyed being with Elaine, who shared his love of camping and other outdoor activities that did not require normal mobility. What ended their relationship, accord-ing to Jim, was that they lived in a small town where everybody knew he was dating her and not one of the other girls in town. Jim worried that people would think there was something wrong with him, that no one else would date him. When he left for college he ended his relationship with Elaine and eventually became pinned to a college class-mate. When his preengagement commitment didn't work out, Jim came to the con-clusion that he could live with other people's reactions if he married Elaine. While Jim was busy resolving his doubts, however, Elaine married one of his friends back home.

Integrated Environments Can Help

The problems of establishing a boy-girl relationship are lessened in situations where young disabled persons live closely with many young nondisabled persons. In large residential colleges, where disabled students live in dormitories which house nondisabled students, mixed-couple dating—disabled women dating nondisabled men, disabled men dating nondisabled women—as well as dating between the disabled is so common that those who have a disabled person as a date are not conspicuous. On smaller campuses, in commuter colleges, and in most high schools where socializing between the disabled and nondisabled is not as openly indulged in, it takes someone who is determined or who has a strong self-concept to break an unwritten social taboo (Goffman, 1963).

Recreation: One Way to Meet a Mate

In addition to the other factors which complicate the disabled adolescent's attempts to establish relationships are the very real limitations imposed by severe physical disabilities on a person's ability to participate in leisure-time activities. Although the disabled now participate in a wider range of recreational activities than ever before, some of these activities require such extensive modifications and accommodations on the part of able-bodied companions that they bear little resemblance to those from which they derived.

Some disabled individuals may feel such activities serve more to isolate them from, rather than integrate them with, other persons. Chute bowling and wheelchair dancing allow severely disabled persons to participate instead of only observing, but do not allow a disabled adolescent to join in the activities popular within her age group—soccer, tennis, disco dancing. A young person who is attracted to someone whose favorite pastime is volleyball will find blindness or a wheelchair a frustrating barrier to establishing the relationship she seeks. Although this situation changes as one's peers become older, that fact offers little consolation to an adolescent.

But if she is patient, the disabled adolescent will discover some activity she is proficient at which others enjoy. Many recreational pursuits require little or no modifications or accommodations. Today the blind bowl, amputees ski, and paraplegics ride horseback, canoe, and fly airplanes. Many severely disabled persons are proficient swimmers, some paraplegics and low-level quadriplegics matching their able-bodied counterparts for speed and agility in the water. Bridge, unmodified bowling, archery, and chess are only a few activities in which many disabled and nondisabled share an interest. But the fact remains, disability limits a person's ability to lead the same type of social life as other adolescents.

TYPES OF PERSONS UNUSUALLY ATTRACTED TO THE DISABLED

Lack of available sexual partners doesn't always concern the disabled as much as lack of suitable sexual partners. Some persons seek the company of disabled persons, not because of shared interests or other personal characteristics, but quite simply because of the disability. Not included among the descriptions which follow are those valued individuals who relate well to everyone, disabled or not.

The Walking Wounded   The "walking wounded" are those persons who have been so deeply hurt in a previous relationship with a "normal" person that they seek out persons who seem unlikely to injure them again. Within this group are divorced men whose first wives were unfaithful. Whether they believe disabled women are more pure or that they are incapable of extramarital affairs, a disproportionate number of nondisabled men married to disabled women had unhappy first marriages. The "walking wounded," however, are composed of both sexes. The fact that many women who marry disabled men are divorcees with children calls into question their primary motive for marriage: financial security, emotional security, or physical and personal attraction.

The Would-Be Dictators   The "would-be dictators" are persons who are so insecure that they feel the need to dominate another human being. Such persons seek out disabled persons because they feel superior to those with physical limitations. Relationships between a "dictator" and a severely physically disabled person follow a set sequence. The "dictator" begins by making himself indispensable, by helping with tasks that a disabled person either is unable to do or can do only with great difficulty. As the disabled person's dependency increases, the "dictator" begins to usurp more and more of the disabled person's time, alienating her from others upon whom she might rely. Eventually theirs becomes a totally encapsulated, one-way relationship, with the disabled person literally at the mercy of the "dictator's" whims. Compliant behaviors are rewarded with needed help and autonomous behaviors punished by the withholding of or threat to withhold that help. If the relationship is marital, the biases of the judiciary and attitudes of the general public, that disabled persons are fortunate when their spouses are willing to remain with them, ensure that the disabled person is trapped until the "would-be dictator" tires of the relationship.

The Unsolicited Missionaries   The "unsolicited missionaries" are persons who develop a relationship with disabled persons in order to save them. The "missionaries" underestimate the types of lives disabled persons can live and believe all the disabled are lacking in social advantages, personal skills, and psychological maturity. The most common type of "missionary" is the person who is convinced that if the disabled believed in Christ, they would be healed and able to resume satisfying lives. Convinced that severely disabled persons cannot be true Christians, these "missionaries" accost the disabled they see in public with religious platitudes, creating a climate more conducive to justifiable homicide than to miraculous cures. Some "missionaries" become intimate with the disabled, offering them love and/or marriage if the disabled only demonstrate the strength of their religious convictions with a physiological miracle. These "missionaries" sometimes precipitate severe emotional disturbances in those they are attempting to save. When a disabled person with a deep faith in God is told he would be healed if he really believed, it causes him to doubt the strength of his own convictions. Moreover, when a disabled person is deceived, ostensibly for the good of his soul, revelation of the truth breeds more cynicism than faith (Pruet, 1976; Eareckson, 1976).

The Gallant Gesturers   The "gallant gesturers" are persons who discount the disabled as sexual beings, and thus view any liaison with them as a basis for self-congratulation. Within this group are men who believe they are doing disabled women a favor when they make love to them and who are affronted when, instead of the gratitude they expect, the women indicate they anticipate more than a casual relationship. Among women who are "gallant gesturers" are those with a "Tea and Sympathy" complex, who have sex with disabled men to restore the men's sense of manhood. Because of their condescending attitudes, these generous males and bountiful females open themselves up to exploitation, but, at the same time, their open discounting of disabled persons does nothing to aid the adjustment of those persons.

U nlike the "walking wounded," who often establish sound relationships with disabled men and women, the "would-be dictators," the "unsolicited missionaries," and the "gallant gesturers" are more likely to irreparably harm those they en-counter. "Dictators" prevent their victims from leading self-governing lives. "Mis-sionaries" threaten the psychological adjustment of persons by casting doubt on their belief in a loving God. "Gesturers" exacerbate the sexual concerns of the disabled by convincing them they have nothing to offer in terms of a mutually satisfying sexual relationship, and therefore should be grateful for whatever attentions they receive.

If rehabilitation programs included counseling designed to alert clients to the various types of social misfits they may meet in the outside world, the newly disabled would be prepared to identify and cope with such persons. Their initial contacts with such persons might then not have such potentially disastrous effects on their ability to adjust and to accept themselves as worthwhile, entitled to the respect of others.

SEXUAL COUNSELING FOR THE SEVERELY DISABLED

Despite the pitfalls of limited early sexual experience, despite the rejection they inevitably encounter, it is important in working with the disabled to keep in mind that large numbers of them marry and maintain lasting relationships. A rehabilita-tion professional's effectiveness is increased if he can differentiate his own fears from the realities of a particular disability, through continual access to reliable sources of information.

Personal Bias as a Substitute for Professional Competence

Personal attitudes toward disability become especially important for those involved in sexual and marital counseling with the disabled. To recognize another person as a sexual being, one must first accept him as a fully human being. Since sexuality lies at the core of our humanness, acceptance of and confidence in our own sexuality are more essential to our self-esteem than any other aspect of ourselves. For example, if your first ventures into the world of work prove fruitless, your despair is limited because there are other openings or other vocational fields you can explore. Not being hired for a job is not as personally annihilating as being turned down for a date, because rejection in the former area is less personal and easier to rationalize than rejection in the latter.

Example 5C   Why the Job Opening Wasn't Filled Today

A secretary who works for a national insurance company related what happened when a young man in a wheelchair came in for a job interview. While the interview was in progress, the women working in the outer office discussed the applicant's looks, his bearing, and whether or not he was engaged or married. Shortly after the interview ended, their boss came out of his office and reassured his staff he had not hired the disabled applicant. His precise words were, "I knew you wouldn't want to look at that all day." He had generalized his own negative reactions to a disability to his office staff, oblivious that the women in the outer office had seen the applicant primarily as a sexually attractive person.

The tendency to attribute one's own reactions to the world at large is a tendency that must be guarded against in sexual counseling with disabled persons. When, for example, a child brings up the subject of marriage or having children, those around him should use the opportunity to discuss how people have many friends before they discover the right person to marry and how everybody has liked someone very much who did not reciprocate the feeling. Disabled children, as well as nondisabled children, should be encouraged to discuss love, marriage, and family responsibilities, in addition to basic sex information. Discouraging such discussions will not end the questions that arise in the minds of children who are surrounded by male-female relationships in their families and in the electronic world of television and movies. Disabled children someday become disabled adults, and so it is irresponsible not to utilize every opportunity to educate them about their sexuality. Above all, whatever a child's or adult's limitations, one should never assume, as Comarr and Hohmann point out, that sex is a dead issue and that disabled persons' expectations are necessarily unrealistic (*Rehabilitating the Person with Spinal Cord Injury, 1972*). Now that "sex and the disabled" has become a flourishing topic in journals (see Appendix D), the disabled are more likely to encounter competent professionals when they seek sexual counseling.

Nevertheless, it is more comfortable to discuss the anatomical and mechanical aspects of sex than to counsel others regarding their sexual problems. Unlike our other needs, our sexuality depends on external validation from others, not on our opinions and attitudes toward ourselves. We may win respect and esteem from others, but at the higher levels of personality development, what we think of ourselves, and how freely we move and act, are typified by the prefix "self-:" self-actualization, self-respect, self-esteem—all of which can be obtained without external approbation. Not so with sexuality. There is no such concept as self-sexuality, because self and sexuality are, to some degree, contradictory. Because we are most vulnerable in the area of our proven sexuality, we find it difficult to objectively counsel others. Each time we try to help someone else deal with their sexual doubts and fears, we resurrect the ghosts of our own past failures, and our fears of the future. This is why Hoch (1977) and Hohmann (1972) emphasize the importance of having those who do sexual counseling "come to terms with their own sexuality." Hohmann states that anyone can do sexual counseling provided he or she (1) is free from or able to deal with any sexual hangups, and (2) has accurate information about the capabilities and limitations of persons with specific disabilities.

Nine Tips for the Counselor

Hohmann offers guidelines, quoted directly below, which are useful in sexual counseling with nondisabled as well as severely disabled persons.

    1 *Don't get people into trouble with their God or their morality.* Many persons have strong moral and religious convictions about various types of sexual activity. For example, certain Catholic priests would consider any kind of sexual activity other than genital-genital contact as a type of masturbation and therefore a sin to be atoned for in the confessional. To urge people to abandon such beliefs without an understanding of their importance in the individual's psychic economy is dangerous and may produce severe reactions of depression, anxiety, suspiciousness, and guilt. Before undertaking counseling, the skillful counselor should explore carefully the person's religious and moral convictions and work within that context, or work together with the patient and the theologies to modify these religious or moral concepts.

    2 *Don't hang your morality on the patient.* Not only do patients have certain scruples, inhibitions, and religious convictions, but so do counselors. The counselor should be well aware of his own biases and convictions, and he should not impose them on the patient. Although he is free to live his own life as he pleases, he should not attempt to persuade the patient to his sense of morality. It cannot be emphasized too strongly that sexuality is an extremely sensitive issue with people whose sexual existence has been severely threatened. They must be treated with great gentleness and understanding.

    3 *Don't force the patient to talk about sex.* The timing of discussions is of utmost importance. If an adequate interpersonal relationship has been developed with the patient, he will introduce the subject at the time he feels a sufficiently pressing need. In interactions with the patient, one should make it clear that sexuality is an open topic. The counselor should then wait until the patient takes the lead in initiating the discussion.

    4 *Don't threaten the patient with your sexuality.* Male counselors, especially those who may harbor some lingering doubts about their own sexual adequacy, may brag about their sexual exploits in the presence of the patient, thus building up the counselor's own faltering ego at the expense of the already injured patient. Likewise, women may sometimes behave in an excessively seductive manner around cord injured patients, confident that their seductive attempts will not be accepted. Contemporary mythology portraying all paraplegics as completely disfunctional in sexual interest or ability should not be fostered by the counselor. . . .

5 *Don't make sex an all-or-none experience.* In discussing sexuality, the wise counselor will keep in mind that sex has many meanings. If a patient does not have and with the best prognosis will not get genital sexual functioning, he should not be told to "forget about sex; your sex life is over" as has happened in some cord injury centers. Rather, the patient should be encouraged to explore whatever relationships are open to him.

6 *Don't assume that once sexuality has been discussed, it is forever resolved for that patient.* Sexuality must be a topic continually open to discussion between patients and staff. Injured men, like anyone else, experience changes in their psychosexual situations. New issues, new experiences, new inclinations and new desires may arise with which the patient may need some help.

7 *Don't assume that there is only one way to convey sexual information.* Too often the assumption is made that adequate information can be communicated only by a formal presentation, followed by discussion. "Latrine talk" with one patient sharing experiences with another is quite as effective in conveying sexual information among the cord-injured as it is among the population at large. One cannot overestimate the efficacy of informal communication among patients in producing effective attitudes and adjustments. Much information also can be conveyed and the general implications of the paraplegic's sexual situation can be introduced in a jocular or kidding environment. Perhaps the method that is most effective is the guidance of a counselor who fills the role of a gentle friend.

8 *Don't expect too much from spouses in their ability to change roles.* Much of the care that must be preferred by the spouse, especially to the severely disabled quadriplegic man, may have the effect of destroying libidinous interest. For example, many wives have told us it is nearly impossible to routinely provide bowel care, feeding, nursing for their husbands and still retain an interest in and image of their husbands as sexual objects. If such tends to be the case, the wise counselor will try to preserve the sexual aspect of the relationship by encouraging the use of outside resources, such as visiting nurses and part-time attendants, in doing these unesthetic chores.

9 *Don't forget all relationships and, in particular, that most intense of relationships, marriage, are a matter of compromise.* The important things to urge upon any cord injured patient and his spouse are attitudes and feelings of mutual trust, willingness to discuss each other's needs, and a sincere search for how they may mutually satisfy each other. The sexual relationships of cord injured men can be as effective a bulwark to marriage and family life as the non-injured person, if they grow out of a deep feeling of mutual respect, love, tenderness and concern (Hohmann, 1972; pp. 56–58).

Chapter 6

Marriage and Family Life

The disabled, like other human beings, place a high value on marriage and family life. If their marriages succeed, their ability to establish such a relationship enhances the process of their metamorphosis. If their marriages fail, their adjustment may be set back temporarily.

Unfortunately, the fear of appearing ridiculous often prevents disabled persons from revealing the extent of their concerns about marriage. Well-meaning professionals may unwittingly force the disabled into concealment by the way they approach the topic of marriage. "You don't ever expect to get married, do you?" results in all but the most self-assured answering, "No." Such a dialogue destroys a disabled person's chance for needed counsel and a professional's chance to gain insight into an area which concerns those with whom he works.

This chapter will:

1 Discuss the various factors affecting a disabled individual's decision to marry
2 Discuss special problems in marriages where one partner is severely disabled and the other is not
3 Suggest ways to minimize these problems

Factors Affecting Marriage Choices

The cultural image of the ideal marital relationship does not include a husband or wife who is severely physically disabled. Instead of expecting that a marriage will succeed when either the bride or the groom is disabled, friends and family often anticipate that the marriage will prove to be a mistake. No matter why such a couple marries, it is certain that the route to their marriage was strewn with negative reactions from others and encumbered by unsolicited advice.

Professional Attitudes

Professionals often harbor negative attitudes concerning a disabled person's desirability as a marriage partner. Such bias is reflected in the following passage from Safilios-Rothschild's work (1970) on the sociological aspects of disability:

> Intermarriage between the disabled and the non-disabled is undoubtedly the best index of social integration. Interestingly enough, an intensive study of mental retardates showed that in effect these retarded men and women used marriage with a normal as the utmost criterion of definitive success in societal integration and adjustment. Here it seems that the disabled woman fares better than the disabled man in likelihood of marrying a normal person, probably because the disabled status is more compatible with the traditional, more passive role of the woman who does not have to support the family. Also, the dependent status of the disabled woman may inspire some insecure man who can then comfortably play the protective role of an "adequate" and "strong" male. (pp. 118–119)

Viewing intermarriage between the disabled and the nondisabled as the best index of social integration assumes that the disabled are less acceptable than the nondisabled to persons who have disabilities themselves. This assumption is typical only of those professionals and disabled persons who are so infused with prejudice that they discount reasons other than social integration for marriage between disabled and nondisabled persons. Such biases often cause professionals to discourage disabled persons from marrying one another, as the following example demonstrates:

Example 6A   Mark and Arlene: Choosing Partners—for Normalness or for Love?

Mark and Arlene, who have been happily married for more than eleven years, received much unasked-for advice from professionals who counseled against their marriage. Mark, an SCI quadriplegic who works as a mechanical engineer, and Arlene, a paraplegic with spina bifida who teaches in an elementary school, met while they were college students. When their engagement became known to the staff of their college's rehabilitation center, Arlene was called in for counseling and urged not to marry Mark. The reasons propounded were: (1) Arlene would regret marrying a quadriplegic because other students who entered into such marriages did; (2) Arlene was attractive and intelligent enough to attract someone who was not disabled if she would only be patient; and (3) if disabled students married each other, it would appear as though the rehabilitation center's attempts to integrate disabled students into the student body were unsuccessful.

Fortunately, Arlene, who was in her early twenties, was old enough and experienced enough to discriminate between what was in the center's best interests and what was in her best interest. Contrary to her counselor's assumptions, Arlene and Mark were not marrying each other out of desperation or loneliness. They had both been active socially, dating both disabled and nondisabled students, until what began as a casual friendship blossomed into something more.

Level of Adjustment to One's Disability

Unlike the couple mentioned above, many disabled men and women do marry disabled or marginal persons because they fear no one else will want them, but marriages of that type appear to be in the minority. Many disabled persons do, like the retardates mentioned above, view marriage with a nondisabled person as confirmation of their personal worth and desirability. But disabled persons who are intent on marrying someone who is nondisabled usually have difficulty accepting themselves and are apologetic about their physical limitations, and are therefore extremely susceptible to social pressures against marriage to other disabled persons.

If intermarriage were a valid index of social integration, it would be difficult to account for Heslinga's findings that more disabled persons are marrying other disabled persons as the disabled, as a group, are increasingly assimilated into society (1974). While thirty years ago it was unusual to see visibly disabled persons in public places, today it is unusual to attend a public event and not see at least one person in a wheelchair, with an amputation, with a white cane, or hearing aid. Not only are severely physically disabled persons shopping, attending sporting events, and appearing at popular night spots, they are also engaging in more dubious pursuits such as hijacking airplanes from their wheelchairs (*Commercial Appeal*, June 6, 1977, p. 1).

Now that the disabled are becoming more socially active, why are they marrying each other in proportionally greater numbers than they were when they led more restricted lives? While integration into "normal" society does increase the likelihood of meeting potential nondisabled marriage partners, this does not invariably mean that a disabled person will choose to marry a nondisabled person simply because he is not disabled. The marriage choices of socially integrated persons indicate that adjustment to one's own disability results in a corresponding reassessment of other persons' physical capabilities (Wright, 1960). To illustrate this point, let us examine one person's fantasies about marriage and the ideal marriage partner.

Example 6B   Ruth: Prince Charming Turned Out To Be Dull, Dull, Dull

Injured in an auto accident at 20, Ruth was totally dependent in all her personal needs following her discharge from a general medical hospital. During the two years immediately after her accident, Ruth was sometimes depressed to the point of considering suicide, and her fantasies concerning love and marriage reflected her physiological and security needs:

"I daydream about meeting a man who is tall, handsome, and strong. In my daydreams he comes to the house to deliver something, fix the television . . . maybe do some yardwork. As soon as he sees me he falls in love and wants to take care of me. He asks me to marry him and promises he'll always look after me. He'll be able to lift me in and out of cars and in and out of bed. He'll stick pillows under my hip when I'm uncomfortable. He'll always be there when I call, even in the middle of the night. He'll dress me and fix my hair just the way I like it."

Ruth's early daydreams mirrored many of the real concerns of newly disabled or extremely physically dependent persons. For them, three of the basic drives in man—hunger, thirst, and the avoidance of pain—predominate over the fourth—sex. Their obsession with alleviating possible discomfort tends to obliterate their sex drive or channel it into atypical concerns. This obsession, common during the early stages of adjustment, leads some researchers to conclude that the physically disabled are sexually immature (Landis and Bolles, 1942).

Sometimes group therapy can help such persons realize that their ideas concerning love and marriage are based on their dependency needs, rather than on a desire to forge an interdependent relationship. Combining well-adjusted persons with those still struggling to come to terms with their disabilities permits those who have resolved their dependency needs to confront other group members with the fact that they are more concerned about finding a live-in nurse, bill payer, or housekeeper than they are a husband or wife. Often the less well adjusted group members are unaware of the extent to which they regard people as objects to be used and more readily accept the insights of their peers than they would the insights of nondisabled authority figures. As metamorphosis proceeds, these individuals' values change (Wright, 1960), affecting the way they view and relate to other people. Ruth became aware that her values had undergone a change when, at 23 and still somewhat physically dependent, she met the man of her daydreams:

Example 6B   Ruth (continued)

"I met Carl at my best friend's house. He was her boyfriend's best buddy. He seemed to take an instant liking to me and I was attracted to him. That afternoon the four of us went on a picnic. Carl picked me up and set me in the car like he had been doing it all of his life. Then he collapsed my chair and put it in the trunk. After we ate, we left E. and K. in the picnic grounds and went for a ride. We spent a pleasant afternoon mainly talking about E. and K. and wondering if they would ever get married. After that Carl and I dated steadily for three months. I was the first woman he had dated since his divorce two years before. He was really bitter about his wife. It used to frighten me the way he'd talk about her.

"Carl lived nearly 200 miles from my home but once a week he'd drive up and spend the whole day with me, leaving late in the evening. He always arrived with a gift for me and flowers for my mother. On our second date, which was the week of my birthday, he brought me a transistor radio. I tried to give it back but he wouldn't take it.

"My mom was very eager for me to keep on seeing Carl. She had always worried about what was going to happen to me when she died. I worried a lot about that too.

"Carl was everything I had dreamed about in a man. He was tall, strong, blonde, and had rugged good looks. He was kind and considerate. I was proud to be seen with him. I liked his gifts and his attentiveness but something was wrong. I didn't like the way he spoke about his wife but it was more than that. Carl was boring. Outside of talking about E. and K. he had very little to say about anything except his wife. Trying to keep up a conversation on the days we spent together gave me a headache.

"During our third month of dating, after hinting about remodeling his house for a wheelchair, Carl asked me to marry him. I refused."

According to Ruth, meeting the real-life embodiment of her fantasies made her realize how inadequate physical strength and normality were as the primary attributes of someone with whom she hoped to spend the rest of her life. While her ideas about love and marriage had changed, Ruth's fears for her future had not. But instead of worrying about who would take care of her, she began experimenting with ways of taking care of herself. She learned to control her bowel evacuations through diet, to prevent pressure sores by periodically checking her skin with a hand mirror, to use her strong reflexes to initiate spasms which allowed her to empty her bladder at will, and to transfer from her wheelchair to car or toilet seat.

During the years she spent in a California college earning her bachelor's and master's degrees, she dated a variety of disabled and nondisabled students. For the last nine years she has been married to a mathematics teacher who became a quadriplegic as a result of a spinal tumor. Expressing satisfaction with her marriage, Ruth laughs, "My husband is often an irritation, but never a bore."

Obviously, not every disabled person can or should marry another disabled person. Those who have not and never can acquire self-help skills have to consider potential partners in terms of their ability to help with daily physical needs. Those with hidden disabilities may seek out nondisabled mates because association with disabled persons might call attention to their otherwise undetectable disabilites. Others may require the reassurance of being able to attract persons who are not disabled.

But the assumption that one will always choose to marry someone who is nondisabled in lieu of someone who is disabled has not been proved to be fact. Past a certain level of adjustment, people marry for a complexity of reasons. Ideally, the disabled should marry those with whom they have the most satisfying relationship. At the low end of the continuum of dependence–independence, high need for social desirability–low need for social desirability, physical dependency or a poor self-concept will preclude marriage to another disabled person, regardless of his other personal attributes. At the upper end of that continuum, factors such as shared interests and common goals may or may not preclude marriage to a disabled partner.

Parental Interference

The reasons for their concern may vary, but few parents want their child to marry someone with a disability. Some dread the reactions of their friends and neighbors. Some believe a disability is the outward sign of an internal flaw, which will affect the marriage or their future grandchildren. Most, however, firmly believe their child will be ruining her life because she cannot anticipate the problems such a relationship involves.

At first, however, parents usually do or say nothing, expecting the relationship to end of its own accord. If it does not, they initiate a heart-to-heart talk, during which they air their objections and describe the practical problems as they see them. Many of the problems they predict will be valid, but many will not, for they typically underestimate their potential son- or daughter-in-law's ability to meet the requisite responsibilities.

If the heart-to-heart talk fails, the next step is to shame the child out of a relationship. This step, which relies on remarks such as "I saw Aunt Mary today and she asked me, 'Can't Charlie find someone else, or won't anyone else have him?'" is effective with some who are already uncertain about the desirability of a relationship. Most persons, however, who are at the point where they are considering marriage to a disabled person are no longer self-conscious about being seen with that person. Emphasizing social desirability is always dangerous with those who pride themselves on their accepting attitudes. If they think someone they care about is being unfairly maligned, they may squelch any lingering doubts they themselves have.

When parents fail in their attempts to influence a child's marital choice, they often divorce themselves from the situation. Some refuse to attend or acknowledge the marriage. Some disinherit their child, their child's spouse, and any children. Sometimes the estrangement is complete. More often a gradual reconciliation occurs over time, often ending with the birth of the first grandchild.

Parents of the nondisabled partner are not alone in their objections to such marriages. Parents of the disabled partner may be as firmly opposed. Why? Because they tend to be overprotective. They often believe their blind, paralyzed, or otherwise handicapped child is more physically and emotionally helpless than he or she actually is.

The vital ingredient in any disabled person's independence is environment. But few parents modify their homes to provide the necessary environment (Blank, 1976). Ramps are expensive, and if thoughtlessly designed can be ugly or dangerous. Thick carpets, which represent a considerable investment and enhance a home's decor, can drain the energy of anyone using a wheelchair. Special storage arrangements are needed both by blind persons and by wheelchair users. Closets, drawers, and shelves arranged for the convenience of a child who stores and finds items by touch and with the aid of memory are organized differently from those used by someone who has vision. And for the wheelchair user, most kitchens, bathrooms, and closets are too cramped or awkwardly arranged to use readily or fully.

What often happens is that ramps aren't built, carpets aren't taken up, bathroom doorways aren't widened, kitchens aren't remodeled, and closets, shelves, and drawers remain exactly as they were. Instead of promoting independence through environmental change, most families with a disabled child promote dependence: "Here, let me help you. It's easier and faster for me."

The consequences of this enforced dependence become obvious when their child begins to talk about marriage. Overprotective parents cannot comprehend how their child, who needs help a dozen times a day, can assume the responsibilities of married life. They fail to realize that their home is an environmental disaster as far as their child is concerned, and that all the fetching, lifting, and reaching they have to do might be unnecessary in a different setting.

Such overprotective parents often tend to feel that their disabled child is emotionally as well as physically helpless. Perhaps remembering the restrictions having a disabled child has placed on them, they fear that the fiancé or fiancée "doesn't know what he or she's getting into," and will tire of the relationship, and that their child will eventually be hurt.

However, most disabled persons, with minimum social skills and training for remunerative employment, become as emotionally and economically independent as their nondisabled siblings. In fact, severe motor or sensory disabilities often keep them from returning to their parents' home, except for short, widely spaced visits, because they can operate more independently in their own homes, where they control the ordering of their environment.

The Disabled as Undesirable Marriage Partners: Common Stereotypes

Common stereotypes perpetuate the myth that the disabled make undesirable marriage partners. The usual stereotype of a disabled husband is that of an embittered male who makes impossible demands on his children and who is a millstone for his wife. The wife, while admired if she perseveres, is excused if she leaves or is unfaithful. Gardner (1978) describes the stereotypes of marriages in which the wife is disabled: (1) The husband is sexually unfulfilled. (2) The husband is an exceptionally self-sacrificing person. (3) Any children are from the husband's previous marriage or must have been adopted.

Stereotypes, however, if applied to a large enough population, are sometimes factual. Some marriages in which one partner is or becomes disabled do end in misery. There are embittered disabled husbands or wives who harass their children and try their mates. But there are also those who shoulder their share of family responsibilities and who are loving, competent parents and companions. Many a disabled man is the primary wage earner in his family (Laurie, 1975, 1976, and 1978), and the traditional role of homemaker as well as employment in a variety of occupations, are within the capabilities of many a disabled woman (Laurie, 1978). Even those women who are bedridden can serve as household managers by organizing and scheduling duties which are then carried out by someone else. The majority of disabled women, however, while they find it difficult to give a large dinner or cocktail party without assistance, can keep their homes in order and provide nourishing meals for their families through careful selection of appliances and organization of household goods. An abundance of publications and books, such as Gilbert's *You Can Do It From a Wheelchair*, advise newly disabled home-makers or disabled brides how to manage a variety of household tasks (see Appendix C).

Counseling the Disabled: Three Marriage Patterns To Beware of

Hohmann (1972) believes the disabled should be counseled that there are three types of marriages which are likely to fail. First is a marriage between a nurse or therapist and a patient.

Marrying a Nurse/Therapist Although many patient–nurse/therapist relationships succeed, two reasons for such marriages result in high rates of failure: marriages for security and marriages in which the nurse/therapist has difficulty changing roles. Widows or divorcees with children may marry men patients with substantial or guaranteed incomes because they desire financial security. Many such marriages end in divorce when the children leave the home or a better marital prospect comes along. As Hohmann points out, "If a nurse marries a patient because she thinks she will have a better deal (more money and a home for taking care of one patient instead of thirty), the chances of a lasting marriage are not very good." Another potential problem in a patient–nurse/therapist marriage is that the nurse/therapist may continue to see himself as a professional rather than a husband and lover. In this situation, as Hohmann points out, "if the home becomes like an extension of the hospital, then the marriage probably will be in trouble."

Marrying (Just Anyone) at a Low Ebb of Self-Esteem The second type of marriage Hohmann cautions against is one entered into within a year or less after the onset of a disability. As a person adjusts to his disability, he will begin to seek out the same type of person he would have before he became disabled. A religious person will rejoin church groups, while a street person will resume his nightly ventures to old haunts. At this stage in adjustment, the person will seek someone of similar intelligence who is emotionally stable and who shares his interests and pastimes. Marriages entered into before this period of adjustment is completed, when self-esteem is low, tend to be based on a belief that the disabled are lucky if they find anyone who will marry them. Desperate and willing to sell their souls to anyone who will take care of them, the disabled may marry persons with psychiatric disorders or drinking problems, believing that someone with a strong need for support and acceptance will be more tolerant and more likely to remain faithful than someone who is self-sufficient. Eventually, however, the disabled person begins to regain his self-confidence and self-respect. As he reassumes his former attitudes and outlook, he may find himself married to a kind of person he would never have chosen had he not been temporarily derailed by a disability.

Marrying the Predisability Boyfriend (Girlfriend) The third type of marriage which has a good chance of failing is a marriage between two persons who were engaged before one of them became disabled. A nondisabled fiancée often feels obligated to go through with marriage plans, although, as Hohmann points out, "the situation has altered completely." The disabled individual may be so fearful of the future that he blocks any indication that his fiancée wants to discontinue the relationship. Sometimes predisability fiancées, like predisability spouses (Pruet, 1976), believe the disability is temporary or a cure will be found eventually. When the permanence of the disability can no longer be denied, and she finds herself in a relationship which pride or religious conviction will not allow her to escape, she may break down emotionally, leaving the disabled person with the double burden of disability and guilt (Valens, 1975; Pruet, 1976; Eareckson, 1976).

If a predisability engagement ends, the disabled person should be made aware that marriages of those who meet their mates after they become disabled have a greater chance of lasting than those contracted before. Although such information may be resented at first, eventually it may help the disabled person to regain his confidence in the future.

MARRIAGE AND DIVORCE AMONG THE DISABLED

According to studies of the marital patterns of people with various disabilities, the disabled marry at nearly the same rate as the nondisabled, but later in life. Their marriages, however, tend to be more stable than average. El Ghatit and Hanson (1976) found a divorce rate among disabled subjects of 23.1 percent as opposed to a national rate of 33.0 percent in 1970. Similar findings in other studies have led researchers to conclude that having a disability does not preclude having a happy marriage (Grynbaum, Kuplin, and Lloyde, 1963; Guttmann, 1964; Weis and Diamond, 1966; Deyoe, 1972).

Nevertheless, while one can infer that a marriage ending in divorce was unsatisfactory for at least one of the parties involved, one should not infer that a marriage which continues is therefore a happy one. Quantitative measures cannot reveal the quality of ongoing relationships. A nondisabled spouse may not divorce a disabled spouse because of a sense of duty, because of religious beliefs, or because of the financial security involved if the disabled partner receives a service-connected disability pension, workmen's compensation payments, or monies from a guaranteed-income policy. A disabled spouse may remain in an unsatisfactory marriage because he or she is too emotionally or physically dependent to leave. A disabled wife may ignore or deny her husband's adulterous behaviors if she has no one else to support her. A disabled husband may tolerate an unloving, sloppy wife because he believes that if he loses her, his only alternative may be life in a nursing home.

Moreover, some disabled persons are denied divorces they seek.

Example 6C   Obtaining a Divorce Can Be Difficult

After Carmen F. was injured in a car accident, her husband moved to an apartment, leaving her in their home with five children. Although he continued to provide his family with a generous monthly income, he said he was too disturbed by his wife's quadriplegia to maintain any relationship with her or their children. He had been gone less than a year when Carmen met Jeff, a nondisabled widower who began to help out in family emergencies and who finally moved in with Carmen and the children. When Carmen and Jeff decided to marry, her application for divorce was denied by a judge who ruled that Carmen could not forego the support of her absent but successful psychologist husband.

What factors contribute to the stability or dissolution of a marriage? According to Hohmann (1972), the most stable marriages are those between two persons who need each other—but not desperately. Physical and psychological independence strengthen a marriage, unless one partner has a strong need to be needed. Although obvious major incompatibilities often keep a relationship from developing, differences in religious affiliation, political allegiance, or even ethnic or cultural background are not the primary factors in the dissolution of marriages (Lederer and Lederer, 1968). Rather, day-to-day annoyances increase marital stress until an additional irritation triggers an outburst which, though it may not destroy the relationship immediately, lessens its ability to withstand the stresses of the future.

SOURCES OF INCREASED STRESS IN MARRIAGES WITH ONE SEVERELY PHYSICALLY DISABLED PARTNER

When one partner is disabled, the number of possible incompatibilities is increased. It is not the physical limitations per se which increase stress, but rather the need to cope with them within the confines of a close relationship. For example, when one person is severely physically disabled, individual differences are accentuated in the areas of (1) pace of life, (2) temperature preference, (3) income allocation, and (4) social activities. To date, research has concentrated on role fulfillment, sexual activities, and stability in marriages in which one or both spouses are disabled. These areas are important, but they do little to clarify the day-to-day patterns of marriages in which the four areas mentioned above have a particular impact.

Because damage to the spinal cord produces a wide range of impairments, each of which is shared by other disability groups, the example of SCI quadriplegia will be used throughout this section to describe disability-related sources of stress in marriage. For example, in spinal cord injury, sensation is lost, as in some cases of hemiplegia; voluntary movement is lost, as in transverse myelitis; spasticity occurs, as in cerebral palsy; bowel and bladder control is lost, as in cancer of the lower digestive or urinary tract or advanced multiple sclerosis; contractures and joint inflexibility develop, as in rheumatoid arthritis; and finally, the homeostatic mechanisms of the body are impaired, as in hypertension and other peripheral vascular diseases.

Although his disability sounds overwhelming, the SCI paraplegic or low-level quadriplegic, with training and careful scheduling of his life, can carry on normal routines of living. The higher the site of injury to the spinal cord, however, the greater the physical impairment and the greater the difficulties of carrying out these routines.

Pace-of-Life Differences

Most severe physical disabilities affect, to some degree, the pace at which a person carries out his daily activities. In fact, recent methods for rating independent living skills base the evaluation on *how long* it takes for an individual to complete a task, rather than on *how* he completes that task. If, for example, a person were capable of getting out of bed and dressing himself, but had to start at 7:00 a.m. to be ready by noon, he would not be truly independent. From the standpoint of social effectiveness, a person is independent if performing necessary skills does not interfere with his ability to meet the other demands of living, such as work, home management, and enjoying other people.

The above example may be extreme, but many disabled persons do spend an inordinate amount of time on self-maintenance tasks. Normally, eight hours a day are spent sleeping, eight working, and eight maintaining self and home and engaging in leisure-time pursuits, community activities, and avocational interests. With no more hours in his day than anyone else, the disabled person is also locked into approximately eight hours of sleep and eight of work, but the remaining eight hours must be utilized differently. A person on dialysis must spend eight to fifteen hours a week attached to the dialysis equipment. After a treatment, the energy level of such persons is high and they feel fine, but hours later toxins again begin to accumulate in their blood, their energy levels drop, and they feel unwell. A woman reports that immediately before a treatment she cannot walk from her car into her grocery store without collapsing. With such disabilities, the pace of life is not only altered, it becomes erratic. Some days a person can keep pace with anyone, but other days he can barely function at all.

The disparity between the time it takes some disabled persons to dress and get out of bed and the time it takes their nondisabled spouse often produces a tense interpersonal situation. In an intimate living situation, what usually happens is that the nondisabled spouse begins to impinge on the time scheduling necessary for the disabled spouse to retain his physical independence. Wanting only to help with the daily struggle to bathe, dress, and toilet, the nondisabled person begins to speed things up. Although she is trying to be considerate, if she continues day after day, she will actually be doing her disabled spouse a disservice. Any severely disabled person, in order to retain the greatest possible degree of physical autonomy, must continually practice his ADL techniques, however awkwardly or slowly he carries them out. Moreover, when another person continues to take over and perform these activities more quickly and easily, the disabled person's psychological adjustment can be threatened. When anyone is constantly reminded of his limitations in performing the simplest self-care tasks, his self-esteem suffers. Eventually, he may give up the struggle to maintain his independence, and in giving up, lose the skills that allowed him to be as self-sufficient as he was.

Not only are hard-won skills lost when the more physically able partner consistently helps a less able partner, but the nature of the marital relationship is altered as well. At first, help is given only with the most difficult and time-consuming activities—putting on socks or lifting a wheelchair in and out of the car. In time, however, the more able person finds herself helping more and being expected to help more. The person who began with an altruistic urge to say, "Here, let me do that. Save your energy for more important things," ends up feeling overburdened and used.

At the same time, the disabled person, sensing the other's growing impatience, is nonetheless seduced into increasingly dependent behaviors, because independent behaviors exhaust him. One day he may try to dress himself. In twice the time it used to take, he gets only half as far. Now, in addition to his guilt because of his demands on his spouse's time, his self-disdain is tinged with fear, for he must rely on the compliance of his partner.

Measures for Reducing Stress Caused by Pace-of-Life Differences

Not all marriages end up as parasite-host relationships, however, Symbiosis is possible, if one continually guards against any dependency-enhancing behaviors. First, if a disabled person is to function at his optimum level, he must have an environment that is tailored to his needs. He is not functioning independently if he can shave but must have someone else get his shaving gear out of an inaccessible cabinet. He is not functioning independently if he can dress but cannot get his clothes out of a closet with a too-narrow door. The problem with arranging the environment for the mutual convenience of two persons with quite different physical abilities is that what is convenient for one is likely to be inconvenient for the other. This problem is not insoluble, however. Dolan and Dolan (1977) describe a kitchen designed for the convenience of a wife with cerebral palsy who uses a wheelchair and her nondisabled, over-6-foot husband. When it is impossible to accommodate two persons equally, the environment should be designed to the requirements of the one who is disabled. A sighted spouse may not be able to read the Braille on a package in a freezer, but she can unwrap it to see if it is a steak or a chuck roast. A blind spouse cannot, and so must rely on some system that allows him to identify objects by touch or by order of arrangement.

Second, spouses must learn to remove themselves from potentially irritating situations. If the faster person is dressed and ready to leave for work while the other is still struggling, he could read the morning paper aloud to both of them or discuss the guest list or menu for an upcoming dinner party. It should be apparent, but often is not, that the disabled person's body is occupied, not her mind. After ADL skills are mastered, procedures which once required time, effort, and concentration still require time and effort, but the steps involved become routine. The boredom experienced in self-care activities may be as great a deterrent to a person's wanting to do things herself as was her fear when she became disabled that if she did something difficult or painful once, she would be expected to do it from then on.

A wise spouse, like an experienced rehabilitator, will encourage a person to utilize this ADL time in some productive way. One Ph.D. who uses a wheelchair developed parts of his dissertation while he wheeled between his home and the library where he was doing his research. By the time he arrived, he was ready to put on paper what he had already written in his mind. Indeed, for the severely physically disabled, making double use of what time they have is necessary to compensate for the many hours they spend on disability-related tasks.

A disabled person's need to use time wisely can complement a partner's need to remove herself from the situation temporarily. At its simplest, this means the person who is consistently faster busies herself with activities unrelated to the other's schedule. Writing letters, reading, removing dishes from the dishwasher, talking to an early-rising neighbor—all are ways of filling one's own time without infringing on someone else's. At a more complex level, this means that both partners recognize the need to develop interests they can pursue independently. The resulting benefits are those realized in any relationship in which two persons share many, but not all, of their interests and spend most, but not all, of their free time together: expanded social networks, increased personal growth, and enrichment of their relationship.

Stress from Varying Temperature Preferences

While differing temperature preferences can cause irritation in any relationship, when a person is disabled, an apparently unreasonable preference may be a physiological need.

To illustrate a physiological basis for varying temperature needs, let us examine what happens in spinal cord injury. An injury to the spinal cord interrupts transmission of nerve impulses up and down the cord. Along with loss of movement and sensation, a loss of temperature control occurs in those portions of the body innervated by the cord below the point of injury.

In the uninjured person a rise in external temperature causes the body to perspire. Evaporation of the perspiration cools the body, keeping its internal temperature constant. A drop in external temperature causes blood to be shunted from the body's surface inward and skeletal muscle fibers to contract. This inward channeling of the blood and shivering of body muscles produce heat, thus keeping the body temperature again constant.

Normally a thin film of perspiration is exuded when the external temperature exceeds 70 degrees Fahrenheit. As the external temperature rises, perspiration becomes more profuse. This homeostatic mechanism is so efficient that, unless the body is exposed to high temperatures for an extended period of time or restricted in fluid intake, body temperature remains within the normal limits. However, when the spinal cord is injured, paralyzed portions of the body do not perspire in response to higher external temperatures. The larger the area of the body which is paralyzed, the greater the impairment of the normal cooling (or heating) process. If the injury is below the neck, much of the body's surface area will still respond appropriately. When an injury occurs in the neck area, however, a rise in external temperature produces a rise in body temperature. In short, when an SCI quadriplegic is exposed to elevated temperatures, he begins to run a fever. The higher the external temperature, the higher his fever tends to be.

On an 80-degree day, a quadriplegic may run a 101-degree temperature or more, if he does not have access to air conditioning. Conversely, when the temperature drops below 70 degrees, quadriplegics often experience hypothermia, a condition where body temperature drops dangerously low (Hylburt and Hylburt, 1979).

These problems with temperature control are compounded by the fact that while someone with SCI quadriplegia will not perspire normally in response to heat, he may perspire in response to stimuli which normally does not trigger the perspiration response, i.e., pain, a full bowel, or pressure in the bladder. The temperature control mechanisms are not destroyed; they are merely no longer under the coordinative control of the lower brain. For some, abnormal perspiration replaces the warning system of pain, thus enhancing rehabilitation. Many have been warned that they were injured—burned by a radiator—or that they had an abdominal infection—an attack of bladder stones—by an outburst of perspiration. Renee, who was injured in an auto accident, perspires across her forehead minutes before her bladder empties reflexively. Once she learned to interpret this perspiration pattern accurately, she was able to dispense with an indwelling catheter—a tube inserted into the bladder to allow free and copious drainage of urine.

Different stimuli produce different perspiration responses in certain SCI persons. An abnormally active digestive tract might result in intermittent episodes of perspiration, much like those of someone with indigestion or the flu. A decubitus ulcer may produce a copious outpouring of perspiration.

Unfortunately, this impairment of temperature control can have adverse physiological and social implications. It is not unusual for a quadriplegic with a pressure sore to perspire so profusely that her clothing is literally soaked with sweat. Because this reaction can be triggered by a variety of internal stimuli, a person can be outdoors in freezing temperatures and suddenly break into a bowel-, bladder-, or pain-induced sweat. In this situation she may not feel uncomfortable for some time, because she can't feel the cold in a major portion of her body. By the time she becomes aware that her body temperature has dropped, the severe physiological stress she has experienced may have lowered her resistance to respiratory infections. The potential seriousness of this situation is underlined by the fact that respiratory infections are the leading cause of death among SCI quadriplegics (Felton, Perkins and Lewin, 1966; Hylbert and Hylbert, 1979).

The health, therefore, of some persons will be endangered unless they live and work where temperatures can be adjusted to their physiological needs. Unfortunately, depending on what internal stimuli her body responds to at any one moment, a disabled person's temperature requirements can fluctuate in a manner incomprehensible to those around her. Even those who are cognizant of the complications associated with certain physical disorders will find it difficult not to think that someone requesting the thermostat to be turned up in an already uncomfortably warm room is behaving capriciously. One who spends a great deal of time with such a person, as does a husband or wife, may find understanding turning into irritation.

Example 6D   Paul G.: Shivering Cold on a Summer Day

Marital stress often arises from situations like the following: Paul G., an SCI quadriplegic, is watching television with his wife on a balmy June evening. The patio doors are open. A soft breeze stirs the air. Suddenly, Paul begins to perspire heavily and to chill. He asks his wife, Judy, to turn the furnace on and set the thermostat at 80 degrees.

Judy, who understands what is happening, is nonetheless tired of being stifled with heat, and rebels. If other people are around, the group's consensus may be, "It's not too cold in here. If you're uncomfortable, Paul, put on a sweater. It's easier for you to keep warm than it is for us to cool off."

Unfortunately, removing clothing when it's too hot or putting on clothing when it's too cold does not completely solve the problem of impaired physiology. But because disabled persons' temperature preferences are judged aberrant, they may be forced to capitulate outwardly. Because of their inability to assert themselves openly in many situations, they may develop passive-aggressive behaviors which begin to predominate in their interpersonal relationships, resulting in increased stress in relationships with others in general, and with marriage partners in particular.

STRESS FROM ALLOCATION OF INCOME

Whatever the disability, there is always some disability-related expense, which can range from minor to catastrophic. A blinded news journalist found he could no longer work for his radio station because he couldn't drive. He either had to take a cab or use buses to carry out his assignments. On his salary he couldn't afford cab fare, and consequently so much of his time was wasted waiting for buses that he was only productive enough to command a half-time wage. He is now considering a degree in psychology, although he enjoys working as a journalist.

Disability-Related Expenses

Severely disabled persons, especially those who are unemployed or under-employed, discover that disability-related expenses excessively strain family budgets. Only veterans with service-connected disabilities are provided adequate pensions and free medical services. It is thought that the stability of these veterans' marriages derives from their substantial pensions and cost-free medical services (Deyoe, 1972; El Ghatit and Hanson, 1976).

For the civilian, however, aid in meeting medical expenses is far from adequate. Civilian benefits from social security are inadequate for normal living expenses, to say nothing of expenses arising from a disability. Physicians' fees, hospital bills, and prescription costs make up only a small percentage of disability-related expenses. For example, the yearly costs of operating an electric wheelchair can almost equal its initial price (Anderson, 1977). Those who are eligible for a prosthetic or assistive device under one program or another may find it impossible to maintain their devices. Moreover, persons who are not eligible for assistance do not receive the discounts given to public and private rehabilitation agencies when they buy services or equipment. In 1980 an unsponsored person may have paid between $1500 and $2000 for an Everest and Jennings (E & J) power chair, but an agency may have paid less than $1000.

"Unlike buying stereo equipment or a new car on which the advertised price may be lower than the manufacturer's suggested retail price, the wheelchair purchaser usually pays the price decided upon by the manufacturer," contends Dr. Lilly Bruck, director of an HEW project concerned with teaching the disabled to become informed consumers (1978). Bruck points out that E & J has 50 percent of the market of 400,000 persons who use wheelchairs in this country, and sells 90 percent of the custom-made chairs for the severely disabled. Because the majority of these chairs are paid for by third parties, i.e., insurance companies or Medicaid, E & J is not encouraged to compete on design or price. Third parties receive sizable discounts and use public funds, and so are not concerned about quality or price. In 1975 the VA bought 20,000 chairs for $3 million—an average of $150 per wheelchair (Bruck, 1978).

Similarly, eight hearing aid manufacturers control 70 percent of their market. Their devices are sold for $350 to $1000 by dealers who, according to Bruck, mark them up as much as 300 percent. A Senate committee investigating the eyeglass industry discovered that frames, which cost $2 and $3 wholesale, retailed for $32.

Special devices for the blind, such as the Optacon (see Chapter 11), cost over $2000. Whether these prices are unreasonable is not the issue here. The issue is that whatever the disability, the disabled have nonnegotiable expenses that the non-disabled do not have. Too many persons are ineligible for financial aid, especially employed nonveterans and families who fall above agency income guidelines based on an estimate of their ability to pay.

Health insurance could solve the problem of medical expenses *if* companies would insure the disabled without requiring them to waive any payments for expenses related to their disabilities. Many persons, unless they are employed and covered under group insurance, cannot obtain hospital or life insurance. Those who are declared eligible may find the waivers so extensive or premiums so high that their insurance offers little protection against bankruptcy.

Many persons, therefore, receive no assistance in meeting the costs of required treatments, modifications, and devices. Those who are eligible for assistance discover that not all expenses are covered and that those devices approved under Medicaid or Medicare may not be suitable for their needs (Bruck, 1978). A family's financial resources are slowly depleted until it either becomes eligible or hovers on the brink of economic self-sufficiency, where other family needs are unmet so that drugs, equipment, and treatments can be purchased.

Disability-Related Expenses as a Source of Stress

Most families go through periods when expenses exceed their alloted budget, but families faced with disability-related expenses differ in that their extraordinary expenses must be budgeted year after year. Instead of decreasing, those expenses tend to increase due to additional medical complications from advancing age. Moreover, disability-related expenses differ because they stem from the unique needs of one family member and not from the needs of the family as a whole.

The stress of continual medical expenses, enhanced by the possibility of additional medical crises, is akin to that incurred during periods of prolonged deprivation such as wars or following natural disasters, with this difference: wars end and damage created by wind, water, or earthquakes is eventually repaired. But when a family devotes one-fourth of its annual income to fixed medical expenses, as did 7.4 percent of the SCI subjects in Zelle and Taranto's study (1976), other items in its budget must be eliminated or curtailed. Items eliminated first are vacations, camp for the children, new furniture and clothing, eating out, and entertaining friends.

Adding to the tensions arising from continual self-denial are those arising from uncertainties of the future. If a disabled person is the family breadwinner, inadequate insurance coverage means there is no financial security should she be unable to work, or die. If a disabled person works, she is ineligible for social security disability payments under existing legislation. Therefore, if she becomes unable to work, her previous medical costs have usually depleted her savings, resulting in her inability to support the family during a period of unemployment, much less pay for additional medical costs.

The constant fear for the future and the continual need to effectively allocate an essentially inadequate income severely strains a marital relationship. In marriages where one spouse is severely disabled, as in marriages where neither spouse is disabled, lack of money may be the primary cause of marital discord.

STRESS FROM DECREASED SOCIAL ACTIVITY

Having a disability almost invariably reduces the number of social activities open to a person. Explanations for lowered social interaction are divided into two categories: (1) lowered social interaction due to ostracization by the nondisabled and (2) lowered social interaction due to concerte physical limitations.

Ostracizing of the Disabled by the Nondisabled

Many of the social restraints upon the severely disabled stem from external causes—social or physical barriers which enforce a certain degree of social isolation, preventing the disabled from being as socially active as they might be (Wright, 1960). Neighbors may shun a family with a disabled member because they want to avoid being expected to sit with a disabled child or shop for a disabled adult. In addition to the fear of social entrapment, some shun the disabled because they believe that disability is caused not by a biological mishap, but by some inward flaw. Some, however, display a greater tolerance for disabled children than for disabled adults. Parents may encourage their children to play with a slow-moving retarded boy in the neighborhood, thinking he will be a stabilizing influence. But when the retarded boy enters puberty, when his voice deepens, his shoulders broaden, and his pants become tight in the crotch, he may no longer be welcome in the homes of his peers.

Time Restrictions Imposed on Social Activity by Physical Limitations

The lowered number of social interactions of the disabled person is often the result of his learning to cope with his physical restrictions. With one foot in the world of the nondisabled, whose influence and company he cannot avoid, and one foot in the world of the physically disabled, whose relationship to him and his well-being he cannot escape, he learns to face his limitations and what those limitations mean in terms of what is best for him and the kind of life he would like to lead. The satisfaction many feel regarding the frequency and quality of their social inter-actions (Dunn, 1967) may stem as much from a reassessment of their own needs and values as from a recognition that they have little choice but to accept what they cannot change.

One thing the disabled person cannot change is the amount of time he requires to maintain his maximum level of independence. To borrow the theatrical meta-phor Goffman (1959) uses to illustrate his theory of interpersonal relationships, "impression management," a severe disability decreases the time available for front-stage activities (social, work, and leisure-time) and increases the time required for backstage activities (self- and environmental management). Let us consider the situation where someone with a spinal cord injury, advanced multiple sclerosis, or severe cerebral palsy is capable of living independently. Such a person may require two to three hours every morning to get up, washed, dressed, and groomed. Add to this the time required to transfer herself and her wheelchair in and out of the car, and by the time she gets to work, she may have used up three and one-half hours of her day getting to her job, while a nondisabled colleague may have used less than an hour. In addition, persons with spinal cord injury or advanced multiple sclerosis may lose several hours every second or third day to bowel and bladder management procedures. Persons who have lost the ability to detect when a bowel movement is imminent, or when their urinary bladder is ready to empty, must maintain rigorous schedules to prevent inadvertent bowel movements or voiding of urine. Several excellent films depicting the procedures severely disabled persons follow to maintain complete independence in bowel and bladder management were produced at the University of Illinois and are listed in Appendix D. Such persons, if they work during the day, must devote eight to twelve nonworking hours throughout the week to these procedures.

In reviewing the hours per week such persons may use up in disability-related tasks—preparing for and getting to and from work equal 23.5 hours; bowel management equals 8 to 12 hours; urinary maintenance, i.e., emptying, rinsing, and sterilizing drainage tubing and collecting devices, equals approximately 9 hours—one realizes that a disabled person may have one and one-half fewer days in his week than do his nondisabled friends and colleagues. Because this time must be subtracted from what would otherwise be free time, a severely disabled person may have little choice but to restrict his social interactions. For him, as for anyone else, the unalterable demands of earning an income, taking care of personal hygiene, and taking care of his home come first, with the needs of his family coming second. Socializing activities, then, are often judged as inconsequential or even as threatening to a person's ability to cope with the physical and psychological stresses imposed by his disability.

In order to meet his potential, a severely physically disabled person must budget his time as carefully as a family of eight budgets its income. Unfortunately, just as lack of money can generate stress within a marriage, so can lack of time for social activities. When the inflexible scheduling of one partner conflicts with the social needs of the other, the relationship may suffer.

Fortunately, however, while having a disability may reduce the number of social activities open to a person, it apparently does not affect his satisfaction with activities which remain. For example, families with a disabled family member report low social cohesiveness with their neighborhoods, having frequent interactions with only one neighboring family (Overs and Healy, 1971). Although social activity decreases, the perceived quality of that activity does not. In an investigation of need satisfaction in marriages where the wife was severely disabled (Fink et al., 1968), it was discovered that both husbands and wives expressed satisfaction with their socializing activities outside the family. While attrition may have limited the sample—those whose needs were not being met may have ended their marriages prior to the study—those couples represented were brought closer because of the disability.

Although not all disabled persons marry or even want to marry, establishing a close, long-lasting relationship with another human being can be the final stage in a disabled person's metamorphosis. As discussed in Chapters 3 and 5, the fear of the social repercussions of having a severe physical disability creates great psychological stress for a newly disabled adult or an adolescent who was disabled as a child. Being able to forge a loving, mutually enriching relationship does more than buttress a disabled person's self-concept and increase his self-esteem, however. It admits him into the society of those who function as couples and allows him to share the concerns and responsibilities of others who function as couples. As Hale (1979) concludes, for the disabled as well as the nondisabled, "a fulfilling, intimate relationship with another human being can be the difference between a lonely, solitary existence and a rich, sharing, rewarding life."

Chapter 7

Ethical Issues and the Future of the Disabled

Medical and social ethics relating to treatment decisions concerning the severely disabled were rarely discussed outside of medical circles until the late 1970s. Through the Karen Ann Quinlan case and the interest and controversy it generated in the public media, lay persons became aware of ethical issues the medical profession had been struggling with previously: the acceptability or unacceptability of either passive euthanasia—withholding of available treatment—or active euthanasia—administration of lethal treatment.

The development of sophisticated methods for maintaining the lives of persons who would previously have died has created new social issues and raised new ethical questions. In addition, genetic counseling and prenatal examination techniques can now predict or detect the presence of numerous congenital disabilities in an unborn child (see Chaper 5). Yet three-fourths of the physicians practicing today know little about such techniques or the questions their use entails. Courses on genetics were virtually nonexistent in medical schools before the 1960s (Stein, 1978). Furthermore, few agree on the proper use of such methods, once a defective fetus is discovered. Do parents have an obligation to abort the fetus (Warkany, 1971) or should they have a choice between an abortion and preparing for the birth of a disabled child (Omenn, 1978)?

Such issues are important not only in the medical profession, but also in the training and orientation of future rehabilitation/special education professionals. Dowd and Emener (1978) stress the need for such professionals to address themselves to these issues in their article "Lifeboat Counseling: The Issue of Survival Decisions." The effect of these issues on helping professionals and the students/clients they serve as the thesis of a presentation by DeLoach, "Medical Attitudes toward the Severely Disabled," at the 1976 national convention of the American Personnel and Guidance Association (APGA).

This chapter will:

1 Examine changing attitudes toward using available medical technology in treating the severely disabled
2 Examine two rationales for these changing attitudes: quality of life and rising medical costs
3 Discuss how disabled persons view the effects of severe physical disabilities on the quality of their lives
4 Discuss how these issues affect rehabilitation professionals and how such professionals can influence the resolution of these issues.

CHANGING ATTITUDES TOWARD MEDICAL TREATMENT

In the past medical practitioners did all they could for their patients because, especially in cases of severe acquired disabilities or severe congenital malformations, they could do so little. Prior to World War II adults with spinal cord injuries rarely survived. During the war, antibiotics and innovative methods of treatment improved the survival rate so that today such individuals, if they receive competent medical care and have enough understanding of their own condition to participate in their own care, are "able to live full and productive lives" (Howell, 1978a).

In 1963, 80 percent of those infants born with spina bifida died. Then a group of English physicians began to use surgical procedures immediately after birth to close the opening in the spine and to implant a permanent shunt (a tube with a valve which drains excess cerebral spinal fluid from the cranial cavity to another area of the body). As a result of these procedures, 80 percent of such children lived and the incidence of mental retardation among the survivors dropped from the previous level of approximately 70 percent to less than 40 percent (Stein, 1978; Howell, 1978b).

With the drop in mortality rates, however, came a change in the definition of appropriate medical treatment. By 1971, the practice of saving children born with spina bifida was being reexamined. In reviewing the records of 848 children he had treated between 1959 and 1968, Dr. John Lorber discovered that 50 percent were still living. Of those who survived, 1.4 percent had no physical or mental disabilities, 80 percent were paraplegics, 17 percent had moderate disabilities such as urinary incontinence, and fewer than 40 percent had any degree of mental retardation. On the basis of these findings, Dr. Lorber concluded, "The indiscriminate use of advanced techniques of all types has kept alive those who should have died" (Lorber, 1971). On March 4, 1974, an article in *The Washington Post* revealed that staff at the Maryland Institute for Emergency Medicine routinely turned off the respirators of mentally alert high-level quadriplegics, although neither the quadriplegics nor their families had requested that respiratory assistance be discontinued.

What treatment is offered a physically disabled person whose condition is treatable but not curable is up to the individual physician. The AMA ethics code has guidelines for certain medical situations: For transplantation, the rights of both the donor and the recipient should be protected; in treating the terminally ill, the decision of the patient or the immediate family to abandon heroic efforts to maintain life when imminent death is irrefutable should be honored. There are no guidelines, however, covering treatment of the severely physically disabled or the 25 percent of children born with Down's syndrome who need surgery to correct intestinal obstructions which otherwise cause most of them to starve to death slowly (Patrick, 1978). In a survey conducted by the University of California School of Public Health at Berkeley, 50 percent of the physicians polled in the San Francisco Bay area favored not operating on such babies (Stein, 1978).

Are these changing attitudes toward saving and maintaining life confined to the medical profession or are they reflected in the larger society? Hardin (1974), Hall and Cameron (1976), Ramsey (1978), and Dowd and Emener (1978) believe Americans, in general, place less value on life than they once did. Cameron surveyed articles on suicide indexed over the last fifty years in the *Readers Guide to Periodical Literature.* His purpose was to investigate attitudes toward suicide in the American culture. He discovered that fifty years ago in the periodical literature suicide was portrayed as a human waste which should be prevented, if at all possible. Today, however, suicide is being presented as a viable alternative to life, in articles often written in a manner that might convince a person contemplating suicide to do so (Hall and Cameron, 1976).

Dowd and Emener (1978), Hall and Cameron (1976), and Ramsey (1978) believe Americans are likewise more accepting of euthanasia than they were in the past. Shortly after Dr. Raymond Duff (Duff and Campbell, 1973) revealed in a medical journal that treatment was withheld from babies with congenital disorders (chromosomal abnormalities, heart defects, and spina bifida) at the Yale–New Haven Hospital, the following item appeared in newspapers across the country: "Yale University pediatrician Raymond Duff . . . deliberately allowed 43 hopelessly defective infants to die. . . . Said Duff . . . 'decisions were made in the best interests of the children, who could not speak for themselves.'" Significantly, no public outcry followed the appearance of the news item and in the author's locality no letter to the editor appeared to question Dr. Duff's definition of "hopelessly defective" (Stein, 1978).

Similarly, persons who are brought to trial for having committed active euthanasia are typically exonerated by their peers (Ramsey, 1978). In 1976 a book was published which dealt with the trial of Lester Zygmanik. Zygmanik smuggled a sawed-off shotgun into a hospital and shot and killed his brother who, three days before, had broken his neck in a motorcycle accident. Not only was Lester Zygmanik acquitted, but his action was interpreted, as the book's title indicates, as an *Act of Love* (Mitchell, 1976).

UNDERLYING RATIONALES FOR CHANGING ATTITUDES

Explicity stated as rationales for the increased acceptance of passive euthanasia in lieu of treatment for severely disabled children and adults are (1) the assumption that the quality of the lives of such individuals is invariably impaired by their disabling conditions and (2) the soaring cost of medical treatment for such individuals. Lorber, when advocating that treatment be withheld from children born with spina bifida, wrote, "These babies now live with distressing physical or mental handicaps or both, often for many years, without hope of ever having an independent existence compatible with human dignity" (Lorber, 1971). In discussing treatment of paraplegic and quadriplegic patients, Dr. Robert Fruin explained, "Costs for catastrophic injuries could be intolerable, but we know these costs can vary, depending on how far we go in treating the men. The ethical issue for most of them is not one of treating or not treating, but of costs" (Stein, 1978).

Disability and the Quality of Life

The assumption that a severe physical disability compromises a child's development toward a full and normal life, or that a meaningful life is impossible for an adult who is dependent on a machine, is accepted as fact by the majority of physicians interviewed by Stein (1978) and the majority of physicians writing for professional journals or presenting papers at medical conferences, as researched by Ramsey (1978). A few, like Dr. Howard Rusk (1972), interpret the effects of severe physical disabilities on a case-by-case basis. In this process evaluation is based on how well an individual is able to manage a disability rather than on the physical limitations produced by it. In his autobiography, Rusk cites the case of Johnny, who was born with a severe congenital defect and was paralyzed, incontinent, and diagnosed as severely retarded. Although Johnny's "situation looked hopeless," he was given all available medical care. Six or seven years later Rusk was attending a meeting at a public school in Brooklyn during recess when students were running up and down the halls shouting at one another. Among them Rusk recognized his former patient "stumping along at a great rate on his crutches, yelling at the top of his voice." When Rusk sought out Johnny's teacher to ask how he was doing, the teacher replied, "Johnny? He's at the top of the class" (Rusk, 1972).

Unfortunately, sophisticated treatment does not ensure that any one individual receiving it will subsequently live a meaningful life, any more than the presence of a severe disability invariably compromises the quality of an individual's life. But the latter assumption, held by many in the medical community, appears to be shared by many laymen. Persons whose attitudes are influenced by the disabling myths discussed in previous chapters share this assumption because if they believe that in order to live a full, productive life one must be physically normal, than they must conclude that those who are not physically normal cannot live full and productive lives.

Disparate views of the meaningfulness of life for disabled persons are highlighted in books, plays, and movies based on the actual lives of disabled persons and in fictional accounts of such persons. Compare, for example, Roy Campanella's (1959) autobiography *It's Good To Be Alive* and the Broadway play *Whose Life Is It Anyway*? Campanella's book is a personal account of his life. Once a successful athlete, Campanella became a high-level quadriplegic in a car accident, but regained his zest for life and was able to begin a new career after he became severely and permanently disabled. The Broadway play is a fictional account of a high-level quadriplegic who is being kept alive by modern science. The character refuses to see any value in his life because of his extensive paralysis, and the whole play centers on his fight to end his life despite medical efforts to keep him alive.

Media Images of the Disabled

Few live less dramatic lives than the severely disabled who have adjusted to and have been trained to cope with their disabilities. They get up, eat, and sleep; some work, some raise children, and all worry about inflation and dwindling energy supplies. Fictionalized accounts of disabled persons are typically unrealistic and milked for their histrionic value. Instead of well-rounded characterizations, the disabled in fiction or theater are often minor characters who serve to highlight or precipitate a climactic situation for the major characters, e.g., Lady Chatterley's husband. If a major character is disabled he either does not want to continue living, like the quadriplegic in *Whose Life Is It Anyway*?, experiences a miraculous recovery, like Tiny Tim in *A Christmas Carol*, or dies heartbreakingly, like Little Nell in *The Old Curiosity Shop*.

When real-life drama is presented, as in the movie *The Other Side of the Mountain*, the story of Jill Kinmont, who became an SCI quadriplegic in a skiing accident, the realistic portrayals may depress individuals who have not gone through the same adjustment process as the disabled themselves. Although Jill Kinmont (now Jill Booth) evolved into a happy, fulfilled young woman in *The Other Side of the Mountain*, a *Time* reviewer in reacting to the movie commented, "She nearly died, and survival was hardly a mercy" (August 11, 1975).

How the Disabled Perceive Their Lives

In researching how severely disabled persons* perceive the effects of their disabilities on their lives, Weinberg and Williams (1978) discovered that 60 percent of their subjects thought of their disabilities as a fact of life or an inconvenience, while only 7 percent thought their disability was the worst thing that had ever happened to them. In fact, 49 percent thought their disabilities had certain advantages. In response to the question that if they had one wish, would they wish they were no longer disabled, 49 percent said yes, 51 percent said no. There was no significant correlation between type of disability and subjects' responses. When those who stated there were positive advantages to their disabilities were asked what those advantages were, one respondent wrote, "I'm so grateful I didn't die from polio. I've prized my being alive even more, since the time I was stricken."

---

*Within the eighty-eight subjects in Weinberg and Williams's study, 22 percent were paraplegics, 6 percent were quadriplegics, 16 percent were cerebral palsied, 33 percent had "other orthopedic disabilities," 9 percent were blind, and 7 percent were deaf.

Weinberg and Williams's findings support previous research that indicates the disabled rate their lives equally as satisfying as nondisabled persons rate theirs (Cameron, Gnadinger, Kostin, and Kostin, 1973). In an article summarizing their research, Cameron and Hall (1976) conclude:

> In eliminating deformed children and pulling plugs on paraplegics, we believe we are sparing them lives of misery. But the trouble is, physical or mental defects do not necessarily mean that people are miserable. When Cameron surveyed people suffering from paralysis, muscular diseases, missing limbs, blindness and deafness, he found that they were as satisfied and optimistic as a comparable group of normal people. The handicapped were also less likely than the normal group to have contemplated suicide. In another of Cameron's surveys, mentally retarded children turned out to be happier than normal children. (Hall and Cameron, 1976, p. 106)

Why do laymen, like the *Time* reviewer, or professionals, like Dr. Lorber, view the effects of a disability so differently than the disabled subjects represented by the studies above? Medical professionals are aware of the physical complications any severe physical disability entails, but tend to be unaware of how well disabled persons can eventually cope with those complications, given adequate psychological support, training, and equipment (see Chapters 3, 4, 5, and 11). To achieve a more accurate outlook on the quality of life of the disabled, Siller (1974) believes it is important that everyone who works with disabled persons on a professional basis make an effort to keep in contact with persons who have been disabled twenty years or more and who are living and working in the community. Without knowledge of the long-term results of medical treatment, special education, and rehabilitation services for congenitally disabled children or adventitiously disabled adults, it is impossible to make "quality of life" judgments based on objective evidence. It is difficult, if not impossible, for someone to predict how she would adjust to a severe disability, unless she has already become disabled and gone through the metamorphosis that occurs after the onset of a disabling condition. For this reason, professionals and laymen alike often view disability as an unmanageable and intolerable situation over which they would prefer death.

To feel oneself fortunate in comparison to someone else's misfortune is human and only one step removed from expecting that person to feel unfortunate in comparison to you. This psychological mechanism underlies what Wright (1960) describes as the "requirement of mourning": the need of those who value physical attributes highly to have those who lose a physical attribute to mourn their loss.

Therefore, when a person is convinced that she'd rather be dead than in another person's situation, it is difficult to convince her that the other person would not also rather be dead. If a severely disabled individual refuses to admit her life is intolerable, the value system of a nondisabled person may be threatened. To protect their value systems, then, some nondisabled persons may discount any evidence that a severely disabled person is fulfilled despite her obvious physical limitations. This could account for Ramsey's (1978) findings that some physicians will continue to believe it is wrong to allow children with severe birth defects to live in the face of evidence that many such persons, even phocomelics who are born with flippers instead of upper and lower limbs, have married, raised families, and had successful careers (Ramsey, 1978; Fiedler, 1978).

Those who have been close to dying through accident or illness, such as Weinberg and Williams's one respondent, realize too well what a thin line separates life from death and that death allows no second chances. In a study comparing amputees who had been injured in combat with amputees who had been injured in noncombat activities, Randall, Ewalt, and Blair (1945) discovered that the noncombat amputees were significantly more depressed immediately following their injuries than the combat amputees. These researchers believe that those injured in combat saw their comrades killed and, given the option of death or amputation, considered themselves fortunate to be alive. Evidence indicates that most individuals, given time to adjust, choose life over death, even under painful or trying circumstances (Stein, 1978). For example, DeLoach was convinced before she contracted polio at 17 that she would rather die than be physically limited.

Example 7A Charlene D.: "Is Life Worth Living without Dancing?"

Months before being hospitalized, Charlene attended a Slavic wedding dance in central Wisconsin. One of the guests was a dark-haired young woman who walked with a cane and who stood with her escort and watched while others waltzed and polkaed.

Several days later, Charlene couldn't stop thinking of the stranger who was so close to her in age but who couldn't join in the vivacious dances. Finally, when she was alone, Charlene tied her legs together and hobbled around her living room thinking, "I'd rather die than not be able to dance." Three months later, she was paralyzed from the neck down and unable to breathe without the aid of a respirator. Instead of wishing she were dead, Charlene was very much afraid that she might die. The fact that she would never walk again, much less dance, seemed inconsequential when she knew she was in danger of losing her life.

Disability and Rising Medical Costs

While "quality of life" continues to be an issue, increasingly individuals in positions to make treatment decisions cite rising medical costs as the rationale for their decisions to offer or withhold life-sustaining treatments to persons with physical disabilities (Ramsey, 1978) or chronic illnesses (Stein, 1978). In 1978, a severely disabled infant who required three months of specialized medical treatment at the Los Angeles Cedar-Sinai Medical Center ran up an average medical bill of $40,278. A hemophiliac whose blood does not clot normally pays more than $20,000 a year for the necessary clotting compounds. Children with leukemia (still a problem for infants) who need transfusions and chemotherapy, children with cystic fibrosis, who are frequently hospitalized, and children with a variety of handicaps have yearly medical bills which, taken together, run into the billions. In 1978, approximately 36,000 persons were being kept alive on artificial kidney machines at a cost to the government of $900 million. It was estimated that the cost would reach $2.2 billion by 1983, and that by 1990, 96,000 persons will require dialysis at a cost of more than $4 billion per year (Stein, 1978).

According to the physicians interviewed by Stein (1978) in *Making Medical Choices: Who Is Responsible?*, whether or not medical treatment is considered extraordinary is determined by how expensive it is. The efficacy of coronary bypass surgery—a $12,500-operation in 1978, with a 1 to 3 percent mortality rate and a 4 percent chance of itself causing a heart attack—is currently being reevaluated as some consider such surgery too expensive "in terms of money, lives and medical know-how." By 1979 criteria had been established in some medical settings identifying only those with an occlusion of their left coronary artery as good candidates for this surgery (Stein, 1978).

Similarly, kidney dialysis, which was developed in the early 1940s, until the 1960s was administered to a limited number of those who could have been kept alive by such treatment because of the scarcity of available machines. In the early 1960s committees decided which patients would get the treatment and live and which would be denied the treatment and die. Only two guidelines were given: reject all children and people over 45 (Stein, 1978). After the government agreed to pay most of the costs of dialysis through Medicare funds in 1972, dialysis became available to all who needed it, as it had been previously in countries with national health insurance programs. But as the cost of terminal kidney disease rose, countries like England reestablished the policy of selection by committee (Stein, 1978).

ESTABLISHING CRITERIA: THE ROLE OF THE SPECIAL EDUCATOR/REHABILITATOR

The entire issue of treatment, whether discussed in terms of "quality of life" or "extraordinary costs," is not one that even professionals are able to discuss objectively and rationally. Strong emotional reactions to the treatment issue cut across lay-professional and religious-secular lines.

A lay person addressing the issue of termination of life-support systems for the comatose or the severely physically disabled expressed her opinion as follows: "It's surprising that so many people are aghast at prolonging life by 'artificial means.' When anyone applies pressure to a bleeding jugular vein, he is prolonging life by artificial means. All of the heart pacemakers, the kidney machines, the organ transplants are designed to prolong life by artificial means. . . . Someone should speak out for the defense of the unconscious. They have a right to live, not a 'right to die with dignity.' There is no dignity in death. That is a term used by those who have put money, comfort or personal belief above the life of another" (*Commercial Appeal*, November 16, 1975).

A physician addressing the same issue in the *New England Journal of Medicine*, however, wrote: "Most citizens pale at the spector of a city filled with nonagenarian stroke victims on tax-supported respirators, while garbage collection has ceased because of a lack of funds" (Hiatt, 1975).

On the issue of euthanasia and children with birth defects, secular scholar Leslie Fiedler contends: "fewer monsters were denied a chance to live in older priest-ridden societies than in an AMA-controlled age like our own in which . . . infanticide is practiced under the name of 'removal of life supports from nonviable terrata'" (Fiedler, 1978).

But Catholic moralist Maguire, according to Ramsey (1978), "points out that many defective children often refuse to die, and from that fact he concludes that we should move to a policy of actively killing them (Maguire, 1974)."

These issues are complex and painful to consider, but they cannot be and are not being avoided. Each day decisions are made that affect the lives of numerous ill or disabled children and adults. Criteria which determine treatment policies have already been established in certain medical settings, such as the Maryland Institute for Emergency Medicine and the Yale-New Haven Hospital. Moreover, criteria for specific disabilities such as severe heart defects and spina bifida have been proposed for adoption by the general medical community (Ramsey, 1978; Stein, 1978; Duff and Campbell, 1973; Lorber, 1971).

While it is impossible to predict what effect dwindling natural resources and the population explosion will have on disabled persons in the future, if the change in attitudes toward offering certain disability groups medical treatment generalizes to other disability groups, special educators and rehabilitation professionals cannot help being affected—most obviously in the nature and the number of disabled persons who will be their students/clients. Dowd and Emener (1978) predict that persons in the helping professions, either individually or as a group, will eventually be unable to avoid playing a role in establishing treatment criteria. They suggest that persons who work with the disabled "will not be able to continue to take refuge in the position that people have no right to make decisions concerning another's life . . ." but rather "need to become proactive in the area of value development . . . to be involved in the generation of criteria by which issues of life and death will be resolved."

Near the end of a graduate course dealing with the rehabilitation of persons with severe disabilities such as blindness, deafness, spinal cord injury, cerebral palsy, multiple sclerosis, and mental retardation, Dowd and Emener gave their students the following exercise:

> You are a rehabilitation counselor living in the year 2001. You have just been informed that the world government has decreed that the earth is overpopulated relative to its resources. It has therefore been decided that some people must be eliminated and that a priority listing must be made for that purpose. Since the government values the opinion of social and behavioral scientists, you have been invited to rank-order the disabilities listed on the board in order of *expendability*. Please remember that the decision has already been made that some people must be eliminated; your decision is *only* concerning which ones. You may refuse to participate if you wish. If you refuse, however, please remember that you have lost any voice in the matter and must accept the results. (Dowd and Emener, 1978, p. 36)

Significantly, although some students reacted with anger and shock, none refused to participate, and a multiplicity of criteria was arrived at.

The discomfort experienced by the students and the fact that they generated conflicting criteria are not surprising in light of the complex physiological, social, and psychological variables involved in how any one individual, whatever his disability, manages and reacts to that disability. If those who work with the severely physically disabled in a professional capacity can keep from stereotyping disabled persons and can free themselves from the influence of the disabling myths, they will not only aid the process of metamorphosis in their clients/students but will also be able to systematically gather objective and representative information with which the validity of existing and future criteria can be substantiated or refuted.

To do so, however, they must guard against acquiring the "zoo keeper" mentality described in Chapter 4. They must do follow-up procedures on existing clients/students in order to develop a basis for predicting beyond a particular student's or client's behavior problem or vocational crisis to what the future is capable of holding for that student or client. Equally important, they must be able to share their knowledge of the benefits society reaps from its disabled members. Few persons outside of vocational rehabilitation, for example, realize that for every dollar spent to return disabled clients to employment—for medical treatment, evaluation, training, or education—approximately 7 dollars are returned to the federal government through taxes from those clients' earnings (Hylbert and Hylbert, 1979). Few persons outside of the rehabilitation-related professions are aware of the vocational successes of severely disabled employees in government agencies like the Tennessee Valley Authority (TVA). In 1979 the TVA hired a man with cerebral palsy who uses an electric wheelchair, expanded its employment of deaf persons to a point where it began offering sign language courses at varying levels of difficulty to non-hearing impaired employees, and employed three totally blind employees—one as a secretary, another as a computer analyst, and the third as a personnel counselor who travels around the country recruiting high school and college students for the TVA network. So successful were these severely disabled employees that the TVA planned to increase the number of such employees in nontraditional jobs throughout the agency by 1980.

But it is difficult for those who work with disabled children or adults, especially at the beginning of their metamorphosis, to comprehend what the future can be like for those with whom they work.

Example 7B   Disabled Children Become Adults with Disabilities: A Physician Becomes Aware

As part of a graduate course in medical aspects of rehabilitation at Memphis State, fourteen physicians lecture to the special education and rehabilitation students on relevant aspects of their medical specialties. When the course was first offered, one of the physicians spent a great deal of time describing the surgical techniques that increased the survival rate of children born with spina bifida, but in 1977 he changed his lecture. He began to discuss how surgery on such children often created more problems than it solved and revealed that it was his personal decision not to operate on such children if they would be left with severe physical and/or mental limitations. He pointed out such surgical procedures were only palliative and that children paralyzed with spina bifida suffered from scolioses (lateral curvatures of the spine), urinary and fecal incontinence, etc.

During his lecture in 1979, an attractive graduate student in a wheelchair asked him what the chances were that a child would be born with spina bifida. When he began to answer in terms of the general population, he was cautioned that the young woman was asking the question in terms of what her chances would be of having a child with that disability. She herself had been born with an open spine and was getting married immediately after graduation.

After class the physician spent twenty minutes in private conversation with the student. Later he remarked that he had never really considered his child patients as someday living as self-sufficient adults.

Well-trained and experienced special educators and rehabilitators can bring to the decision-making process an expertise that others lack. In many medical settings the personnel are not trained in rehabilitation or special education and do not know the wide range of lives disabled persons lead outside of institutional or agency settings, or the contributions various disabled persons can make to the wider society after they have been the recipients of the services and the technology society presently offers (see Chapters 9, 10, and 11).

LEGAL RIGHT TO MEDICAL TREATMENT

Persons with certain disabilities may have a greater need for acute or chronic medical care than do nondisabled individuals. Yet the disabled often have more difficulty acquiring the necessary treatment for a variety of reasons: inaccessible public transportation (Chapter 11), inaccessible medical facilities (Chapter 11), and discriminatory practices of those who provide medical services (Hogue, 1980). When discriminatory practices result in legal action, however, courts have ruled that it is illegal to deny a disabled person any medical treatment which is available to others, regardless of whether the disabled person is an adult or a child.

In *Lyons* v. *Grether*, 239 S.E.2d 103 (Va. 1977), a blind woman won a damage suit against a physician who had refused to treat her for a vaginal infection. When the woman, accompanied by her guide dog, arrived for her appointment, she was told the physician would not treat her unless her dog was removed from the waiting room. When she insisted her dog remain with her, the physician "evicted" her, refused to treat her, and did not help her obtain treatment from anyone else (Hogue, 1980).

More vulnerable to discriminatory practices, however, are the several thousand defective newborns who are estimated to be allowed to die each year, either because parents refuse to permit treatment or because physicians refuse to administer treatment. In *Maine Medical Center* v. *Houle* (Superior Court, Cumberland, Maine, 1974), the court intervened between the parents of a newborn child and the attending physician. The child was born on February 9, 1974 without a left eye, with a rudimentary left ear with no canal, with a deformed left thumb, and with a fistula (opening) between his trachea and his esophagus. Without surgical closure of the fistula, the child could not take nourishment or breathe normally. When the father directed the attending physician not to operate and to discontinue intravenous feeding, the matter was placed in the hands of the court. On February 11, by the time the court issued a temporary restraining order to prevent the parents from issuing any directive injurious to the well-being of the child, the child had already suffered brain damage due to his impaired breathing. In view of the deteriorating condition of the child, the attending physician then recommended that all life-supporting measures be abandoned, because he judged the quality of the child's life would be severely compromised if he survived. The court ruled that all life-supporting measures should be continued, that "the doctor's qualitative evaluation of the life to be preserved is not legally within the scope of his expertise" (Hogue, 1980).

Chapter 8

The Rise of Consumer Activism among the Disabled

The physically handicapped—who comprise an estimated 35 million Americans—are emerging as the nation's newest civil rights movement. And they are demanding what the majority of Americans take for granted: the ability to get on or off a bus or subway, to get in and out of a building, to attend the schools of their choice, to take full part in the community and to live independent lives with dignity.

Newsweek, *December 21, 1976*

In the wake of the civil rights movement of the 1960s and early 1970s, a new minority group began to make itself heard. Labeled by *Newsweek* as "the next minority," disabled persons from California to Massachusetts, from Michigan to Texas, began to organize. Their purpose was practical rather than philosophical. Not included in the Civil Rights Act of 1964, they were not covered by legislation banning discrimination in education, transportation, housing, or employment until nearly ten years later.

Due largely to the input of disabled activists, the 1973 Rehabilitation Act, Sections 503 (affirmative action) and 504 (nondiscrimination), extended basic civil rights to disabled persons. But they soon discovered that getting a law passed was far removed from having that law implemented. Four years passed between the time the 1973 act was signed into law and May 1977, when the regulations for Section 504 were released. Even then success was elusive. Pressure from business and professional groups created a movement in Congress to amend and weaken the act. In 1978 Senator Stevenson from Illinois introduced a bill to extend municipal transit authorities' time limits for making their fleets of buses accessible to everyone, including persons using wheelchairs. The senator withdrew the bill after disabled consumers picketed his office, but resistance to the act in the House continued to gain strength.

Reactions of helping professionals to the attempts of the disabled to obtain their legal rights have been mixed. Some organizations, such as NRA, have actively supported the disabled. Others have adopted the stance that civic concerns of the disabled are not the concern of organizations concerned with rehabilitation. Many individual professionals support disabled consumers, while others are impatient with consumer complaints and fear any reforms initiated will make their work more difficult.

This chapter will:

1 Discuss factors which prevented unification of the disabled in the past
2 Discuss the forces which are now welding the disabled into a social movement
3 Discuss consumer impact on new legislation and implementation of old
4 Discuss the need for communication and cooperation between professionals and consumers

The rise of consumer activism reflects the growing unity of persons with a variety of disabilities. This rise also reflects the realization of the disabled that they must unite if they are to prosper socially and legally. But in order to unite, they must surmount some formidable obstacles. They must eliminate rivalry and factionalism among organizations for persons with different disabilities. They must learn the proper legal and political channels to use to secure and maintain their civil rights.

OBSTACLES PREVENTING THE UNIFICATION OF THE DISABLED IN THE PAST

As Safilios-Rothschild (1970) points out, there is more diversity among the disabled than among members of any other minority group. The disabled do not share the same distinguishing physical characteristics, as do the blacks or the elderly, or the same culture, as do members of ethnic or religious groups. The disabled not only cut across racial, religious, and ethnic lines, but they also face different problems depending on the type or severity of their disabilities.

People who are concerned with removing architectural barriers quickly learn that solving an accessibility problem for one disabled group may create a problem for another. Curb cuts which allow persons in wheelchairs to move freely from city block to city block may be hazardous for blind persons who may trip over the edge of a poorly constructed cut. Similarly, persons who use crutches may have more difficulty maintaining their balance on ramps designed for wheelchairs than on steps with horizontal treads.

In addition to requiring different solutions for the same problems, members of one disability group may be reluctant to join forces with the members of another, fearing that demands of other groups for benefits may cost them special considerations they now enjoy. For example, other disabled persons want the same disability-based income tax deduction the blind receive. But if all 35 million disabled persons in the United States received an extra deduction, much tax revenue would be lost. Conceivably, instead of all disabled persons' paying lower income taxes due to the extra expenses they incur as disabled persons, a reevaluation of the existing tax break for blind persons might end all disability-related personal deductions.

The tendency of some disabled persons to view advances of other groups of disabled persons as threatening is enhanced by the fact that the disabled, in general, have negative attitudes toward disability. Because they are members of the larger society, it is not surprising that many who are disabled share the societal aversion toward disabilities that differ from their own. Persons with quadriplegia may fear persons with epilepsy; persons with epilepsy may be repelled by persons with quadriplegia; and both epileptics and quadriplegics may shun persons with cerebral palsy.

The severity of a person's disability may influence how much she identifies with her own or other disability groups. Someone with a marginal disability, e.g., a partially paralyzed arm or controlled epileptic seizures, may be unable to accept the fact that she is disabled. Someone with a profound disability, e.g., total paralysis or advanced congestive heart failure, may be too ill or too incapacitated to concern herself with social and economic issues.

With all these factors working against the social and political unification of the disabled, it was slow to gain momentum and still is far behind that of other minority groups.

ROLE OF EDUCATION IN PROMOTING UNIFICATION OF THE DISABLED

Before World War II, one seldom saw visibly disabled persons outside their homes. The severely physically disabled were not educated or trained on a systematic basis and, without education or training, couldn't obtain the money they needed to enter society and actively fight for their rights.

With the end of World War II, this situation began to change. Suddenly there were thousands of severely disabled young war veterans who received disability pensions and who, during lengthy hospital stays, had formed a network of friendships with one another. Young, active, and financially independent, they refused to be barred from community participation (Deyoe, 1972). Many wanted to return to school under the GI Bill, which provided for the training or education of returning veterans. Veterans with disabilities soon discovered, however, that no university was willing to make the accommodations necessary to incorporate them into its regular student body.

Example 8A   Direct Action Begins: Winning Access to the University of Illinois

In Illinois, veterans in wheelchairs attended classes in a former tuberculosis hospital in Galesburg, but in the late 1940s the Galesberg campus of the University of Illinois was reconverted to a sanitarium. While others were allowed to transfer to the main campus in Urbana, disabled students were not, because the Urbana campus was inaccessible. But the disabled veterans wanted to continue their educations, and so, in the company of disabled and nondisabled supporters, they marched to Springfield, where they camped on the lawn of the Governor's mansion to publicize their desire for a college education. Eventually, Governor Stevenson acceded and the University of Illinois admitted a few disabled students on a regular basis.

At first, only minimal accommodations were made. Buildings containing classrooms for basic courses were ramped, but many ramps were inadequate or dangerous. Some were installed over existing stairways, and were so steep that even the most muscular wheelchair students could not go up or down without assistance. And until new dormitories were built in the early sixties, many students, disabled and nondisabled, were housed in ramshackle wood-and-tarpaper relics of World War II, known as the "parade ground units." These quarters, located in a section of the country known for its extremes of hot and cold weather, were so cold in winter that students often had to break through ice in the toilet bowls in the morning before disposing of urine from their overnight drainage systems.

But they persevered and prepared the way for other disabled persons, veteran and civilian. Slowly the university incorporated changes making it easier for disabled students to live more comfortably and get around more easily. New dorms had rooms designed to be used by all students interchangeably. Older buildings were ramped, and existing bathrooms made accessible, while new buildings had accessibility features built in. Timothy J. Nugent, who supported disabled students from the outset, assumed directorship of the university's program for disabled students, and established the university's Rehabilitation-Education Center, which is still the model for rehabilitation centers at colleges and universities throughout the nation.

Those first disabled students, however, did more than open the doors of higher education. After they graduated, they settled in all sections of the country, paving the way for a nationwide consumer movement. It would be difficult to find any major organization of disabled consumers which does not have among its leaders an alumnus from the University of Illinois.

ROLE OF ORGANIZATIONS OF DISABLED VETERANS

Organizations of disabled veterans have had a successful history of securing the rights of their membership. Disabled veterans are assured a measure of public support, because even with the antipathy against the military engendered by the Vietnam war, most people respect those who became disabled serving their country. Moreover, these veterans carefully guard the rights they do have, because they fear that without a politically powerful organization, they could lose the benefits they now receive.

When the need arises, the Paralyzed Veterans of America (PVA) are not slow to use the communications media to arouse public support.

Example 8B   PVA Safeguards Rights of the Individual against Hospital Policy

A situation which stirred one chapter of PVA to action stemmed from a confrontation between a spinal cord injury center and H. Kohn, a paraplegic patient. Due to a change in hospital policy, efforts were being made to discharge all long-term patients, some of whom had lived in the hospital for fifteen years. In this case, PVA intervened when the hospital attempted to discharge Kohn, who had a massive, incurable decubitus ulcer (pressure sore). The staff argued that since the ulcer would remain unhealed within a hospital setting or outside, and since Kohn could come in as an outpatient, there was no need for him to use valuable hospital space.

Kohn did not want to leave the SCI ward for an inner-city apartment from which he would have to make semiweekly trips to the hospital for dressing changes and infection checks. He consulted the regional PVA officers. PVA responded by threatening to release a local news story, complete with pictures, that a VA hospital was refusing full medical services to a disabled veteran with a large, unhealed decubitus ulcer. Kohn still lives in the center, but a fellow patient who also had an incurable ulcer but who did not protest his discharge has since died from an infection he incurred while being treated as an outpatient.

Disabled veterans' organizations are equally effective in combating discrimination against disabled veterans as a group. During a national convention in Chicago several years ago, some conventioneers were turned away from a downtown restaurant because the manager said their presence would depress other patrons. When the story appeared in the Chicago papers, the manager found himself looking for another job, and all disabled persons, veteran and civilian, found themselves being denied admittance to public places less often.

To some degree, public attitudes toward veterans and the benefits acquired by veterans' lobbies have had a positive effect on all disabled persons. But many veterans' benefits are denied to civilians, and there is even a great disparity between the benefits received by veterans with service-connected disabilities and those of veterans whose disabilities are not service-connected. The phrase "disabled vet" often conjures up visions of an accessible home in the suburbs, a generous monthly pension check, and an unlimited supply of adaptive equipment and medical services. For the veteran with a non-service-connected disability, however, that vision does not apply. He receives a small monthly pension and some medical services, but an infraction of hospital rules can result in a loss of even limited medical benefits. That is why organizations of disabled veterans realize their influence has limits. They do not attempt to intervene in situations where they will not readily get public support, because they realize that with the unpopularity of the Vietnam war, the high unemployment rate causing increased criticism of veterans' advantages in civil service employment, and the taxpayers' increasing disgruntlement with many publicly supported programs, they could easily lose the gains they have made.

ROLE OF ORGANIZATIONS OF DISABLED CITIZENS

In the civilian sector, the realization that unification was necessary grew slowly. By 1977, over 100 agencies existed in HEW to provide services to the disabled (Fay, 1977). Outside of the federal government, hundreds more, such as the American Foundation of the Blind, the United Cerebral Palsy Associations, and the National Association of the Deaf, worked for the betterment of disabled civilians. The services of each of these agencies were invaluable to the persons it represented, but an agency's need to raise funds sometimes conflicted with the disabled's need to be viewed and treated like anyone else. Early fund-raising appeals stressed the succumbing aspects of disability (Wright, 1960). By playing on the sympathies of potential donors, fund-raisers left the impression that the disabled were "poor, helpless cripples" (PHCs)—as the image was labeled by the disabled themselves. An early television appeal for the Muscular Dystrophy (MD) Associations consisted of Jerry Lewis standing behind an empty wheelchair saying, "The man who sits in this chair will never work again!" Such appeals had an understandably negative influence on employer attitudes toward disabled job applicants—especially men in wheelchairs.

Recent fund-raising appeals portray the disabled in a more realistic, hence more favorable, light. Telethons feature the abilities and the limitations of the disabled by utilizing those who require services but who are successful, such as an executive of a national airline who "sits in" a wheelchair due to MD.

Until 1977, despite the raising of funds for services and research and despite the establishment of public and private agencies to deal with disability-related problems, little progress was made in securing competitive employment for disabled persons and ensuring that job sites, streets, public buildings, and transportation were accessible. The problem was not the lack of job qualifications or accessibility standards. The problem was that employer attitudes remained unchanged, and architects, builders, and municipal transit authorities were unaware of or ignored the need for and means of creating a barrier-free environment.

It was this lack of social progress that stimulated disabled persons to organize. Purely social organizations, like "indoor fun clubs" or "sunshine clubs," which offered members outings and chitchat, began to give way to activist organizations which offered members a chance to, as *Newsweek* wrote, "take full part in the community and to live independent lives with dignity."

Some of these organizations focus on one problem area, such as the Austin-based Mobility Impaired Grappling with Hurdles Together (MIGHT), which works toward accessible public transportation. Others have multiple goals, such as the eastern-based Disabled in Action (DIA). The activist orientation of these groups is often reflected in their names or acronyms: the World Association to Remove Prejudice Against the Handicapped (WARPATH), headquartered in Florida; and the Student Organization for Every Disability United for Progress (SO FED UP), consisting of students on university campuses in New York City (Laurie, 1978).

But the attempts of these disparate organizations to produce wide-reaching changes were nearly as ineffectual as were efforts of the public and private agencies before. All these splinter groups needed to combine their efforts through a nationally based consumer organization, which could weld the disabled into a potent political force.

Washington, 1974: the Founding of the American Coalition of Citizens with Disabilities

In Washington, D.C. early in 1974, the American Coalition of Citizens with Disabilities (ACCD) was founded. The ACCD was designed to accomplish two major tasks: (1) coalesce organizations of disabled persons and federal, state, and private organizations for the disabled; and (2) enlist the support of the government, the private sector, and the general public in eliminating attitudinal, environmental, and occupational barriers impeding disabled persons.

The ACCD membership, guided by strong, assertive leadership, exemplifies the commitment of well-established disabled persons to the institutionalized, the poor, or the inarticulate, who do not have the means to express their concerns effectively. Based in the nation's capital, the ACCD, although still a young organization, has an impressive list of accomplishments to its credit. When the Secretary of HEW delayed issuing the regulations defining Section 504, the ACCD sponsored sit-ins across the country. As an umbrella organization which could coordinate geographically dispersed groups of regional protestors, the ACCD succeeded in carrying out a nationwide protest which resulted in the regulations' being released. Among those making up ACCD's political base are the American Council of the Blind, the Epilepsy Foundation of America, the National Association for Retarded Citizens, the National Association of the Deaf, the National Association of the Physically Handicapped, the Paralyzed Veterans of America, the United Cerebral Palsy Associations, and individuals who did not belong to any specific organization.

Washington, 1977: the White House Conference on Handicapped Individuals

Even before a national umbrella organization became a reality, the disabled had had some impact. Input from consumers led to the Rehabilitation Act of 1973's provision for a White House Conference on Handicapped Individuals. Three years after the passage of the act, the machinery for the conference was put into action. Prior to the conference in May 1977, state and territorial conferences were held to elicit and prioritize the concerns of the disabled, their parents, and professionals in disability-related fields. Among the issues covered were education, health care, housing, transportation, and recreation. Recommendations compiled in each territory and state were sent to the planners of the White House Conference, along with the names of delegates and alternates who would attend; 50 percent of the delegates were disabled, 25 percent were parents of disabled persons, and 25 percent were professionals.

At the 1977 conference, delegates had access to experts in available sources of funding, provisions of existing legislation, and legislation currently under consideration. During the day delegates attended workshops; in the evenings they met in state or territorial caucuses where information was exchanged and recommendations from individual workshops were voted on. Those recommendations passed were compiled and forwarded to the President and individual members of Congress for consideration. By 1978 some recommendations were being implemented, but a strong countermovement began to arise to delay or negate some of the gains which had been made (see Chapter 9).

SPECIFIC CONSUMER ISSUES

The ACCD encapsulated disabled consumers' concerns in its first newsletter (1977): ". . . improved education, expanded rehabilitation programming, accessible housing, effective transportation, civil rights, enhanced employment, self-determination and integration into the mainstream of American life." The common element in these concerns is the desire of the disabled to control their lives and to be integrated into their communities. In order to achieve this, jobs, transportation, and housing are necessary, but an adequate income is indispensable.

Adequate Family Incomes

Regardless of the disability, there is always some disability-related expense. The expense can stem from the astronomical costs of kidney dialysis, for those not covered by social security or other government programs, to the lesser costs of transportation to do food or clothes shopping for those who cannot use public transportation to shop.

During a year when neither of them is ill, the DeLoaches spend more than $2000 on maintenance drugs, prosthetic equipment, repair of that equipment, and structural modifications. In one year, they spent more than $3000 on the purchase of two electric wheelchairs alone. The DeLoaches are fortunate, however, since they are both employed and able to buy the services and assistive devices they require, including a modified van. Persons who cannot work because they have no transportation and cannot live independently because they can't afford accessible housing are, unfortunately, more common.

Professionalism and Commitment

At one of the state conferences preceding the White House Conference, a parent joined a discussion concerning mainstreaming of disabled school children. What she said drew a spontaneous round of applause, and summarizes, as well as any brief formulation could, a main concern of disabled consumers: "You can't teach a teacher love." Society responds to the needs of the disabled with money, but what the disabled need most from those who would help are things that money can't buy: dedication, commitment, zeal, energy, insight, action, courage, imagination—and even, if necessary, unpaid overtime.

Providing the things that money can't buy is the distinguishing mark of the true professional. But too many rehabilitators believe they are behaving like professionals when they concern themselves only with their narrowly defined area of expertise. If rehabilitators are true professionals, they will be concerned about the global goals of rehabilitation as well as the duties outlined in their job descriptions. Access is by far the most overriding of these global goals, because it is impossible to work, run a home, and participate in community affairs without being able to move about freely within a community. Yet many rehabilitators, professional rubric aside, regard and treat rehabilitation segmentally (Siller, 1974). Medical rehabilitators concentrate on physical restoration, the social worker helps with family problems, the psychologist is concerned with psychological adjustment, and the rehabilitation counselor works toward job placement.

Each rehabilitator sees his responsibility as one finely delineated area of the overall problem. Seldom do rehabilitators work together or with disabled persons to eliminate the environmental or social barriers which prevent the disabled from becoming well established in society. Unfortunately, a person can receive the best medical care, adjust psychologically, learn a marketable skill, and still be a rehabilitation failure if accessibility and transportation problems are unsolved. What concerns consumers most is not that professionals who serve them are often oblivious to the importance of accessibility and mobility for rehabilitation success, but that professionals who are aware are often reluctant to act, when a word from them could influence those who are in a position to effect needed change.

**Example 8C   Sin of Omission: for Lack of a Phone Call, the
Park Remains Inaccessible**

Massachusetts has a law that when streets are torn up, curbs will be rebuilt with curb cuts. Several years ago in preparation for the Bicentennial, the Boston Gardens across from the Massachusetts Commission on Rehabilitation were being renovated, but the adjacent sidewalk was replaced without a cut. Not only was this against the law, but it meant persons in wheelchairs could not get to the Gardens without assistance.

Shortly after the work on the Gardens was finished, an employee of the Commission was backing a man in a wheelchair off the curb in front of the Commission. When the wheelchair user commented on the absence of curb cuts, the rehabilitation "professional" remarked, "Yes. They've just finished working on the Gardens but they didn't bother to ramp the curb." Although the rehabilitator knew the law, was familiar with the problem of getting around in areas with no curb cuts, and had noticed before construction was completed that the sidewalk was not going to be ramped, he had not been concerned enough to pick up his phone and call City Hall to attempt to rectify the situation. He saw the presence or absence of curb cuts as inconsequential to his job as a rehabilitator.

The apathy of individuals often reflects the apathy of the agencies for which they work. Policies of such agencies contradict the purposes for which they were founded.

**Example 8D   Consumer Advocacy: the Interference of the
Unpaid in the Activities of the Paid**

In Austin, MIGHT had been working for some time with public transit authorities to work out an accessible mode of public transportation. MIGHT, experiencing active opposition from the authorities, contacted twenty-four agencies serving the disabled in the Austin area and asked them for their support. MIGHT is an organization of consumers who have other jobs, but who donate their time to the problems of those who cannot attend meetings because they don't have transportation. People in the agencies they contacted receive salaries for dealing with problems of disabled persons. Nevertheless, not one agency was willing to work with or lend support to MIGHT's members. Rather than committing themselves or voicing their concern about the lack of accessible transportation, these agencies openly criticized MIGHT's members as being self-serving and publicity-seeking.

Such criticisms are based on fact: disabled consumers are self-seeking and do utilize the communications media to publicize their concerns. But they are forced to be self-seeking when agencies founded to look after their interests fail to do so.

Every profession—law, medicine, teaching, nursing, counseling—has a mixture of hacks, heroes, and those who fall in between. Stressing the need for commitment among those who work with the disabled doesn't imply that rehabilitators must always be heroes. People do burn out, and the most dedicated, especially, need to pace themselves. Eventually, if society metamorphoses into a barrier-free society, the need for heroism will become less, not greater.

The metaphor "metamorphosis" refers both to the process of change an individual undergoes as he adjusts to a severe disability and the process of change our society is now undergoing, as it discontinues the segregation of the disabled. In the later stages of metamorphosis, as the transition becomes more complete, efforts that once were extraordinary become routine. In this transformation, society as a whole is benefited. For example, a person who is traumatically blinded or paralyzed is rushed to an emergency room, but twenty yeas later, he makes an appointment for an infection or a bad cold and sits in a waiting room like anyone else. The disabled look forward to a society in which outmoded attitudes, buildings, transit systems, and treatment methods will have been transformed in such a way that the disabled may become contributing members rather than burdens to that society. At such a time, there will be need for fewer miracle workers and more ordinary, competent mainstream teachers. But this change hasn't happened yet, and now, during the transformation stage, more rehabilitators are needed who will see to it that the trailblazing laws the disabled have been waiting for so long are actually put into practice.

Understandably, consumers are concerned that large amounts of money may go toward providing services which they never receive. If consumers received more support from professionally oriented persons concerned enough to ensure enforcement of existing legislation, then a certain cartoon that springs to mind, featuring a Rube Goldberg-type machine and aimed at bureaucracies in general, would not so aptly apply to rehabilitation. At the top of this cartoon Uncle Sam pours gold coins into the machinery. Along the twists and turns of the machine's inner workings are numerous spigots, out of which coins stream into the waiting hands of rehabilitators stationed along the way. At the far end sits a man in a wheelchair. A single coin makes its way past the grasping hands and rolls into his lap.

During a class presentation on advocacy, a student asked why he, as a future rehabilitation counselor, was expected to concern himself with attitudinal and architectural barriers. The answer he got was that these concerns are part of a counselor's territory, that a true rehabilitation professional is willing to use any legitimate means to pursue a development vital to his clients' success.

Implementation of Existing Legislation

The political activity of disabled citizens is based on the belief that legislated behavior change precedes attitude change. The continuation of the practical problems disabled persons face, i.e., inadequate income due to unemployment or underemployment, has caused them to shift from efforts aimed at winning acceptance to efforts aimed at obtaining legislation that will secure their right of access to public places, jobs, schools, and every mode of public transportation. Acceptance, plus access, would be ideal, for no one wants to encounter the "five o'clock" prejudice experienced by Jewish executives who work and lunch with Gentile colleagues, but whose existence is not acknowledged after the end of the working day or week. But if a person has spent years fruitlessly searching for employment, it becomes unimportant whether she is liked, as long as she is hired.

Through experience, the disabled discovered that depending on others to do the "right" thing did not noticeably improve their social situation. Therefore, the disabled learned to demand their rights, to be more assertive. For example, a speaker at a national rehabilitation conference urged disabled participants, when they were refused admittance to restaurants or theaters, not to passively leave but to block the entrance so others could not enter. The speaker believed it would be more effective to behave disruptively and publicly embarrass a businessman than to allow him to discriminate with impunity.

Much like the militancy of other minority groups, the militancy of the disabled is a reaction to decades of discrimination and ostracization. But behaving assertively in isolated instances will never effect the widespread changes the disabled seek. Even legislation alone is not the answer. Since the early 1970s much enlightened legislation has been passed, but the disabled are discovering, as did others before, that laws are worthless unless they are implemented. The words of Section 504 seem starkly simple: "No otherwise qualified handicapped individual shall, solely by reason of his handicap, be excluded from participation in, be denied the benefits of or be subject to discrimination under any program or activity receiving federal financial assistance." The civil rights extended under this section should guarantee handicapped children a public education in line with their needs and abilities, and handicapped adults and children equal access to public housing and transportation. But even a law cannot affect the behavior of a school district, a university, a housing authority, or a public carrier unless that law is implemented and penalties for noncompliance are enforced. The disabled point out that, while blacks objected to sitting in the back of the bus years ago, today persons using wheelchairs cannot even get onto the bus even though the technology required to board and unboard them is available at the cost of only $95 per bus per year (*Paraplegia News*, May 1977).

Unfortunately, while an appeal to the collective public conscience may loosen purse strings during a muscular dystrophy telethon, it will not open the doors of public schools or ramp urban area transit buses. Lawsuits initiated by the disabled have ensured that qualified teachers cannot be denied a job because they are disabled and that inaccessible subway stations in Washington, D.C., could not be opened until they were made accessible. More recent lawsuits have involved an airline which refused to transport a woman unless she bought two tickets, one for herself and one for an attendant; a supplier of prosthetics for allegedly overcharging customers; and numerous transit authorities who have ordered replacement buses which are not accessible. Many such lawsuits are being lost, however.

Example 8E   "A Precedent for Public Exclusion?"

After Robert Marsh, a quadriplegic, was forced to leave a theater because he was unable to sit in a regular theater seat, a verdict in Marsh's favor in the Los Angeles Superior Court was overturned. The state court of appeals ruled that state law does not require (1) admission of patrons whose wheelchairs block aisles in violation of fire codes or (2) modifications of such facilities for use by the handicapped. The court said, "The statute requires only that the operator of a business opens its doors on an equal basis to all that can avail themselves of the facilities without violation of other valid laws and restrictions" (*Paraplegia News*, May 1977).

What victories there have been, such as the eventual signing of the 504 regulations, have been hard won.

Example 8F   Direct Action against Government Stalling:
the Battle for 504

Early in 1977, after other methods to induce Secretary Calipano of HEW to sign the 504 regulations failed, consumers staged sit-ins in HEW regional offices to publicize their cause. The sit-ins received national coverage but the military tactics—surround, starve, and subdue—used to combat the demonstrators are known to few.

According to B. J., one of the demonstrators in Washington, when the sit-in began, the Secretary of HEW met with the demonstrators, welcomed them, and said that food and beverages would be available to them in the evening. Believing him, the demonstrators consumed the supplies of food and drink they had brought with them, but by evening discovered that all telephones had been disconnected, a cordon of police surrounded the area, and no one was permitted to enter or leave, including reporters or food vendors.

The following morning, an employee of HEW who had become aware of the demonstrators' situation on his way into work left his office and then returned with a large bag filled with fruit and vegetables. He had passed through the cordon when a policeman, realizing what he was carrying, tackled him, knocking him to the ground. As he fell, he tossed the bag to one of the demonstrators, who began passing out its contents. But the police, moving quickly, passed through the crowd, seizing the food from the hands of the then-hungry protesters. Several hours later, the Secretary sent a message offering the demonstrators a doughnut and a cup of black coffee if they would accept a weakened version and delayed implementation of the regulations. They refused, but the spirit of the Washington-based protest was broken.

Outside of Washington, however, other groups of protesters could not be as easily encapsulated. In California over 150 persons, with a reserve force of fifty more who served as substitutes or intermediaries with the news media, settled in, determined to stay until the regulations were signed. Their determination, coupled with nationwide press coverage, resulted in the original regulations' being signed in April 1977, over three years after the act was passed.

The political activism of the disabled, however, is not based solely on self-interest. The desire to be self-sufficient and a part of the community underlies their more obvious desire for employment, housing, education, and transportation. Deyoe (1972) found evidence of this in his twenty-year follow-up of disabled World War II veterans. A significant percentage of his subjects, who received service-connected benefits, spent their time doing volunteer work ranging from visiting the newly disabled to serving as scout masters for disabled Boy Scouts.

NEED FOR COMMUNICATION AND COOPERATION BETWEEN CONSUMERS AND PROFESSIONALS

The relationship between consumers and professionals is, necessarily, a symbiotic one. If no one needed rehabilitation services, there would be no need for rehabilitation professionals. Without rehabilitation professionals, disabled adults or parents of disabled children would have no one to help them secure appropriate medical treatment, financial aid, special education, training, and employment. Even though experts are sometimes less than expert and their attitudes sometimes antithetical to adjustment, poor services are better than no services at all, while the best services can change the course of a disabled person's life for the better. In Greer's case, the intervention of a neurosurgeon resulted in his being admitted into a specialized school, over the administrator's protest. In DeLoach's case, the intervention of a psychologist was instrumental in her receiving services previously denied her by a vocational counselor. Since the 1973 Act, client assistance projects (CAPs) systematize client advocacy within vocational rehabilitation, but similar support is not available to clients in other agencies or institutions.

At the root of the distrust and disaffection between professionals and consumers lies inadequate communication. On the one hand, professionals work under constraints which clients know nothing about. Many newly disabled adults, or parents of children with physical or mental defects, believe professionals could solve their problems if only the professional were competent or were willing to expend the necessary effort. The fact is that for many disability-related problems, there are no solutions. Parents who deplete their financial and emotional resources in a quest for some physician, some treatment that will cure their infant often blame the physician or the treatment for failure arising from an irremediable condition.

On the other hand, disabled individuals, or their parents, often invent techniques or discover resources that remedy seemingly insoluble problems. Some books listed in Appendix E contain information not found in professional journals or publications. But often when disabled persons attempt to share their experiences, their experiences are discounted, because they are laymen (Kaufman, 1976).

Example 8G   Self-Imposed Deafness: All the Answers Are in Print

Art R. is an SCI quadriplegic who was being rehabilitated in a VA hospital. Art was independent in everything except his bowel management, because he lacked the finger movement necessary to use usual methods of bowel evacuation. Art's psychologist was also a quadriplegic and knew other persons, similarly disabled, who used suppository inserters to carry out this activity. But when the psychologist asked Art's physician for permission to try an inserter, the physician, who knew nothing about inserters, refused to allow Art to try one. Sometime later, the psychologist was summoned to the physician's office and told to bring along an inserter. A medical journal had just recommended the use of such devices, thereby changing the physician's opinion of their usefulness.

Too often, when professionals deal with problems, they do not ask disabled persons who live with such problems for advice.

The disabled, unless they happen to be professionals, lack the training and hands-on experience of those professionals who work with a variety of disabled clients, while professionals lack the personal experience the disabled have garnered by living with a disability. Successfully rehabilitated disabled persons can form a valuable resource pool for those who work with less experienced disabled persons, and often feel an obligation to share the information they have accumulated. But disabled resource persons are usually volunteers, whereas it is the rehabilitation professional's job to concern herself with the overall goals of rehabilitation and to master the more technical aspects of rehabilitation.

Once two-way communications and mutual respect have been established between professional and consumer, they can more effectively cooperate toward their mutual goals. Neither the professional nor the consumer should be more concerned with being respected or appreciated than with the primary goal of rehabilitation—optimum adjustment of all disabled persons. Open confrontation between professionals and consumers could endanger the future of essential training, rehabilitation programs, and technological development, if legislators and private philanthropists learn of existing limitations in services. Instead of trying to improve these services, they may reduce or curtail them. A time when the economy is weak and when government spending is closely scrutinized is no time to publicly question the effectiveness of any program in which one has a vested interest.

Based on the mutual experiences of professionals and consumers, the following suggestions could lead to increased trust, understanding, and cooperation between them.

Suggestions for Professionals

1   Professionals must be open to criticism and secure enough to judge when criticism is well founded and when it is not.

2   If a criticism is aimed at a condition over which professionals have no control, they should share this with consumers and enlist the consumers' aid in reducing the constraints under which professionals work.

3 Professionals should neither discount the knowledge of consumers without formal training in rehabilitation, nor expect consumers to have all the answers, becoming disillusioned when they do not.

4 Professionals should not expect too much of consumers in terms of the time and effort they can expend on rehabilitation-related problems. While professionals are compensated, financially and professionally, for their rehabilitation-related efforts, consumers in other occupational fields are motivated primarily by their altruism.

Suggestions for Consumers

1 Consumers should be certain that their criticisms are valid before taking action which might be harmful to others. When a now well-established consumer organization was new, its members obtained an injunction against construction work on a civic center, because news reports stated that all parking lots were to be eliminated by the plans. Afterwards, the group discovered that the plans had actually included special handicapped parking facilities and a number of curb cuts and ramps.

2 Consumers must carefully weigh the cost of ventilating grievances against the cost of possible loss of current services and alienation of concerned, competent professionals.

3 Consumers should attempt to join forces with dedicated professionals to enlist the support of others and should substantiate their criticisms with constructive solutions.

4 Consumers, after enlisting the support of professionals, should follow through by working with them until common goals are reached.

POSSIBILITIES FOR THE FUTURE

Already, there are indications of a growing unity between professionals and consumers. The National Council of Rehabilitation Educators (NCRE) has a task force on consumer affairs whose charges are to contact consumer organizations and seek consumer input and support for rehabilitation counseling programs. Members of NRA joined forces with consumers and disabled professionals to successfully protest the illegal opening of inaccessible subway stations in Washington, D.C.

Whether this increased unity is occurring rapidly enough, only the future will tell. Many fear a backlash if consumers and professionals become too vociferous in their demands for continuing and increased rehabilitation services and if the cost of providing those services seems to outweigh the eventual benefits (see Chapter 9).

Countering that fear are the increased numbers of disabled persons who are obtaining educations in universities and colleges across the country. If the experience of the first graduates from Illinois is repeated in the 1980s, the existence of well-educated persons with a variety of sensory and motor impairments bodes well for the future of the disabled. Sociologists have long predicted that if the disabled are to improve their status, they must move into positions of power and prestige, where they can act as leaders and spokespersons for others (Safilios-Rothschild, 1970).

In retrospect, it is unfortunate that the extent of President Franklin D. Roosevelt's paralysis was so carefully concealed from the public. More open coverage of his physical limitations might have corrected some of the misconceptions about disabled persons today. In FDR's day, of course, only a President could inhabit an almost-magical world in which someone using a wheelchair was not handicapped by environmental restrictions. For FDR, ramps were built, elevators installed, limousines and airplanes made accessible. The tools of access were invented long before medicine learned to keep alive the vast numbers of disabled individuals who are now joining together to pursue their rights.

It is unfortunate that the access created for FDR was temporary and benefited him alone—ramps built before he arrived were torn down as soon as he left. The metamorphosis now taking place in American society will extend to all disabled Americans the kind of access once available only to a President. And to the disabled who need them, accessible buses are better than accessible limousines.

Chapter 9

Legislative Breakthroughs

During the 1970s, legislation was passed by Congress and state legislatures which significantly changed the opportunities available to handicapped citizens (Graves, 1979). As Graves indicates, this legislation went far in enhancing the rights of the handicapped in such areas as civil rights, education, health, and access to public facilities. Although federal legislation for the handicapped dates back as far as the 1800s (Oberman, 1965; Malikin and Rusalem, 1969), not until the 1970s were laws stating that services *must* be provided for the handicapped passed and enforced, replacing laws stating that services *could* be provided. Due to the recency of the passage of most of these laws, their legality is presently under some dispute.

The number of such laws passed since 1970 is impressive, and a complete listing of such legislation would be outside the scope of this book. Our intent here is to highlight the most significant legislation and its purpose. The reader is referred to such sources as *Amicus* (National Center for Law and the Disabled), *Handicapped Americans Report* (Plus Publications), *Word from Washington* (United Cerebral Palsy Association), and *Programs for the Handicapped* (Office of Handicapped Americans) for more detailed information regarding legislation and court decisions involving persons with disabilities. Addresses for these organizations can be found in Appendix D.

This chapter will review:

1 Landmark legislation of the 1970s
2 Other legislation affecting handicapped individuals
3 Significant court decisions involving the education and employment rights of the handicapped

LEGISLATIVE LANDMARKS OF THE 1970s

This section will examine in some detail two pieces of federal legislation which have the potential for significantly enhancing opportunities for the disabled population of the United States. The first of these, the Rehabilitation Act of 1973 (Pub. L. 93-112), provided unprecedented revisions of the state-federal vocational rehabilitation system. This system works to provide vocational training and other opportunities for adults with disabilities. Similarly, the Education for All Handicapped Children Act of 1975 (Pub. L. 94-142) mandated that all handicapped children be provided education through the state board of education. Between 1975 and 1979, Congress also passed several acts which amended aspects of both these laws.

The Rehabilitation Act of 1973

The state-federal vocational rehabilitation system has a lengthy legislative history (Malikin and Rusalem, 1969; Malikin and Rusalem, 1975). Prior to 1973, the criteria which had to be met in order for an individual to receive services from the vocational rehabilitation program were rather loosely defined (Rubin and Roessler, 1978). The three basic criteria were: (1) the individual must have a physical or mental disability; (2) this disability must constitute a handicap to employment; and (3) there must be a reasonable expectation that rehabilitation services would render the individual employable (Rubin and Roessler, 1978). It had become a common practice in many vocational rehabilitation agencies to serve the less severely disabled as often as, or more often than, the more severely disabled. Congress, in passing the Rehabilitation Act of 1973, conveyed its opinion of such practices. In part, Congress stated:

> The purpose of this act is to . . . authorize programs to . . . develop and implement State plans for meeting the current and future needs for providing vocational rehabilitation services to handicapped individuals and to provide such services for the benefit of such individuals, serving first those with the most severe handicaps. . . . (Pub. L. 93-112, p. 2.)

This law contained several new and unique features not found in prior rehabilitation legislation. Probably the most important aspects of this law were: (1) its emphasis on serving the most severely disabled; (2) its emphasis on expanding the freedom of handicapped individuals through the removal of architectural, transportation, and employment barriers; and (3) its establishment of a civil rights provision for the handicapped.

Public Law 93-112 contained provisions that have since become the focus of much public attention and bureaucratic interpretation, as well as lawsuits. Sections 501, 502, 503, and 504 were the aspects of this act which addressed the expanded civil rights of the disabled. In summary form, the essence of each section is as follows:

Section 501—established within the federal government an Interagency Committee on Handicapped Employees. This section, in general, charged the Committee with (1) coordinating affirmative action plans for employment of the handicapped by each department and agency within the federal government; (2) encouraging state governments to formulate employment plans to hire and promote handicapped individuals being rehabilitated with federal monies; and (3) reporting to Congress annually on progress in hiring and promoting the handicapped (Pub. L. 93-112).

Section 502—established the Architectural and Transportation Compliance Board. This board was charged with responsibility for (1) ensuring compliance of federal agencies with architectural standards; (2) removal of architectural and transportation barriers to the handicapped in public facilities; and (3) determining what, if anything, could be done to encourage public and nonprofit organizations to adhere to barrier-free design of facilities (Pub. L. 93-112).

Section 503—states that organizations having contracts with the federal government above the amount of $2500 per year must "take affirmative action to employ and advance in employment qualified handicapped individuals . . ." (Pub. L. 93-112).

Section 504—"No otherwise qualified handicapped individual in the United States . . . shall, solely by reason of his handicap, be excluded from participation in, be denied the benefits of, or be subjected to discrimination under any program or activity receiving federal financial assistance" (Pub. L. 93-112, p. 39).

In 1978, Congress passed amendments to the 1973 Rehabilitation Act, in the form of Pub. L. 95-602 (Comprehensive Rehabilitation, Comprehensive Services and Developmental Disabilities Amendments of 1978). This law added another section to the provisions of the 1973 Rehabilitation Act:

Section 505—sets forth several procedural conditions regarding complaints filed under Section 501, 503, and 504. Among its provisions, Section 505 provides for the reimbursement of attorney's fees under certain conditions. This new section establishes a strong connection between Section 504 and the Civil Rights Act of 1964 (*Amicus*, vol. 3., no. 6).

Many handicapped individuals who had previously been served through vocational rehabilitation agencies found themselves unable to benefit fully from these services due to inaccessible places of employment, negative attitudes of employers, and other discriminatory practices. With its mandates to the state-federal vocational rehabilitation system to serve the most severely handicapped, Congress felt compelled to provide for the removal of many of the more common hindrances to the training and employment of the severely disabled. Through the provisions of Sections 501, 502, 503, 504, and 505, Congress addressed itself to such problems.

The Comprehensive Rehabilitation, Comprehensive Services and Developmental Disabilities Amendments of 1978 (Pub. L. 95-602) mentioned above also included a provision for "comprehensive independent living services." This new provision, probably the most significant aspect of this law, was designed to meet needs of individuals so severely disabled that they did not have the potential for employment, but who would benefit from services designed to assist them to live independently (*Programs for the Handicapped*, Office for Handicapped Individuals, 1979).

The Education for All Handicapped Children Act of 1975

During the latter part of the 1960s and the early part of the 1970s, Congress passed several acts which greatly assisted states in providing educational services to handicapped children (Lavore, 1976). The Education for All Handicapped Children Act of 1975 (Pub. L. 94-142) was a comprehensive act which included all provisions of prior legislation and extended some of the services which could not previously be offered with federal assistance. Like the vocational rehabilitation programs, many special education programs for handicapped children were serving only milder forms of handicapping conditions. The intent of Congress in passing Pub. L. 94-142 was that *all* handicapped children, no matter how severe their disabilities, would be served through public special education programs. The purpose of the law was stated as follows:

> . . . to assure that all handicapped children have available to them . . . a free appropriate public education which emphasizes special education and related services designed to meet their unique needs, to assure the rights of handicapped children and their parents or guardians are protected, to assist States and localities to provide for the education of all handicapped children and to assess and assure the effects of efforts to educate handicapped children. (Pub. L. 94-142, p. 3.)

Subsequent amendments to this act in 1977 (Pub. L. 95-49) and 1978 (Pub. L. 95-561) extended its authority and allowed states to submit a single annual count of eligible handicapped children in December instead of the previously required twice-per-year census procedures (Office for Handicapped Individuals, 1979; *Handicapped Americans Report*, vol. 1, no. 1, p. 7).

Both the Rehabilitation Act of 1973 and the Education for All Handicapped Children Act of 1975 were legislative breakthroughs. These acts, for the first time, mandated that vocational rehabilitation and special education must serve the most severely disabled. In so doing, they made accessible many services and opportunities which had not previously been provided to all handicapped individuals.

OTHER LEGISLATION AFFECTING HANDICAPPED PERSONS

Although the Rehabilitation Act of 1973 and Pub. L. 94-142 were important legislative acts, during the 1970s Congress passed many other acts extending privileges and opening opportunities for certain members of the handicapped population. Much of this legislation from 1970 to 1976 has been summarized and discussed elsewhere (Lavore, 1976; Rubin and Roessler, 1978; Malikin and Rusalem, 1975). In the next section we will concentrate on laws passed during the 95th Congress (1977–1979). In Table 9-1 a summary of this legislation will be found.

As indicated in Table 9-1, the 95th Congress enacted a considerable amount of legislation affecting handicapped individuals in the areas of housing, transportation, job training, and social services. It should be noted that the portion of Table 9-1 titled "Provision(s)" represent summaries only, and the complete provisions of the acts should be consulted if the reader is interested in the exact stipulations of these laws. The rehabilitation act, the education act, and other acts passed during the latter part of the 1970s indicate that the U.S. Congress is aware of and is making efforts to eliminate many barriers to handicapped individuals' full participation in the community. Its legislative record indicates a general consensus with the central theme of this book, i.e., that providing more opportunities for individuals with disabilities will reduce the maladjustment and tragedy which heretofore accompanied such conditions. Some might say that congressional legislation, by itself, can do only so much toward promoting the rights of the disabled. But Justice Brandeis of the Supreme Court stated, "government—for good or ill—is a teacher to society and that society will imitate what it learns from government" (*Amicus*, vol. 1, no. 5, p. 12).

COURT DECISIONS INVOLVING EDUCATION AND EMPLOYMENT RIGHTS OF THE HANDICAPPED

In discussing recent legislation for the handicapped, Graves (1979) states: "The civil rights of handicapped people extend to all areas of life from hospitalization to the interrogation process in the courts" (p. 14). Graves appears to be interpreting the intent of Title V of the Rehabilitation Act of 1973, which contains Sections 501, 502, 503, 504, and 505, already discussed in this chapter. It is a fact that certain rights of the handicapped have been stipulated through the provisions in Pub. L. 93-112 and its subsequent amendments, Pub. L. 95-602. The rights have also been reinforced to some extent by regulations issued by the Department of Health, Education and Welfare. However, the true test of the validity of these rights rests with what the courts hold to be the intent of these provisions and the legal restrictions applicable to them. Here we will examine some of the more crucial court decisions involving the education and employment rights of handicapped individuals.

Sources for this review include all available issues of *Amicus* (volume 1, no. 1 through volume 4, no. 1),* supplemented with issues of *Handicapped Americans Report*, volume 2, no. 1 (January, 1979) through volume 2, no. 12 (June, 1979). Since the focus of this book is the handicapped individual's entry into the community, and since such entry is primarily through education and employment,

*The authors express their gratitude to the staff of the National Center for Law and the Handicapped for providing the necessary back issues of *Amicus* to assist us in this review.

Table 9-1 Significant Legislation Affecting Handicapped Citizens Passed by the 95th Congress

Act	Provision(s)	Target Population
Tax Reduction and Simplification Act of 1977 (Pub. L. 95-30)*	A tax credit of $35/year for the elderly blind; 10% credit for the year 1977–78 for businesses hiring clients referred from Vocational Rehabilitation; also provides deductions for day care of the handicapped in the home.	Elderly blind; businesses employing VR clients; families of the handicapped
Automobile Allowances and Adaptive Equipment (Pub. L. 95-116)	Extends authorization for the provision of an automobile (one-time grant) and grants for adaptive equipment to veterans with service-connected disabilities involving the loss or impairment of the use of limbs.	Handicapped veterans
Housing and Community Development Act (Pub. L. 95-128)	Provides for housing assistance (rent subsidies, etc.) for the handicapped and elderly under housing constructed using Housing and Urban Development funds. Also provides for monies for rural group homes for handicapped and elderly. Requires HUD to issue regulations for assuring accessibility for the handicapped in housing constructed with such monies.	Handicapped eligible for HUD housing
Reduced Air Fares (Pub. L. 95-163)	Authorizes reduced air fares for the handicapped and elderly on a space-available basis. Not mandatory for airlines to do so.	Handicapped air passengers
Housing and Community Development Amendments of 1978 (Pub. L. 95-557)	Makes provisions for financial assistance to nonelderly (ages 18 to 62) handicapped for both single unit and congregate dwellings. Sets aside $50 million in loans for meeting housing needs of handicapped.	Handicapped
Revenue Act of 1978 (Pub. L. 95-600)	Raises spending ceiling for Title XX funds (basic ser-	Low-income blind and disabled

Table 9-1   Significant Legislation Affecting Handicapped Citizens Passed by the 95th Congress *(Continued)*

Act	Provision(s)	Target Population
	vices to the low-income groups, including the blind and disabled)	
Comprehensive Employment and Training Act (CETA) Amendments of 1978 (Pub. L. 95-524)	Requires prime sponsors of CETA training programs to file plans for the inclusion of handicapped individuals in their programs.	Handicapped individuals eligible for CETA training
Comprehensive Older Americans Act Amendments of 1978 (Pub. L. 95-478)	Authorizes funds for demonstration projects for delivery of various social services to the homebound elderly, blind, and disabled.	Homebound blind and disabled

*Complete provisions for each act may be found by locating the act using its Public Law number, in this case 95-30, in the Government Documents section of most libraries.

Source: This material is adapted from *Handicapped Americans Report,* vol. 1, no. 1, and *Programs for the Handicapped,* Office of Handicapped Individuals, January/February 1979.

specific court cases were selected involving these two major issues. There have been many court decisions involving other issues, including institutionalization, sterilization, and transportation barriers. Reference to selected cases involving accessibility of transit systems is made in Chapter 11.

General Rights of the Handicapped

Two recent court decisions have affirmed the rights of disabled persons within the courts to bring civil action (suits). In *Cherry et al.* v. *Mathews et al.*, No. 76-1255 (D.D.C.),* James Cherry (a disabled individual) and a consumer organization (Action League for Physically Handicapped Adults) brought suit against then Secretary of Health, Education, and Welfare Mathews to issue long-delayed regulations implementing Section 504. The plaintiffs contended that Congress fully intended such regulations to be issued and that by refusing to promulgate them, Mathews was violating their rights under Section 504. On July 19,1976, a district court ruled in favor of Cherry and ordered such regulations to be issued promptly. Although the court's order was stayed for ten days, the decision upheld Cherry's right to action against HEW (*Amicus,* vol. 2, no. 2).†

   In *Sites* v. *McKenzie,* No. 76-24-W (N.D.W.Va.), a district court ruled, on November 13, 1976, in favor of Thomas Sites, a mental patient and convicted

*The numbers following the name of a case are legal references provided to assist readers who desire to research the case themselves.

†Throughout this section of the text, references to issues of *Amicus* are to the department in each issue entitled "In the Courts." A reference such as (*Amicus,* vol. 2, no. 5) refers the reader to the "In the Courts" department of volume 2, number 5 of this publication. When a portion of the reference is quoted directly, page numbers are given (*Amicus,* vol. 2, no. 5, p. 17).

criminal. Sites contended that he had been refused the right to participate in rehabilitation programs at the prison in which he was confined. The court decided he did have the right to participate in such programs under the provisions of Section 504 (*Amicus,* vol. 2, no. 2).

These cases seem to support the general rights provided to the handicapped under Section 504.

Right to Education Provisions

Court decisions involving the rights of handicapped individuals to appropriate educational programs are here classified into four categories: (1) right to regular (mainstreamed) education, (2) right to special programs, (3) right of institutionalized individuals to educational programs, and (4) right to higher education.

Right to Regular (Mainstreamed) Education   In a 1976 case, *Hairston* v. *Drosick,* No. 75-0691 CH (S.D.W.Va.), a federal district court ruled that Trina Drosick, a child with spina bifida, must be provided an education within the regular classroom. School officials contended that Trina's special toileting needs must be furnished by her mother and not by the school; thus, she could not attend regular classes. The court stated that denying Trina this opportunity violated her rights under Section 504, and that "a major goal of the educational process is the socialization that takes place in the regular classroom, with the resulting capacity to interact in a social way with one's peers" (*Amicus,* vol. 1, no. 3, p. 6).

In *Unified School District No. 1* v. *Thompson,* No. 416-488 (Cir. Ct., Dane County, Wis.), Michael Byrd, a mentally retarded pupil, was refused the right to participate in the regular physical education program by the Unified School District. Michael's father then appealed to the Superintendent of Public Instruction for Wisconsin, Thompson, who ordered the school district to provide such services to Michael. The Unified School District then brought suit against Thompson. In May 1976 the Circuit Court of Dane County ruled that Thompson had no authority to issue such an order, and severely criticized the Wisconsin state legislature for such vague laws regarding special education. Later, Unified School District No. 1 voluntarily provided Michael Byrd with an individualized physical and academic education program (*Amicus,* vol. 1, no. 6).

Right to Special Programs   In April 1976 a class action* suit was filed in Federal District Court of the Virgin Islands on behalf of handicapped children. The suit, *Harris et al.* v. *Kean et al.,* No. 76-323 (D.V.I.), alleged that the children were being denied an appropriate educational program in violation of the provisions of Section 504. The federal judge rejected the motion for an injunction against the school district, noting that the Virgin Islands was at the present time attempting to implement a special education program. The judge stated that placing handicapped

---

*Paraphrasing *Black's Law Dictionary,* a "class action" is a civil suit in which one person or several persons [the plaintiff(s)] represent a larger group, or class. In this example, Harris et al. represents all handicapped children not receiving special services in the public schools of the Virgin Islands. The holding of the court in such matters applies, in theory, to all members of the class represented.

children into such programs before they were fully implemented would be disadvantageous to the children in question (*Amicus,* vol. 2, no. 4).

In July 1977, in *Mattie T.* v. *Holladay,* C.A. No. D.C. 75-31-S (N.D. Miss., 1977), a class action suit was filed against the state of Mississippi on behalf of twenty-six handicapped students. (Mattie T. was one of the twenty-six handicapped students represented in this action.) The plaintiffs in the case held that the state was not complying with the Education of the Handicapped Act, Part B, on several counts: (1) The plaintiffs claimed that the federal act applied to all school districts in the state whether or not they were receiving federal funds. (2) It was claimed that this state was not taking the necessary steps outlined in the federal law to identify all handicapped students in the state. (3) When handicapped students were identified, particularly as educable mentally retarded, the identification procedures were racially and culturally discriminatory (evidence cited in the court indicated that while 49 percent of the public school population was black, 76 percent of children in special education were black). (4) Federal law states that when handicapped children are identified, they must be provided education with their nonhandicapped peers, if at all possible. Plaintiffs presented evidence that 85 percent of all mildly retarded children ages 6 to 12 in Mississippi were being educated in self-contained classrooms.

This case is unique in that two distinguished social scientists, Jane Mercer and Milton Budoff, were expert witnesses for the plaintiffs. In January 1979 a Federal District Court judge issued a final consent decree in the case of *Mattie T.* v. *Holladay.* It ordered that the state issue specific criteria for placing handicapped students in settings not considered the "least restrictive environment" to avoid large-scale segregation. It also required the state to hire "outside experts" to evaluate the state's processes for classifying and placing handicapped children, to avoid culturally biased identification procedures. All school districts which have misclassified children as mentally retarded must identify them and provide them with compensatory education. An identified handicapped child cannot be removed from school for more than three days without a review of the child's educational program. Finally, the state must provide to all parents of handicapped children a book detailing their rights as parents (*Amicus,* vol. 2, no. 3; vol. 2, no. 5; vol. 4, no. 3).

In *Sherer* v. *Maier, North Kansas City School District et al.,* No. 77-0594-CV-W-4 (W.D. Mo. 1977), the parents of 8-year-old Kimber Sherer, a child with spina bifida, brought suit against the school district for refusing to catheterize the child. The parents had been advised by their physician that their child needed this procedure once a day. The suit alleged that this refusal by the school district violated the child's rights under Section 504. The court, on November 2, 1977, dismissed the case, concluding that the parents had not exhausted all administrative remedies available to them. The court also indicated that the suit could be filed again if such administrative relief* was not subsequently received (*Amicus,* vol. 3, no. 1). This

---

*Administrative relief consists of filing complaints with the institution in question and with the Office of Civil Rights, Department of Education. In many cases, the courts urge the plaintiff to seek such relief first before filing suit.

case stands in contrast to *Mattie T.* v. *Holladay*, where the subject of administrative relief was not considered and the right to private action was affirmed.

Howard S. v. *Friendswood Independent School District*, No. G-78-92 (S.D. Tex.), involved Howard S., a young man suffering from minimal brain damage and emotional disturbance. After attending special education classes in the school district through junior high school, he began developing severe behavioral problems, was expelled from school, and subsequently attempted suicide. He was then placed in a private school in Austin, Texas. In this case, the Federal District Court granted the parents temporary relief, ordering the Friendswood Independent School District to provide their son a free, appropriate education through payment of the private school tuition until the school district could develop its own educational program for such individuals. The basis for this ruling was Section 504 (*Amicus*, vol. 3, no. 4).

Right of Institutionalized Individuals to Educational Programs The following case involves the rights of children within institutions to educational and other programs. In a New York federal court decision the commitment to the concept of deinstitutionalization of the retarded even in the face of other factors can be seen. In *New York State Association for Retarded Children and Parisi* v. *Carey*, 72-C-356 (E.D.N.Y.), a large group of residents of Willowbrook State School had been placed in the public schools of New York City by a previous consent decree. Some of these children were later found to be hepatitis-B carriers. The Board of Education of New York City decided to exclude these retarded children found to be hepatitis-B carriers from the public schools. Of the fifty children excluded, forty-two were former residents of Willowbrook. The New York State Association for Retarded Children (NYSARC) sought court action to prevent the children from being excluded. The association's case was upheld in federal court. Following this court decision, the New York City Board of Education established a special program for the children involved which was physically segregated within the public school program. The NYSARC again appealed this action, contending that such a segregated plan violated Section 504 and the rights of such children under the Fourteenth Amendment. On February 28, 1979, the Federal District Court upheld the association's appeal. It would seem that the initial consent decree deinstitutionalizing the forty-two children from Willowbrook was of primary importance to the court even in the face of other health concerns.

Right to Higher Education Several cases have been decided in courts, stipulating the rights of handicapped persons in institutions of higher education under Section 504 and other provisions. In *Borden* v. *Rohr et al.*, No. 75-844 (S.D. Ohio), Michael Borden was refused the right to play on the junior varsity basketball team at Ohio University because he had the use of only one eye. In December 1975 a federal judge issued a temporary restraining order against the university, but also exempted the university from liability for any injuries incurred by Borden while he was participating in basketball. The suit was later dropped when the plaintiff received a letter from the state attorney general of Ohio stating that he would be allowed to play junior varsity and to try out for varsity basketball (*Amicus*, vol. 1, no. 3).

In *Barnes* v. *Converse College*, No. 77-1116 (D.S.Car.), Nelda Barnes, a deaf teacher, was required to attend college to update her teaching certificate. In July 1977 a lower court ruled that under Section 504 the college she attended, Converse College, had to pay for the cost of interpreter services for Barnes to attend the required course. This ruling was reversed by the U.S. District Court in March 1978, which found that the plaintiff had not exhausted her "administrative remedies." Barnes petitioned this court again, claiming that to exhaust administrative remedies would be futile. In May 1978 the same court again denied her petition, stating that the plaintiff could not judge the "adequacy of the administrative mechanism without making any effort to test the remedy" (p. 20). However, the court added that she would be reimbursed for her interpreter expenses if such administrative proceedings ruled she was entitled to such, and that she could also file suit again if such administrative relief was not satisfactory (*Amicus*, vol. 3, no. 4; vol. 2, no. 5).

In a similar case, *Camenisch* v. *The University of Texas*, No. A-78-CA-061 (W.D. Tex.), Walter Camenisch, a deaf individual, was required to attend classes at the university to maintain his position as dean of students at the Texas School for the Deaf. Camenisch sued the University of Texas for payment of interpreter services. On the basis of Section 504, the district court granted a preliminary injunction which ordered the university to provide such services, on the basis that administrative action could take a year or two and the plaintiff's position would be in jeopardy. The plaintiff was requested to file a complaint with HEW and to post a bond of $3000 pending the outcome of administrative procedures (*Amicus,* vol. 3, no. 4).

In these cases it can be seen that the courts have become more cautious in ruling for handicapped individuals. They have begun to encourage such individuals to pursue administrative procedures before filing court action, and, in the case of such action, to post a bond pending the outcome of their administrative complaints.

Probably the most widely publicized case involving a handicapped person's rights in higher education in *Southeastern Community College* v. *Francis B. Davis*, No. 78-711 (U.S.Sup.Ct.). This was the first such case involving rights under Section 504 to reach the U.S. Supreme Court. Later in this chapter, an entire section and discussion will be devoted to the details of this case.

Employment Rights of Individuals with Handicaps

Court cases involving employment rights fall into two general categories: (1) those involving initial permanent employment and (2) those involving discrimination against handicapped employees. In some of the cases to follow, the right to "private action" will be cited in the courts' decisions. This is a legal question involving the right of an individual to bring civil action (suit) in regard to a federal law and its regulations. In 1975 the U.S. Supreme Court heard a case, *Cort* v. *Ash*, and in rendering its decision in this case set forth four criteria which must be met for the right to private action to be granted. Paraphrased, these criteria are:

    1 Is the individual filing suit one of the class for whose benefit the statute was enacted?
    2 Is there any implicit or explicit intent of the legislation either to create or to deny the right to private action?

3 Is it consistent with the underlying purpose of the legislative scheme to imply such a right for the plaintiff (individual)?

4 Is the cause of action one traditionally relegated to state law, in an area basically of concern to the states, so that it would be inappropriate to infer cause of action solely on the basis of federal law? (422 U.S. 76).

Therefore, when a decision indicates the individual had no right to "private action," that court is stating that one or more of the above criteria were not met.

Decisions Involving Refusal to Employ Disabled Job Applicants   *Drennon* v. *Philadelphia General Hospital*, No. 76-239 (E.D. Pa.), was one of the first cases involving refusal to hire a handicapped job applicant. LaVon Drennon was refused permanent employment as a laboratory technician by the hospital because she had a record of epileptic seizures, although she had completed a successful period of training and trial employment without incidents. Drennon filed suit claiming that the hospital's refusal violated her rights under Section 504. The district court, in January 1977, denied the hospital's motion to dismiss the case, but refrained from issuing a ruling until the plaintiff had sought federal administrative relief (*Amicus*, vol. 1, no. 6).

In another case involving a history of seizures, *Fast* v. *Ross*, No. G. 78-775 C.A. (W.D. Mich.), a federal court in December 1978 ordered the Michigan state police to administer all necessary admission tests for entrance to the state police academy to David Fast, the plaintiff. Fast, who had a history of seizures at the age of 13, had been denied such admission tests on the basis of his medical history. In this case the court ruled that denying such tests violated Fast's rights under Section 504 and was an "irrebuttable presumption"* which also violated his rights under the Fourteenth Amendment. This concept of "irrebuttable presumption" is unique to the extent that it is another legal avenue by which the disabled may contest denial of rights (*Amicus*, vol. 4, no. 1).

The concept of irrebuttable presumption was used in another case, involving the refusal to employ a sightless teacher. In *Gurmankin* v. *Costanzo*, Nos. 76-1730, 76-2297, 77-1273 (3rd Cir., 1977), the U.S. Court of Appeals, Third Circuit, ruled that denial of the right of opportunity to demonstrate one's teaching ability because of a disability (blindness) was an unconstitutional irrebuttable presumption that the plaintiff was not qualified to teach sighted students. The ruling, issued in April 1977, did not address the rights of Gurmankin under Section 504 directly. However, the court noted that prior cases had established a disabled person's right to private action under Section 504 (*Amicus*, vol. 2, no. 4).

Another case involving the employment of a person with visual problems is ironic because the employer in this case was the Connecticut Institute for the Blind. Ellen Schuman lost her position as a teacher's aide at the institute due to budgetary

---

*An "irrebuttable presumption" is a legal concept regarding how evidence can be presented. If one side presents evidence ruled to be established fact, rules of evidence forbid introduction of evidence by the opposing side to rebut the "fact." In this specific case, the court did not rule on the established "fact," but the state police department did in its administrative hearings. The concept of an "irrebuttable presumption," once used widely in courts, has only recently experienced a rebirth in its usage and is a most questionable practice (Bergdorff, 1980).

cutbacks. Since the position lost was in the upper school, Schuman reapplied for a similar position in the lower school, but she was denied employment due to her limited vision. The case went before the Supreme Court of Connecticut. In *Connecticut Institute for the Blind* v. *Connecticut Commission on Human Rights and Opportunities,* No. 8756 (Conn. Sup.Ct.), it was ruled that the institute could not make a blanket decision that all persons with visual problems do not qualify as teacher's aides in its lower school. The court directed the lower court to settle the amount of back pay and benefits owed to Schuman. Schuman's arguments in this case were based on employment under Connecticut state law (*Amicus,* vol. 3, no. 6).

In *Gibson* v. *U.S. Postal Service*, No. 77-2453 (W.D. Tenn.), Anthony Gibson was denied a permanent part-time job as a mail handler after having held a temporary position with the U.S. Postal Service. The denial was based on the discovery that Gibson suffered from a convulsive disorder. In April 1978 a district court issued a consent order that Gibson be hired. The court in this case stipulated a probationary employment period, allowing dismissal of Gibson only on the grounds that he could not perform his job satisfactorily (*Amicus,* vol. 3, no. 4).

Cases Involving Discrimination against Handicapped Employees Several cases decided in courts have dealt with discriminatory employment practices toward employees having some type of disability. Some of these cases involve employees hired with a preexisting disability, while others involve employees who have become disabled subsequent to their employment.

Not all cases involving job dismissal of a handicapped employee disregard the physical requirements of the job in question. In *Coleman* v. *Darden et al.*, C.A. No. 76 M 686 (D. Col., 1977), Michael Coleman, a blind law-school graduate, was employed as a law clerk for the Equal Employment Opportunity Commission in Colorado. After two years, Coleman was dismissed for failure to pass the bar examination. He reapplied for a position as a legal research assistant, a position requiring heavy amounts of reading, and was denied employment. He filed suit, claiming rights under Section 501. The district court dismissed the case, stating his rights had not been violated since the reading requirements were reasonably related to the job of legal research assistant. The court ruled also that Coleman had no right to private action. This case, like *Southeastern Community College* v. *Davis* (to be cited later), tends to indicate that the courts do often take into account the physical requirements for jobs (*Amicus,* vol. 2, no. 5; Bergdorff, 1980).

Howard McNutt, legally blind, was an employee of the Department of Housing and Urban Development (HUD). The plaintiff was transferred to another department and had no formal evaluation of performance for two years, thus eliminating his chances for promotion. In *McNutt* v. *Hills et al.*, C.A., No. 75-1422 (D.D.C., 1977), McNutt filed suit against HUD. Meanwhile, an administrative grievance hearing revealed that McNutt had been discriminated against, that he should be promoted four grade levels, and that he should be awarded back pay. HUD did not comply. In January 1977 a district court judge found that the plaintiff had been discriminated against and ordered HUD to implement appropriate affirmative action in this case (*Amicus,* vol. 2, no. 5).

Raymond Holland, an electronics technician having cerebral palsy, was transferred to a new position within his company requiring considerable eye-hand coordination. When he failed to perform adequately in this new position, he was demoted by his employer, Boeing Company. In *Holland* v. *Boeing Company*, 90 Wn. 2d 384 (Sup. Ct. Wash. 1978), the Supreme Court of Washington ruled that Boeing was unfair in refusing to make reasonable accommodations for physically handicapped employees. The court ordered the company to reinstate Holland to his prior position and to award him deserved back pay, attorney's fees, and reimbursement for vacation time (*Amicus,* vol. 4, no. 1).

Charlotte Smith is a licensed airline pilot employed by NASA. She is also a paraplegic confined to a wheelchair. Even though employed, she failed to be promoted at the same rate as two similarly qualified nondisabled male employees. She filed suit on the basis of discrimination against her sex and her physical disability. The U.S. Court of Appeals, in *Smith* v. *Fletcher*, No. 75-3948 (5th Cir., 1977), ruled that Smith had in fact been discriminated against on the basis of her sex. The court failed to rule explicitly on the role of her disability in the case, but indicated that both sex and physical disability appeared to be interrelated in this situation. The court, in its ruling, cited a statement by one of Smith's supervisors: "I know it would be difficult for a young woman to travel all over the country, getting in cabs, airplanes, with a wheelchair" (*Amicus,* vol. 2, no. 6, p. 20).

In the case of *Trageser* v. *Libbie Rehabilitation Center*, No. 77-2224 (4th Cir., Dec. 18, 1978), the district court rendered a decision which narrowly interpreted the 1978 amendments to the Rehabilitation Act of 1973. In its ruling, the court indicated that the new amendments, which in effect made Section 504 a part of Title VI of the 1964 Civil Rights Act, restricted the interpretation of "federal assistance" to mean only federal monies designated to provide employment opportunities (*Amicus,* vol. 4, no. 1). This ruling has serious implications for further litigation under Section 504. Court decisions had up to this point taken the phrase "federal financial assistance" to mean any federal funds received by the institution, company, or organization. If the *Trageser* ruling is adhered to in future cases, "federal financial assistance" will be restricted to mean only federal monies designated to provide employment, such as in CETA programs. The case was appealed to the U.S. Supreme Court, but on June 18, 1979, the high court declined to hear the case (*Handicapped Americans Report*, vol. 2, no. 12).

The Supreme Court's Decision: A Blow to 504?

On June 11, 1979, the U.S. Supreme Court issued its decision after hearing the case of *Southeastern Community College* v. *Francis B. Davis* (*U.S. Law Week*, vol. 47, p. 4693). This was the first case in which the high court had ruled on the provisions of Section 504 (*Handicapped Americans Report,* vol. 2, no. 1, 1979). In its decision, the court ruled that Southeastern Community College had not violated the plaintiff's rights under Section 504 by denying Davis admission to a clinical training program in the field of nursing. Davis was deaf and contended that she could succeed in this program if certain modifications of the curriculum were made as indicated by HEW's regulations for Section 504. The court's ruling has been described in the media as a setback to the rights of the handicapped. "The movement to protect the handicapped against discrimination suffered a major setback with the court's ruling . . ." an editorial stated (*Memphis Press-Scimitar*, July 4, 1979, p. 6). In an Associated Press article, Richard Carelli wrote concerning the Davis decision: "Handicapped persons have no legal right to attend a college when they cannot meet the physical requirements" (*Memphis Commercial Appeal*, July 8, 1979, p. 14). However, when the ruling itself is examined, there is no indication that the court ruled against Section 504 per se. Paraphrased, the Supreme Court stated:

> No violation of Section 504 occurred when the college denied the plaintiff admission. Nothing in the history or the language of Section 504 states an institution can not require reasonable physical qualifications to enter a clinical training program. The modifications of the college training program to make it appropriate for the plaintiff would be so pervasive that they would render such training invalid as a nurse's training program. (*U.S. Law Week,* vol. 47, p. 4689.)

The court ruled that: (1) the terms of 504 prohibit exclusion from a program solely because of a handicap, but this does not prevent a program from requiring certain "legitimate physical requirements"; (2) the affirmative action necessary to dispense with oral instruction for the plaintiff goes beyond the "modifications of post-secondary curricula" referred to in the 504 regulations; and (3) the line between lawful refusal to extend affirmative action for a handicapped individual and illegal discrimination is not always clear, but in the context of this case, the college's refusal to make appropriate modifications in its curriculum did not constitute discrimination (*U.S. Law Week,* vol. 47, p. 4689).

It would appear that the coverage of this case in the media as indicated by the above editorial statement may give an erroneous impression of what the ruling said. As paraphrased above, however, the ruling upheld Section 504, but held that Davis's contention went beyond its provisions. There is a note of finality about U.S. Supreme Court decisions; debates or protests will not change them. Only another case brought to the high court which addresses the discrimination provisions of Section 504 in another context will modify the Davis decision.

Conclusions Regarding Rights of the Handicapped in Litigation

What conclusions can be drawn from this review of court cases involving the education and employment rights of individuals with handicaps? It appears safe to conclude the following:

1   The courts generally have recognized recent federal legislation, specifically Pub. L. 93-112 and 94-142 and their amendments, as valid laws.
2   The application of rights afforded by these laws must meet a number of specific legal requirements.
3   As time progresses, the courts have become more strict in their interpretation of these rights, as seen in the Supreme Court's decision in *Southeastern Community College* v. *Francis B. Davis.*
4   In seeking relief from injustice through the courts, the handicapped individual generally must be able to prove that (a) arbitrary and capricious dis-

crimination occurred, (b) the situation meets the "right to private action" requirements, and (c) the individual has sought and did not receive satisfactory administrative relief.

FUTURE PROSPECTS

The future of the legal rights of the handicapped will be interesting to observe. Whether legislation and court decisions of the future further or retard the progress of the 1970s will be determined by the general mood of the country. To extend Justice Brandeis's statement quoted earlier in this chapter, government, through the laws and court decisions of the 1970s, has taught society much regarding the rights of the handicapped individual. In the most desirable state of affairs, society will heed the "lessons" of government and the general citizenry will demonstrate their commitment to guard these established rights. This will signal the metamorphosis of society described in other sections of this text.

Chapter 10

Preparing the Disabled Individual for Community Life

An individual with a severe physical disability needs a wide array of services to realize her full potential for assuming a role in society. This chapter examines the services necessary to provide a disabled individual with the skills she requires to be fully integrated into community life. These services are presented in the following categories: (1) self-care, (2) educational services, (3) vocational services, (4) transportation services, and (5) residential services.

In the following discussion, many references will be made to the concepts of "potential" and "skill." In this context, "potential" may be defined as an individual's remaining physical, intellectual, and social abilities which may be developed, through training, to assist her in adapting to various life situations. "Skill" is defined as a specific potential ability developed for the achievement of a specific task. Potential, then, refers to something such as muscle function, intelligence, or social perceptiveness. Skill, on the other hand, refers to the ability to walk, to read, to conduct oneself appropriately in social situations, and so on.

This chapter will present a discussion of services available to assist individuals in transforming potential into skills, focusing on:

1 The nature and role of available services
2 The nature of personnel and agencies providing these services
3 The current and future status of the effectiveness of such devices

SELF-CARE

Nature and Role of Self-Care Services

Before an individual can become a full participant in community living, he must, to some degree, be capable of dressing, feeding, and grooming himself, and of performing the routine tasks of life, such as housekeeping and similar activities. These tasks are often referred to as ADL (activities of daily living) skills.

Interestingly, ADL skills are often taken for granted by those so fortunate as to have developed them during the process of growing up. In order to illustrate this point, the authors frequently have their students assume a disability for a 24-hour period as a part of their course requirements. These students invariably discover that major daily activities, such as going to class, going to work, or going shopping, are not the most frustrating for them. Rather, the "simple" tasks of getting bathed, shaved, dressed, and fed are the activities which become their psychological undoing. Since these "simple" tasks are the first ones of the "disabled day," by the time the students get around to the major tasks, they find themselves so exhausted and exasperated that they have little or no motivation to attend to their other affairs.

Assisting severely disabled individuals to achieve competence in self-help and activities of daily living comprises a vast area. Entire volumes have been written on this subject, including the texts of Goldenson, Dunham, and Dunham (1978) and Laurie (1976). Rusk's (1977) recent edition deals with specific procedures for teaching skills in activities of daily living and other areas. Here we will deal with the personnel and programs providing such services rather than the procedures per se for developing and/or teaching such skills.

Personnel and Agencies Providing Self-Care Services

The assessment of basic potentials and the initial teaching of skills in self-help and ADL are usually the domain of physical and occupational therapists. Such therapists, trained in the anatomy and physiology underlying such potentials and skills, provide these services through a variety of procedures and in a variety of settings.

If the individual in question is a child or young person, his potential for self-care is evaluated and training is initiated in this area. Frequently, these services are performed by or with the consultation of a physical or occupational therapist. If the child is of school age, he receives these services, as needed, as part of his educational activities. Often physical or occupational therapists work directly with the child, supervise aides who involve the child in specific procedures, or train the child's parents in rendering the needed exercises and activities. In most communities, the limited number of such therapists cannot provide all the services needed. Programs that utilize aides and parent training constitute one method of circumventing the shortage of such personnel.

With the development of infant stimulation programs, more emphasis has been placed on the entire area of early childhood programs, and on providing continuity in programs for children from infancy through the initial stages of formal education (Quick, Little, and Campbell, 1974). Many early childhood programs are designed to facilitate development and training in feeding, toileting, and other self-help activities. With the advent of mandatory education legislation (see Chapter 9), the number of such programs should increase. As a result, preparing a child to care for himself, totally or partially, *before* he enters the formal school years will allow more time in later years for the development and training of other strategic skill areas.

With regard to adults who have become disabled, the assessment, development, and training of self-help and ADL become somewhat different. Instead of learning to achieve such tasks from scratch, they must learn different ways of doing what they had previously been able to do. Again, physical and occupational therapists play a vital role in assessing potential for and initiating training in skill development in this area. The services and activities provided with the supervision of the physical and/or occupational therapist may have much broader goals than self-help and/or ADL, but the latter are always important components of such activities.

This training, or retraining, is usually provided within medically oriented rehabilitation facilities operated through local, state, and/or federal sponsorship, on either an inpatient (live-in) or an outpatient basis. For example, the Veterans Administration has a national network of such centers for veterans of military service throughout the United States. Many individual states have centralized rehabilitation centers, such as Hot Springs Rehabilitation Center in Arkansas, Warm Springs Rehabilitation Center in Georgia, Rancho de los Amigos in California, and the Woodrow Wilson Rehabilitation Center in Virginia, to name only a few.

For adults, self-help and ADL training become critical in forming their attitudes toward the limitations placed on them by their conditions. If newly disabled adults can be assessed accurately and trained adequately to develop such skills, routine life is somewhat less burdensome. However, if an adult cannot, or at least is told he will never be able to, bathe, dress, or feed himself through the development of skills and/or the assistance of technological devices, it is little wonder if he is not motivated to be retrained for a vocation and other broader goals of rehabilitation. Compared to a child with a severely disabling condition, a newly disabled adult is frequently provided fewer formal opportunities to develop fully his self-help and ADL skills. Since most of his formal assistance in this area is provided within a specific time frame and location, i.e., following the onset of disability and within the rehabilitation facility setting, he does not have the opportunity for extended specific training in this area. Unlike a child, he does not go to a preschool or school setting where such efforts are provided over an extended period of his life. In addition, he is often sent home with only minimal instructions and training for himself and for his family members regarding self-help and ADL skills. Here the attitudes of the persons in his immediate environment become crucial if supplemental development in this area is to be achieved.

Whether the individual is a child or an adult, however, self-help and ADL skills are developed in one of three major ways. First, and most ideal, the individual is trained to perform such tasks totally independently. Second, technological devices may be developed to aid him in accomplishing such tasks. Third, other persons within the individual's immediate environment can be trained to assist him in certain of these tasks, although this is obviously the least desirable alternative. In actuality, many severely disabled persons learn to achieve the multitude of tasks within the general area of self-help and ADL through a combination of these three methods. As elaborated upon in Chapter 11, recent advances in rehabilitation engineering are making the development of sophisticated technological assistive devices a more feasible and viable alternative than ever before. However, it must be remembered that technological devices become inoperable at times and will always be less desirable than the development of independent living skills by the individual.

Current and Future Status of Self-Care Services

The services available to assist the individual in developing self-care skills have become highly effective in the recent past. As pointed out by Goldenson, Dunham, and Dunham (1978), Laurie (1976), and Neisworth and Smith (1978), advances in the areas of rehabilitation engineering and behavior management technology which enhance training in feeding, toileting, dressing, and other self-care activities are now being utilized with individuals evidencing very low initial potential. It is likely that in the near future even more sophisticated developments in electronics technology and advanced training techniques will make self-care, and independence, a reality for most severely disabled persons.

EDUCATIONAL SERVICES

Nature and Role of Educational Services

Once an individual acquires some self-help and ADL competencies, or even while she is still in the process of achieving such skills, educational needs become pertinent. In the United States today, education still remains the major avenue through which one enters the mainstream of society. Although certain aspects of this fact are changing, individuals with severe disabling conditions still need some degree of educational competency to attain self-sufficiency. Many differences of opinion exist among both professionals and lay persons regarding the role of education in the lives of severely disabled individuals. Education is seen by many as the only salvation for those with severe impairments. By others, education is viewed as a useless endeavor if an impairment is extreme. In actuality, the truth lies somewhere in between.

Since the passage of Pub. L. 94-142, the Education for All Handicapped Children Act, many misconceptions regarding the intent of this legislation have arisen. Although this act allows for a variety of different settings in which handicapped children's education may be carried out, it encourages placement of such children into the "least restrictive environment," which implies "as normal an educational environment as possible" (Suran and Rizzo, 1979, p. 444). Many parents and professionals, however, have interpreted Pub. L. 94-142 to mean that the regular education classroom, the mainstream of the educational environment, meets the ideal criterion of the least restrictive environment. Thus, the term mainstreaming has gained much popular acceptance. As Suran and Rizzo (1979) point out, "Mainstreaming, however, involves not only the placement of the special child in the regular classroom with nonhandicapped peers but also the addition of whatever supportive services are needed to ensure a successful educational experience" (p. 444).

The critical point is that this mandate *does not* state that every special child must be mainstreamed. In fact, many special educators are now stating that for severely disabled children, the concept of mainstreaming is inappropriate and irrelevant (Burton and Hishoren, 1979). It would be unwise, for example, to place a physically handicapped child with multiple, associated disabilities in a regular classroom with a teacher untrained in the nature of the needs of such a child. Similarly, deaf children who have not totally mastered some communication system would be lost in a regular class. Burgdorff (1980) cites an educator of deaf children who states that four out of five young deaf children could not have their needs met in the regular classroom.

The law does mandate that the severely disabled, who had previously been excluded from public school programs due to the severity of their handicaps, must be provided a free appropriate education. This mandate has encouraged the development of many educational programs whose objectives extend over a much broader spectrum of objectives than the traditional "three R's" of regular education. Public school programs are now being developed with training in basic self-care and other areas as the central focus of the curriculum.

With a new mandate to serve all handicapped children, education has become more receptive to advanced behavioral technology (Haring, 1979). Great strides have been made in applying such methods to the severely physically handicapped. According to Haring (1979), when technological advances such as the engineered classroom are applied to the education of the physically handicapped, ". . . not only is close attention given to the arrangement of the physical environment, but also to the arrangement of conditions which reinforce learning" (p. 28). Bigge and O'Donnell (1976) have devoted an entire text to the application of such technologies to the education of the severely physically handicapped.

In essence, these new educational programs focus on the development of specific short-term, intermediate, and long-term teaching objectives. Using every available type of aid and method, the child is taught to perform specific tasks which, measured behaviorally, indicate whether or not she has achieved the desired teaching objective. A teaching objective is stated in very specific, measurable terms. For example, an objective to teach a child eye-hand coordination might state that, given a small container and five pennies, the child will be able to place four of the five pennies in the container unassisted. If the child does not reach the desired objective, teaching methods are modified accordingly in order to assist her to do so.

Throughout the entire process of teaching severely disabled students, the crucial factor is communication. Many such children cannot communicate in ordinary ways. The essence of any educational program, therefore, will be to develop ways for the student to indicate her grasp of the content which is being taught. For this to be possible, the student needs to know how to use language. Language is a uniform set of written, spoken, and/or gestural symbols which have meaning to both the sender (writer, speaker, etc.) and the receiver (reader, listener, etc.). The process by which such symbols are sent and received is communication.

There are many severely disabling conditions that drastically limit the ability to communicate. Blind, deaf, cerebral-palsied, quadriplegic, and autistic individuals have different types of communication problems, with varying degrees of difficulty. The cerebral-palsied individual who cannot speak, write, or even gesture consistently is often labeled retarded. Autistic persons, for unknown reasons, do not communicate in conventional form, despite having an apparently adequate language system. For the quadriplegic individual, some conventional forms of communication, e.g., speech, may be simple enough, while other forms, e.g., writing, may be extremely laborious and time-consuming. Deaf or blind individuals may, in certain respects, be more fortunate, since special communication systems have been developed for them and are used routinely. Even these systems, however, are limited to the extent that only certain "outsiders" acquire competency in using them.

Communication is vitally important in determining the extent to which certain severely disabled individuals will not only become educated but also participate in community life. A study reported in Vanderheiden and Grilley (1977) indicates that in rank-ordering several different abilities, a group of severely disabled adults ranked communication as the most important. Communication has a twofold relationship to the educational process. First, if the individual must use a nonconventional method to communicate, this method should be acquired and developed during the process of his formal education. Second, unless an efficient, reliable means of communication is developed, a complete education is almost impossible.

In the chapter concerning the deification of normality (Chapter 3), it was pointed out that there is a prevailing attitude among many nondisabled individuals, as well as some disabled persons, that performing a function "normally" is the only acceptable goal, rather than performing a function in the most efficient manner possible for the individual concerned. To a certain extent, this attitude complicates the development of alternative methods of communication by the disabled.

Example 10A

Tom P. was a young man who, because of diabetes, recently lost his eyesight. He was fired from his job as a computer programmer because he had failed to inform his employer of his diabetic condition. Tom went for many months without a job, not because the computer printouts with which he worked were not available in Braille, but simply because most firms which he contacted were not comfortable with the prospect of hiring a programmer who used Braille: who could double-check his work? The case of Tom P. is not at all unique in the area of communication problems of the severely disabled.

In the area of assessing the potential of the disabled, the basic problem is that most intelligence, aptitude, achievement, and other assessment instruments are based on, and assume some level of competence in, the more conventional methods of communication. The special communication problems of the severely disabled are just now beginning to attract attention to the dire need for what is generally and broadly termed nonvocal communication. Vanderheiden and Grilley (1977) have written an entire text dealing with the use of nonvocal communication in educational settings. Communication boards,* the "Bliss" system, and other methods have been developed to enhance communication potential and skills of severely and multiply disabled individuals. New devices utilizing electronic technology, including computer-based communication methods, are being field-tested. Some of the factors impeding a broader-scaled application of the developments in this field are: (1) the experimental nature of many such devices, (2) the expense of developing and marketing such devices, (3) the lack of personnel trained in the engineering of such devices, and finally, (4) the lack of personnel trained to make efficient use of such devices in the classroom.

Once the basic skills needed to perform academically are acquired through the use of specialized teaching procedures and/or technological aids, the academic preparation of the severely physically disabled student runs parallel to that of her nonhandicapped counterpart of similar intellectual ability.

Personnel and Agencies Providing Educational Services

For the most part, the above types of services are provided through personnel within the public school systems. In special cases, individuals of school age are provided such services through various types of private facilities. With the passage of Pub. L. 94-142, more appropriate and desirable programs will be found within the public school system without the need for sending a child away from his own community and expending large amounts for tuition for special private facilities.

The above discussion of the educational needs of the severely disabled has assumed an early onset of disability. What about newly disabled adults who require educational services? In many rural areas, recently disabled adults frequently are also high school dropouts and need a G.E.D. (Graduate Equivalency Diploma). In other cases, the persons cannot return to their former employment and must meet certain educational requirements to prepare for another form of vocation. What services are available to these individuals? In most large communities, there are remedial education programs for adults who need to meet certain minimal education requirements. Some of these are operated within the confines of rehabilitation centers, some are available through adult education programs of the public schools, and still others are provided through private volunteer organizations. Most Veterans Administration hospitals have an educational therapy component designed to assist disabled veterans in achieving minimal educational skills.

What about higher education for individuals with severe disabling conditions?

---

*Communication boards are manually operated devices that indicate to the "listener" what the individual wants to say. For example, a symbol on such a board might mean "I am thirsty." By pointing to that symbol, the sender conveys a message, "I am thirsty." The receiver then confirms this message by responding in an appropriate manner to the message, e.g., "Would you like a drink of water?"

For some such persons, higher education is inappropriate and/or of questionable value in developing skills which they can use to attain suitable vocational goals. There are other individuals, however, who may greatly benefit from achieving advanced degrees. For such persons, special consideration must be given to which educational institution is best suited for them, from both an academic and an environmental standpoint. If an institution has the appropriate course of study as well as the facilities to accommodate the student in regard to living arrangements, transportation, special assistance when needed, etc., then it is a suitable choice. However, if the course of studies available to such a student is inappropriate and/or the facilities are inadequate, the student's experience with higher education could be disastrous. More will be said about the role of higher education in equipping the person for community life in the following section on vocational rehabilitation services.

A wide spectrum of specific educational services is available for the severely disabled individual. The more restrictive (special) such services, the fewer persons there are who, ideally, need them. In regard to special education in public or private school settings, this is termed the "educational cascade" (Suran and Rizzo, 1979, p. 444). The interested reader is referred to Suran and Rizzo (1979, pp. 444–445) for a complete description of such services. Here we will limit our description of educational services to those serving adults.

Adult Education Programs

Public School Adult Education Programs   These are designed for adults who, during their school years, did not receive full educational opportunities. For many participants, these programs are designed to help them acquire a G.E.D. Some programs, however, offer courses in basic academic areas (reading, math, accounting, etc.) or for enrichment purposes. Because these programs are designed for all adults needing such services, there should be no reason why individuals with severe disabling conditions should not avail themselves of them if they fulfill specific educational needs.

Adult Education Programs within Rehabilitation Facilities   Most rehabilitation facilities—state, federal, or private—have adult education components. The major objective of these programs is to assist clients to master basic academic skills to meet minimal job-entry requirements.

Current and Future Status of Educational Services

As Haring (1979) indicates, the behavioral technology to achieve educational objectives for the severely physically disabled is available. In many programs around the country, this technology is applied routinely and effectively. However, such application of stringent scientific methods is not as widespread as some would like. Many programs are still using curricula which are less than effective. It will probably be some time before all severely physically handicapped children and adults will have the full benefit of available educational advances.

At present, it can be stated that there are two developing areas which hold great promise for advancing the educational opportunities for the severely physically disabled child. First, the behavioral technology described by Haring (1979) will continue advancing and improving teaching techniques. Second, advancement in computer and engineering technology will produce instructional aides which, when combined with advanced behavioral techniques, will greatly enhance the educational opportunities for the severely handicapped.

VOCATIONAL SERVICES

It is estimated that of all employable disabled persons, 85 percent are unemployed (Mosher, 1978, p. 71). If this figure is accurate, the provision of vocational services for the severely physically disabled apparently is at present less than effective.

Nature and Role of Vocational Services

The major program designed to assist disabled individuals in acquiring vocational competencies is the state-federal vocational rehabilitation system. This system is designed to assist handicapped individuals in preparing for and obtaining vocational placement and, theoretically, will assume any cost directly involved in this process, within stipulated guidelines.* To qualify for such services, (1) an individual must have a verifiable disability; (2) the disability must constitute a handicap to securing employment; and (3) there must be a reasonable expectation that services rendered will result in vocational placement (Rubin and Roessler, 1978, pp. 54-55). It is the last of these three criteria that has come under a great deal of criticism and that has been, at least theoretically, eliminated by recent legislation. The term "reasonable expectation" is, of course, very subjective and judgmental. Prior to the passage of the Rehabilitation Act of 1973, with its mandate to serve the more severely disabled, this third criterion for eligibility was sometimes used to disqualify the more severely disabled individuals from services.

Although many strategic services are provided by vocational rehabilitation, including referral, treatment, maintenance, and training, the three critical services of counseling, prevocational evaluation, and vocational placement will come to have utmost emphasis in the rehabilitation process for the severely disabled if recent legislative mandates are actually carried out.

Vocational counseling with the severely disabled individual can be a long, complicated, and perplexing process. Its purpose is to select an objective which is appealing to and desirable for the client and, at the same time, realistic in terms of the client's potential and skills. In the following example, competent vocational counseling could have either prevented a poor plan from being developed or helped alleviate, to some degree, the results of poor vocational planning.

Example 10B

Dave T. was in his late thirties and was employed in a sheltered workshop, earning less than 50 cents per hour. He had a rather severe case of cerebral palsy which affected his mobility and eye-hand coordination, with some speech impairment. Dave had above-

*The specific services of the state-federal vocational rehabilitation system are discussed in detail by Malikin and Rusalem (1969, 1975).

average intelligence, although he had only completed the ninth grade in school. He detested working at the sheltered workshop and wanted very much to hold an executive position in order to "be his own boss." His counselor felt that Dave's relatively high aspiration resulted from his being totally frustrated with his current situation. Eventually, through the assistance of vocational rehabilitation services, Dave purchased a small business operation in a rural town. This was his attempt to establish his independence and become "his own boss." Lacking business acumen and experience, Dave failed in his business enterprise, and at last report he was back working in the shop. Dave's venture might have been more successful had his counselor helped him to better appraise himself and arrange for him to work in an on-the-job training situation in a small business before striking out on his own. This would not have guaranteed the success of Dave's venture, but would have better prepared him for it.

The above example is intended to show the critical role vocational counseling can play in the future of a disabled individual. It should be remembered that there are a wide range of problems involved in counseling severely disabled clients regarding vocational objectives. Each client presents a different set of circumstances. Sometimes a person's disability per se appears to be the major stumbling block to vocational success. At other times, situational factors are the paramount obstacles. Even when it appears that the physical and/or mental condition of the person is the primary barrier to an adequate vocational pursuit, the obstacle may actually be inappropriate goal setting, restricted employment possibilities, or a lack of creativity on both the counselor's and client's part in pinpointing a reachable vocational niche for the client.

Arriving at a feasible vocational goal for the client involves considering a myriad of factors. Among those of prime import are (1) the nature of the physical and/or mental condition, (2) the age of onset, (3) the client's family, (6) the client's present financial situation, (5) the attitudes of the client's family, (6) the client's marital status, (7) the client's educational achievement and social and psychological attributes, (8) the client's prior vocational experience, (9) the client's attitude toward his present situation, including his personal aspirations, (10) the nature of the local job market, and (11) the competence of the client's counselor. Much could be written about the influence of each of the above factors in the counseling process. When one considers that for every client a totally different combination of the above factors is involved, it is not difficult to understand the complexity of and the necessity for adequate vocational counseling.

Fenoglio (1974) describes three approaches to counseling and evaluating a severely disabled client: the "whole-man theory," the "loss-of-earning-capacity theory," and the "actual-wage-loss theory" (p. 300). Actually, unless the first theory prevails, vocational success on the part of the client is almost doomed to failure. A vocation is not merely a means of earning an income; it is a *raison d'être*. In our society, a person's work is to a large degree the essence of the person.

Arriving at an adequate vocational objective for the severely disabled client requires a high degree of creativity on both the client's and the counselor's part. The current job market is changing in that certain trades and other submanagerial positions are becoming more attractive. The conception that many severely disabled persons must seek white-collar and/or professional fields because they are less physically stressful is now less salient than once was the case. This is not to say that such positions are no longer desirable, but rather that social prestige and/or financial remuneration are no longer restricted to these occupational areas. Self-employment and homebound industries are becoming much-sought-after goals for many persons, disabled as well as nondisabled. Care must be taken, however, not to use such terms to justify inadequate vocational placement and goals. The blind person selling pencils on the street corner could be considered "self-employed"! What may be required more and more in this area of vocational counseling will be consideration of heretofore unimagined positions which will satisfy both the criteria of economic security and psychological well-being. The vocational counselor cannot afford to maintain stereotypic thinking in regard to vocational objectives.

With certain severely disabled persons, extensive prevocational evaluation, work adjustment services, and vocational evaluation are necessary to determine the abilities and skills influencing the choice of vocational objectives. These three processes are coming to play a more critical role in vocational services for the severely disabled.

"Prevocational evaluation" is a term which refers to evaluation of behaviors essential for functioning within a vocational situation—behaviors such as promptness, ability to relate effectively with peers or supervisors, persistence at assigned job tasks, etc. (Rubin and Roessler, 1978). If, at the end of the prevocational evaluation, the client is found to be lacking in such basic behaviors, the client is then placed in "work adjustment." In this training, basic skills such as promptness, work relations, etc., are stressed through training in a joblike situation. Prevocational evaluation and work adjustment are often performed in sheltered workshops, vocational training units, or other similar facilities. Usually, the vocational counselor contracts through such facilities to have such evaluation and training performed. These services are usually provided when the client has had little or no work experience and before he is provided with more specific vocational training.

After it has been ascertained that the severely disabled client has the basic behavior patterns to function in a work situation, he often will undergo vocational evaluation. This is a process of assessing his basic vocational aptitudes, such as eye-hand coordination, muscular strength, and sorting ability, as well as many other work skills. When a profile of the client's work skills are developed, he and his counselor are better able to match his abilities with an appropriate occupational choice. Vocational evaluation is also often performed by a facility such as a vocational training center, a sheltered workshop, or a rehabilitation center.

After a thorough assessment of the severely disabled client's vocational needs, a vocational training program is developed. The array of possible training programs ranges from on-the-job training for a specific job to college and/or graduate training. Once trained, the client is ready for placement on a job.

Vocational placement is the procedure whereby the client secures some work position. All other services of vocational rehabilitation may be provided, but if this does not result in the client's attaining a productive place in society, the previously provided services are only partially successful. In more recent references to placement (Rubin and Roessler, 1978), the term "selective placement" is beginning to be used. Selective placement implies that a concerted effort is made to place the client not just in *any* position which is appropriate for him but in one position where minimal architectural, transportation, and job requirement problems will be encountered. This means that the client and his counselor must not seek out a specific position in accounting, data processing, or counseling, for example, without taking into consideration (1) the attitudes of the personnel with whom the client will be working, (2) whether or not the client can get into, and be physically mobile within, the job setting, and (3) whether the client will have access to transportation to and from the job site without such transportation being an insurmountable problem.

A selective list of the possible outcomes of job placement would include competitive employment (the primary outcome for the self-sufficient), sheltered employment, homebound employment, volunteer work, unpaid domestic care (care of home and other family members), and total dependence on others (VEWAA, 1975, p. 88). Each type of outcome can be functional and effective depending on the nature of the potential, skills, and aspirations of the client in question.

Personnel and Agencies Providing Vocational Services

Vocational counseling, evaluation, and placement may be provided for the disabled individual by a number of different professionals through a number of different agencies. Frequently, the specific locale of the handicapped client is critical in this respect. Here we will discuss the traditional personnel and agencies commonly providing such services. The reader should keep in mind, however, that the provision of such services can deviate in a number of ways from the view presented here.

When a client is served through vocational rehabilitation, her counselor must devise, with her cooperation, an individually written rehabilitation plan (IWRP). This plan states the services that will be provided by vocational rehabilitation and other agencies and the objective of these services. Normally, the primary objective of such a plan is some type of employment. In devising this plan with the client, the rehabilitation counselor usually becomes involved to some degree in vocational counseling with the client. What does the client wish in the way of employment? Why does she desire such a position? Through these and other related questions, the counselor engages in exploring with the client the vocational goals possible for the client. Other personnel, including vocational evaluation and placement specialists, may also assist the client in this process. However, the vocational rehabilitation counselor usually has primary responsibility for assisting the client in this task.

The vocational evaluator works with the vocational rehabilitation counselor in assessing the client's potential and skills. This assessment procedure may include psychometric tests, job samples, simulated job samples, and on-the-job evaluations. The vocational evaluator may be employed in a state-federal vocational rehabilitation facility or in a private agency which contracts with vocational rehabilitation to provide evaluative services to clients. Goodwill Industries, private sheltered workshops, and other similar facilities often provide such services to clients of vocational rehabilitation. At the end of the vocational evaluation, a summary report is provided to the vocational rehabilitation counselor and the client, and this information is incorporated into the client's rehabilitation plan.

After vocational counseling, evaluation, and other services are provided to meet the client's rehabilitation objectives, the vocational placement specialist begins to assist the client in placement. Although for many years placement was considered part of the job duties of the vocational rehabilitation counselor, job placement is becoming so complex that many state and private agencies are now employing full-time placement specialists. Such persons spend a large portion of their time familiarizing themselves with the job market in their area and working with employers. Frequently, they are in the best position to place clients selectively.

Current and Future Status of Vocational Services

As was indicated in the first part of this section, the statistics indicating the success rate for employment of the disabled are not impressive. This is not to state that vocational services fail to achieve anything. Ideally, employment is the ultimate goal of such services; but if employment is not achieved, this does not always indicate failure of the entire process. In some cases, providing the client with skills to engage in a constructive avocation is preferable to her sitting idle day after day. Despite such partial compensations, however, it must be stated that the effectiveness of vocational services currently falls short of that of other services. With the mandate of recent vocational rehabilitation legislation to seek out viable alternatives to competitive employment, the outlook for a brighter success rate is good. Also, technological advances of rehabilitation engineering in job-site modifications, discussed in the following chapter, will assist many severely disabled clients in finding their niche in the job market.

TRANSPORTATION SERVICES

Thomas O'Brien, director of special projects for the Massachusetts Bay Transit Authority, once stated, "The greatest barrier for handicapped persons is the attitude of people toward the disabled." He continued, "Organizations such as the Urban Mass Transportation Administration don't really understand that the handicapped want to do their own thing and that lack of accessible public transportation is one of the main roadblocks to the employment of the handicapped" (*Amicus,* January 1976, p. 8). O'Brien estimated that "60 to 70 percent of handicapped persons are unemployed," with the implication that lack of adequate public transportation may be one major factor in such a high unemployment rate.

Dunham (1978) puts it more succinctly, stating that "having a doctoral degree is of little consequence if one cannot get from home to a job" (p. 124). This same author estimates that, despite what is said concerning congested urban traffic, despite the masses of automobiles on our streets and highways, from one-third to one-half of the U.S. population is without any type of transportation at all. Therefore, to achieve the ultimate goal of rehabilitation and metamorphosis, the transportation needs of individuals with disabilities must be addressed.

Nature and Role of Transportation Services

To receive appropriate education, medical care, vocational training, employment, etc., the disabled person must leave her residence and travel to the necessary facilities. The more fortunate of us do not give transportation a second thought. We go to our driveways, start our automobiles, and drive to our destination, not thinking about how someone too young or too disabled to drive or too poor to afford public transportation (or unable to avail herself of public transportation even if she could afford it) would achieve this feat. According to Dunham (1978), the two major obstacles to transportation are technology and attitudes.

With respect to mass transit systems, most buses, subways, taxis, etc. cannot be utilized easily by persons in wheelchairs, with severe visual problems, or having other types of ambulatory difficulties. Technology currently available is such that most mass transit systems *could* be made accessible if there were a widespread need expressed by the general public for such modifications. As is pointed out in other chapters, however, throughout the country there are over twenty lawsuits involving accessibility to mass transit systems for the handicapped currently in the courts. The focus of these lawsuits generally involves the excessive cost and effort of making such systems accessible. Here the unwillingness of the public to expend large amounts of public funds for the benefit of the handicapped, not the technology per se, is the real problem.

Certain types of handicapped individuals can satisfy their transportation needs through the use of modified cars (with hand controls), modified vans, and other types of vehicles such as golf carts. These types of transportation enable such individuals to move about their communities independently. For many, however, such as the blind, technology will never enable them to be independent in terms of long-range travel. Such individuals must rely on the assistance of others, transportation provided by private organizations, or public transportation. In large urban areas, most travel required *is* long-range, i.e., outside walking distance. Some types of accessible public transportation, then, is necessary for such individuals to be full participants in their communities.

In many locales, private health organizations are providing transportation services for the handicapped. The services offered by these operations, however, are limited, consisting of transportation to and from medical and rehabilitation services, etc. Such systems are not designed to serve the handicapped in the same way that public transportation is designed to serve the general public. Therefore, to achieve full integration of the handicapped into the community, some type of public transportation service is needed.

Current and Future Status of Transportation Services

At present the transportation services available to handicapped individuals are, for the most part, inadequate. While public reluctance to expend the money necessary to render mass transit systems accessible is often cited for this deficiency, this is not the only obstacle. As was alluded to in Chapter 8 ("The Rise of Consumerism"), the handicapped are still not unified on many issues. Transportation is one such issue. One can bewail the public's apathy, but one must also recognize that the advocates of the handicapped have failed to agree on a desirable goal to meet the transportation needs of the majority of handicapped citizens. When some advocates demand Transbus, while others want door-to-door services, and still others press for other types of systems, the public cannot take full blame for the lack of progress in this area. Until such issues are resolved in the form of a unified goal, transportation will be a problem, and some handicapped individuals will still, for instance, hold a doctorate but be unemployed for lack of transportation.

RESIDENTIAL SERVICES

There is a facility designated "The Home for Incurables" which demonstrates the failure of our society to achieve a full metamorphosis for the institutionalized disabled individual. In visiting the facility, one is initially favorably impressed with the modern, clean building which has such a depressing and pejorative name. However, this initial impression is gradually eroded upon observing the facility for any length of time, as one encounters many severely disabled, intelligent adults between the ages of 20 and 60 who have nowhere else to reside. The majority are unemployed and spend their days consumed by the activities within the home. This example is to highlight the immediate need for more concerted efforts in the area of residential services for the disabled. Considerable effort is currently being expended to provide community facilities for former residents of institutions for the mentally ill and mentally retarded. However, fewer efforts are being made for those individuals in residences like The Home for Incurables.

Nature and Role of Residential Services

Many disabled persons, due to lack of family assistance, financial resources, or basic self-care skills, must depend on public facilities to meet their needs for shelter. Such facilities may be nursing homes, institutions for the mentally ill or retarded, or other institutionlike residential care units. Although such facilities meet a most basic need, the nature of their operations often does not facilitate integration of the individual with a disability into the total community.

A multitude of housing arrangements have developed in order to meet the need for more appropriate living conditions for the severely disabled. In several large communities, such as Berkeley, California, centers for independent living have been established. In the majority of urban, suburban, and rural areas, however, individuals with severe disabilities live in the usual apartment or residential facilities. Those in need of attendant care must depend on others to come in periodically and care for them.

For individuals who are disabled with no family to care for them and little or no money to pay for such services, the problems of residential care services fall into three general categories: (1) securing services without relinquishing their personal freedom to participate fully in society, (2) finding these services without undue expenditure of money, and (3) securing such services without becoming shackled to others, i.e., relatives, church groups, volunteers, etc. The state of the art in the provision of residential services for the semi-independent physically disabled individual is not very advanced. In fact, one might say that it is still very much in an embryonic stage. There are some exemplary programs in this area, but they are not available on a wide enough geographic basis to serve a significant portion of the population needing such programs.

Personnel and Agencies Providing Residential Services

Although the need for residential services is not new, development of and provision of such services on a large scale are among the most recent innovations in the field of rehabilitation. Therefore, the personnel and agencies providing these services are by no means standard across locales, in comparison to special education or vocational rehabilitation services. The majority of residential facilities are operated by private, nonprofit organizations. These organizations often receive funding through federal and state agencies, such as HUD mental health and vocational rehabilitation.

The personnel operating these facilities usually consist of full-time administrative staff members and full- or part-time house parents, counselors, self-care aides, etc. At present, there are few formal training programs for such personnel. The private organizations sponsoring these facilities usually provide their personnel thorough on-the-job or in-service training to prepare them for their duties. Many different types of persons, such as college students, neighborhood young people, mildly mentally retarded persons, etc., have been utilized to provide such services (Laurie, 1978). However, these attendant-care personnel often are in states of transition and therefore present certain problems in respect to counting on their long-term availability to provide such services.

Current and Future Status of Residential Services

Laurie (1978) summarizes a study by HUD of eight projects specifically designed to serve the disabled. This study revealed several findings. Among them were the following:

1 The severely disabled cannot use such facilities independently without attendant care.
2 Such projects will facilitate freedom of the less severely disabled only if other essential services are also available.
3 Housing, transportation, and rehabilitation are interrelated.
4 Small facilities scattered throughout an area are better than large, consolidated units (Laurie, 1978, p. 105).

In summary, Laurie states:

> In short, the problems of housing for the disabled will be solved when living in the community is as feasible as subsistence in a nursing home, when vocational rehabilitation assumes its rightful responsibility for ongoing rehabilitation and adjustment to independent living. . . . (p. 108)

CONCLUSIONS

In the present chapter, we have attempted to review the services needed to prepare the disabled individual for a role in society. The services reviewed are crucial in order for most disabled citizens to participate in community life. We have not begun to describe all possible services needed by particular individuals. The reader is referred to the *Disability and Rehabilitation Handbook* (Goldenson et al., 1978) for a more extensive examination of this area. Neither have we attempted a detailed description of any of the services included here. We have, however, provided a general overview of some of the types of procedures and personnel available for assisting severely physically disabled individuals with their assimilation into society.

Chapter 11

Making Community Life More Accessible for the Disabled

If one accepts this book's premise—that independent living is the result of successful metamorphosis—one cannot overlook the importance of an accessible environment for rehabilitation success. For many persons, it is impossible to accommodate themselves to existing barriers in architecture, housing, and public transportation. But with available knowledge and resources, it is possible to design buildings and transit systems that are both aesthetically pleasing and usable by the disabled and nondisabled alike.

What is needed to eliminate environmental barriers in our society? Legislation? The necessary laws are on the books. Standards? The necessary heights, widths, slopes, etc. are covered in a multitude of standards, from those of the American National Standard Institute (ANSI) to the North Carolina Building Code. Money? Barrier-free design adds little to a new building's overall cost. Awareness and implementation of existing laws? Most accessibility laws do not provide for enforcement. Contractors sometimes ignore blueprints or build buildings with steps at the top of ramps or drop-offs at the base of curb cuts, proving they don't understand what accessibility entails.

If barriers are to be successfully eradicated, public service announcements must appear continuously on television and radio, handicap awareness days must be held in schools, barrier-free design must become a basic requirement for a degree in architecture, building inspectors must be made aware of the importance of barrier removal, and penalties must be established and enforced for violations of accessibility laws. People can be well educated and trained to make the most of their mental and physical capacities, but their education and training will be useless if they are unable to move about within their communities. People can receive therapy and training in routine tasks of living, but medical rehabilitation will be wasted if there is nowhere for them to live after discharge except an institution or nursing home. A rehabilitation effort which addresses itself to one aspect of a person's life is useless unless it dovetails with all the aspects involved in rehabilitation of the total person.

This chapter will:

1   Discuss architectural barriers and how they can be eliminated
2   Discuss barriers to independent local and cross-country travel
3   Cite changes needed in housing design so that various living accommodations can be used by persons with varying disabilities
4   Describe the role of rehabilitation technology and the need for continued development of adaptive aids and devices

---

Example 11A   Francis W.: a Quad Who Went from Near-Total Dependence to Total Independence

Francis W., a C5-C6 quadriplegic, is one of the many severely disabled persons who live independently after attending the University of Illinois in Champaign-Urbana. Francis, like many other disabled Illinois graduates, had been told he would need attendant care for the rest of his life. Therefore, when Francis applied for admission, he assumed, as did his physicians and therapists, that a family member would have to attend him to help him with his dressing, bathing, toileting, and transportation needs.

During his preadmission interview at the university's Rehabilitation-Education Center, Francis quickly discovered what being a disabled college student at Illinois entailed. Unless an applicant was capable of functioning independently, he would not be admitted, because no attendant care was allowed in university dormitories. The reasons for this policy were twofold: to encourage better relationships between disabled and nondisabled students and to enhance the placement of disabled graduates. Early trials, where roommates doubled as attendants, had resulted in increased dependency on the part of disabled students and alienation of roommates/attendants who experienced academic difficulties due to excessive demands on their time. Furthermore, the outstanding placement record of disabled graduates was believed to be based on employer confidence that these graduates expected no reduction of job responsibilities because they were physically disabled.

At the outset, Francis was told he would be admitted only if he learned to care for himself. Francis, however, believed that was impossible. He argued that he might manage to put on trousers, but not undershorts too. The center's physical therapist, in rebuttal, responded that none of the male paraplegics or quadriplegics wore underwear, because of the danger of getting pressure sores from wrinkles in two layers of clothing. Then Francis asked how he could tuck the back of his shirt into his trousers, when he needed both arms to maintain his balance when he leaned forward. The therapist pointed out that it wouldn't matter if Francis's shirt hung out in back, because no one could see the back of his shirt while he was sitting in his wheelchair.

By this stage of his interview, Francis was feeling desperate. He knew a college degree would give someone with a disability as severe as his a chance to get a job that would pay his disability-related expenses, but he was afraid to live without help. In a final attempt to impress the therapist with how truly limited he was, Francis brought up what he believed was an insoluble problem. "How," he asked, "can I manage my bowel movements? I can't give myself a bedpan or clean up afterwards." The therapist, however, who had had experience with many quadriplegics with Francis's degree of involvement, replied, "I could suggest several methods that might work for you but I'd rather have you talk to some students who are quadriplegics. They use a variety of methods and one should work well for you."

With that, the therapist made several phone calls and then he and Francis set out for the men's dormitories. By that time Francis was not surprised when he found himself laboriously wheeling himself down the center's ramp and up the sidewalk toward the men's dormitories. But he was confident that, after a few token pushes, the therapist would grab his wheelchair and start pushing. No such luck. Unlike anyone else Francis had met since his diving accident, the therapist seemed content to adjust himself to Francis's pace, making casual conversation while he and Francis slowly moved along a seemingly endless stretch of concrete.

By the time they reached the dormitory, Francis was exhausted. He had pushed himself farther than he ever had before. His exhaustion, however, was tinged with elation. The fear that had clouded his mind began to give way to stirrings of hope, of germinating self-confidence. And there were more new experiences to come. By the time he reached the room where a fellow quadriplegic, Dennis R., waited to share his bathroom techniques, Francis had opened two doors and had pushed himself up a ramp to the first floor of the dormitory.

Francis's home was unramped and had five steps at the lowest entrance and a sidewalk which was heaved up by tree roots. To go anywhere, he had to be carried down and up steps and lifted in and out of a car. In Illinois, however, he found smooth sidewalks, ramped buildings, and buses equipped with wheelchair lifts. More-over, dormitories, married student housing, and nearby off-campus apartments were accessible, allowing severely disabled students to choose from a variety of living situations.

HANDICAP: A MATTER OF ENVIRONMENT

Between the time Francis applied for admission and the day he graduated with a Ph.D., he became self-sufficient: able to live alone in an apartment, transfer himself and his wheelchair in and out of a car, and drive using hand controls. His success was based not only on the university's barrier-free environment and the techniques he learned from fellow students, but also on the unending encouragement and support he received from the center's staff, who insisted that he could live independently and who invented and refined a variety of assistive devices that allowed him to do so.

It is impossible to exaggerate the importance of an accessible environment to the rehabilitation of any mobility-impaired person. The best help the center's staff gave disabled students was no help at all. Because the staff had helped design the accessible dormitories, they never had to lift students up or down a flight of stairs. Because there were ramps into buildings, curb cuts at corners, and accessible buses running fixed routes every hour, the staff never had to help a student cross a street or push him to class. And because they had the patience many hospital personnel lack—patience to help extensively paralyzed students learn to dress and undress, to transfer into and out of their wheelchairs, and to manage their own bladder and bowel routines—the staff never had to serve as attendants or orderlies. The therapist who refused to give Francis a push gave him something more valuable— independence. More rehabilitators need to substitute planning and learning for direct care. "No help" can lead to a slow but permanent solution to the problems of independent living, while direct care is the kind of "help" that keeps the disabled helpless.

Francis was reminded of the importance of a barrier-free environment every time he left the university setting, whether to vacation with his family or to look for a job. All his new-found expertise could not get him up the five steps into his parents' home without help. Once he was inside, the arrangement of the kitchen made it impossible for him to make his meals or clean up afterwards. Because of the arrangement of the bathroom, he could no longer manage his bowel movements or bathe himself. The only area in which he retained his independence was in dressing, and even there he had to have someone bring his clothes from inside the narrow closet door.

One might ask of what use were those years of experimentation and effort if Francis could only function in a special environment. First, Francis had learned that he could be independent in the proper environment. Second, Francis had obtained an education which permitted him to find a job in a city big enough and progressive enough to be largely accessible. Eventually, he was able to afford extensive modifications in the home he bought, making it even easier for him to maintain an independent life style. And third, the 1973 Act means that special environments, which once were found only in a few places like the University of Illinois, are now the law of the land.

Unfortunately, many severely disabled persons are not as lucky as Francis. Those more severely disabled may never attain physical independence, and so their efforts to live within the community and to find jobs which pay enough for attendant care are necessarily more complicated. Environmental barriers often force these persons into social prisons not of their own making.

Example 11B   Lucy P.: Job, Yes; Access, No

Even persons with moderate physical limitations may be defeated by barriers in areas where they live and work. Lucy P., an art history major who wanted to work in a New York museum, obtained the job she wanted but was unable to keep it. Lucy, who is 3 feet tall and has some degree of weakness in her lower limbs, cannot drive a car and so found herself paying over $75 a week for cab fare to and from work. Her transportation expenses, in addition to her medical expenses, made it impossible for her to keep working.

A disability can prevent persons like Lucy from reducing their transportation costs by moving closer to where they work. In older cities, especially, many jobs are located in areas where apartments are in brownstone walkups, i.e., buildings with outside stairs and small or nonexistent front yards where there isn't enough room to build a ramp. While small electric elevators, which lift a person up to 6 feet off the ground, are useful in certain situations, such elevators require a large outdoor landing so persons in wheelchairs or using crutches can exist safely and enter the building directly, without encountering a step or high threshhold. Many older buildings either do not have suitable landings or have flights of stairs immediately inside their entrances. Moreover, such external elevators, because they are necessarily close to the street, are vulnerable to theft or vandalism; and because they depend on electrical power, they may trap users inside or outside during power outages.

Therefore, the most convenient, or most readily modified housing—on a close-to-ground-level conventional or slab foundation—is usually located in outlying areas, where transportation is indispensable. Unlike those who can drive or use mass transit, persons like Lucy cannot afford to get to and from areas with the most job opportunities. Of all the barriers which limit opportunities for the disabled, transportation barriers create the greatest difficulties. But solving their transportation needs would not, in and of itself, guarantee the disabled access to the same social rewards enjoyed by the nondisabled, for accessible and affordable transportation means little if, once a person gets to her destination, she cannot enter or use the facilities there.

ACCESSIBILITY IN ARCHITECTURE

What comprises an architectural barrier is a difficult concept to explain to persons who are not disabled. In the main, architectural barriers are invisible to those whose ability to function is not affected by them. Handicap awareness events, where legislators and business persons attempt to carry out their daily routines using a wheelchair or other assistive device, are limited in their usefulness, because participants know they can discard their disabilities at any time. Such events are, however, useful in clarifying what is an architectural barrier and what is not. Just as every crack in a sidewalk takes on a new significance to a child on roller skates, so does a curb to a pseudoparaplegic who, knowing little about wheelchair management, rolls off a curb frontwards.

Architectural barriers, as Mace (1977) points out, are not problems only for people with physical disabilities:

> The child or small person who needs to use a coin telephone and cannot reach the high coin slot is handicapped. The elderly person whose impaired vision makes it impossible to read scarcely legible signs and markings, the student whose study space is poorly lighted, the pregnant woman who must climb long flights of stairs, the mover who must carry a piano through a narrow door, as well as a person who uses a walker or a wheelchair and cannot climb stairs or enter a toilet stall—all are handicapped by facilities. An environment that has been designed for a mythical average or "normal" person who is of average size and who possesses full and complete use of all physical, mental, and emotional faculties will not meet the needs of most people.

To clarify what an architectural barrier is, let us examine three types of man-made barriers: (1) approach barriers—getting *to* the place; (2) entrance barriers—getting *into* the place; and (3) functional or total-use barriers—making *full use* of the place.

Approach Barriers

Often when barrier-free design is discussed, the discussion is limited to design elements which prevent unassisted disabled persons from entering government buildings, sports arenas, motels, restaurants, churches, etc. While entry is essential, accessibility encompasses more than getting in and out of a building with ease. Nevertheless, for the mobility-impaired (those using wheelchairs or crutches), the endurance-impaired (persons with cardiac disorders), or the energy-impaired (persons on dialysis), their entire lives and physical well-being may be affected by their inability to climb steep steps or open heavy doors into businesses, schools, or physicians' offices.

There are two kinds of approach barriers which prevent persons from getting to places without assistance. First, there are parking barriers. The disabled need wide parking spaces so they can get out of and into their vehicles without being blocked by other cars. Nothing frustrates a motorist who uses a wheelchair more than to leave a store or restaurant only to find her car or van parked in. The normal distance between two parked vehicles, 1 to 2 feet (12″ to 24″), is inadequate for someone using a wheelchair, which is 2 feet, 4 inches wide (28″).

Since there is no known way to prevent Americans from parking anywhere they can fit their vehicles, motorists who use wheelchairs will eventually become trapped, faced with two possible solutions: (1) waiting for the other driver to move or having him paged if a public address system is available, or (2) entrusting their keys to a stranger passing by who can move the vehicle.

Wide parking spaces need to be located where the disabled will not have to cross heavily trafficked streets or pass behind many other parked cars. Persons seated in wheelchairs are approximately 48 inches tall and therefore cannot be easily seen in the rear- or side-view mirrors of most cars and vans. Many a person in a wheelchair has been run into by someone backing out of a parking space who did not realize anyone was behind him.

Second, there are walkway barriers. A person must be able to move from the surface of a lot or street to the walkway leading to where she is going. Many times, lots with parking spaces specially designed for handicapped persons are encircled by a high curb, except for the driveway in from the street. Every parking area should have one space where the level of the lot slopes gradually to the level of the walkway so that persons with mobility problems can move out of the parking area with ease.

Entrance Barriers

Every building, public or private, should have one front entrance which is ramped or at ground level. When a ramp is required, its slope should be no greater than 12:1, it should be 3 feet wide, and it should have a 4-foot-deep landing at the top and a 5-foot-deep landing at the bottom. The ratio of 12:1 means that for every inch in height, the ramp must be 1 foot long; e.g., a 6-inch curb requires a 6-foot ramp to meet ANSI standards. A house with an entrance 30 inches off the ground requires a 30-foot ramp for mobility-impaired persons to enter and exit easily and safely. Paraplegics with strong arms and good trunk balance can wheel up steeper grades, but as the grade increases, so do their chances of flipping their chairs over backwards, somersaulting themselves back down the ramp.

Once a building's entrance is reached, doors must be light enough to be opened easily and wide enough to allow passage through. Doors with pressure closers should require no more than 8 pounds of pressure to open. Doors which open outward must have platforms deep enough and wide enough so that someone in a wheelchair can swing the door open and wheel around it without either hitting the side of the building or falling off the side of the ramp.

Sometimes one encounters a situation where an architect has designed inac-cessible "accessibility features" into a building, or a contractor has built access-enhancing features—but not according to plan. One common error is constructing a ramp with a step at the top. Another is installing curb cuts with poles for street or traffic lights in the middle or with an inch or more drop-off at the bottom. Such blunders are discouraging, because unusable "accessibility features" are not likely to be rebuilt and buildings with such features remain inaccessible. At Memphis State University, the cost of rebuilding a 30-foot, too-steep ramp was estimated to be $12,000, while the original cost of a properly built ramp was estimated to be $6,000.

At times entrance accessibility is affected by societal conditions unrelated to the handicapped. For example, to prevent the theft of shopping carts, many stores install narrow gates at their entrances. These gates keep the carts from leaving but at the same time keep persons in wheelchairs from entering.

Total-Use Barriers

Once inside a building, persons still may encounter barriers that prevent them from accomplishing what they came to accomplish. Many buildings with accessible entrances have one or more steps inside. Many motion picture theaters have no special section where persons in wheelchairs can sit, and fire regulations will not permit them to sit in the aisle. Many retail stores have aisles too narrow for those with walkers, on crutches, or in wheelchairs. An office with vertical files and poorly placed furniture prevents persons from holding jobs as file clerks or secretaries. In libraries upper shelves of books and card catalogs are out of the reach of persons who cannot use step stools or ladders. In grocery stores items are often displayed in areas inaccessible to many customers, not just the disabled.

Some total-use barriers are simple to correct; some are not. Some can be eliminated by simply rearranging furniture or merchandise displays. Some require removal of walls or installation of movable partitions. Some might require able-bodied employees to assist persons as part of their job responsibilities.

Persons with sensory impairments are particularly beset by total-use barriers. The blind need Braille elevator markings, building directories, and emergency directions, so they know where they are or where to go in case of fire. The hearing-impaired need alarm systems with flashing lights and telephone amplifiers, or they will be as effectively prevented from utilizing telephones as are the mobility-impaired when booths are narrow or coin slots more than 48 inches off the floor.

Some total-use barriers, such as inaccessible bathroom facilities, cafeterias, and drinking fountains, keep persons from spending long periods of time on job sites or in museums or other recreational settings. Few persons can or should work eight hours with no access to bathroom facilities, and such access is especially important to those with chronic infections or who are susceptible to disorders of the urinary system.

Nonetheless, bathrooms continue to be built with stalls too narrow to admit wheelchairs. Cheryl T. had muscular dystrophy and attended public school in central Wisconsin. Because her school had no accessible bathroom, Cheryl restricted her fluid intake so she could go for an entire day without needing to urinate. Cheryl died of kidney failure in her early twenties after having had a series of urinary infections throughout her school years. Other disabled persons attempt to solve the problem of inaccessible bathroom facilities by padding themselves with towels or wearing diapers or rubber-lined underpants.

Due to increasing compliance with architectural accessibility laws, many new public buildings have at least one bathroom stall wide enough to admit a wheelchair. Unfortunately, compliance is sometimes uninformed, so that while a stall may be wide enough, the hall leading to a bathroom with a wide stall may be too narrow to allow wheelchairs to turn into the bathroom lobby. In some situations, lobby doors are too narrow to admit wheelchairs, although if one could get in, one would find grab bars around the toilet, stools hung at recommended heights, insulated water pipes, and faucets even persons with limited hand function can operate.

Again, lack of comprehension rather than willful noncompliance with the law is most often the cause of inaccessibility in buildings which were intended to be accessible. For this reason, consumers in many cities have volunteered to be on-call advisors whenever architects or builders have questions concerning barrier-free design. An alternative might be for architects and builders themselves to ride through framed-in buildings in wheelchairs while needed alterations can still be made without excessive cost.

Codes and Costs

Public building codes, such as the North Carolina code or the ANSI standards, clearly describe what features are necessary to make buildings accessible to everyone. Unfortunately, many disregard such codes. When a contractor in Massachusetts who has a son with cerebral palsy asked a building inspector about the lack of accessibility features in blueprints for a new city building, he was told, "Don't worry about that law. That's just a lot of damn fool nonsense anyway." This situation followed the establishment of an architectural barriers board in 1974. The Massachusetts board was given the responsibility of developing and enforcing regulations for barrier-free publicly funded buildings in that state. Moreover, Massachusetts trains building inspectors in both the letter and the spirit of the standards, so inspectors are aware that they face a court action in case of noncompliance.

Each of the fifty states has legislation aimed at eliminating architectural barriers. Some states, such as North Carolina and Massachusetts, have attempted to remove existing barriers, to prevent barriers in new construction, and to put teeth into existing laws by providing penalties for violations. North Carolina is unique in regard to the scope of the handicapped section of its building code and its efforts to implement that section. In 1968 the North Carolina Building Code Council recommended that ANSI A117.1 standard for accessibility be used in North Carolina. Because the code used "should" instead of "shall," the handicapped section was not taken seriously and nothing changed. In 1973 and 1974 the code was expanded to include all new and remodeled public and privately owned buildings, and compliance was mandated. The only structures not affected are single- and two-family residences and certain sections of specific industrial facilities, such as refineries.

Unlike that of Massachusetts and North Carolina, however, antibarrier legislation in most states has proved as ineffectual as was North Carolina's prior to the 1973–74 revision and expansion. Eight states do not have any laws to comply with federal legislation (Pub. L. 93-112, the Rehabilitation Act of 1973, Section 502; and Pub. L. 90-480, the Architectural Barriers Act of 1968), which requires any building whose construction was paid for with federal funds or any facility which received federal funds to be barrier-free in terms of the ANSI standards. Seventeen of the fifty states which have legislation have waiver clauses which eliminate any benefits meant to accrue from that legislation. One such waiver clause, Connecticut's House bill No. 3863, which was enacted in 1965 and amended by House bill No. 3518 in 1973, states: "The public works commissioner can set aside or modify any particular standard or specification when it is determined that it is unpractical and would cause unusual hardship or unreasonably complicate the construction, alteration or repairing of a site or building" (*Barrier Free Site Design,* 1976).

Any legislation, to be effective, must provide for the following: (1) training and education of those in a position to influence the construction of barrier-free facilities and sites, (2) clear-cut and severe penalties for noncompliance, and (3) a board which is empowered to review cases and institute court actions against violators. One problem a state faces when it attempts to fulfill the above provisions is the shortage of professionals who have the expertise to adequately implement the functions of such a board. Few architects are aware of the needs and capabilities of the various disability groups or of how buildings can be designed to meet these needs and match these abilities. Few schools of architecture have incorporated barrier-free design requirements into their curricula. Only six schools in the country have an elective course or seminar dealing with design concerns of the disabled. According to Mace (1977), questions on barrier-free design are now included in licensing exams for architects. As Mace points out, if such questions are specific enough and numerous enough to make a real difference as to whether or not an individual receives a license, both architects and schools of architecture may begin giving attention to the architectural needs of the disabled.

For architects who are aware and who want to solve access problems, lack of uniform standards can be a hindrance. The VA has standards for barrier-free design, as do individual states and professional organizations of architects. To reduce the confusion from these many, often contradictory, standards, many legislators and consumers specify ANSI standards as the preferred guidelines.

Lack of awareness or confusion over standards alone does not account for the fact that inaccessible buildings continue to be built. Engineers, contractors, and administrators might be more willing to remove barriers if their anxieties concerning increased cost could be allayed. Two conclusions about the cost factor can be drawn with confidence: first, it is often twice as expensive to modify a structure after it has been built as to incorporate accessibility into the original plans; second, although accessibility features will increase the overall building costs, the percentage of the increase will be less than 1 percent of the total cost.

In a study by Perkins and Will, less than 10 percent of the architects surveyed believed it would be prohibitively costly to build totally accessible structures (*Barrier Free Site Design,* 1976). A study conducted by the Department of Urban Studies used several existing and several hypothetical buildings to estimate the cost involved in constructing these buildings according to ANSI standards without infringing on any of the buildings' normal functions or ruining their aesthetic appearance. Each existing structure could have been made fully accessible for less than 1/10th of 1 percent of the total construction costs. In the cases of hypothetical buildings, accessibility was estimated at less than 1/2 of 1 percent of the total construction costs (*Barrier Free Site Design,* 1976). Contractors who believe exessive construction costs make accessibility infeasible point out that existing standards call for wide doorways and that wide doors cost more than narrow doors. But as Mace (1977) points out, a door that is 6 inches wider requires 6 inches less wall space, and since it costs more to construct walls than doors, total construction costs tend to even themselves out.

Constructing barrier-free buildings from the start does not cost significantly more than constructing buildings which are not barrier-free, but modifying existing buildings can be expensive. The materials to construct ramps to a building 30 inches above ground level will cost more than designing a ground-level building or one whose approaches slope less than 5 degrees. Similarly, installing 32-inch doors in toilet stalls is less expensive than tearing out partitions to widen narrow doorways. Unfortunately, in certain sections of the country, many buildings are totally inaccessible and difficult or impossible to modify without excessive cost.

Example 11C   Access Hassles Can Mar the Charm of Famous Places

In 1974, William D., who uses a wheelchair, received a grant to do research at Harvard's Houghton Library. Although he discovered a barrier-free path across the Harvard campus, the only buildings he could enter had entrances with nearly vertical ramps, except the library, where the university had installed a more horizontal temporary wooden ramp.

Finding accessible housing was even more difficult than finding his way around campus. A fairly accessible Holiday Inn close to Harvard offered temporary lodging, but no university housing was both accessible and available to visiting faculty. Five months before his arrival, William contacted rental agencies, university housing, disabled individuals, and agencies such as Easter Seals for help in finding a place to live. Inquiries made in a 20-mile radius from Harvard revealed that not only was there a lack of accessible short-term housing, but many disabled persons in the area were forced to live in second- or third-floor flats from which they had to be carried by families or friends.

Finally, William was referred to a couple who lived across the street from Harvard's divinity school. The couple had a 10-year-old son with spina bifida and for years had been carrying him up and down the five steps into their first-floor apartment. Since the family was going to spend the summer in New Hampshire, the couple was willing to sublet their apartment to William, who paid half the cost of having a ramp built.

Even with accessible housing and an accessible place to work, however, William was barred from most of the places visitors to the Boston area enjoy. Most historical sites in Boston and the surrounding areas are inaccessible. The Old North Bridge, from which "the shot heard round the world" was fired; Nathaniel Hawthorne's home; much of the Freedom Trail; and the Plymouth Plantation—all are impossible for mobility-impaired persons to tour alone, and some are impossible to navigate even with the aid of several strong friends. Before the Bicentennial, curb cuts were installed on some historic streets, but barriers in buildings are so numerous and the area is so highly congested that accessibility is, at best, a formidable task. Moreover, there is the problem of violating historical authenticity by adding ramps to colonial structures. New buildings and reconstructed streets and sidewalks should, however, be barrier-free.*

Inaccessible Voting Sites—Taxation without Representation

One area where accessibility is a concern is not covered by state or federal legislation: voting sites. Many polling places are in buildings covered by existing legislation, but many are not. To date, legislation concerning accessibility, with the exception of the North Carolina Building Code, only affects publicly funded buildings. The Massachusetts Architectural Barriers Board, for example, develops and enforces standards only for buildings built with public funds, not for all buildings used by the public. In addition, churches, theaters, and the like come under the board's jurisdiction only if they seat more than 150 persons. Other places of business must be two stories high and employ more than forty persons before they have to comply (Mace, 1977). When sites which are not covered are used as polling sites, it is assumed that disabled persons will vote by absentee ballot and will not, therefore, be disenfranchised. This is not possible. Aside from the inconvenience of having to have a doctor certify that a disabled person is unable to come to a polling place every time she wants to vote is the fact that absentee voting is not allowed in certain types of elections. Despite the Fourteenth Amendment, which states, "Nor shall any state . . . deny to any person within its jurisdiction the equal protection of its laws,"

*Harvard has since developed a plan to comply with Section 504 of the 1973 Act (Pub. L. 93-112). When the "Harvard Plan" is implemented, it should make much of the campus—and all of the classroom facilities—accessible.

many states do not permit absentee voting in school, park, primary, bond, and runoff elections. Political disenfranchisement not only violates the rights of the severely physically disabled by limiting their access to the legislative process, it reduces their chance to gain an equal share of the social, economic, and educational opportunities open to others in our society.

BARRIERS IN TRANSPORTATION

In no other area do severely disabled persons encounter more unnecessary restrictions than in the area of public transportation. Even for those who live the most limited lives imaginable outside of custodial institutions, transportation is, at times, indispensable. Everyone must, if no one else is available, go grocery shopping himself on a regular basis, and must sometimes seek health care.

Going for Groceries

In most urban areas the neighborhood grocery store which would deliver free of charge or at a minimum cost is a thing of the past. Those few markets which still provide delivery service have higher overall markups or charge sizable fees for delivering food to your door. Therefore, persons who are confined to their homes and unable to engage in remunerative employment cannot afford such services where they still exist. Moreover, the lack of mobility of such persons usually means that they have not had the opportunity to form the relationships which would ensure them of a pool of volunteers willing to shop for them regularly. Meals-on-Wheels or similar programs, which bring low-cost meals to homes of those unable to shop for or prepare their own food, are not available in all areas. Where such programs are available, senior citizens and persons recovering from temporarily incapacitating diseases or accidents are given first priority. Seldom do younger permanently disabled persons receive such meal services.

Trips to the Physician or Dentist

Because of their lack of transportation, disabled persons do not receive adequate health care. Many such persons avoid trips to physicians, dentists, or clinics quite simply because they have no way to get there. Friends or relatives may be unable to assist them—lift them into cars or buses, along with their walkers or wheelchairs; up curbs and up steps into buildings; and finally onto and off examining tables or dental chairs. Implementation of existing accessibility laws would, of course, result in modified transit systems, physicians' and dentists' offices, and clinics. Without implementation of laws pertaining to mass transit systems, however, many disabled persons would still not obtain the health care they desperately need. While public health nurses are often available for long-term medical services such as changing dressings, irrigating catheters, and giving baths, such services exceed the financial resources of most disabled persons, because to qualify for aid under most public and private programs they must receive care in a medical setting, not in their own home.

In addition to requiring long-term health care, however, disabled persons are subject to the entire gamut of acute illnesses and disorders which require a physician's attention. Few physicians make house calls for any patient under any circumstances, particularly for persons without influence who, because of the chronicity of their conditions, will need the same service again and again.

Therefore, when severely physically disabled persons ask for medical assistance, they are told, "Have someone bring you to my office," or "Meet me in the emergency room of the hospital." Unfortunately, in many instances there is no one available to bring these people anywhere for any reason. In a similar situation, most desperately ill persons can call a cab or ambulance, but these options may not be open to the desperately ill disabled. Too many times in noncrisis situations, these persons have had a summoned cab pull up only to drive off when the potential fare is found to be in a wheelchair or otherwise severely disabled. If a cab company is informed at the outset that a customer needs assistance, it may send a cabbie who is willing to assist. More often, however, when a person's special needs are described in advance, the promised cab never arrives.

Although ambulance drivers expect their customers to be injured or ill, their services are too expensive for all but emergency situations. Moreover, some ambulance companies do not provide service to impoverished areas, where many disabled persons live, because of the high crime rate in such areas; while others demand advance payment from persons who have no money.

The end result is that many disabled persons neglect their minor health problems or treat them with home remedies. In this way minor disorders which with early diagnosis and treatment might have been easily checked flare into more serious disorders, sometimes producing secondary disabilities, sometimes resulting in death.

Independence in Driving

For a limited number of individuals, the transportation picture is not so bleak. Since the advent of the collapsible wheelchair after World War I, anyone who is strong enough to transfer into a vehicle, lift her folded wheelchair behind the front seat, and use one of a variety of commercially available hand controls can transport herself whenever she wishes.

Until the early 1970s, independence in driving depended on the ability to move oneself and one's wheelchair into and out of a vehicle. For those who could transfer themselves but not their chairs, a variety of effective and not-so-effective wheelchair-loading devices were available. By the early 1970s, modifications had been developed which were to make independence in driving a reality even for persons too disabled to transfer but able to drive from a wheelchair.

Modifications which permit a person to enter and drive while remaining in a wheelchair consist of a commercially available van—Dodge, Chevrolet, Ford, among others—equipped with a wheelchair lift, wheelchair tie-downs, and hand controls for driving. The proliferation of wheelchair lift designs since the early 1970s has created serious problems for would-be van owners. Some designs are reputedly unsafe, with a history of giving way and dropping the lift's occupant to the ground. Others have poor repair records, stranding their owners while repairs are being made.

Once a would-be van owner has decided which modification is best in terms of performance and ease of operation for someone with his degree and type of disability, a major problem remains—money. In 1972 the total cost of a typical van, including all modifications, was approximately $7,000. By 1979 the cost of such a van was approximately $14,000. Since the VA in 1973 approved modified vans as alternatives to cars with hand controls, the VA will purchase such vans for veterans with service-connected disabilities. Civilians who are sponsored by DVR must buy their own vans, but DVR may pay for modifications if a client's ability to work depends on his having his own transportation. Like all government agencies, however, DVR is required to obtain bids from different lift manufacturers and then accept the lowest bid. In some areas, a company that manufactures an unreliable lift makes the lowest bid, and therefore a client will be equipped with a lift inferior to others currently available. Even though DVR may assume the cost of modifications, the cost of the van itself may be prohibitive for clients who, being unemployed, are not considered good risks by potential lenders. Furthermore the frequent need for repair makes the cost of maintaining such vehicles high, and thus limits ownership to those with healthy, steady incomes. For many disabled persons, however, getting a job depends on having reliable transportation; but without a job they cannot afford reliable transportation.

Access and the Wheelchair Driver

The increased availability, if not affordability, of vehicles which can be entered and driven by severely disabled persons has increased the ease with which these persons travel, as long as they provide their own transportation. Outside of a suitable vehicle, two other problems face the disabled traveler: overnight lodging and usable rest stops. One wheelchair couple, when traveling from their home in Minnesota to either of their parents' homes in Georgia, had to check as many as fourteen motels in one night before they found one which was accessible. Some motel chains have, within the last ten years, provided accessible accommodations in many areas of the country. Holiday Inns, Travelodges, and Quality Inns put out guidebooks which indicate with an accessibility symbol which motels have one or more rooms equipped for wheelchairs, i.e., with wide bathroom doors, grab rails, lowered towel and Kleenex dispensers, and sometimes a ring in the ceiling over the bed from which a transfer trapeze may be hung. The wheelchair traveler soon learns, however, that such symbols indicate that the motel in question has wheelchair-accessible rooms, and only that. The symbol does not necessarily indicate that the motel's entrance is accessible or that there are curb cuts from parking areas.

Indispensable to travelers with any mobility impairment, from those with an impaired gait to those needing an electric wheelchair, is a guide entitled *The Wheelchair Traveler*, which is edited by a paraplegic. *The Wheelchair Traveler*, in addition to accessibility information about motels, hotels, and tourist attractions in the fifty states and many foreign countries, gives traveling tips, such as whom to call in case of illness or when needing a catheter changed. Most disabled persons who are traveling alone use *The Wheelchair Traveler* in conjunction with access guides published in many cities by Easter Seals or Junior Leagues. Such guides list and describe accessible banks, churches, restaurants, motels, etc. in cities from Detroit to San Antonio, from San Francisco to Boston.

Not all persons make periodic trips cross-country, but most, unless they are forced to remain home by physical or financial concerns, do occasionally spend an entire day on the road. Until the mid-1970s, travel was complicated by a lack of accessible comfort facilities along the nation's highways. Until the mid-1970s, very few rest areas had accessible bathroom facilities or picnic areas. After 1975, changes began to occur. Where earlier one might see an occasional rest stop designed to accommodate the mobility-impaired, by the summer of 1977 all rest stops in several states were totally accessible. The Federal-Aid Highway Act of 1973 requires that projects funded by the Highway Trust Fund "shall be" designed to be used by all persons, including the elderly and the "non-ambulatory wheelchair bound."

Despite an occasional step backward, the disabled made great advances in the area of private transportation during the seventies. How well they will fare in the future is a matter of concern in light of certain economic and political trends, such as decreasing energy supplies. Added to the cost of obtaining modified vehicles is the increasing cost of continuing to operate such vehicles. Compact cars, which give good gas mileage, are not large enough to hold collapsed, lightweight wheelchairs, to say nothing of chairs with special features, such as power models. Unless a person has gargantuan strength, she needs a car which is large enough to fit a folded wheelchair easily behind the driver's seat. Such cars, which get low gas mileage, are energy savers compared to modified vans, which average about 7 miles to the gallon in urban areas. Those whose jobs depend on their ability to operate modified cars and vans are concerned about keeping their jobs as the gas shortage worsens. The energy shortage, coupled with their realization that for every person who can provide her own transportation, hundreds more cannot, provides the impetus for the struggle to make all public transportation accessible to all persons.

Access to Mass Transit: Technological Progress but Political Reluctance

Despite legislative mandates, local transit authorities are reluctant to comply with the law that all buses purchased after 1979 must be wheelchair-accessible. As these authorities point out, the law says buses must be accessible but does not provide funds to incorporate accessibility features. In certain areas alternative methods of transporting the disabled are proposed or in effect. Dial-a-Ride is such a system. Dial-a-Ride provides door-to-door service on a demand basis, thereby eliminating the problem of getting to and from bus stops or of running buses in areas and at times when demand is light. Such systems, however, typically give priority to certain types of transportation needs, such as first priority to medical appointments and second to senior citizens' activities. There is no denying that medical care or travel requirements of the elderly are important, but the problem with a Dial-a-Ride system is that very few buses make up the fleet, and nonunion drivers are used to cut operating costs. Therefore, when several vehicles are out for repair or several drivers quit or call in sick, the system ceases to operate. In cities with Dial-A-Ride, persons dependent on the system for reliable transportation to work have lost their jobs because of excessive absenteeism or consistent lateness. In addition to the unreliability of Dial-a-Ride as a mode of transportation is the difficulty of trying to accommodate work schedules to limited transportation services. The disabled often work shifts or, if they are professionals, have schedules which vary from week to week due to evening meetings or weekend work at the office. Services like Dial-a-Ride cannot provide the same extensive services as can regular bus systems.

If the disabled are to become contributing members of society, they must be able to use all forms of public transportation. According to a study conducted for the Urban Mass Transportation Administration (UMTA), approximately 13,370,000 Americans have difficulty using unmodified public transportation. Yet many of these persons are supporting the existing systems with their tax dollars. What prevents them from using public transportation varies: steep steps, narrow aisles, dim lighting, illegible signs, or policies which state that public carriers, which load, transport, and unload millions of tons of inanimate goods daily, will not make similar provisions for assisting human beings to likewise reach their destinations (Goodkin, 1977).

The first federal legislation which specifically stated that conveyances paid for by federal funds should be usable by the elderly and the handicapped was the 1970 Biaggi Amendment (Pub. L. 91-453) to Section 16 of the Urban Mass Transportation Act of 1964. The Federal-Aid Highway Act of 1973, the 1974 amendments to that act, and the National Mass Transportation Assistance Act of 1974 together provide for the following: (1) projects funded by the Highway Trust Fund "shall be planned, designed, constructed and operated" so they can be used effectively by all persons, including those with severe mobility impairments (Pub. L. 93-87); (2) no project will be approved which does not provide the elderly and handicapped with equal access to all "public mass transportation facilities, equipment and services" (Pub. L. 93-643); and (3) special services and funds will be provided for assisting disabled and/or elderly persons. The legislation with the most potential, from a consumer's point of view, is the Department of Transportation (DOT) Appropriations Act of 1975, which specifies that no funds available under the act shall be provided to public carriers for "passenger rail or subway cars . . . motor buses or for the construction of related facilities unless . . . designed to meet the mass transportation needs of the elderly and handicapped" (Pub. L. 93-391).

The extent to which the above legislation has increased the accessibility of public transportation and public transportation facilities varies. Modifications of facilities along expressways lie at the positive end of the continuum, while the lack of modifications in rail and subway cars and buses lies at the other. Estimates at the time the 1975 act was passed were that if implementation began immediately, the modifications needed to make all public transportation accessible would take thirty years. Although the design for a wheelchair-accessible transbus is available, no such buses have been built, so transit authorities cannot select the size and model they prefer. In tests such transbuses ran more quietly and more smoothly and reduced the loading time of passengers to approximately one-half that on existing buses. Moreover, studies conducted by DOT indicate that the low-floor, ramped transbus is more attractive to persons who are not disabled than buses now in use.

Few communities, by the end of the 1970s, had more than a token barrier-free bus within their fleet of vehicles. Despite existing laws, the outcomes of lawsuits conducted by consumers have not been encouraging to those who need barrier-free transportation. In 1975 a suit against the Jefferson County Transit Authority in Birmingham, Alabama, was lost when the judge decided the plantiff was not denied bus service because nothing stopped her from riding if she had someone carry her on and off (Goodkin, 1977).

Opponents of wheelchair-accessible public transit systems fear the cost of accessibility might run as high as 2 billion dollars. Yet in 1975 the cost of public and private services to the disabled was more than $86 billion, of which a sum of $16 billion was for income maintenance. According to a DOT study in 1969, 59 percent of the disabled live in families with combined incomes of less than $3,000 a year. While 47.8 percent of the disabled were employed, 67 percent of those unemployed were evaluated as able and willing to work. What they lacked was reliable transportation. If those 67 percent became employed, the minimum yearly economic benefit would be $824,000,000 in goods and services, not counting the decreased cost in welfare and social security payments or the increased tax revenues.

Of those 47.8 percent who meet their own transportation needs, however, many rely on high-cost, door-to-door taxi service, when they can make special arrangements with companies or individual drivers. Even those who have others to help them usually choose to use cabs rather than inaccessible buses for two reasons: it is less strenuous for an attendant to lift someone in and out of a car than to carry him up the steps into a bus; and, as parents of disabled children will testify, bus drivers and passengers become irritated by the time it takes to load first a disabled person and then his mobility aid into a barrier-ridden public conveyance. Therefore, taxi service is the only alternative for those who cannot use public transportation and cannot drive themselves. For example, 14 percent of the trips made by disabled persons are by taxi as compared to 2 percent for the general population (Goodkin, 1977).

Before 1977, DOT had exerted no pressure on providers of transit services to consider accessibility in ordering new equipment, although federal legislation requiring reduced fares during nonpeak hours and reserved seating for those elderly and handicapped persons who could use unmodified transportation was enforced. In fact, these special fare and seating considerations have been given wide publicity, causing the general public to believe that accessibility problems have been solved, because they "have just read that the handicapped pay reduced rates, so they must be able to get on and off somehow."

Access to Airlines: Barrier Roulette

Although day-to-day requirements tend to focus consumer concerns on local transportation systems, serious problems exist in long-distance transportation systems too. Because of the difficulty the disabled have in trying to travel by air, train, or bus, most, if possible, travel by car or van. Driving long distances, however, is not feasible for those who travel for a living or whose jobs require a great deal of traveling. But air travel, while less time-consuming, is especially stress provoking for the disabled. Whether or not such persons will be allowed to board a plane depends not only on which airline is involved, but also on which airline employees are on duty when a would-be passenger arrives at the airport.

Example 11D   Stranded in Chicago: Friendly Skies, Hostile Airlines

The first two years DeLoach was in college, she flew home and back during Christmas vacation. The third Christmas, however, she left Urbana as usual on Ozark Airlines and at O'Hare transferred from Ozark to North Central. When she reached North Central's boarding area and checked in, she was told she would not be allowed to travel without an attendant. That decision created quite a dilemma. She could not return to Urbana, because her dormitory was closed for vacation. She could not take another airline, because North Central was the only airline that provided service to her hometown. She didn't know anyone in Chicago and didn't have the money for a hotel, if she had had a way to get to one. So she argued with the airline's personnel. Finally, they relented but warned her never to fly North Central again. Fortunately, since then she has lived in areas serviced by a variety of airlines.

A federal regulation stipulates that a disabled passenger must be attended by a nondisabled person during a plane trip. Since 1930, when the first blind person was allowed to fly, disabled passengers have created so few problems that most airlines, most of the time, disregard the regulation. Occasionally, however, some employees still refuse to allow an unattended disabled passenger to board. This results in the nerve-racking uncertainty for the disabled as to whether or not they will be stranded if they transfer to another airline or allowed to return after they have reached their destination. This can be unbearably stressful when one is attending a business meeting or presenting a paper at a national convention.

Persons who depend on power chairs have additional problems with airline policies and personnel. The unanswered question for them is how best to transport their wheelchair batteries. The same airline at different times will tell would-be passengers that they will be allowed to travel only with dry-cell batteries, drained wet-cell batteries, or no batteries at all. Sometimes when a power chair owner makes his reservation, he is told he can fly with his battery, but when he gets to the terminal, the airline may let him fly (1) without any battery or (2) without his wheelchair and battery. Recently, Clarissa J. flew to Seattle for a rehabilitation engineering conference. She arrived with her power chair and wet-cell battery. When the conference was over and she arrived at the Seattle airport to return home, she was told by the same airline that she could not return with her battery. When she objected, she was assured that the airline would store her battery for her until she returned to claim it. Since that was the first time she had been to Seattle, her battery may be in storage for a long time. What bothered Clarissa most was not that she had to buy a new battery when she returned home, but that she was completely helpless until someone got a battery and installed it in her chair. Anyone who depends on an electric chair is completely immobilized when the chair's power source is interrupted, whether by malfunction or human arbitrariness.

Access to Amtrak

One positive change in long-distance travel is Amtrak's announced plan eventually to make all facilities accessible. Already trains with modified cars are running on the East Coast, and in time, each train will have at least one car outfitted with (1) a bathroom with grab bars, low commodes and lavatories, and a transfer seat; (2) special seating areas for passengers who remain in their wheelchairs; and (3) available food service. Even now aisles in Amtrak cars are wide enough to allow persons in wheelchairs or on crutches to pass. Although cars are increasingly accessible, few Amtrak stations have been remodeled so that disabled persons can enter trains easily from station platforms. In stations which have been remodeled, such as Union Station in Washington, high platforms allow persons to wheel directly into trains.

Train travel, except for excessively long trips, has certain advantages over airplane or car travel. Traveling by train is less expensive than traveling by plane and less tiring than traveling by car. Many cities with no airports have train stations. Train stations are usually in the heart of cities, close to hotels and business areas, while airports are often on the outskirts of cities. And finally, airlines expect disabled passengers to arrive early and to board before and disembark after other passengers. If Amtrak carries out its plans, long-distance travel may become as enjoyable and affordable for the disabled as it now is for others who travel for pleasure as well as business.

ACCESS TO EMPLOYMENT

Although all architectural barriers are undesirable, few have a more negative impact than those in potential job sites. Physical limitations and employer prejudice can be overcome, but unless job openings occur in totally accessible sites, disabled applicants face the formidable task of trying to sell their expertise to employers over that of applicants whose physical condition requires no job or job site modifications. Once disabled applicants are hired, however, their lower absenteeism and lower rate of turnover far offset any initial disadvantage to the employer from having to make changes which allow them to function productively (Sinick, 1968; Goodyear and Stude, 1975).

The two types of modifications which help disabled persons meet job requirements and compete successfully with nondisabled persons are: (1) job-site modifications, which eliminate barriers in offices, factories, and other job sites and (2) job modifications, which use adaptive aids to improve performance. Both types of modifications have received increased attention because Section 504 requires employers who do business with the federal government to make "reasonable accommodations" for disabled workers. Those engaged in vocational placement must approach barriers on job sites or affecting job performance as placement problems which are unique to specific individuals preparing for specific jobs. The solutions that are developed, however, will tend to overlap from placement situation to placement situation.

Modifying the Individual To Meet Job Requirements

To reduce the effect of limitations resulting from disease, developmental condition, or injury, assistive devices have been developed to (1) extend a person's reach vertically and horizontally, beyond the limits imposed by a sedentary position, muscular weakness, or inflexible body joints; (2) strengthen a person's grip; (3) improve a person's ability to move about quickly and easily; and (4) compensate for a person's impaired sensory abilities.

Standing Aids   Those who are confined to wheelchairs have difficulty with certain jobs because of their stature. Seated, such persons are approximately 48 inches tall, so unless they can vary their height according to the situation they are in, they are proficient only at tasks which are normally done from a sitting position or which can be adapted to someone in a sitting position. Ironing is one example of a common task which can be done as easily by someone sitting as by someone standing, if an adjustable ironing board is used. Many occupations are difficult if not impossible for those who cannot stand for even a short period of time. Secretarial work, classified as a sedentary occupation according to caloric charts, may require one to file items in vertical files or cabinets. Persons who stand 48 inches tall are not as limited as someone who must remain seated since they may use step stools or ladders to extend their reach.

Those who use wheelchairs but who have strong trunk, arm, and shoulder muscles can use commerically available, modified wheelchairs to bring themselves to a standing position. An SCI paraplegic works as a welder with the aid of such a device. In addition to these "Stand-Alones" are wheelchairs in which the seat adjusts to various levels. Such variable seating heights allow one man who had polio to work as a printer and one woman who is a paraplegic to work as a beautician.

Reach and Grip Aids   Job opportunities are limited for those with hands weakened from muscular dystrophy or who cannot reach up, down, or to the sides. To offset these impairments, a wide variety of "reachers" can be used. These are modified to meet the special needs of a particular individual or particular job. Although reachers come in various lengths and require varying degrees of strength to use properly, most consist of a scissor-type handle at one end and a pinching apparatus at the other.

Some have corrugated rubber on the pincers to prevent slipping when items like a heavy catalog are being lifted from the floor or when a sheet is pulled over a bed. Others have foam rubber or magnets attached to their tips to allow manipulation of small metal objects. Homemakers with cardiac or neuromuscular disabilities find reachers essential for such tasks as pulling meat packages out of a freezer and inserting electrical plugs into outlets blocked by pieces of furniture. Employees find that the uses of such devices are as varied as the imaginations of those who use them. Many libraries stock these devices for their disabled patrons.

One type of reacher is really a modified mouth stick. By squeezing one end between the teeth, a person can grasp and move a variety of objects or work the controls on tape recorders or radio equipment.

Persons with cerebral palsy, with no control of their extremities but some control of their head movements, type, write, draw, or spell out messages on an alphabet board by means of a pointer attached to a headband or a construction-type hard hat.

Mobility Aids   A variety of mobility aids—e.g., wheelchairs, crutches, walkers, electric golf carts—help persons move swiftly and easily in barrier-free environments. Some aids, constructed out of different materials and in various styles, are more durable, safer, and easier to manage than others. Some persons subject their mobility aids to so little stress that their devices last for years. Others subject their equipment to such hard use that even the most well-constructed aids wear out quickly.

Persons with different degrees of impairment require different aids: canes, crutches, or walkers for those with minimal limitations; manual or power wheelchairs for those whose limitations are more severe. Each mobility aid must be carefully prescribed according to the individual's needs: some crutches extend from beneath the armpits, while others extend from the forearm down; some are wood, others aluminum; some have a fixed length, while others can be adjusted so a child can use the same pair of crutches through several stages of growth.

Selecting crutches, however, is simple compared to evaluating the options available in wheelchairs. There are adult-sized wheelchairs, child-sized wheelchairs, extra-wide wheelchairs for the extra-wide person, and narrow wheelchairs for the slightly built. Some wheelchairs have reclining backs to rest or relieve pressure on the buttocks, some have high backs to support those with weak shoulder or neck muscles, and some have low backs to allow users to engage in wheelchair sports without having their arms hampered when they are shooting for baskets or tossing javelins. A wheelchair may be ordered with fixed or removable arms that extend straight to the front or dip down halfway toward the front so that it fits under the edge of a desk or table. Legs are either removable, able to be extended horizontally, or permanently attached in a semivertical position. Tires vary from solid rubber to pneumatic and the type of tire chosen is of paramount importance. Pneumatic tires, which give a more comfortable ride, are easier to push over rough terrain or ice, but are not recommended for use on job sites where sharp bits of metal lying around may cause repeated flats, although thorn-proof inner tubes can greatly decrease the probability of getting a flat tire. Because of the complexity of proper wheelchair selection, anyone faced with the need to order a wheelchair should consult guides such as *Rehabilitation: A Manual for the Care of the Disabled and Elderly* (Hirschberg et al., 1976) or secure the services of a therapist or prosthetist who has experience prescribing chairs.

Many who have been disabled for a long time know what mobility aids best suit the type of life they lead. Some who can manage with a cane, walker, or crutches under normal circumstances discover that they get around faster and safer in snow or ice or on wet grass by using wheelchairs with pneumatic tires. Those who obtain jobs which require them to move about constantly may use wheelchairs at work and their canes, crutches, or walkers during nonworking hours. Amputees discover that the function of the missing body part can be partially restored by modern prosthetics which operate by using adjacent muscle tissue or tiny, high-powered electrical cells. Paul, who has had four extremities amputated, far from being totally helpless as one might expect, learned to be independent in his ADL, to walk and climb stairs without canes or crutches, and to continue to do his own farm work, including operation of farm machinery. Paul's achievements have been recorded on film by the Texas Institute for Rehabilitation and Research as an example of the importance, not only of client motivation, but of the expertise of dedicated rehabilitators.

Sensory Impairment Aids   Devices such as hearing aids, white canes, or Optacons provide assistance to those with sensory impairments in managing their personal care, homemaking, and occupational activities. For example, the Optacon, which is about the size of a cassette recorder, and which translates the written word into symbols which can be "read" by the fingers of a trained person, has opened up the world of print by permitting blind computer programmers to read computer printouts or blind secretaries to read what they type, make corrections as they go, read telephone directories, and file items with ease.

The advantage of retraining or outfitting persons with adaptive aids is that they can then carry their rewon skills with them and will not have to be placed in a special setting in order to comprehend, communicate, and function physically. Their independent living skills will remain with them even if they change jobs, move to different homes, or leave one region of the country for another. For example, a welder who owns his own Stand-Alone can manage any job for which he is qualified and in which he needs to work in an upright position, as long as he can get to and from his place of work and in and out of his job site.

Modifying the Environment To Fit the Individual

In certain instances, however, it is infeasible or impossible to adapt the individual to a particular job, but possible and practical to adapt the job to a particular individual. With today's technology, no artificial hand allows a person to type with the same speed and accuracy as did his original hand. To bring a typist with an amputated hand up to his maximum level of performance, therefore, he must be provided with and trained to use an electric typewriter with a keyboard modified for one-handed typing. While admittedly an equipment modification, rather than a job-site modification, a one-handed typewriter is more likely to be provided by an employer as a reasonable accommodation than by the employee as a self-owned piece of adaptive equipment.

In many cases, a person's ability to fulfill particular job requirements depends on simple, inexpensive modifications of the environment—rearrangement of furniture and relocation of tools and equipment. Repositioning office furniture can make the difference between a disabled employee's being someone who does her job slowly and awkwardly or someone whose work compares favorably with anyone else's. Furthermore, rearranging storage cabinets, files, and bookcases and storing the most often used supplies in the most accessible areas may improve the working capacity of all employees, not just the disabled.

Example 11E   Walter H.: Paraplegic and Plant Manager

Walter H., a plant manager for a national drug company, has been recognized by his business peers for his contributions both to his company and to his community. In Walter's office the desk is placed in the center so he has access to all sides of the room. Along the room's periphery are horizontal storage units no more than 30 inches high. His desk, raised on blocks painted black, is high enough so he can sit comfortably without his knees or the wheelchair running into the top of the kneehole. Adjoining his office, an executive washroom with a wide sliding door has a sink 30 inches above the floor and a wall-hung commode with grab bars with a seat high enough so he can transfer easily from his wheelchair and back again.

The layout of the above office typifies the modifications which allow disabled employees to be productive employees: (1) a carefully thought out arrangement of furniture and equipment; (2) use of carefully selected, commercially available furniture, i.e., a desk with a large knee hole and horizontal storage units; and (3) custom alterations demanding little expertise, i.e., a pocket sliding door and wall-hung bathroom fixtures installed at ANSI standard heights.

Job Modification in Practice

George Washington University's Job Development Laboratory has successfully solved problems its severely disabled clients face in carrying out their personal maintenance and occupational duties. Building on the premise that the major difference between a homebound person and a remuneratively employed person is the ability to move about freely in the community, the laboratory has proved that severely disabled persons who are motivated and who have reliable transportation are as productive as nondisabled persons doing the same work (Mallik and Sablowsky, 1975). The Job Development Laboratory moves severely disabled persons into competitive employment through job modifications that range from modifications to existing equipment, such as snap-on switch levers on tape recorders, to custom-designed equipment, such as open vertical files which allow wheelchair-bound employees to sort mail. After a modification has been developed, the designs for it go into a pool so that it is readily available when anyone else encounters a similar functional or occupational problem.

In addition, the laboratory has compiled a listing which matches occupations with aids that allow persons with severe limitations to be successful in those occupations. For example, a disabled insurance claims adjuster may require (1) a telephone on an extension arm with a spring lever to depress the phone cradle buttons, allowing one-handed use of a regular desk phone; (2) a filing system composed of metal drawer dividers stacked on the desk's surface; and (3) a dictating machine remotely controlled by slight pressure of a hand, chin, or elbow. Clients who wish to be receptionists may require (1) the telephone modification above and (2) a microfilm viewer with a knob adapted for simple hand motions, which allows access to documents, reference books, and telephone listings without turning pages or handling heavy books. For those who wish to be magazine editors, the aids might consist of (1) the modified dictating machine above and (2) a rotating bookshelf allowing access to heavy books with a minimum of reaching and lifting (Mallick and Mueller, 1975).

The majority of the laboratory's clients are functioning as quadriplegics from disabilities including cerebral palsy, spinal cord injury, rheumatoid arthritis, multiple sclerosis, and muscular dystrophy. These persons are now competitively employed in jobs as computer programmers, mail clerks, insurance claims adjusters, receptionists, magazine editors, microfilm inspectors, clerk-typists, keypunchers, and microthin jacket fillers (Mallick and Mueller, 1975).

As the expertise of persons specializing in job and job-site modifications increases, the match between client and occupation may improve to where any job failure will stem from work-adjustment problems rather than from the limitations imposed by a disability.

ACCESS TO HOUSING

Within the last decade, a major concern of both professionals and consumers has been the lack of housing for disabled persons. Many who live in nursing homes or with relatives do not require custodial care but have no alternative living situation available in which they could function independently. The perennial lack of housing suitable for disabled persons has been exacerbated by the trend toward deinstitutionalization,* by improved rehabilitation techniques which result in persons' being able to live independently in accessible environments, and by the growing expectation of such persons that they should be given the chance to control and manage their own lives.

Deinstitutionalization

The trend toward deinstitutionalization has meant that institutions such as mental hospitals or developmental centers are experiencing legal pressure to move their residents back into their communities. To smooth the transition from sheltered institutional life to the complex world outside, semisheltered environments, i.e., half- or quarter-way houses, were planned to provide former residents both security and a place to learn necessary coping skills. But institutions found themselves having to move numbers of persons out into communities without having places to house them or trained personnel to teach them socially acceptable behaviors and simple survival skills. The appearance in many areas of physically or mentally disabled persons who looked strange and acted stranger did nothing to reduce community opposition to the establishment of group homes or transitional living centers. In middle Tennessee, an attempt to move a group of moderately retarded residents into a residential community failed to gain either community or resident acceptance. Community members were disturbed by the behavior of their new neighbors, who thought nothing of sitting in the middle of a sidewalk eating

---

*Although this nine-syllable word appears to represent professional jargon at its worst, it describes a humane but cost-conscious effort to allow people more control over their own lives by helping them make the transition from institutional to community life.

watermelon and spitting seeds into the street. The retardates, ostracized by those around them and unused to living without institutional supervision, asked to return to the more companionable structured life they had lived before.

Community resistance is not limited to the mentally retarded, however. An attempt to establish a group home for the physically disabled in New England met such strong resistance that the would-be founders of the home had to recruit support from those who participated in the 1977 White House Conference on Handicapped Individuals.

Adding to the demand for housing due to legislative mandates aimed at deinstitutionalization is the fact that, since the early 1970s, an increasing number of physically disabled persons have received the training and devices they needed to live with a minimum of outside help. Even without transportation to allow them to be remuneratively employed, some living on public monies found they could live by themselves if they had a home that was barrier-free and arranged for their, not someone else's, convenience. In a study of the housing needs of the disabled in Massachusetts, the Massachusetts Association of Paraplegics (MAP) discovered that 41 percent of their membership lived in inadequate housing and that 68 percent of their membership would move into accessible housing were it available. These figures, if projected to the entire state, indicate that 33,000 disabled persons in Massachusetts alone live in inadequate facilities and that 72,000 are ready to move into specially designed housing. If one assumes that Massachusetts is representative of other states, the need for accessible housing, nationwide, is phenomenal (Riel, 1977).

Housing needs of the disabled are compounded by (1) their extraordinary living expenses and (2) their high percentage of unemployment or underemployment. In Riel's study, 52 percent of the respondents were unemployed and therefore unable to finance the construction or remodeling of homes designed to meet their accessibility requirements. What deinstitutionalization means in terms of housing is that severely disabled young persons now compete with the elderly for limited space in special housing facilities and in nursing homes, for as Hirschberg, Lewis, and Vaughn have discovered, they are increasingly unwelcome in their family living units (1976).

Living with Family?

The increasing reluctance of families to accept disabled family members back into the home may have its roots in the demise of the extended family.

Example 11F   Gloria F.: Disabled but Fully Functional in an Extended Family

Gloria F., now in her sixties, was born with club hands and feet. She has lived with her sister Sophie and Sophie's husband Troy since they were married nearly fifty years ago. At one time the "family" included Sophie's 94-year-old mother, Sophie's other sister Ida, an unmarried son, a married son, the son's wife and their three children, and a disabled family friend who had broken her hip and could no longer live alone. Troy, who supported the entire family, bore his responsibilities willingly and proudly. Later his married son supplemented the family's income with his wages, allowing his dad to retire from his job as a foreman in a paper mill.

Such communal families, which incorporate friends and relatives who have nowhere else to go or who are temporarily or permanently incapacitated, still exist but are becoming increasingly rare. More common is the nuclear family, consisting of a husband, wife, and one or two underage children, which often has moved from its original hometown, thus severing geographical ties with other family members or lifelong family friends. Therefore, when a family member acquires a disability, no one is readily available to volunteer for nursing or housekeeping duties. High salaries of licensed or practical nurses have eliminated skilled at-home nursing care for all but the independently wealthy. Many families cannot even afford a part-time, unskilled attendant, since many insurance policies do not pay for nursing services outside of medical settings and make no provisions for attendant care (Hirschberg, Lewis, and Vaughn, 1976). Therefore, when a person sustains a severe and permanent disability, his family often finds it difficult to care for him or to afford the modifications and adaptive devices which might allow him to care for himself and even, in some cases, assume housekeeping and child-care responsibilities.

Living in Convalescent or Nursing Homes

For these reasons, many young, potentially active persons are placed in nursing homes or convalescent care homes, where they remain until they die. In such situations, young, alert persons live with elderly persons who are often passive and senile. Because the young disabled are in the minority, because such homes are typically understaffed, and because what staff exists is not trained in or aware of techniques necessary to prevent secondary disabilities, e.g., pressure sores or contractures, a young disabled nursing home resident exists in a situation that is potentially dangerous physiologically, psychologically, and socially (Kiser, 1974).

If more convalescent care hospitals were available, the situation would improve for those with no family to depend on or without the ability to care for themselves. Unfortunately, many convalescent care hospitals actually operate as nursing homes and so do not provide the therapy and medical supervision the disabled require. Furthermore, any capabilities such persons may have, which in the appropriate setting would allow them to live fuller, more independent lives, are eroded by impersonalized hospital routines. True convalescent care hospitals would both provide long-term skilled care and at the same time allow residents some alternative choices in life style within their specialized environment.

Low-Cost Alternatives: Group Living and/or Shared Attendant Care

A frequently heard argument concerning the feasibility of living facilities geared to young disabled adults—facilities which would provide (1) varying degrees of care, (2) activities initiated by and attuned to individual interests and abilities, and (3) spacious living quarters with private kitchens and public dining areas—is that such facilities would be prohibitively expensive. If one considers the costs over a lifetime, however, living situations geared to the disabled proved to be less expensive than situations where they are warehoused in homes or hospitals and thus prevented from contributing in terms of goods produced, services rendered, or taxes paid into the economy.

For example, the average severely disabled person does not require around-the-clock supervision and could live in bed-and-board accommodations—if he were permitted to. Bed-and-board living situations can be small-scale—as when a private home is subdivided into a few living units—or large scale—as when a high-rise facility is built to house many. What bed-and-board living situations have in common is that they provide private living space where residents can sleep, relax, and cook their meals if they want to, as well as communal space where residents can socialize or eat food prepared by others. Since such facilities do not provide nursing or attendant care, admission or continued residence depends on a resident's being able to care for himself. When someone becomes ill or permanently incapacitated, he must leave. One guideline commonly used to screen applicants for residency is whether or not the applicant is ambulatory. The premise underlying this guideline is that nonambulatory persons cannot be independent in their ADL, and therefore many persons are excluded from bed-and-board living situations unnecessarily.

For those who do require attendant care, group homes or communal living situations provide inexpensive alternatives to other long-term care facilities. Like bed-and-board residence, group homes can be established in homes which were once private or can take the form of high-rise units where the disabled live with other disabled persons or with nondisabled, sometimes elderly, persons. In either situation, individual units are built to meet the needs of disabled residents—wide doors, grab bars in bathrooms, Braille markings, flashing alarms, and amplified telephones. Residents who require help can share attendant services because few, regardless of the severity of their disabilities, require more than an hour or two of care in a twenty-four-hour period. Typically, a severely disabled person might require assistance in getting in and out of bed, bathing, going to the bathroom, and putting on certain articles of clothing, such as shoes and socks for someone with an artificial hip joint. Occasionally, residents may be confined to bed with the flu or a broken limb and temporarily require more extensive care, but still not skilled nursing care. With careful scheduling several persons can share the services of one attendant on weekdays and of another on weekends and holidays. Such sharing of service benefits both the disabled and their attendants: the disabled can hire more dependable and competent persons because they can offer more attractive salaries; the attendants are assured better-paying, full-time employment.

In university settings, group living situations utilize the part-time services of students who need extra money but who don't have the time for full-time jobs. At Boston University, the severely disabled live on one floor of the theology school and theology students form a pool from which attendants are selected.

Group living situations have proved a responsible way of moving persons out of institutions back into their communities. Neighborhood cooperative living situations function successfully in areas of the country where strong nursing home lobbies do not actively work against the establishment of limited-care, long-term residential units *(Commercial Appeal*, October 23, 1977).

A Home of One's Own: Ideal and (Comparatively) Affordable

Some persons, however, do not need regular attendant care and so prefer to live in their own homes as opposed to apartments or cooperative living facilities. In Riel's (1977) survey of housing preferences of disabled Massachusetts residents, 32 percent preferred cooperative living facilities, 32 percent preferred regular rented apartments, and 34 percent preferred their own private homes. A disabled individual's desire to own her own home cannot be dismissed as a wish-fulfilling fantasy, because many severely disabled persons do enjoy and cope successfully with home ownership.

As rising building and maintenance costs have made the American dream of homeownership more difficult for the nondisabled to realize, so they have made it more difficult for those with higher-than-average living expenses. In analyzing the comparative costs of housing alternatives, Frieden (1977) indicates that establishing long-term, low-interest loans to allow the disabled to purchase and modify their own homes might prove less expensive than maintaining them in institutions simply because there is nowhere else for them to go:

> Some general trends and dimensions regarding costs may be briefly noted. First, it is almost axiomatic that the more extensive and enriched the total program offering is, the more expensive the residential care will be; therefore, facilities which provide counseling, re-socialization, therapy, medical follow-up, vocational training and the like, as part of the total program, will show higher operating costs. Next there is a tendency for free-standing facilities to be less costly than those associated or affiliated with parent organizations. This may be the result of duplication of certain administrative overhead and/or personnel costs.
>
> Auspices of the facility will also tend to influence costs. The findings of a national survey of halfway houses, completed in 1975, show that municipal or state-operated facilities tended to have the lowest average number of clients per facility, followed by private, non-profit facilities, then federally-auspiced facilities, then finally profit-making facilities. Moreover, when per diem costs were examined, it was found that the for-profit facilities reported higher per diem costs ($18.30) than either federal ($12.30), state ($14.70), or private non-profit programs ($13.80). According to this survey of halfway house type programs, it can be generalized that large private, profit-making facilities are characterized by a large number of clients, higher per diem costs, a large full-time staff, and relatively few professional staff. Public (i.e., federal, state) facilities have a higher proportion of professionals on their staff and report lower per diem costs.
>
> According to national statistics, per diem costs for halfway houses currently fall within the general range of $12 to $18 per day, with the average at approximately $16. Boarding homes and long-term care facilities (which generally afford fewer services) operate at a noticeably lower per diem cost rate; a fair estimate would be that the per diem costs in such facilities would fall within the range of $7 to $15.
>
> Apartment programs are still less expensive to operate because of lower plant and staff costs and fewer on-site services are required. Per diem costs for supervised apartment living may be estimated to fall within the range of $3 to $8 per client—although this is by no means a well-documented figure. Supervisory costs, as distinct

from the apartment rental, for providing these services may be as low as $1 to $2 per diem. At the other extreme, skilled and intermediate level nursing homes require the highest per diem expenditures; a reasonable estimate of per diem costs for such facilities would be between $20 to $30 or even higher. It should be noted that cost of living arrangements may be both material and nonmaterial, while benefits are mostly nonmaterial. Material costs may be relatively low for those persons who live in multi-resident dwellings and share life support services. On the other hand, material costs may be relatively high for those persons who choose to live alone and hire a full-time attendant, or those who live in more institutionalized settings.

Nonmaterial cost includes frustration caused by waiting and compromising, insecurity caused by undependable attendant services, or uncertainty about arrangements, and boredom resulting from routinization and segregation. Some nonmaterial costs, like frustration and boredom, may be higher in institutionalized settings while other nonmaterial costs, like insecurity, may be higher in less institutional arrangements.

The Swedish approach to housing for handicapped individuals suggests that a reorganization of priorities is needed in planning alternate living arrangements for institutional living. The Fokus model, in Sweden, arranges accessible housing at two-thirds the cost of living in a nursing home, including rent and service, charging about twenty per cent of the resident's income. "Urban and rural districts have communally employed home helpers who serve old, sick, and disabled people (*Barrier Free Design*, 1975)." Fokus enables handicapped people to live securely under the same conditions and with the same opportunities as non-handicapped, in a chosen geographical area with access to reliable personal service, transportation, work and satisfying free-time activities. (Frieden, 1977, pp. 328–329.)

There is little doubt, based on experiences in other countries, that accessible and affordable private housing would allow many to live in a more independent and dignified manner than is now possible. In making a variety of housing alternatives available, society would reduce the cost of maintaining facilities which primarily serve as human storage depots and would restore the freedom of choice now denied many who happen to have a severe physical disability.

TECHNOLOGY MAKES THE DIFFERENCE

After medical specialists have exhausted their expertise, after antibiotics have eliminated pathological organisms, after surgeons have removed pressure impinging on nervous tissue, after various therapists have strengthened or restored movement to impaired muscles or joints, the last hope of the severely disabled lies with those who work in the area of technology. Disabled persons wanting to lead productive and self-satisfying lives no longer need to be physically normal. Technological advancements substitute wheels for malfunctioning legs, laser beams for malfunctioning eyes, and batteries for malfunctioning nerves, i.e., pacemakers, which control the beating of a heart or the emptying of a bladder.

When related to the functional problems of human beings, technology is appropriately defined as the systematized application of scientific knowledge to the multiplicity of problems which the disabled face in day-to-day routines of living. More than the pool of devices which solve specific functional problems, technology involves basic research—the development of new advances—and transfer—the application of existing technology to practical problems. Already, many advances from the space program have been transferred into devices for the severely disabled: an environmental control which allows paralyzed persons to use their eyes or breath to activate switches that turn lights on and off, raise and lower window blinds, open and close doors, and activate or deactivate televisions, radios, intercom systems, or telephones; and a polyurethane silicone plastic foam more effective in preventing pressure sores than previously used foam rubbers. But existing technology has not yet invented devices that can eliminate the effects of loss of physical functioning. To make that possible, future technological breakthroughs are necessary. Unfortunately, much basic research must precede any major breakthrough, and there is no guarantee that any such breakthrough will ever occur.

The role technology will play depends largely on how much our society values technology that benefits the disabled. Decisive technology, which prevents disabling diseases and conditions, is highly valued, for few would question that the funds poured into research to develop a polio vaccine were well spent. Halfway technology, the development of assistive devices such as the Optacon, which improves physical functioning in a manner reflected in increased potential for employment, is also highly valued. The economic or humanitarian value of research that may result in a mechanical feeding device for a person too disabled to engage in sheltered employment is more difficult to determine. Therefore, the most important aspect of technology for rehabilitation lies in the area of transfer. Technological transfer can be described as the development of as many secondary uses of scientific breakthroughs as possible. According to those in technology, there are many developments that could be applied to functional problems, but no one who could recognize their rehabilitative potential is aware of them. Much duplication of effort exists, even among rehabilitation engineers, because of poor communication within technology and between technology and other fields.

This problem is not new in rehabilitation. Once a device has been developed, the problem is always how to let those who need such devices know the devices exist. Rehabilitation is replete with Sunday mechanics and Saturday engineers who devise a specialized hand control, energy-saving lift, or computerized system which auditorily reproduces the written word. These mechanics and engineers seldom have any official connection with rehabilitation, but are friends, relatives, or neighbors who set out to solve a specific problem of a disabled individual. Sometimes these home workshop endeavors mushroom, as did the folding wheelchair. According to Everest and Jennings, Harry Jennings designed the first folding wheelchair for his friend Herbert Everest, who lost the use of his legs in a mine cave-in. Similarly, the Roycemobile, a modified wheelchair van, resulted from a collaboration between Robert Royce, an engineer, and a disabled friend who eventually became his partner. Everest and Jennings is now the leading manufacturer of wheelchairs in the United States, and Roycemobile dealerships were found throughout the nation before Royce's death.

Unfortunately, many innovations are not available to those who need them the most. Before full advantage can be taken of present technological advances, three questions must be answered: (1) How can the transfer of existing technology into marketable devices be financed and coordinated? (2) How can private industry find it profitable to produce these devices, or will production have to be subsidized by public or private organizations? and (3) How can those who need the devices afford to purchase them? In 1976, NASA testified before the House Committee on Science and Technology that space-age technology which can solve many functional problems of the disabled already exists. The NASA representative implied that while there is a need for continuing research, there is a more pressing need for translating existing technology into practical devices and for distributing these devices to the disabled in the least expensive and most efficient manner possible.

Again Sweden offers a model, based on a national health insurance program which absorbs extraordinary costs associated with chronic disease and severe disability. In Sweden, manufacturers of assistive devices are guaranteed a market and disabled persons are guaranteed access to the adaptive aids they require. The government subsidizes manufacturers' research and development of devices judged to have commercial potential and, under the National Health Program, supplies devices free of charge to those who need them. This public backing of private enterprise, common in countries which are leaders in rehabilitation, may explain why for years leak-proof female urinals had to be imported from West Germany.

Ideally, medically related technology would result in disabilities' being prevented, rather than being dealt with after they occur. Such decisive technology would concentrate on the development of preventive procedures such as the rubella vaccine, which has reduced the incidence of congenital blindness, deafness, and/or mental retardation resulting from infection by the rubella virus during the first trimester of pregnancy.

But because man is a biological being, subject to invasion by multitudes of ever-changing organisms and vulnerable to innumerable accidental traumas, disabilities will continue to occur and to persist. Well-financed research leading to a vaccine or an antibiotic takes years, while rapidly reproducing virulent organisms are capable of developing a resistant strain in a matter of days. Genetic counseling and amniocentesis can prevent many congenital defects, but the occurrence of mutant genes is largely unpredictable and uncontrollable. So, although the need for technological innovations that will prevent disabilities from occurring cannot be overemphasized, neither can the need for more research and development of halfway technology, to reduce the handicapping effects of existing disabling conditions. Properly utilized, halfway or "stop-gap" technology can become interchangeable with decisive technology, in terms of outcome. Halfway technology is capable of allowing the blind to "see," i.e., travel through and interpret their environment, and those with paralyzed limbs to be mobile, i.e., move about within their homes and communities.

Even present technology, which will seem very primitive years from now, can make available devices which, while not eradicating the effects of disabling conditions, make having a disability less catastrophic. Three factors, the first two of which were discussed previously, contribute to ineffective utilization of existing devices: (1) often the disabled cannot afford and so cannot avail themselves of the devices they need; (2) those who provide services to the disabled are often unaware that certain devices exist; and (3) some persons have a low tolerance for devices and find it difficult to utilize them. There is a psychological relationship between "gadget tolerance" and the ability to make optimum use of remaining physical abilities. Some are unable to use devices properly, or become so obsessed by such devices that they concentrate their energy on finding the ideal device rather than on learning to use what they have as best they can. For example, because a daily living task takes much time and effort, such persons may refuse to dress themselves, while they wait for the ideal dressing aid to be developed. For optimum functioning, severely disabled persons must learn to regard such devices, from dialysis machines to voice-controlled wheelchairs, as what they are—aids to enhance but not substitute for their own efforts.

Technology Applied: Rehabilitation Engineering Enters the Scene

Rehabilitation engineering, a relative newcomer on the rehabilitation scene, is a discipline which combines the expertise of trained engineers with the expertise of medical and paramedical personnel to develop technological advances which will enhance the functioning of severely disabled persons or simplify the duties of those who care for the disabled. Many rehabilitation engineering clinics concentrate on bioengineering, i.e., the use of microswitches and electrodes to replace the function of destroyed or damaged body tissues. One man, who is totally paralyzed with the exception of a miniscule muscle group around one eye, effects simple communications by using those remaining muscle fibers to activate an electromyographic electrode.

Such devices have their drawbacks, however. First, they often solve only the problem of one person. Second, since specialized knowledge and equipment are required, such devices are expensive to design, maintain, and replace. Third, they allow persons who are disabled enough to require them independence only in one small area of their daily lives. As Hirschberg, Lewis, and Vaughn (1976) point out, an environmental control may enable a person who can only move his head to turn on a hot plate to heat water for coffee, but not to fill the pot with water, place it on the hot plate, pour the coffee in a cup, and wash the dishes afterwards.

Despite these drawbacks, rehabilitation engineering clinics have made and are making invaluable contributions to the physical and emotional well-being of severely disabled children and adults, their parents, and their families. For persons who have been totally dependent on others for their every need, simply being able to turn a light switch on and off at will can result in as great a sense of accomplishment as becoming a skilled player would to a nondisabled tennis buff. Moreover, each rehabilitation engineering breakthrough, added to the growing store of bioengineering knowledge, benefits many disabled and nondisabled persons alike.

Take, for example, the evolution of dialysis technique and equipment. Until recently dialysis was an expensive, complex treatment which was available only to a chosen few. Dialysis boards screened candidates to decide who should receive treatments that could not be made available to all. Today, thousands are on dialysis, many using home units which reduce the costs in money, time, and energy of hospital treatments. Portable dialysis units, about the size of a lunch box, are being refined, so that persons can cleanse toxins from their blood with little disruption of their daily routines. An increasing number of vacation areas are making dialysis equipment available, so vacationers and traveling business persons can continue their treatments away from home.

While the achievements of rehabilitation engineers to date cannot restore full physical functioning to disabled persons, such achievements have lessened or eliminated specific functional problems. Consequently, greater numbers of disabled persons live by themselves and are competitively employed, while many others now require only part-time attendant care and are successful in competitive or sheltered employment.

Chapter 12

The Self-State, Stigma Incorporation, and Adjustment to Physical Disability

How does an individual with a disability (stigma) achieve psychological adjustment to his disability? What are the mechanisms, or psychosocial dynamics, involved in this adjustment? This chapter will present a theoretical frame of reference from which adjustment to physical disability may be examined. Some of the concepts utilized here and in the following chapters will be taken from other theories, primarily Goffman's (*Presentation of Self in Everyday Life* and *Stigma*) and Wright's (*Physical Disability: A Psychological Approach*). Theories abound in this area (Shontz, 1970; McDaniel, 1969; Roessler and Bolton, 1978; Wright, 1960). The theory presented here is unique in its potential for systematic utilization in the area of rehabilitation. There is as yet little hard research to support many of the premises of this theory. However, we consider it of heuristic value to present such concepts as being operative in the psychological adjustment to physical disability, hoping to encourage new research, even if such research is done for the sake of disproving these concepts.

This chapter will:

1 Review some of the classical self-concept theories
2 Introduce the concept of the self-state
3 Present the psychodynamics of stigma incorporation
4 Discuss some issues and considerations related to stigma incorporation

REVIEW OF SELF-THEORIES

Before a discussion of the self-state and stigma incorporation and their relationship to adjustment to disabilities, it might be well briefly to review other theories regarding the self, the self-concept, and other related constructs. Bernard and Huckins (1971) delineate the following three aspects of the self derived from the many theories regarding its functions: (1) how one views oneself (self-as-subject); (2) how others appear to think of the individual (self-as-object); and (3) the ability to act, think, etc. (self-as-doer). These same authors review the major self theories and their respective conceptualizations of the self. For example Margaret Mead's "social self" is what the individual discovers about himself or herself through interactions with others. Prescott Lecky conceives of the self as a consistent set of values one holds regarding oneself (Bernard and Huckins, 1971). Finally, Harry Stack Sullivan conceives of the self as a protection against anxiety that functions similarly to ego defense mechanisms [(Chapter 3) (Bernard and Huckins, 1971)]. W. Fitts (1965), in developing his self-concept scale, conceptualized the self to be comprised of several aspects, including the physical self, the moral-ethical self, the personal self, the family self, the social self, and self-criticism. Bigge (1976) reviews the relation between self-concept and self-awareness with regard to the physically handicapped individual. She provides some specific tasks that educators and others can employ in developing self-concept and self-awareness in the physically handicapped person.

Although these and many other similar theories make use of various conceptualizations of the self, the following method for conceptualizing an individual's overall evaluation of himself has been chosen because it most fully clarifies stigma incorporation and its ramifications for rehabilitation.

Roessler and Bolton (1978) present a thorough review of theory and research regarding the relationship between self-concept and disability. Two points noted by Roessler and Bolton need to be mentioned here. First, the results of research regarding any relationship between self-concept and disablement are, at this point, ambiguous. Second, for scientific reasons some authorities, particularly Guilford (1959), seriously question the use of the self-concept construct in the study of personality. The question of the validity of Roessler and Bolton's theory and research is centered around the methodological problems involved in assessing self-concept in a physically disabled population. One of the present authors has utilized the Tennessee Self-Concept Scale with a group of very severely disabled adults and found that their scores on this scale were extraordinarily higher than those of the nondisabled. This chapter will not offer any practical resolution to such methodological problems. However, the self-state construct will still be utilized for the sake of presenting a theory of adjustment to physical disablement. Some concepts to be presented here may, in the future, lend themselves to empirical validation.

THE SELF-STATE

As indicated above, many theorists have conceptualized one aspect of personality to be the *self-concept*. The self-concept is often conceived to be a static aspect of one's personality, consisting primarily of how the individual views his or her abilities, talents, defects, and overall state of being. The *self-state,* as posited here, deviates from this form of conceptualization to the extent that although many of the individual's concepts concerning his or her state of being are static, other such conceptualizations are fluid and vary considerably over a period of time. The self-state, then, is here conceptualized as one's overall appraisal of oneself at a specified time and place. Many events impinge on the person hourly, daily, etc., which may alter the self-appraisal and, thus, the self-state.* When certain events, changes, or interpersonal encounters have a relatively permanent effect on the individual's self-state, such changes are said to be *incorporated* into the self-state. What is still unknown and subject only to speculation, however, is the factors determining whether or not a specific event, change, etc., will or will not have such an effect as to be incorporated in a relatively static nature into the self-state. As conceived here, the self-state is most similar to Fitts's "dimensions of self."

The self-state is here conceptualized as being more vulnerable to events which produce relatively permanent alterations in one's self-appraisal at certain times than at others. This vulnerability is conceived to be the *self-state threshold.* This construct is directly related to how difficult or easy it is for the self-state to be altered by the incorporation of newly formed concepts of self. The self-state threshold is raised and lowered during different stages of one's development and by the intensity of certain life events. For example, for most persons, becoming physically impaired is, generally, of such intensity as to lower their self-state threshold. Physical impairment then produces a varying period of vulnerability in the self-state, with the result that events occurring during or shortly after disablement can have lasting effects on one's self-state. The fluctuation of the self-state threshold is not directly related to the sequential stages of human development. That is, this threshold is not necessarily lower at an earlier stage than it is at a later stage. For example, the authors believe that this threshold is generally higher during prepuberty than it is during adolescence. Therefore, events, encounters, etc. during adolescence may have a more profound and lasting effect on the self-state than very similar events prior to adolescence.

We have defined the general nature of the self-state and the self-state threshold. However, in dealing with the effects of physical disablement on these constructs, with particular reference to the self-state, it is hypothesized that the self-state is a gestalt of several dimensions of a person's being. Although it is somewhat mechanistic to do so, we will specify some of the major components of the total gestalt of the self state.

The major components as described here are:

1   The physical self-state
2   The independence-support self-state
3   The interpersonal self-state
4   The industrious self-state
5   The creative-relaxation self-state

*The term *self-state* will be used here to the exclusion of the term self-concept. Although the two constructs may seem very similar to the reader, self-state is preferred here to highlight the changing fluidity of one's perceptions of oneself. If the reader prefers to conceive of the self-concept as one's relatively unchanged appraisal of oneself over time, he is free to do so.

The Physical Self-State

This is perhaps the most basic part of the self-state since it is one of the first states to evolve. In a classic sense, this aspect of the self-state is directly related to the body image concept as discussed by Schilder (1950) and Fisher and Cleveland (1958). This aspect encompasses the person's perception of her physique, body symmetry, boundary, and agility, along with the aesthetic appearance of her total physical presence. This aspect begins to develop as early as 6 months of age and is one of the pillars of the person's total self-state. However, *as is true for all the components of the self-state, for different individuals each component has a differential value in the total self-state and such values are uniquely derived mainly through experience.*

The Independence-Support Self-State

This is actually an extension of the physical self-state just discussed. Included here are the most basic abilities to care for oneself, which are frequently required in activities of daily living or self-help skills, such as dressing and caring for the body, feeding skills, and mobility skills, at the most basic level. At higher developmental levels this would include the ability to "strike out on one's own," skill in solving the problems of everyday living, etc.

The Interpersonal Self-State

This component of the self-state begins to develop somewhat later than the two previously discussed components. It involves the acquisition of skills in relating on a meaningful, rewarding level with other individuals. As with all other self-state components, there exist many individual differences in this area. In our society, this area is frequently the one which is most critical for social adjustment in adulthood.

The Industrious Self-State

From their early beginnings, human beings have been toolmakers and workers. The industrious self-state is used to refer to a wide variety of activities having as their objective the achievement of some type of productive goal or service. In present-day America, one may think of this state in relation to remunerative employment. However, this is a restricted view of this concept. It is possible to develop a comfortable, industrious self-state without holding a job or position. Behavioral scientists tend to recognize in human beings a drive for constructive activity. White (1956) postulates striving for competency even in small children. One has only to watch the persistence of most infants in their initial attempts at walking to realize that this persistence is a striving for competence in moving about their environment. This innate human drive to achieve control (competency) over one's environment becomes a critical self-state component.

The Creative-Relaxation Self-State

This self-state component is a derivative of the industrious self-state. "All work and no play makes Jack a dull boy" is a truism. Individuals engaged in routine industrious activities generate a derivative need for some diversion which satisfies other competency needs. An increasingly important area for enhancing feelings of self-adequacy, it is a particularly crucial area for members of the population with a great deal of leisure time at their disposal, such as some severely disabled individuals.

A particular individual's self-state may comprise more components than the five outlined above. However, the components listed and briefly described are those which are most frequently involved in the dynamics of physical disability. It is axiomatic that an individual's development will determine which of these or other components of the self-state will be most prominent and valued for that person. One may grow up valuing physical appearance and/or ability. Physical disability involving physical disfigurement and/or deformity will, at least temporarily, have a devastating effect on the total self-state of such a person. On the other hand, a rugged individualist's self-state would be most endangered by a disability which severely limits the independence-support component. In summary, the total effect of a physical disability on an individual's self-state can never be ascertained from merely knowing the nature and extent of the disability. Rather, one must be familiar with the disabled individual's self-state.

THE SELF-STATE AND PHYSICAL DISABILITY

Physical disablement will have a significant impact on the self-state. During the natural history of the development and outcome of the condition of the physical disability, the self-state will undergo many changes, sometimes swiftly, sometimes slowly; sometimes negatively and sometimes positively. These changes and their final outcome are the true essence of what is here termed *stigma incorporation*, in which a disability becomes an integral part of the self-state. However, before dealing with this concept, it must be stated that self-state has been conceptualized for the express purpose of emphasizing the constantly changing impact a physical disability may have upon an individual's overall appraisal of his worth. A physical disability will have different effects on the different components of the self-state. That is, a disability may have, temporarily at least, more impact on the physical self-state and the interpersonal self-state than it does on other components. At different times, during different circumstances, other self-states, such as the industrious self-state, may be most affected by the disability.

The concept of the *self-state threshold* is proposed to highlight the observation that the impact of physical disablement is often accentuated at certain times or periods of the individual's life. It is hypothesized that the onset of a physical handicap and/or the full realization of the implications of a handicap for an individual's life-style renders the individual more vulnerable to her experiences immediately following such an event. Whether these experiences are positive or negative, their influence on specific components of the self-state and on the global self-state are more strategic and frequently have long-lasting effects. Thus, the onset of a physical disability during adolescence, a time when the interpersonal self-state is in a crucial stage of development, will have a greater impact on that component of the self-state than it would if it occurred before or after this critical developmental period for this component of the self-state. Likewise, disablement during early adulthood, at a time when the individual is just beginning to establish economic independence, will temporarily impair this self-state component more than it would had the handicap occurred at a different period of life.

THE PSYCHODYNAMICS OF STIGMA INCORPORATION:
A THEORETICAL FRAME OF REFERENCE

This section will attempt to explore the influence of physical disablement on the self-state. The transition from the trauma of disablement through the final and ideal stage, stigma incorporation, will be traced, and the concepts involved in such a transition will be defined as they occur in the psychodynamic process of stigma incorporation.

Physical disability imparts to the individual a stigma. "Stigma," as used by Goffman (1963), has two aspects. First, there is the physical mark, or in this case, the disability. The second aspect of stigma is the social disgrace that has come to be associated with the physical disability. Related terms are "stigmatizing" and "stigmatized." Such terms, as they will be used here, refer to the social process of assigning negative values to certain physical stigmas. Therefore, to begin with, physical disability is, to a greater or lesser degree, socially stigmatizing. Either the physical stigma and/or the inability to perform certain functions due to the presence of the disability lead to what is here termed "disability-related stress." In Chapter 3 the relationship between physical disability and stress was explored. Disability-related stress refers to the adjustive demands placed on the individual that can be directly attributed to the physical disability. If, as is usual in the initial stages of disablement, the frequency, intensity, and amount of disability-related stress are excessive, the self-state threshold is greatly lowered. The events, impressions, and frustrations experienced during such a period then become, at least temporarily, a significant part of the self-state. Since most of the experiences during the initial stages are negative, the individual must deal with these events, impressions, and frustrations as they relate to his overall worth as an individual. Stewart and Rossier (1978) point out that depression often closely follows the onset of disability. Depression is also listed as one of the restorative adjustments to disability (Roessler and Bolton, 1978). It is proposed that the depression observed following disablement is a manifestation of a temporarily lowered overall evaluation of self-worth, i.e., of the self-state.

To combat this phenomenon, as was explained in Chapter 3, the individual has two alternatives. First, he may employ one or more of the ten ego defense mechanisms that do not change reality as such but alter the individual's perception of reality data. The second alternative is to develop and employ task-oriented approaches, which are techniques by which situations may be divested of their stress-inducing aspects. This second approach requires experience, knowledge, and planning. In the majority of cases, the first approach is usually the one employed by individuals when they first come to the realization of disablement. As time passes and other factors come into play, task-oriented behaviors will, ideally at least, come to be employed more frequently.

Whatever strategy is employed is directed at stress reduction and a more positive self-state. It should be noted that not all stress is necessarily negative, even when it is disability-related. The discovery of a skill or function which the individual thought was lost will produce disability-related stress to the extent that it will require a temporary or permanent alteration of one's self-state. Hans Selye, the pioneer investigator in the field of stress, utilizes the concept of "eustress" to refer to positive events producing stress, and "distress" to refer to negative stress (Selye, 1976).

Agreeing with this observation that positive changes can produce disability-related stress, Shontz (1970) states, "The common sense view of disability as a negative psychological experience does not prepare us for the possibility that improvement from illness or that removal of disability or threat to life may produce depression" (p. 58).

Overuse of ego defense mechanisms as stress reducers often leads to what will be termed *stigma isolation.* Stigma isolation leads a severely disabled individual to perceive disability-related stress as the result of external events, situations, and attitudes on the part of others, i.e., out of his control. This tends to keep the stigma an isolated, separate aspect of the self-state. The majority of the individual's experiences are, to him, unrelated to his stigma. The result of the psychological phenomenon of stigma isolation is that since it is based on strategies which are not reality-based (ego defense mechanisms), it has little effect upon the reduction of the frequency and/or intensity of disability-related stress that will arise in future experiences.

It must be pointed out that during the early natural history of disablement, stigma isolation and its accompanying use of ego defense mechanisms plays a critical role in easing the bleak reality of disability. To expect an individual to cope with the intense stress resulting from severe physical disability immediately after injury and/or learning of his stigma is unrealistic. The employment of ego defense mechanisms such as denial, repression, etc., is to be expected for a period of time. However, the continued use of this strategy of coping with the resulting stress can result in the nonintegration of the stigma into the self-state and its components. For example, if an individual continually has his self-care needs fulfilled for him by someone else and is never allowed to learn to accomplish such tasks independently, his independence-support self-state will rely on persons external to himself as an integral part of this self-state component. The failure to meet self-care needs and the resultant stress will be displaced onto those external to himself who are normally responsible for meeting such needs. Such an individual will fail to view such frustrations as limitations of his own self-state, but will blame them on the irresponsibility of others.

When an individual begins to acknowledge the fact that many of the frustrations, conflicts, and pressures she encounters are the direct result of limitations placed upon her by the disability, she will of necessity begin to develop methods for avoiding, resolving, or minimizing such occurrences. This is the beginning of what will be termed here *stigma recognition.* Stigma recognition is the process by which an individual (1) acknowledges the fact of her disability and (2) begins exploring the implications this fact will have on her life-style. The methods and strategies resulting from this process will begin to be more task-oriented to the extent that they are employed to reduce future experiences of disability-related stress. Stigma recognition involves not only the individual's coming to view herself as disabled, but also her beginning to seek others, either professionals and/or disabled persons, who have the expertise to assist her in developing stress-reducing strategies. In the beginning of this process, the individual may not fully realize the myriad ramifications her disability will have upon her self-state. She may begin by seeking strategies to reduce stress in only one area of her existence. If such an individual experiences success in seeking such a stress-reducing strategy, this will eventually lead to other explorations for task-oriented strategies. The premises upon which this exploration is based are that (1) there is a problem; (2) it will probably not go away by itself; and (3) someone or something will enable her to cope more effectively with problems in stress-producing situations. Lack of success in such ventures will result in further employment of the less efficient ego defense mechanisms.

It should be noted that no matter how many successful task-oriented strategies an individual develops in reducing disability-related stress, there will be occasions when she will still employ ego defense mechanisms in order to maintain her achieved self-state. Insensitive individuals, inaccessible buildings, restaurants, or movie theaters, and the like leave even the most resourceful person with little recourse but to utilize such mechanisms. However, as the process of stigma recognition progresses, the individual comes to acknowledge more aspects of her self-state which are stress-prone due to the fact of her physical disability. Since many instances of physical disability begin with convalescence in a medical setting, the process of stigma recognition usually begins with the development of strategies designed to reduce stress in the physical and independence-support components of the self-state. This is why the attitudes and techniques of professionals staffing medical rehabilitation facilities are so critical to the future restoration of an individual's self-state. Beginning with the basic physical functions and developing these functions to facilitate strategies for taking care of personal needs as independently as possible is most critical. "You can't do that!" or "You can't do it that way" not only negate initial attempts at developing task-oriented strategies; more importantly, such remarks may actually restrict the stigma recognition process.

With minimal abilities and limited values placed on the physical and independence-support self-state components, an individual can begin to explore his strategy alternatives in the interpersonal, the creative-relaxation, and eventually, the industrious self-state. It is here posited that this can only come from the entry into the stigma recognition stage of adjustment. If the individual is forced to rely too heavily on ego defense mechanisms, thus experiencing the same level and intensity of disability-related stress, his self-state, and its respective components, will not be developed to a sufficient level to allow for future exploration of task-oriented strategy alternatives.

After a variable period of time, the individual, recognizing his stigmatizing condition and having developed a significant number of strategies for reducing stresses associated with physical disablement, begins to fully assess the implications of his condition for his life-style, and more specifically, the different components of his self-state. He seeks out more and more sources of reliable, useful information concerning additional task-oriented strategies. He begins to use sources such as books, consumer literature, and other individuals who have lived through what he anticipates, which act as reality checks on his self-state assessment. He then enters the phase of *stigma incorporation*. Stigma incorporation, being the final stage of this theoretical frame of reference, is the state in which the fact of the individual's stigmatized condition becomes an integral part of both the majority of the components of the self-state as well as the total self-state. After reaching this point, the frustrations, conflicts, and pressures resulting from disability-related stress are minimized by task-oriented strategies.

To differentiate stigma recognition from stigma incorporation, one can compare the thought processes associated with each. The individual in the former state will often think of his disability first and foremost when planning some activity. This is not necessarily negative. In the latter, stigma incorporation, disability is not always first and foremost, but it is almost always taken into account. A critical aspect of stigma incorporation is that an individual begins to assess the positive things which accrue from disablement as well as the negative—such things as being free of armed services duty, having access to convenient parking facilities when and where they are available, and being eligible for certain programs such as vocational rehabilitation. Any of these listed benefits could also be perceived negatively, but their being seen as positive is an indicator of stigma incorporation. Such positive "fringe benefits" do not entail using one's disability as a convenient excuse, but rather realizing that there are benefits unique to individuals with such a disablement.

It must be remembered that both stigma recognition and stigma incorporation are phases that take lengthy periods of time to come to full fruition. It is quite difficult to distinguish where one ends and the other begins. It might also be stated that the beginning of stigma incorporation is not always totally positive. In fact, since stigma incorporation is achieved through an individual's integration of the stigmatizing condition into her total self-state, there is a reasonable expectation that the initial entry into this phase may be briefly accompanied by periods of emotional despondency. During such periods, self-destruction may even be contemplated. However, since the very hallmark of this stage is the use of task-oriented as opposed to ego defense methods for stress reduction, resolution of such despondency will usually be rapid and task-oriented. It is possible, however, under the most undesirable circumstances, that an individual could reach this phase and revert back to stigma isolation, with its almost sole reliance on ego defense stress resolution strategies.

In summary, stigma incorporation is very similar to what has been termed "self-actualization." It remains, for most disabled persons, an ultimate goal, not a fully achieved state. In this particular frame of reference stigma incorporation is very much a matter of degree. While never fully achieved, it can be achieved to varying degrees by the development of stress resolution strategies with a reality base.

STIGMA INCORPORATION: SOME ISSUES AND CONSIDERATIONS

With this brief outline of the process of stigma incorporation, we will examine some issues and considerations involved in applying this theoretical frame of reference to some of the more salient problems involved in the psychological adjustment to severe physical disability. The topics to be addressed in this regard will be: (1) the process of stigma incorporation as it applies to age of onset of disability and (2) some research-methodology issues created by this theory.

Stigma Incorporation and the Age of Onset of Disability

Earlier writing on the psychology of adjustment to physical disability (Wright, 1960) addressed the issue of congenital versus acquired disability to some extent. More recent reviews (Shontz, 1970; English, 1971b; and Roessler and Bolton, 1978) do not deal directly with this matter. ("Congenital" disability refers to disability occurring extremely early in life, usually from birth. "Acquired" disability refers to a condition occurring sometime later in life.) Wright (1960) reviews many "common sense" postulations regarding adjustment to the two types of onset. As Wright indicates, although common logic dictates that growing up with a disability would usually entail a different level of adjustment than would acquiring a disability later in life, little or no empirical research supports the advantages of one type of onset over the other.

Stewart and Rossier (1978) selected three critical points in the life cycle regarding adjustment to spinal cord injuries: birth, adolescence, and middle age. Children born with defects, according to this source, do not have predisability capacities with which to compare their current functioning, but do learn to "envy" abilities of others which they have never possessed. Disability occurring in adolescence, a tumultuous time of development, greatly interferes with the normal experiencing of career choice, personal identity, and sexuality. Middle age marks the initial decline in certain abilities, which is accentuated by physical disablement. How does physical disablement at these critical life cycle points affect the process of stigma incorporation? We will examine these three stages of development and attempt to illustrate the unique variation of stigma incorporation at each point.

Birth It was stated that a stigmatizing condition such as physical disability affects the self-state through disability-related stress. For a child born with such a stigmatizing condition, disability-related stress is, like most other things, learned. The extreme physical exertion of propelling oneself on crutches and/or in a manually operated wheelchair is "natural" to such a child. To him, in the social isolation of his home, family, etc., his walk, manner of speech, and eye-hand coordination are normal. He will, however, learn that he is different. Until he encounters such learning experiences, there will be little or no disability-related stress. Once such experiences are encountered, the induced stress will be handled in a manner psychologically similar to that of a person acquiring a disability later in life. The qualitative difference will be in the temporal spacing and intensity of such learning experiences. If the child is gradually exposed to situations in which his difference becomes obvious to himself, the resulting disability-related stress will be experienced by increments. If, however, he is protected from such learning experiences, the inevitable will someday occur and the intensity of the resultant stress will be almost identical to that of the newly disabled adolescent or adult. Gradual or sudden exposure to such learning experiences do not necessarily determine the quality of adjustment following such experiences. That is predicated on a complexity of factors, many of which were discussed in relation to disability and stress in Chapter 3.

Since an individual's evaluation of herself depends to a large degree on the impressions gained from significant others, the attitudes, reactions, and coping strategies of her family become critical to her approach to stress-reducing strategies. The reactions of parents, in particular, are important. It has been the authors' observations that the ego defense mechanisms employed by individuals to cope with disability-related stress are often also employed by other family members, especially parents. If denial, depression, anger, and hostility are very much evident in the family's view of the child, these mechanisms will be evident in the individual's stress reduction repertoire. If such strategies are in an overabundance in relation to more task-oriented ones, the child may internalize such an imbalance. Thus, she begins to rely too heavily on denial, repression, rationalization, or other such mechanisms. As will be pointed out more than once, the use of such ego defense mechanisms is constructive and serves "restorative" functions, to use Roessler and Bolton's (1978) phrase. It is only when they are used to the virtual exclusion of more reality-based, task-oriented approaches to stress reduction that they impair the stigma incorporation process. Thus, the perception and reactions of family members are most critical to the child's own perception of the meaning of her difference.

Depending on the nature of the child's immediate environment, stigma isolation, in a sense, could possibly develop more easily here than at other stages of the life cycle. If stigma isolation is the psychological process of externalizing the origin away from self, and one's disability in particular, it is conceivably easier to develop such a process if one learns to externalize such stress early in life. Also, it must be remembered that a child disabled from birth has no predisability state with which to compare current experiences. She cannot say, "They did not laugh at the way I walked (or talked, or ate, etc.) before 'it' happened." Particularly if such externalizing is reinforced by significant others, stigma isolation could develop to a greater degree than at other stages of disability onset.

It is difficult to identify specifically the factors promoting the development of task-oriented strategies in physically disabled children. A few general observations could be made. The first factor is whether the child is allowed to develop skills enhancing his independence. Here, other factors come into play, the most critical being the nature and severity of the child's disability. In the case of extremely severe disabilities, it is difficult for the persons caring for the child to assess the amount of independence which can reasonably be encouraged in him. The nature of the disability specifically influences whether or not the effects of the disability improve as a result of the natural history of the condition. For example, a child with a condition similar to cerebral palsy may gain abilities and functions as a result of chronological development and other factors. On the other hand, certain disabilities exhibit little spontaneous improvement, and may even become more disabling. For example, muscular dystrophy is a progressive disease and children with this condition exhibit continued deteriorating functions and abilities. Whatever is the case, the parents are frequently in a quandary as to the amount and kind of independence to encourage. Time is a most critical factor here. If parents and friends continually offer assistance in achieving tasks which the child could do, time permitting, the task-oriented strategies for achieving such tasks fail to develop. Patience in letting a child take twenty minutes to accomplish something which he could do in five, with some help, is difficult for many persons to sustain.

Accessibility to persons with knowledge regarding techniques and devices to promote task-oriented strategies is another critical factor. Those caring for the child may desire him to develop certain basic abilities. However, their limited knowledge regarding the techniques, devices, and other sources of assistance are limited in many instances. It becomes essential, then, that those assisting parents and others with disabled children have an extensive knowledge of the sources to which these persons might go to obtain various types of assistance.

Adolescence   The second critical stage of self-state development is the period of adolescence. During this period many physiological changes are occurring. Physical growth and sexual maturation are two of the more important such changes. Externally, the individual is experiencing changes in his social status. For the first time, in many instances, he is experiencing another group, his peers, as more important to his developing self-state than his parents or other adults in his home environment. With such internal and external changes in progress, the individual frequently experiences many new feelings and emotions which are unfamiliar to him. These unfamiliar experiences often make such an individual, disabled or nondisabled, feel "different." He is no longer a dependent child; nor is he an independent adult. He can no longer identify with and rely on the advice and comfort of his parents. As a result, he turns to his peers, who are undergoing the same internal and external changes. This group becomes almost omnipotent in its influence on the adolescent's self-state. All these interacting processes may result in a significant lowering of the adolescent's self-state threshold.

With the above processes in mind, one can understand how an adolescent who becomes physically disabled while he is undergoing such dramatic and significant internal and external changes is often overwhelmed by stress. He has just begun to explore who, what, and where he is, as well as who, what, and how he will meet adult life. Since physical adroitness and attractiveness are prized during adolescence, a physical disability which diminishes either or both induces considerable stress. Most importantly, disablement at this time confuses the individual's evolving schema of self. The lowered self-state threshold, the disrupted identity related to disablement, and the ensuing struggle to reestablish a conceptualization of one's self-state can result in an excessive state of stress.

To portray the situation of the adolescent experiencing physical disability as totally negative and devoid of any positive aspects would be a distortion. Since the self-state threshold is normally lowered during this period and since the total self-state is not fully crystallized, the process of stigma recognition can sometimes be facilitated. If it is recalled that stigma recognition consists of the acknowledgment of the fact of disability and the beginning of exploration of the effect the stigma will have on one's life-style, it may be seen that in certain instances the turbulence of the adolescent period may be one of the "better" times for the process to take place in the natural course of development. The physically disabled adolescent, with sudden restrictions on her freedom imposed by the disability, comes face to face with the fact of disablement. The resulting intense stress may lead to ego defense mechanisms for a period, but the rebelliousness normally characteristic of this developmental stage may also promote the development of certain task-oriented strategies, as antiauthoritarian as such strategies may be at this point. The reactions of the young man in *Easy Walking* are excellent examples of such strategies (Nasaw, Appendix B). Willie Nasaw's first venture to the "outside" after his medical rehabilitation consisted of riding wildly through his hometown with his friends, smoking pot, and going to a rock concert. The companionship of his peers and the positive mood induced by his "joint" carried him through his first encounter with the public.

Since the typical adolescent has not yet completely formed a static picture of where she is going and what she wants to be when she gets there, the ramifications of stigma might more easily be encompassed in such formulations. Also, as pointed out by Stewart and Rossier (1978), the hospitalization and confinement of newly disabled adolescents frequently places them in direct contact with older persons in the same newly disabled predicament. Such experiences frequently cause the adolescent to "age before her time." The rebelliousness, the lack of a fully developed self-state, and the experiencing of aspects of life "beyond one's years" all combine frequently to enhance stigma recognition in adolescence. If stigma recognition does take place as the result of these factors, stigma incorporation is more likely to follow closely.

Middle Age   Physical disability occurring during middle age presents problems that often differ from those of earlier developmental periods. The individual has usually achieved a well-defined social role. This stage, as pointed out by Stewart and Rossier (1978), is characterized by a "sense of decline and loss" of previous characteristics and abilities, e.g., loss of hair, endurance, memory abilities, etc. Physical disablement acts to accelerate the already sensed loss and decline. As pointed out by Safilios-Rothschild (1970), it is sometimes the case that physical disability is a welcome relief from a life-style which is dull, boring, and hated. For example, if an individual has worked many years at a job which she detests and has done so only to fulfill some social responsibility, physical disability with the accompanying impairment of the work role is, then, a blessing in disguise. More often, however, the middle-aged individual takes great pride in her achieved status and life-style. Disability, to such an individual, is an enormous threat and source of stress. If she is already threatened by younger, more capable persons, in whatever social role, the physical disability takes on all the trappings of an overthrow of the individual's perceived self-state. Such an individual, then, can be expected to employ a number of strategies, both of the ego defense variety as well as the task-oriented variety, in order to fend off the threat of social displacement due to impaired physical abilities.

As pointed out by many authorities (Wright, 1960; Safilios-Rothschild, 1970; McDaniel, 1969), a multitude of variables influence one's adjustment at this stage. The abilities most used to maintain one's self-state and whether these are seriously impaired will determine the intensity of disability-related stress. For example, a cardiovascular accident with minimal physical residual damage but considerable language involvment (aphasia) will have a very different effect on a mechanic than it will on an attorney, college professor, or an auctioneer.

The reaction of the middle-aged disabled individual's immediate family members will also influence his realignment of the self-state. The nature of his predisability role in the family nucleus will have a definite influence on the perceived postdisability status within the family unit. If he played the role of major breadwinner, problem resolver, or family leader, the other family members will possibly have more adjusting to do than he will. The floundering of these other family members to reestablish some semblance of stability within the unit will, no doubt, have an influence on the disabled family member. If, on the other hand, the individual played a more passive role in the family, his disablement might not be as stressful to the family unit, so that other family members might become directly supportive of the disabled member, focusing more on assisting him to develop task-oriented strategies to compensate for the loss and reduce disability-related stress.

At the period of middle age, the financial resources of the individual become critical. In some cases, the medical and other expenses incurred due to the disability may be deferred through insurance companies, Medicaid, Medicare, or other resources. If, however, the individual has been self-employed, or in a type of employment where little or no security in the form of insurance coverage was available, the economic impact of disablement, in and of itself, may be so overwhelming that the pending financial crisis consumes all the available coping energy of both the individual and the family. Before any other rehabilitation work is accomplished, such financial concerns must be resolved.

This has been a brief overview of how physical disability influences adjustment of the self-state in three critical developmental periods. The purpose has been to highlight the variations of the stigma incorporation theory at three different life stages. Incorporating a stigmatizing physical disability into one's self-state depends largely on the other developmental stresses impinging on the self-state at a particular point in time. Some such stresses enhance the process of incorporation, while others render such incorporation extremely difficult. By way of speculation, one might say that incorporation may be more difficult later in the life span of the individual, all other things being equal (which they never are).

STIGMA INCORPORATION REVISITED

In tracing the structure and dynamics of stigma incorporation, it might be well to review and summarize the total concept. Stigma incorporation has to an extent been achieved when the stigmatizing condition is integrated into the relevant component and/or all components of the self-state. Through this integration, task-oriented strategies are built into these components to reduce excessive disability-related stress. Unfortunately, there are no simple rules by which to assess an individual's degree of stigma incorporation. However, typically the individual neither ignores the condition which is stigmatizing nor dwells on it endlessly. Neither does he use his disability to manipulate others. The primary characteristics of stigma incorporation are reduced disability-related stress, minimal use of ego defense mechanisms; maximum use of workable task-oriented strategies for confronting major and minor problem areas, and recognition of the stigmatizing condition as a characteristic (but not the primary characteristic) of the self-state.

In the above description of stigma incorporation, we have attempted to set forth certain constructs which are possible to examine empirically, in order to confirm or refute their validity. Several stress surveys have been created. The one generated by and outlined in the publication by Dohrenwend and Dohrenwend (1974) could be used as a model to construct a disability-related stress survey. In their work, these authors presented a number of studies relating what they termed "stressful life events" to physical and emotional illnesses. A number of different lists of such events are to be found in this source, but generally most include such life events as change of job, trouble with superior at work, divorce, etc. The studies reviewed appear to indicate that the number of such stressful events over the preceding twelve-month period is related to both physical and emotional health.

It might be that differentials in perceived stress levels could be related to global adjustment. If such a relationship is demonstrated—if stress is found to be a crucial correlate of adjustment—then it might be better to study the nature and type of disability and its relation to stress rather than to more global measures of adjustment. Many projective devices, such as the Rorschach, Thematic Apperception Test, etc, with their obvious limitations, are still capable of assessing the employment of defense mechanisms. Mason and Muhlenkamp (1976) have used an interesting and validated way of assessing the defense mechanism of denial. These researchers, using the Multiple Adjective Affect Check List (MAACL), found that care givers (RNs, LPNs, etc.) tended to exaggerate the distress of patients who had undergone some type of surgical loss, as was demonstrated when the ratings of these care givers were compared to ratings completed by the patients themselves. Vander Kolk (1976) has also developed a voice stress test to measure the reactions of the nondisabled to certain types of disabilities. Although this study used the nondisabled for subjects, it is quite conceivable that such voice stress methods could be used to measure the intensity of areas of stress in the lives of the disabled. If the conceptualizations presented in this chapter are valid, then such stress indicators should correlate positively with measures of adjustment. With such measures and others, stress level and the tendency toward ego defense mechanisms could also be investigated. Task-oriented strategy may present more difficult measurement problems. However, empirical strategies for investigating these constructs can and should be developed in order to assess accurately the factors impacting on adjustment to disability. The results of such research will provide professionals with a clearer picture of strategies which can enhance their clients'/patients' adjustment to severe disability.

Chapter 13

Disability and Social Impression Management

In preceding chapters, task-oriented strategies for adjustment to disability have been discussed. There are many different types of task-oriented strategies: using adaptive devices, arranging one's living environment to accommodate physical limitations, and structuring one's daily routine to avoid excessive and unnecessary stress. However, one area in which it is difficult to reduce stress-producing effects, at least in any structured way, is social interaction. Social interactions may be a source of considerable stress, but they can also be, at the same time, a source of much personal fulfillment.

This chapter will:

1 Introduce the concept of stigma barrier
2 Relate the concept of social impression management to stigma incorporation
3 Describe crediting and discrediting performance from a nonverbal perspective
4 Apply the concept of social impression management to rehabilitation practices and research endeavors

THE CONCEPT OF STIGMA BARRIER

When a nonstigmatized person encounters an individual with a stigmatizing condition, the nonstigmatized person may initially feel set apart from or uncomfortable with the stigmatized individual. This reaction, which was discussed at length as a source of social stress in Chapter 3, may be conceptualized as the *stigma barrier.* An excellent example of stigma barrier is found in an article by Bogdan and Taylor (1976) entitled "The Judged, Not the Judges: An Insider's View of Mental Retardation." The subject being interviewed is relating his experiences as a former resident of a state school. Parts of this interview describe the devastating effects of stigma barriers:

> Take a couple of friends of mine Tommy McCan and P. Tommy was a guy who was really nice to be with. You could sit down with him and have a nice conversation and enjoy yourself. He was a mongoloid. The trouble was people couldn't see beyond that. If he didn't look that way it would have been different, but there he was locked into what other people thought he was. (Bogdan and Taylor, 1976, p. 51.)

This concept has many widespread implications. For example, naive students in the helping professions, when first exposed to certain populations of disabled individuals (for example, residents of a mental institution), feel this stigma barrier intensely. Such students are at once in a conflicting position, i.e., they have a fleeting and common feeling of aversion, yet at the same time, they feel guilty concerning this common reaction because of their commitment to their profession. They are ashamed of themselves, yet would not dare divulge this feeling.

What many people do not realize, however, is the fact that with persistence and reciprocal positive relating on behalf of both parties, such barriers disappear in most cases. The length of the stigma barrier period varies with the type of stigma, the personal attributes of the person with the stigma, the attitude of the nonstigmatized person, and the nature and course of the social interchange. The biggest problem appears to be that one party or the other is frightened away before the barrier can really be broken. Bringing the concept of stigma barrier to light may be one way to hasten its demise! More will be said regarding the role of stigma barriers in social interactions throughout this chapter. The purpose here is merely to introduce the concept. How it applies in specific situations will be dealt with in relation to specific aspects of impression management.

WHAT IS IMPRESSION MANAGEMENT?

Impression management applies to one of three major dimensions of what Goffman (1963) might term "stigma management," or others' adjustment to disabling conditions. The three major dimensions are (1) physical/psychological management, (2) environment management, and (3) social/interpersonal management. The first of these dimensions, physical/psychological management, refers to those behaviors one should observe to remain physically and psychologically healthy. (Although the term "healthy" is somewhat subjective and judgmental in nature, it is used here for lack of a better term.) Included in this category would be such actions as following medical advice and observing sound psychological counseling. Environmental management refers to those behaviors that ease day-to-day routine activities and facilitate the reduction of excessive stress which results from performing perfunctory chores. Ample literature and availability of professional advice, along with knowledge existing among specific affected populations, can assist the individual in the first two dimensions. For example, the book *You Can Do It From a Wheelchair* (Appendix E) is designed to assist persons in wheelchairs in environmental management. The *Archives of Physical Medicine and Rehabilitation* abound with articles on specific topics of interest to both the physical/psychological and environmental management areas for persons with physical handicaps. Social/interpersonal management, the focal point of this chapter, refers to those facets of a person's interpersonal exchanges which facilitate rewarding social contacts.

There is a paucity of practical, how-to-do-it material on social/interpersonal management, of which impression management is one facet. Impression management, for our purposes, consists of those conscious behaviors performed by a person for the express purpose of enhancing others' evaluation of that person. Zunin and Zunin (1974), in their book *Contact: The First Four Minutes* place emphasis on the initial impression which sets the overall tone of any interpersonal exchange. Kleinke (1973) also considers first impressions very influential in interpersonal evaluations. The purpose here is not to overemphasize the importance of superficial, brief encounters, but rather to suggest concrete ways in which brief encounters can be extended in order to break the stigma barriers and thus promote more rewarding social encounters for persons with handicapping conditions.

SOCIAL IMPRESSION MANAGEMENT AND STIGMA INCORPORATION

In the preceding chapter the concept of stigma incorporation was proposed and described to some extent. At this point, the reader may well ask, "How does social impression management relate to the theory of stigma incorporation?" Stigma barrier, which has just been described, is probably one of the major sources of disability-related stress in interpersonal situations. A condescending smile, raised eyebrows, and related reactions often produce stress within the stigmatized person. A question here might be: When is a smile actually condescending and when is the condescension merely in the mind of the stigmatized? To delve into this question here would entail a diversion from the main point of this chapter. For our purposes, condescending smiles, raised eyebrows, etc., are assumed to be validly perceived.

Such stigma barriers, being a source of threat or frustration, must be dealt with in some manner. Social impression management consists of an array of task-oriented strategies designed to accelerate the breakdown of the stigma barrier. The acumen of the individual in the use of such strategies is partly a function of the stage of stigma incorporation in which she is currently operating. If she is still struggling with stigma recognition, her astuteness in applying such strategies may not be as well developed as if she were in the final stigma incorporation stage. A related question here might be whether social impression management techniques result from the process of stigma incorporation or enhance it. Empirical research may eventually shed light on such questions. However, it must be remembered that social impression management as presented here is a concept with great potential as a task-oriented strategy for adapting to interpersonal stress. It is also a promising area for research into the psychosocial adjustment to severe physically disabling conditions.

CREDITING AND DISCREDITING PERFORMANCES: A NONVERBAL PERSPECTIVE

Goffman (1959), in his book *The Presentation of Self in Everyday Life* discusses the concept of crediting and discrediting performances. Goffman defines a performance as ". . . all the activities of a given participant on a given occasion which serves to influence in any way any of the other participants" (p. 15). In this regard, Goffman states that any major or minor "flaws" in such a performance will lead the intended audience to question the entire performance. In such a case, according to Goffman, the performer is giving a *discredited* performance. On the more positive side, when a performer's minor and major behaviors are congruent with (agree with) the impression that is intended to be conveyed to the audience, this is a *credited* (believable) performance.

For example, a performer (individual) with a speech defect gives a discrediting performance to the naive person (audience) merely by not producing a speech pattern in the expected manner. Or, an observer (audience) is frequently made uncomfortable and suspicious by a person who, having suffered a stroke resulting in facial paralysis on one side, smiles unilaterally. Often these are not conscious perceptions by observers, but rather register preconsciously as a feeling that "something is wrong here." Therefore, the credibility of the performance is called into question. If persons who, because of some physical impairment, routinely engage in behaviors which automatically call their performance into question, the most direct countermeasures are to: (1) make them aware of this fact and (2) give them some practical additional behaviors to add to their performance repertoire to dilute the effect of the other, discrediting, behaviors. A smiling face can go a long way to overshadow a speech defect. The distracting techniques described in Chapter 3 are another example of practical behaviors which enhance impression management.

Knapp (1972) states:

> The term *nonverbal* communications is commonly used to describe all human communication events which transcend spoken or written words. At the same time, we should realize that many of these nonverbal events and behaviors are interpreted through verbal symbols. In this sense, then, they are not truly *non* verbal. The theoretical writings and research on nonverbal communication can be broken down into the following seven areas: (1) body motion or kinesics. . . , (2) physical characteristics, (3) touching behavior, (4) paralanguage (vocal qualities such as tone and pitch), (5) proxemics (the distance between two persons interacting), (6) artifacts (articles adorning one's person), and (7) environment (pp. 20–21).

To summarize what Knapp classifies as nonverbal would result in including almost all human behavior except for spoken words which can have symbolic meaning.

Most discrediting or crediting performances involve a great deal of nonverbal behavior. Major authors in the field of nonverbal communication or behavior (Birdwhistell, 1970; Kleinke, 1973; Knapp, 1972; Morris, 1978; and Nierenberg and Callero, 1971) cite Goffman's concept. If it is assumed that a physical disability constitutes a discrediting performance or appearance, then the nonverbal communications conveyed by the presence of the disability play a major role in the discrediting performance. "Social impression management," then, is a way of describing a strategy for manipulating, altering, or in other ways controlling certain aspects of nonverbal behavior for the sake of performing more creditably.

WHAT IS AN "IMPRESSION"?

As implied in the preceding discussion on nonverbal communications, certain aspects of our behavior influence others' evaluation of us. Physical appearance, manner of dress, and gestures (body language) are all elements of "impression." One definition of impression could utilize Goffman's concept of crediting versus discrediting performance. Whether or not an audience views an individual's performance as real or unreal would then constitute the individual's impression. However, such a definition is, for our purposes, too general. Stated more explicitly, and borrowing from Gestalt psychology, *the total impression conveyed by a person is greater than the sum of the specific elements (behaviors).* It is important for the reader to understand that the consistent use of a specific behavior, for example, to convey a positive impression, may not always work. One cannot *always* display a pleasant smile (a specific, positive element of behavior). Any behavior can be inappropriate in some situations; for instance, one does not ordinarily attend a funeral ceremony displaying a pleasant smile! The key is the appropriateness of the behavior for the situation. In order to convey a positive impression, a person's behavior must be, in its totality, congruent and appropriate to the situation in which he finds himself. We can define an impression, then, as the sum total of behaviors a person displays in specific situations, which lead others to formulate a positive, neutral, or negative evaluation of his behavior.

AREAS OF IMPRESSION MANAGEMENT

Although we have defined an impression as the gestalt conveyed by many specific behaviors, in this chapter we will discuss selected aspects of nonverbal behaviors which we believe have the most potential for impression management for persons with severe physical disabilities. These selected aspects are: (1) physical demeanor, (2) physical distance, (3) facial expression (including eye behavior, gestures of the mouth, and postures of the head), and (4) vocal behavior.

In the discussion which follows, the reader may begin to feel that for every movement, look, or way of saying something, there is some deep, dark psychological reason behind that behavior! It may be well to remember an observation of

Morris (1978), who states that a nonverbal behavior functions on three levels: a physical level, a social level, and finally, a psychological level. Let us take the example of scratching oneself. On the physical level, one scratches because one itches. On the social level, scratching might be a desired behavior in order to exhibit conformity to some social group's rules. Finally, theorists in nonverbal communications say that scratching can, at the psychological level, indicate doubt, guilt, and a whole array of negative meanings. It is important to note that before a nonverbal behavior is interpreted for its underlying psychological meaning, it must first be examined for a physical or social meaning.

Physical Demeanor

Physical demeanor encompasses several areas of impression, including manner of dress, general physical stance, and overall facial expressions. As Nierenberg and Callero (1971) point out, the total impact of these elements on impression must be considered. If one element is incongruent with others, this will detract from the other congruent elements. A gross example in the area of dress is that of the well-dressed man in a custom-tailored suit, perfectly matched tie and shirt, and matching colored alligator shoes, with his fly unzipped! This single incongruent element detracts from the total impression of the well-dressed man which he is attempting to convey. In this example, the congruent element is especially detracting due to its total dissonance with the remaining elements. If the same man were shabbily dressed, the unzipped fly would still be somewhat incongruent, but not nearly so much as in the former case.

Most persons have an underlying belief that people should be respected for their inner worth and do not want to admit that the way a person is dressed influences whether he is generally accepted and shown respect. However, it is a basic finding in the area of nonverbal communications and impression management (Kleinke, 1973; Knapp, 1972) that dress does, in fact, have a most definite influence on how others view a person.

A major function of dress is to facilitate one's acceptance by peers within a specific situational context. This brings us to the recognition of differing dress codes for different situations. A commonplace error frequently made in rehabilitation is permitting or complicitly accepting a dress code congruent only for the rehabilitation setting, which may mislead the client to believe that all people in all settings should accept the same manner of dress. The attire one might wear while in evaluation or training in a rehabilitation setting is not necessarily the attire one should wear to a job interview or in some other social situation. This applies equally to dressing up for a situation as to dressing "down." The manner of dress one would wear to interview for a job as a mechanic in a garage differs considerably from the attire one would wear while interviewing for a position in a bank! Many persons do not realize that dressing up for certain situations can be as detrimental to impression management as dressing "down." Applying Goffman's concept of discrediting performance, if our hypothetical garage manager were interviewing a person known to him as a client of some rehabilitation agency, the client's wearing a suit and tie to the interview might reflect to that manager a lack of knowledge about the job setting. The client might be perceived as uppity, unrealistic, or otherwise unaware of his proper role in the situation.

Knowing a person to be a rehabilitation client may subconsciously "program" an interviewer to be more sensitive to any type of discrediting behavior. The general rules of thumb in any social situation are common sense, appropriateness, and neatness.

Another pertinent facet of physical demeanor is general physical stance. A client with a disability who keeps her head bowed and has a shuffling gait conjures up in the mind of others an image of inferiority, while a natural head-up, relaxed gait aids immeasurably in presenting a favorable impression. Also, it has been shown in some unpublished research (Johnson, 1977) that gait training in clients through the use of videotape feedback improves their own self-concept!

There are some physical conditions which pose definite problems in the area of physical stance. An example of this type of physical condition is extreme kyphosis (hunchback). Such clients naturally tend toward the head-bowed position in walking or sitting. Training these clients to hold their heads in a position which increases eye contact with others will facilitate their being more readily accepted by others. (As will be shown in the section on facial expression, eye contact, along with other aspects of facial expression, can increase interpersonal closeness.) Another example of a physical condition which poses physical demeanor problems is cerebral palsy. Here, however, the nonverbal aspects of communication become complex. Does the contracted or dysrhythmic bodily movement from the neck down disrupt interpersonal communications? Or is it the combination of this body movement plus facial grimaces which creates a negative impression? In the following section of this chapter we will be exploring some of the positive actions one might take to compensate for detracting aspects of physical demeanor.

Physical stance can create extremely subtle impression-management problems for those confined to wheelchairs. As indicated in the book *Bottom High to the Crowd* (see Kirkendall and Warren, Appendix B), persons who use an upright, standing position cannot understand how it feels to be always, literally, looked down upon. Therefore, being "bottom high" to most other persons may increase one's tendency to be more submissive, on the one extreme, or more aggressive, on the other. The authors know a number of adults in wheelchairs who are strongly attracted to all types of vehicles: all-terrain vehicles (ATVs), three-wheeled motorcycles, speedboats, etc. This attraction may serve one of two functions: (1) to put them in equal status with others, or (2) to allow them more freedom to move about in what would ordinarily be off limits to their "wheels." In either case, the old, simplistic explanation of "overcompensating" will not suffice. The use of vehicles allows for the satisfaction of needs that would also have been present were those individuals able to walk.

In many types of physical disability, physical stance is in some way impaired. The task of rehabilitation personnel should be twofold. First, the physical effect must be minimized if possible. For example, if an individual's gait is such that she often looks down to see what her feet are doing, she could possibly be trained to walk with her head upright. Second, if the physical stance is discrediting to the individual's impression, other features of her appearance which have greater aesthetic appeal should be emphasized. For example, if a woman's deformity of limbs, gait, or other physical features distract from her impression, and if she happens to have very attractive eyes, they could be emphasized through the use of cosmetics, etc.

Physical Distance

The concept of physical distance refers to the proximity between persons engaged in interactions. Subsumed under this topic is the actual physical contact between people, otherwise termed "touching behavior." In regard to physical distance, Hall, in *The Hidden Dimension* (1972), states that there are four distinct spatial areas surrounding a person during day-to-day social interaction. These four areas are (1) intimate, (2) casual-personal, (3) social-consultative, and (4) public. Intimate space extends from a person's exterior to a distance of 18 inches; casual-personal from 1½ feet to 4 feet; social-consultative, from 4 to 12 feet; and public, from 12 outward. These personal spaces can expand and contract depending on the culture as well as the specific situation. At a crowded social gathering, these four spaces would be different from those on a public thoroughfare. Nierenberg and Callero (1971) point out that certain other nonverbal behaviors are regulated by the personal space situations in which we find ourselves. For example, in an overcrowded elevator, each person's intimate space will be intruded upon by strangers. In such a situation, unwritten social etiquette dictates that each person in such an elevator *avoid* eye contact with strangers on the elevator with him!

The concept of personal space may be used to illustrate the psychosocial aspects of stigmatizing conditions. In the beginning of this chapter, the concept of stigma barrier was introduced. If any behavior would tend to heighten one's stigma barrier, it would be the intrusion of a presumably stigmatized person into one's intimate or casual-personal space. One instance highlighting this aspect of behavior is the tendency of some mentally retarded individuals to routinely violate other persons' intimate and casual-personal spaces. An opposite situation would be one in which a person in a wheelchair might have difficulty entering another's intimate space when to do so would be appropriate. If unaware of the caution a wheelchair user is taking to avoid causing physical injury, the other person might subconsciously perceive this behavior as a rebuff.

In entering these various areas of a person's personal space, one should actually observe the same (nonverbal) social etiquette as one does in entering another's place of residence. One at first stands in the other's public space (his front porch) and looks for appropriate nonverbal cues (knocks on the door) before entering the more proximal personal space areas, depending on the type of interaction to be transacted. A stigmatized person will normally be expected to "keep his distance" (stay well within the public space) until invited. If a stigmatized person ignores these social rules, he will tend to increase the other's stigma barrier. The saying "I'd walk on the other side of the street to avoid him" is a verbal expression of the reality of personal space codes. In the section on application of these concepts we will focus on ways of encouraging another person to grant nonverbal permission to enter his personal space. Here our objective is to point out the importance of the physical distance concept.

Kleck and his colleagues in a number of experiments (1966, 1968, and 1969) have indicated that nondisabled subjects engage in avoidance behaviors when interacting with the physically stigmatized. Included in such behaviors are greater speaking distances, terminating interaction prematurely, and being less expressive in the spontaneous body movements. Persons working with the disabled should be aware of these findings, since such avoidance tendencies on the part of others will have definite implications for the reciprocal actions of the disabled. For example, would it be wise for the disabled person to attempt to close such speaking distances too obtrusively? Should the disabled develop more "courting" gestures (to be discussed later) in an attempt to prolong the interaction? As stated earlier, subsumed under the heading of physical distance is the act of actual physical contact, or touching. Several publications dealing solely with this topic have appeared on the bookshelves. The foremost of these is Montagu's *Touching: The Human Significance of the Skin* (1971). Montagu postulates that to be touched is an essential need both in young animals as well as in infants and children, for later healthy emotional growth.

A study of university students cited by Knapp (1972) and Kleinke (1973) indicates that within our culture there exist prescribed social codes not only for who touches whom, but also for where particular persons (either same or opposite sex friends) may touch others. In adults the most frequent area of physical contact is the hand. In the above-mentioned study, it was found that females' bodies were touched more often and over a wider area than those of males. In general, adults in our culture are nontouching compared to adults in other cultures. It has been found in the United States that in even the most intimate relationship, i.e., courting, touching behavior is much less frequent than in other countries.

With respect to the concept of personal space, it must be realized that to touch another, one must be well within the casual-personal zone, if not the intimate zone. It is generally felt that touching is a sociable, positive behavior; however, a recent source (Henley, 1977) has a different view of the act of touching. Henley believes that nonverbal behavior can be classified along two dimensions: horizontal and vertical. Horizontal nonverbal behaviors are those exhibited between equals, i.e., sitting close together, relaxed postures, etc. Vertical nonverbal behaviors are those which demonstrate status between unequals. A boss walking into a subordinate's office without waiting to be invited in is a good example of the use of vertical nonverbal behavior. Henley is very emphatic in pointing out that touching behavior can be very much a part of the vertical dimension of nonverbal behavior. She states that ". . . the use of touch (especially between sexes) . . . [serves] to maintain the social hierarchy" (p. 95). Later, she further states, "It is, in fact, often considered an affront, an insubordination, for a person of lower status to touch one of higher status" (p. 95). It should be pointed out that the recurring theme of Henley's book is that we live in a male-dominated society and that the nonverbal rules for males are very different from those for females. Henley's thesis, however, is intriguing from the impression-management viewpoint. If, in fact, the physically disabled are perceived as occupying lower social status (Wright, 1960), Henley's observations regarding females and minority groups would apply as aptly to the physically stigmatized.

For the person with a disability, physical contact can, literally, be a "touchy" matter. Both as initiator and as receiver, the person with a disability must interpret behavior in this area in a special way. If the recipient of such behavior, he must determine if it represents true acceptance or a nonverbal put-down. If initiator of the action, he must consider how such behavior will be received (interpreted) by the other person. It is almost impossible to generalize here, because each such act must be interpreted in its particular context. Many stigmatized persons might subconsciously be "programming" themselves for rejection and isolation by either rushing in and touching inappropriately or, at the other extreme, avoiding physical contact when such would be normal and appropriate.

Persons with disabilities frequently encounter situations in which they feel (accurately so) that they are being patronized, but internalize these feelings by attributing them to their own paranoia. If, however, they were to review all the specific nonverbal, particularly touching, behaviors involved, they might not feel so paranoid. What they may have been observing was certain vertical nonverbal behavior directed toward them. For example, did the other person give the "politician's handshake" (the normal handshake, but with the person grasping the individual's forearm with his other hand)? This specific gesture, according to Nierenberg and Callero (1971), is seen by most Americans as "insincere and falsely ingratiating" (p. 33) if initiated by a relative stranger. On the other hand, a person with a disability might feel she was rejected or isolated in a situation, but if she reviewed her own specific behavior, she might recall behaviors on her part that set her up for such a reaction. Did she avoid close physical distance? Did she avoid physical contact even when openly invited? Are our nonverbal behaviors in such situations one form of self-fulfilling prophecy? In counseling and other less formal relationships, it might be well to explore such possibilities and encourage experimentation with alternate types of nonverbal behaviors to assess differences in the reactions of others.

Facial Expression

Probably the most influential aspect of nonverbal behavior on casual-social interactions is facial expression. Of all areas of nonverbal behavior, it has probably received more attention from both the speculative as well as the controlled research sectors than any other aspect. Since 1965, Ekman and Friesen (1975) have continuously conducted research on what they term "facial affect." They identify three areas of the face and six basic emotions. The three areas of the face consist of the upper face, a center strip running across the eyes and bridge of the nose, and the area from this center strip down. The six emotions are surprise, anger, fear, disgust, happiness, and sorrow. The complexity of facial affect displays is a result of the mixture of different emotions in the three anatomical areas. That is, a person may show surprise in the upper face, fear around the eyes, and disgust in the lower portion of the face. This is why it has taken years to accurately assess facial affect. A "pure" facial affect occurs when the same emotion is displayed in all three anatomical areas simultaneously, which is very rare in day-to-day interactions.

Another factor brought out by Ekman and Friesen is that an emotion in one area of the face may be there for only a millisecond. In fact, they liken the face to the sea, with waves of different emotions passing over it constantly. Even videotape or motion picture film, operated at the normal speed, cannot capture the waves. It can be seen, then, that study of facial affect is very complex, and oversimplified generalizations should not be made.

For present purposes, three specific elements of facial expression will be highlighted: expressions of the eyes, gestures involving the mouth, and the general posture of the head.

Eye Behavior   A great deal of material has been compiled from literary works concerning the eyes and their relationship to an individual's character, personality, and momentary reactions. "The eyes are the windows of the soul" is an expression which aptly describes the importance of eye behavior. Knapp (1972) classifies eye behavior into two categories: (1) mutual glances, more commonly referred to as "eye contact," and (2) pupillary reactions (dilation or constriction of the pupils). Pupillary reactions are difficult to observe except within a special laboratory setting. Therefore, we will concentrate on eye contact in this section.

According to Knapp, eye contact plays several roles in interpersonal interactions.* First, it provides feedback regarding the other person's reactions. Second, it is involved in what is termed "channel control," or the regulation of who is to speak and who is to listen. In fact, there is a complex interplay of eye behavior constantly occurring when two or more people are interacting. Third, eye contact can be indicative of the nature of the relationship between the interactants. Eye behavior between casual friends differs greatly from eye behavior between two persons involved in a romantic relationship, and these behaviors differ greatly from the nature of eye contact between two antagonists. Finally, eye contact can serve to decrease distance between two persons.

Much of what is written concerning mutual glance involves its use in intimate relations. However, according to Henley (1977), ". . . eye contact, like touching, has its negative side too. We don't like to be stared at, and believe it's impolite for us to stare at others ourselves" (p. 152). Therefore, when using eye contact one must be extremely careful. Henley also points out that gazing at another can indicate intimacy or the desire to be seen favorably by someone of superior status. On the distinction between gazing and staring, she writes:

> How may aggressive staring, however, be distinguished from non-aggressive "visual attention"? People may get cues from the length and type of eye contact (e.g., eyes wide open or half-closed, tracking the other's movements or riveting the other in space), as well as from other body cues (such as head slightly raised or lowered) and external circumstances (relationship, nature of interaction). Much further study is needed, though, to spell out these distinctions satisfactorily (p. 154).

---

*It is recognized that the rules of eye contact behavior vary with the culture or subculture being discussed. For example, Henley (1977) points out that eye contact behavior among American blacks varies according to the race of the interactants. The reader is cautioned that the present discussion concerns the general rules of eye contact behavior in the United States.

An interesting study cited by Knapp (1972) involved an interview between two persons, one of whom had been told the other was epileptic. In this study, it was found that the naive interactant tended to *increase* eye contact when told the other person was epileptic. Knapp attempts to explain such results by stating that the naive person was ". . . desperately seeking information which might suggest the proper mode of behavior" (p. 154).

It can readily be seen, then, that a high degree of eye contact cannot simplistically be equated with liking. Research also indicates that in competitive situations or in situations involving deception on the part of one of the interactants, there tends to be decreased eye contact. However, in a paper presented at the First National Conference on Body Language in November 1977, findings were presented that indicated that during the exact moment of deception, the deceiver tended to increase eye contact with the person whom he was attempting to deceive. As Nierenberg and Callero (1971) indicate, ". . . when [persons are] asked a question or when reacting to a statement that makes them feel defensive, aggressive or hostile, their eye contact increases dramatically" (p. 25). Eye contact can also be used to increase anxiety in others by gazing at them longer than, say, ten seconds, commonly called staring. This is especially true when the persons involved are strangers or are not well acquainted. In this type of situation, as indicated earlier, eye contact can indicate a display of dominance.

The preceding complex rules for eye behavior present many problems for persons training disabled clients in rehabilitation settings. The principles involved are abstract, and it is difficult, for instance, to teach clients the very fine difference between attentive gazing and staring. But, if our clients are to fully participate in society, teach them we must!

The knowledge that eye contact can influence the nature of a relationship is particularly relevant in working with persons with disabilities. The client who feels inadequate and thus avoids eye contact with others is programming himself for isolation and, possibly, rejection. Clients who walk differently, talk differently, or in other overt ways behave differently may induce extended gazing behavior in others. These clients may become threatened or defensive in this type of situation. One's initial reaction is to become hostile and stare back. However, stares can also be met with a pleasant smile and/or greeting that often elicits positive reactions and promotes constructive relations.

Eye contact is also used to decrease physical distance between two interactants. The courting couple at a social gathering will tend to increase their eye contact when physically separated, particularly when across the room from each other. As the couple comes closer together, their overall eye contact will decrease. At this point, little can be said about how this particular aspect of eye behavior applies to persons with disabilities.

Pupillary dilation or constriction has also been discovered to relate to certain aspects of behavior. Dilation is associated with arousal of interest while constriction is associated with disinterest (Kleinke, 1973). Some research has attempted to determine whether or not this aspect of behavior might be used to investigate attitudes; however, preliminary findings in this area are equivocal. On a practical level, it is difficult to apply the efficient use of pupillary reaction to increase positive social impressions.

Gestures of the Mouth   In combination with expressions of the eyes, the general way in which the mouth is held determines a large number of facial expressions. The small "smilie" stickers with the corners of the mouth turned up or down exemplify this aspect of nonverbal communication. Generally, when the corners of the mouth are pulled back and upward, this is considered a smile. According to Nierenberg and Callero (1971), there are three types of smiles.

The first is the *simple smile,* where the corners of the mouth are pulled slightly back but the teeth are not exposed. People usually use this smile when observing (reading) something amusing or interesting. According to Nierenberg and Callero, the individual is "smiling to himself." However, one of the authors has observed this smile used as a confirmation or acknowledgment when directed toward another. For example, if two persons are listening to a third party discussing some topic and stating an opinion or fact, the interactants will use the simple smile to acknowledge the fact that one of them has already stated something similar.

In the *upper smile,* the corners of the mouth are pulled back and the upper lip exposes portions of the teeth. According to the above source, this is used to greet friends.

The *broad smile,* with corners of the mouth pulled far back and both upper and lower teeth exposed, is used mainly as an expression of hilarity or laughter. A hybrid of the broad smile is the *oblong smile,* a tense exaggeration of the former.

In general, smiles convey positive emotions, except for the oblong smile, which conveys insincerity. When we force or coerce others to smile against their will, the oblong smile is usually the result. Naive persons attempting the broad smile may inadvertently produce the oblong smile, with disastrous results. In an unpublished pilot study, one of the authors developed some slides of disabled individuals in various social situations. In one particular slide, a young woman with a usually pleasant smile was instructed to strike a pose showing extreme interest. She extended her usual broad smile to the extreme, so that many persons viewing and rating adjectives from the slides later checked the adjective "phony" a sizable percentage of the time.

The mouth in a nonexpressive, closed, tense position or with the corners turned down generally conveys a noncommital or negative impression. This is usually termed a "serious" or "frowning" expression. The corners of the mouth turned down in the frown position convey such a common message that it will not be dealt with here. The serious look, when improperly used, can convey the wrong impression. Many persons, concerned with their image, equate intellectuality or professionalism with a serious expression. Used inappropriately, such seriousness can convey the absence of spontaneity.

Postures of the Head   Postures of the head are often determined by the physical heights of the interacting persons. The 5-foot 7-inch individual cannot very easily "look down" on a 6-foot 6-inch person with whom she is talking! In general, the vertical posture of the head is influenced by certain factors outside the control of the individual if she is to maintain minimal eye contact with the person with whom she is interacting.

However, the horizontal position of the head can be appropriately controlled by the individual. This position Nierenberg and Callero (1971) call the "head tilt." They point out that tilting the head to one side while looking at a person usually indicates interest. There are, of course, many variables involved here, but a slight tilting of the head can convey interest in the other person and in what she is saying. This gesture, combined with appropriate eye contact, can also convey the impression of intelligence, since most of us are somewhat egotistical and feel that anyone interested in what we are saying has to be intelligent! It would be an interesting experiment to teach appropriate head tilting beheavior, along with eye contact behavior, to mildly retarded individuals, to ascertain the effect of such behavior on others' impressions of their intelligence.

We may include the movements of the head along with head posture. The two most widely recognized movements of the head are horizontal rotation (shaking the head) and vertical movement (the head nod). In our culture, shaking the head generally has a negative connotation, while nodding the head has an affirmative or positive connotation (Morris, 1978). According to Zunin and Zunin (1974), a single, quick nod indicates agreement, while a slow, repeated nod is an encouragement to the speaker to continue. An effective counselor learns to use this latter gesture efficiently. The rapidity of these head movements, along with other contextual cues, can change the meaning of the gesture. Slowly shaking the head may indicate, "I'm not sure I understand."

Since the head and facial regions are the most critical in interpersonal relationships, it would seem advisable to devote considerable time to training the disabled in the use or misuse of cues of this nature. An attentive face, a pleasant expression, or an encouraging movement of the head might encourage others to focus on the person, not the disability.

Vocal Behavior

"It wasn't *what* he said, but the *way* he said it!" is a commonly heard statement that demonstrates the important impact vocal behavior has on impressions. Vocal behavior, in nonverbal communications, encompasses pitch of voice, rate of speech, vocal expressions (yawning, belching, etc.), unique speech patterns and/or characteristics (accents, nonfluencies, etc.), intensity, and a myriad of other qualities. For our purposes, the focus here will be on variations in pitch, rate of speech, and certain unique voice characteristics encountered in various types of speech difficulties.

The pitch of the voice (raising or lowering the tone) enables us to place emphasis on certain words. Raising pitch emphasizes words, while lowering pitch tends to decrease emphasis. As Knapp (1972) points out, we tend to lower pitch on the last word in a declarative statement, while raising the pitch (emphasis) on the last word in a questioning statement. For example:

"We are *going* to town."
"We are going to *town?*"

The italicized words signify increased pitch. This same mechanism can be used in a multitude of ways to vary the meaning of identical statements:

"*I* love you."
"I *love* you."
"I love *you*."

These three statements convey three distinct messages. Much of our pitch variation behavior is performed unknowingly, but it has a definite impact on the message conveyed.

Both Knapp (1972) and Kleinke (1973) review studies involving the pattern of speech on impressions of the speaker. Knapp reports that during a particular sentence, rate of speech increases over phrases which the speaker wishes to deemphasize, while the rate of speech slows, generally, on elements of the sentence the speaker wishes to emphasize. Kleinke cites research to support the belief that an overall increase in speech rate is indicative of increased anxiety and/or enthusiasm. It is also a common observation that raising or lowering the loudness of one's voice has definite interpersonal impact. Persons communicating with others whom they believe to be not very adept at language (the deaf, hard of hearing and/or "foreigners") tend to raise their voices, as if increased loudness compensates for a language barrier. Increased loudness thus has come to connote a feeling of being subordinated or otherwise put down on the part of the listener. At the opposite extreme is a slowed, elaborately enunciated speech pattern, which also connotes a put-down.

Frequently when a disabled individual is reacting to someone who has raised and/or slowed his speech noticeably when conversing, the disabled person, almost unconsciously, becomes irritated. At the conscious level, he will experience a vague feeling that the other individual is condescending, or does not respect him. If the disabled person then relates this feeling to a third party (e.g., a rehabilitation counselor or a friend), the disabled person will often be admonished that he is too sensitive, or paranoid. A task-oriented strategy for the disabled person to use with someone who raises and/or slows the voice when speaking to him is to comment in a very even, matter-of-fact tone, "Don't shout, I'm not deaf" or "I can't walk, but I'm not retarded, so don't speak so slowly." With a slow, overly enunciating speaker, a more aggressive strategy would be for the disabled person to mimic the speaker's vocal pattern.

Another aspect of vocal behavior which has particular relevance to rehabilitation is encompassed under the term "unique vocal characteristics." Included here are the range of deviant speech patterns often encountered in persons with disabilities. Studies reported by Kleinke (1973) tend to indicate that listeners' aesthetic preferences with respect to speech patterns do not affect their comprehension of verbal messages if they are interested in what is being said. Knapp (1972) points out that listeners' comprehension appears to become affected in the case of extremes of vocal qualities, such as severe stuttering, etc. Some studies even tend to support the fact that mild "negative" voice qualities, under certain conditions, increase the listeners' retention of what is being said.

Since verbal content is, superficially at least, the common ground of most human interaction, persons with speech variations frequently find such interactions extremely taxing. One of the authors, who has a mild speech impediment, is frequently reluctant to converse extensively via telephone, CB radio, etc., outside his normal professional and social situations. These media inhibit his ability to use compensating nonverbal cues, thus creating a stressful situation. Many persons without speech defects appear to share this reluctance. However, in face-to-face interactions cues, used properly, can be helpful in relegating a vocal deficiency to the background while bringing the individual's more personable qualities to the foreground.

Global Nonverbal Clusters

Up to this point we have considered specific elements of nonverbal behaviors influencing impressions on human interactions. There are, however, clusters of behaviors comprising many specific gestures which, when taken together, convey a general attitude or tone. Nierenberg and Callero, in *How To Read a Person Like a Book* (1971), give an explicit and well-outlined review of such clusters. They describe openness clusters, defensive clusters, evaluative clusters, suspicion clusters, etc. It would be redundant and too extensive to review the specific gestural composition of such clusters here. At the same time, some ways in which such clusters can be used in increasing interpersonal effectiveness will be cited.

The stigmatized person, if his goal is acceptance in a particular situation, might want to familiarize himself with Nierenberg and Callero's openness, readiness, and confidence clusters. If he feels he is being set up or badgered into compliance because people think he is a pushover, evaluative or self-control gestures might be appropriate. Nervous, frustration, and other negative clusters may also help protect an individual from someone else who is openly aggressive. A few examples of the constructive use of some of these clusters may help to illustrate their meanings.

The *openness cluster* generally conveys a message of open, honest, and accessible communication. Some specific gestures comprising the openness cluster are: palms pointed outward, arms unfolded, appropriate head and facial posture (a slight tilt and a pleasant, interested expression), sitting forward in one's seat (if sitting), moving closer to the other person, etc. This cluster generally gives the impression of friendliness and personableness. When used in an interview situation or in attempting to establish a casual social conversation, it is extremely effective. Another component of this cluster is appropriate eye contact. For some persons with certain types of disabilities, anatomical limitations will limit their ability to initiate certain types of openness gestures. For instance, the person confined to a wheelchair may not be able to sit on the edge of his chair. However, compensatory gestures such as the head tilt, increased eye contact, and arms unfolded with palms extended outward can help to offset such an anatomical limitation.

Many persons with disabilities frequently find themselves being pressured by well-meaning friends and/or salespersons—even by "helping" professionals. In such situations, the use of the evaluative, the self-confidence, or even the suspicious cluster might be effective in buying the disabled time to make their own decisions.

A hand-to-cheek gesture coupled with a furrowed brow and narrowed eyebrows at the inside corner comprise the *evaluative cluster* and will make any would-be persuader back off a bit. Straightening one's posture to an erect position, even if sitting, looking the person square in the eye, and putting the tips of the fingers together in a steepling fashion connote confidence and may be used to convey one's firmness in regard to a particular stand or opinion, once a decision is made. These are components of the *confidence cluster.* If the would-be persuader persists in his attempt to change one's mind, one may then want to turn one's body at a right angle and give him a sideways glance to convey that his persuasive efforts have aroused the *suspicious cluster* in the listener. Much has been said recently regarding "assertiveness training." The foregoing evaluative, confidence, and suspicious clusters will go far to support any verbal assertiveness on the part of a client learning to be more independent in his thinking.

The above summary is a cursory treatment of the use of gesture clusters in certain interpersonal situations. A thorough reading of *How To Read a Person Like a Book* or other sources such as Fast's *Body Language* will give the professional or client clues to nonverbal clusters and their uses in interpersonal situations. For the disabled who desire to feel that they are not alone in feeling oppressed by nonverbal put-downs, a must for reading is Henley's *Body Politics: Power, Sex, and Nonverbal Communication.* In her preface, Henley states, "This book is for those people who have felt oppressed by power, yet confused about some of the ways it is used to oppress them" (p. vii).

The Total Context: The Essential Link to Success

As has been stated earlier, the constructive use of nonverbal behavior in impression management of persons with disabilities depends on the total context and situation. One incongruent element may destroy the remainder of creditable impressions. Therefore, designing any program to teach such behavior would be an extremely laborious and complex task. If such a program were developed, it should consist of the following elements or phases: orientation to the role of gestures in impression management; the use and misuse of specific gestures as well as gesture clusters; situational role-playing practice using these behaviors; feedback on the effectiveness of role playing; and finally, actual practice in real situations with follow-up critiques and discussion of outcomes. Videotaping of the role-playing phase would be an important component of such a program.

These training programs could be used with a variety of disabilities. However, specific modules would be appropriate for particular disability types presenting unique problems in certain aspects of behavior. In particular, such programs for the mentally retarded would have to be highly structured, and multidimensional contingency training would be essential to accommodate the complexity of teaching nonverbal behaviors appropriate to the total context of any specific situation. Too often we teach generalities and do not focus on specific concepts adapted to varying circumstances. This practice would lead to total disaster in impression-management training. Caution must be exercised to avoid an overly simplistic approach to this type of training.

APPLICATION OF IMPRESSION MANAGEMENT TO REHABILITATION

The foregoing section has reviewed the elements of impression management with some attention to its application in specific situations. The present section will focus on a review of the possible applications of impression-management techniques to rehabilitation. In this text, we have extensively used global terms such as "adjustment," "coping," etc. This section is intended to specify techniques that, when used propitiously, will promote social acceptability and to this extent promote adjustment.

Living By "Their" Rules: Pros and Cons

When the subject of impression management for the disabled is broached, one is confronted with a basic philosophical and ethical question. Why should a person with a disability, or anyone for that matter, orient her behavior to impressing others? This is a valid question. A basic premise of democratic society is one's freedom to behave, within certain moral and social parameters, as one desires. Why, then, must it become essential to alter our usual behavior for the sake of acceptance, respect, or any other valued response from others?

There is no straightforward answer to this question. The answer will be individually derived, based on one's own personal values. If an individual wants to be accepted by others, then modifying her overt behavior is a desirable goal. If, however, she values her own personal freedom to be what she is above any type of social acceptance, then it becomes her choice not to change her behavior. This question then becomes: does one want to live by "their" rules ("their" meaning society as a whole), or does one want to live in a more individualistic style? The resolution of this question has definite ramifications for persons with stigmatizing conditions. If a person with a disability chooses the more individualistic style of behavior, she should recognize others' personal rights not to accept her. She should also recognize that lack of acceptance may eventually affect her perception of herself. From the introduction of these basic ethical issues, we can proceed to discuss the application of impression management.

The Four-Minute Barrier versus the Stigma Barrier: An Interesting Problem

Zunin and Zunin (1974) give the following explanation of why they feel the first four minutes of any interpersonal encounter are so critical:

> Why *four* minutes? It is not an arbitrary interval. Rather, it is the *average* time, demonstrated by careful observation, during which strangers in a social situation interact *before* they decide to depart or to continue the encounter. By watching hundreds of people at parties, offices, schools, homes, and in recreational settings, I discovered that four minutes is approximately the minimum breakaway point—the socially acceptable period that precedes a potential shift of conversational partners. Since people are not machines run by electronic timers, four minutes is an *average*, both real and symbolic, throughout this book (p. 6).

At the time that this four-minute barrier is operating, particularly between a person with an obvious disability and a stranger, both interactants are also coping with the stigma barrier. This might seem an impossible social task, unless the person with the disability is firmly convinced of two premises.

The first concerns the "tragic figure myth." This myth springs from the deification of normality myth (see Chapter 3) and operates within the nondisabled to the effect that they think the disabled are tragic figures who should be pitied. Such a ridiculous belief and attitude can operate to the advantage of a disabled person if she realizes that *anything* she does, particularly nonverbally, to convey the congenial "good guy" impression will disarm a nondisabled person and influence that person to perceive her as even more congenial than would normally be expected.

The second premise that must be kept in mind concerns the "his problem-my problem" quandary. This quandary frequently operates when a disabled individual confronts someone who behaves in an impolite, obnoxious manner. Unless very sure of herself, the person with a disability might tend to think her disability is the stimulus eliciting such behavior. However, if the other person tends to be obtrusive and obnoxious to *anyone* in *any* social situation, the individual with a disability can resolve this quandary quickly by assuming that the behavior is the former's problem and not her own. This assumption will probably be correct in most instances, and will produce within the disabled person a feeling of confidence.

The adoption of these two assumptions within the ongoing mental set of the disabled individual may be long and arduous, but once accomplished, it greatly eases social interaction. In addition, the firmness with which these premises are held will play a large role in determining how well the person displays appropriate nonverbal behavior in specific situations. As has been stated, if both the four-minute barrier and the stigma barrier are operating simultaneously, there is considerable tension in the situation. If the disabled person is relaxed and is impervious, nonverbally, to this tension, often the other person will begin to relax. There is, of course, no magic trick the disabled individual can perform to set the other person at ease. But if the person with a disability is convinced that she is not a tragic figure and that any tension in the interaction is usually the other person's problem, her nonverbal behavior will follow suit. This, in turn, will tend to help put the other person at ease and enhance the possibility of a positive interaction.

The Constructive Use of Openness, Readiness, and Courting Gesture Clusters

We all like people who appear to be honest and willing to cooperate and who, above all, appear to like us. The use of the openness cluster (a relaxed stance, eye contact, uncrossed arms and legs, etc.) conveys honesty, i.e., the person is being himself. When encountering strangers, a person who adopts these nonverbal gestures will, more often than not, be perceived by the other person as friendly. Likewise, those not adopting such gestures will often give the impression that they are unfriendly and do not wish to be approached. For example, one of the authors was passing through a student cafeteria when he noticed a disabled individual who he knew had previously experienced a lack of success in meeting new acquaintances. In this light, the author took a few mental notes regarding this person's nonverbal posture. He sat at an isolated table, had a stiff posture, wore a sour expression on his face, and stared down at his food, cutting off any possible eye contact. In addition, he was not dressed in characteristic student attire. He appeared to be lonely and bitter, and, by prohibiting any possible rewarding social contact, thus reinforced the tragic figure myth.

The openness cluster can be used effectively in encountering strangers, interacting with coworkers, and in many other social situations where friendliness is appropriate. This style is particularly effective in the classroom for relaxing students and establishing a freer atmosphere.

Readiness clusters are particularly conducive to expressing one's motivation and enthusiasm, and are useful when interacting with potential employers and/or superiors at one's work. Readiness is conveyed with both hands on the hips (if standing), chin jutting out slightly, intent eye contact, and sitting on the edge of the chair. It is important to emphasize that both hands on the hips are necessary to convey readiness; only one hand on the hip conveys femininity and/or impatience. This is a classic example which illustrates how the misuse of a gesture could produce erroneous and undesirable results.

Why should *courting gesture clusters* be included as a part of impression management techniques for disabled individuals? The reason is that the term "courting" is used to convey the idea of vying for approbation and attention. Gestures included in this cluster consist of straightening or curling one's hair, putting particular emphasis on certain articles of clothing, and other preening gestures. Scheflen (1972) also includes unobtrusive directing of one's palm outward, such as brushing back one's hair with the back of the hand so that the palm extends outward. Eye contact, appropriate smiles, and head-tilting behaviors are used sometimes to reinforce courting gestures.

The almost immediate effect such courting gestures have in the right social setting, e.g., parties and public gathering places, can be amazing. In an informal experiment, one of the authors taught a person totally unfamiliar with these gestures their use at a cocktail party. He had the person, a female, pick a male out of the crowd at random, the ultimate objective being to have that particular male, who was across the room at the time, come over and talk to the "trainee" in fifteen minutes. At the end of the experiment, the selected male had the trainee cornered; meanwhile, the perpetrator of the experiment left the room, receiving a furtive "What do I do now?" look from the "trainee." Such gestures when used unobtrusively during Zunin's four-minute interval can prolong social encounters and create an atmosphere for rewarding interpersonal exchanges.

The Constructive Use of Cooperation, Readiness, and Confidence Gesture Clusters

The reader may wonder why we again mention readiness within another group of clusters. This is because the ultimate goal of most rehabilitation efforts is successful vocational adjustment, even though other types of adjustment are desirable by-products. And again, readiness is an essential element of conveying enthusiasm and motivation, which are critical to one's evaluation by superiors on a work site. Looking busy and/or looking willing to work are desirable traits to display on the job. Along with the aforementioned readiness gestures, hand touching the face, unbuttoned coat, and an intent tilt of the head all convey interest and willingness to listen and cooperate. Conversely, folding one's arms and sitting back and/or slumped in one's chair (or slouching while standing) connote disinterest, defensiveness, and unwillingness to listen. Many employers will say about a client, "He just isn't motivated (or just doesn't care)." This is probably a result of the client's assuming such counter readiness-cooperative clusters too many times.

Confidence is first of all a state of mind, but when actually adopted it becomes manifested in certain gestures. An erect posture (even if one is sitting in a wheelchair), much eye contact, squared shoulders, infrequent blinking of the eyes, and the chin held forward all convey confidence. This cluster, when combined with readiness and cooperative clusters, is most impressive to employers. Again, practically speaking, a person with a disability cannot *constantly* display these gestures in his job situation, but at critical times (such as when receiving instructions, listening to new plans, etc.), they become effective displays of competence.

The Constructive Use of Defensive, Evaluative, and Dismissal Gesture Clusters

Up to this point we have intentionally focused on positive nonverbal gestures. However, just as nonverbal communication can be effective in promoting favorable impressions, it is also a handy weapon to use in undesirable situations. In fact, nonverbal communication is even more effective than verbal retorts or assertiveness because the latter actions leave the offenders an opportunity to retaliate. Nonverbal gestures, used appropriately, convey the same message without bringing up the issue.

Persons with disabilities frequently are confronted with problems of social rejection, e.g., a rude waitress or an obnoxious stranger. Such rejecting circumstances frequently stack the deck against the disabled person, since any retaliatory action on his part conjures up the tragic figure myth. In addition, verbal retorts are often welcomed by such people. On the other hand, in certain situations, sitting, crossing one's arms or legs, and moving toward the other person are all effective countermeasures. Appropriate retaliatory nonverbal action on the part of the disabled person satisfies his need for assertiveness, and yet often leaves the rejecting person in a confused, frustrated state.

For example, let us envision a situation in a restaurant where the waiter or waitress is rude. Sitting back in one's chair, with furrowed brow, a hand-to-face evaluative type of gesture, and continued eye focus on the object of one's wrath will tend to make the offender extremely uncomfortable. If he or she becomes so uncomfortable as to say something, a downward shaking of the head, an annoyed rolling of the eyes upward, or totally ignoring the verbal remark will suffice as a response to the remark. If, as usually happens, the offender goes back to his or her routine, one then resumes one's prior askance evaluation, which completely unnerves the rejecting person. Above all, one should remain calm and say nothing.

Another cluster which is effective in specific situations is the dismissal cluster, a nonverbal manner of "unrecognizing" a person conspicuously. The dismissal gesture is very effective with some persons who insist on inquiring about a person's disability. Such inquiries are often made by persons with the best of motives, but there are certain people whose nonverbal behavior betrays the fact that they are merely satisfying a morbid curiosity. For these persons, the dismissal cluster is extremely appropriate. In these situations the disabled person need not bother with niceties or verbal sarcasm, but may dismiss the person nonverbally.

The foregoing comments are not intended to instruct anyone in "kinesic karate," i.e., putting down someone merely to satisfy one's aggressive drives. They are intended to offer an alternative to not-so-effective verbal retaliatory measures in the face of obtrusive social rudeness. Nonverbal defensive, evaluative, and dismissal clusters are techniques which may be used discreetly in appropriate situations to avoid verbal altercations, which usually end with both parties losing.

Fortifying themselves with the contents of *How To Read a Person Like a Book, Body Language, Body Politics,* and other books on nonverbal communication (see References) can teach persons with a disability methods for dealing with varying social situations in a new and effective manner.

Despite the authors' enthusiasm for the potential of the nonverbal approach to social impression management, this approach should not be viewed as *the* answer to the reduction of interpersonal stress. It must be remembered that such enthusiasm is based on its unexplored potential as a task-oriented strategy for managing stressful situations. Nonverbal communication is a relatively new and unexplored field. Because of the complexity and the situationally relative nature of this aspect of behavior, there are many variables involved; therefore, simplistic rules and sequential, "cookbook" procedures are useless.

If what is now known about nonverbal communication can be accepted, however, there is a pressing need for applied research and development of practical methodologies for training persons with disabilities to use nonverbal communications in their day-to-day social interactions. Use of these nonverbal techniques may enhance their behavioral repertoire and facilitate the process of metamorphosis.

Chapter 14

Conclusion: Metamorphosis of the Individual and of Society

We hope this book has enlightened the reader about the factors involved in the process of adjusting to physical disablement. Severe physical disability does not have to be seen as a tragic end of things. It is, as the process of metamorphosis unfolds, also a beginning. What appears tragic and depressing today will not necessarily be perceived as tragic and depressing tomorrow, or five, ten, or twenty years from tomorrow. Even tragedy gets boring after months or years, and depression finds little room to grow in a life in which the days and weeks are too short for all the things one would like to do. Happiness tends to be a comparative thing, and if a severely disabled person finds his salary as good, his job as exciting, his house as attractive as those of his neighbors—is he deluded if he claims to be happy?

Surveys of research studies which explore the relationship between disability and psychological adjustment (Barker et al., 1953; McDaniel, 1976; Pringle, 1964; Roessler and Bolton, 1978; and Wright, 1960) show the same result again and again: no significant differences can be found between physically disabled people and normal, nondisabled people when measurements of both the type and the quality of their psychological and social adjustment are compared. Only those who still subscribe to the deification of normality myth will be surprised to find that the disabled are just as well adjusted and just as happy as anyone else. It isn't the final state of *being* disabled that's especially stressful—it's the *transition* to that state: the metamorphosis.

We are not saying that every cloud has a silver living—that every ugly duckling turns into a swan—or that everyone lives happily ever after, disabled or not. By no means. In this book we have criticized negative attitudes toward the disabled, but we have no interest whatsoever in pseudoprogress toward a more positive outlook if that "progress" is based on a fallacious wishing-will-make-it-so mentality. The human being who experiences permanent physical disablement sometime during his life should not be misled into expecting the miraculous return of whatever ability—walking, hearing, speaking, seeing—has been lost. But neither should he be misled in the opposite direction: into expecting to feel miserable as long as the loss remains unrestored. Both the miracles we hope for and the miseries we fear are failures of the imagination, which tends to use the imagery supplied by daydreams and nightmares to fill what is at first a vacuum, virtually devoid of any experience with relevant facts.

That vacuum fills rapidly for the person with a recently acquired physical disability. After the initial shock of the realization of a less-than-desirable physical state which will probably not go away, a person begins to learn new ways of doing what she did before—and ways of accomplishing, as well, some brand-new things. These new, different ways are, at first, awkward, stress-producing, and frustrating. But daily chores must be done, and some of them one enjoys doing, despite the hassle; thus, little by little, a person gets accustomed to a new modus operandi. What at first was awkward, painful, or embarrassing becomes just a regular part of living, incorporated into one's routine. After such habituation, the person begins to concentrate more on participation in life now rather than on what used to be or what might have been. It helps, too, when those around her cease to marvel at how "wonderful" and "courageous" she seems, and begin to take her contribution for granted. The blind musician is admired for his music, and not for the "tremendous effort" it requires; the wheelchair-using executive is honored or criticized (as the case may be) for how he runs his company, not for how he drives his car. To be taken for granted, oddly enough, is a major milestone toward metamorphosis.

By now it should be obvious to our readers that the process of metamorphosis we have been discussing has almost nothing to do with medical care and almost everything to do with education into an alternative life-style for people who are born or suddenly become physically different. Most of the troubles encountered by either an individual or society itself during a metamorphosis could be accurately filed under: Change, resistance *to* or Differences, fear *of*. And it's not enough for disabled individuals, one by one, to outgrow their resistance to change, or to conquer their fears of being and appearing different. The two kinds of metamorphosis are interdependent: the alternative living skills mastered by the disabled —using arms and wheels to get around instead of legs; reading with fingertips instead of eyes: communicating via a pay teletype instead of speaking/listening with a pay telephone—will be of slight use to them if society does not meet them halfway.

Society's metamorphosis has only begun, however. Even after the legislative breakthroughs of the 1970s, many parts of society are still very slow to change, very reluctant to meet the disabled halfway. That's why, in most places in America, the nation that put a man on the moon still can't put a wheelchair user on a bus. That's why a blind person with one or two college degrees still has a hard time finding a job. That's why millions of deaf Americans are finding that the phone company is still not very cooperative about helping them to communicate. That's why, in some areas, society's metamorphosis appears to be stalled by a backlash that asks, in effect: "What's in it for us? Why should *we* have to change just because *they* are different?"

The answer is, to alter a famous line: "What's good for the disabled is good for everybody." Let's look at the three principal goals of the disabled—(1) access, (2) independence, and (3) equal opportunity—to see what they mean for society at large.

1 *Access benefits all.* In the large meaning of the term, access includes not only removal of architectural barriers that impede the mobility-impaired, but also the elimination of communication barriers that hinder those with vision and hearing impairments. If you have ever lingered near an accessible building and seen a rock band moving heavy speakers and amplifiers, parents pushing a baby stroller, people using, perhaps temporarily, crutches or a cane, or someone who was old, or pregnant, or just tired, you probably saw them head straight for the same curb cut or ramp or automatically opening door or elevator which is essential only to the disabled—but convenient for a lot of people. Similarly, a recent newspaper article on the local book review page pointed out that the same Talking Book concept developed for the blind is now being marketed (on handy cassette tapes) to the general public—especially to commuters and salespersons who would rather spend their hours on the road listening to *Walden* or *Robinson Crusoe* than to a chattering radio or the passing traffic. Many disabled individuals have come to recognize that their necessities are everyone's conveniences. If history is any predictor, when accessible mass transportation ("kneeling" buses with ramps for wheelchair entry) is finally in general use, it will benefit more than wheelchair users who can't drive or can't yet afford a car. Such vehicles should prove just as helpful to those with a heavy suitcase on wheels, or a week's groceries in a folding cart, or a golf bag, or—who knows?—to bike or moped riders who would rather take their vehicles home inside a dry bus than outside in the rain.

2 *Independence benefits all.* Insurance companies are beginning to realize that it is vastly cheaper to restore the independence of an employee who becomes disabled—to rehabilitate and reemploy him—than it is to leave that employee dependent for life on a lengthy, expensive disability pension. The teaching of independent living skills to a disabled child or young adult can also liberate parents or relatives—or the welfare system—from the exhausting burden of providing total care to someone who is personally helpless and socially unproductive. Even when the prospects for gainful employment *seem* rather slim (and we emphasize *seem* because we know too many well-paid workers with extreme disabilities whose job success confounds all ordinary formulas for predicting employability)—even then, independence of any kind, to any degree, is a boon to be cherished. Whether the task is working or driving, dressing or bathing, feeding oneself or even just stirring one's own coffee, the urge is universal: "I'd rather do it myself." And when one person accomplishes what would otherwise require two, both are liberated: the weaker one gains power, a measure of control over his own life; the stronger one gains freedom from having to hover over someone, waiting to be asked for help.

3   *Equal opportunity benefits all.* We believe that human rights must be universal: that rights cannot be restricted to a privileged class or condition without losing much of their meaning; that full civil rights are just as vital to the disabled as they are to any minority; that segregation is bad for any group; and that the desegregation that mainstreaming and architectural accessibility are now bringing about for the disabled is the very same "idea whose time has come" still unfolding in human history. We believe that Martin Luther King was right when he said, "When any man is bound, *I* am less free."

When the disabled, through metamorphosis, become unbound, the freedom they experience ramifies and resonates through all the lives adjacent to theirs like a chain reaction. Example: a distant uncle and aunt came to visit a disabled niece and her husband. Seeing their pleasant apartment, their two plywood ramps for getting their wheelchairs from the parking lot to the sidewalk and from the sidewalk into their unit, and their new van, equipped with a lift and hand controls, the uncle's face broke into a smile that just wouldn't quit. "Well!" he declared. "After this I'm not going to worry about you any more!" It became clear that he and his wife had discussed their disabled niece many a time in the years since they had seen her last (which was before she had achieved independence and married). Her image as a largely helpless and dependent person, and the thought of the many hardships her disability then entailed, had been recurrent stresses troubling their conversation and gnawing at their souls for all those years. The visit became a festive one: instead of fixing or fetching things, as they had expected to do, the aunt and uncle could relax, enjoying their niece's hospitality, discussing Texas, travel, and retirement, and comparing the merits of vans and campers. The metamorphosis of one disabled couple had liberated another couple, who until then had been less free because someone a thousand miles away, whom they had known years before, had been known and remembered as bound.

Multiply that example by all the aunts and uncles, cousins, brothers and sisters, parents, grandparents, friends, neighbors, and acquaintances of America's 36 million disabled citizens, and you have an image of the psychic burden, the mental chains, that the mere awareness of physical disability places on the minds and hearts of *those who are not themselves disabled.* Metamorphosis can change—is changing—all that. Metamorphosis makes thoroughly obsolete the former notion of what it means to have a disability, to be handicapped: the tin cup, the cheap pencils, the eyes that plead for a handout—and replaces it with a new reality: the active, independent disabled person who works her own job, manages her own home, and looks the world straight in the eyes when she says: "Do me the favor of *not* doing me any favors. Just give me the tools to be independent, and I can do for myself."

References

Administrative order no. 78-7. *Amicus*, July/August 1978, *3*, 4.

Anderson, M. Power to the crips. *Human Behavior*, 1977, *6*, 48–49.

Anderson, T. An alternative frame of reference for rehabilitation: The helping process versus the medical model. *Archives of Physical Medicine and Rehabilitation*, 1975, *56*, 101–104.

Barker, R. S., Wright, B. A., & Gonick, M. R. *Adjustment to physical handicap and illness: A survey of the social psychology of physique and disability.* 2d Ed. New York: Social Science Research Bulletin 55, 1953.

Barker, R. S., Wright, B. A., Meyerson, L., & Gonick, M. R. *Adjustment to physical handicap and illness: A survey of the social psychology of physique and disability.* New York: Social Science Research Council, 1953.

Barkman, A. H., Weissman, H., & Frielich, M. H. Sexual adjustment of spinal cord injured veterans living in the community. *Archives of Physical Medicine and Rehabilitation*, 1978, *59*, 29–33.

Barnes v. Converse College. *Amicus*, July/August 1978, *3*, 4; September 1977, *2*, 5.

Barrell, R. P., DeWolfe, A. S., & Cummings, J. W. A measure of staff attitudes toward care of physically ill patients. *Journal of Consulting Psychology*, 1965, *29*, 218–222.

———, ——— & ———. Personnel attitudes and patients' emotional responses to hospitalization for physical illness. *Journal of Psychology*, 1967, *65*, 253–260.

Barrier Free Design, United Nations Expert Group Meeting on Barrier Free Design, Rehabilitation International, June, 1975.

Barrier Free Site Design. Washington, D.C.: Department of Housing and Urban Development, U.S. Government Printing Office, 1976.

Becker, E. *Denial of death.* New York: Free Press, 1973.

Bennett, R. L., & Knowlton, G. C. Overwork weakness in partially denervated skeletal muscles. *Archives of Physical Medicine and Rehabilitation,* 1965, *46,* 22–29.

Bernard, H., & Huckins, W. *Dynamics of personal adjustment.* Boston: Holbrook Press, 1971.

Bigge, J., & O'Donnell, P. (Eds.). *Teaching individuals with physical and multiple disabilities.* Columbus, Ohio: Charles E. Merrill, 1976.

Bills that have become law in the 95th Congress. *Handicapped Americans Report, 1,* 1, 7.

Birdwhistell, R. *Kinesics and context.* Philadelphia: University of Pennsylvania Press, 1970.

Bitter, J. A. *Introduction to rehabilitation.* St. Louis: C. V. Mosby, 1979.

Black, H. C. *Black's Law Dictionary.* 5th ed. St. Paul, Minn.: West Publishing, 1979.

Blank, J. P. *19 steps up the mountain: The story of the DeBolt family.* Philadelphia: J. B. Lippincott Company, 1976.

Blue, R. *Sex education and the mentally retarded.* Unpublished manual, 1974.

Bogdan, E., & Taylor, R. The judged, not the judges: An insider's view of mental retardation. *American Psychologist,* 1976, *30,* 50–56.

Borden v. Rohr, et al. *Amicus,* March 1976, *1,* 3.

Bradfield, R., & Heifetz, J. Education of the severely and profoundly handicapped. In J. Bigge & P. O'Donnell (Eds.), *Teaching individuals with physical and multiple disabilities.* Columbus, Ohio: Charles E. Merrill, 1976.

Bregman, S., & Hadley, R. G. Sexual adjustment and feminine attractiveness among spinal cord injured women. *Archives of Physical Medicine and Rehabilitation,* 1976, *57,* 448–450.

Brown, C. *Down all the days.* Greenwich, Conn.: Fawcett Publications, Inc., 1970.

Bruck, L. *Access.* New York: Random House, 1978.

Burgdorf, R. *The legal rights of handicapped persons: Cases, materials and text,* Baltimore: Paul H. Brooks, 1980.

Burton, T., & Hirshoren, A. The education of severely and profoundly retarded children: Are we sacrificing the child to the concept? *Exceptional Children,* May 1979, *45,* 8, 598–603.

Camenisch v. the University of Texas, *Amicus,* July/August, 1978, *3,* 4.

Cameron, P., Gnadinger, D., Kostin, J., & Kostin, M. The life satisfaction of nonnormal persons. *Journal of Consulting and Clinical Psychology,* 1973, *41,* 207–214.

Camp. F. *Two wheelchairs and a family of three.* Wheaton, Ill.: Tyndale House Publishers, 1973.

Cardwell, V. *Cerebral palsy: Advances in understanding and care.* New York: North River Press, 1956.

Carelli, H. High court hands down mixed bag of rulings on minorities. *Memphis Commercial Appeal,* July 8, 1979, p. 14.

Carpenter, J. O. Changing roles and disagreement in families with disabled husbands. *Archives of Physical Medicine and Rehabilitation,* 1974, *55,* 272–274.

Carty, L. A. Advocacy. In R. M. Goldenson, J. Dunham, & C. Dunham (Eds.), *Disability and rehabilitation handbook.* New York: McGraw-Hill, 1978.

Cherry, et al. v. Mathews, et al. *Amicus,* February 1977, *2,* 2.

Childress, J. Who shall live when not all can live? *Surroundings,* 1970, *53,* 339–362.

The Coalition, February 1977, *1,* 1.

Cobb, A. B. (Ed.). *Medical and psychological aspects of disability.* Springfield, Ill.: Charles C Thomas, 1973.

Cochran, P. Pejorative terms and attitudinal barriers. *Archives of Physical Medicine and Rehabilitation*, 1977, *58*, 499–504.

Cohen, S. *Special people*. Englewood Cliffs, N.J.: Prentice-Hall, 1977.

Coleman, J. *Abnormal psychology and modern life*. Chicago: Scott, Foresman, 1964.

Coleman v. Darden, et al. *Amicus*, September 1977, *2*, 5.

Colen, B. D. Doctors decide on life support end. *Washington Post*, March 10, 1974, A1, A10.

Comarr, A. E. Marriage and divorce among patients with spinal cord injury I through V. *Proceedings of the Veterans Administration Spinal Cord Injury Conference*, 1962, *11*, 163–215.

Comer, R. J., & Piliavin, J. A. Effects of physical deviance upon face-to-face interaction: Other side. *Journal of Personality and Social Psychology*, 1972, *23*, 33–39.

Commercial Appeal, Memphis, Tennessee, November 16, 1975.

———. Memphis, Tennessee, May 16, 1976.

———. Memphis, Tennessee, August 6, 1977.

———. Memphis, Tennessee, October 23, 1977.

———. Memphis, Tennessee, February 5, 1978, p. 22.

Connecticut Institute for the Blind v. Connecticut Commission on Human Rights and Opportunities. *Amicus*, November/ December 1978, *3*, 6.

Conner, J. R., & Leitner, L. A. Traumatic quadriplegia: A comprehensive review. *Journal of Rehabilitation*, 1971, *37*, 14–20.

Cook, D., Psychological aspects of spinal cord injury. *Rehabilitation Counseling Bulletin*, 1976, *19*, 535–543.

Cort v. Ash (422 U.S. 76), 1975.

Crawford v. University of North Carolina. *Amicus*, September 1977, *2*, 5.

Cripples Journal. Oswestry, England: Central Council for the Care of Cripples, 1925.

Davis, F. Deviance disavowal: management of strained interaction by visibly handicapped. *Social Problems*, 1961, *9*, 120–132.

Davis, M. S. Attitudinal-behavioral aspects of the doctor-patient relationship as expressed and exhibited by medical students and their mentors. *Journal of Medical Education*, 1968, *43*, 337–343.

Davis v. Bucher. *Amicus*, September/October 1978, *3*, 5.

Dembo, T. Utilization of psychological knowledge in rehabilitation. *Welfare in Review*, 1970, *8*, 1–7.

Department of Health, Education, and Welfare. *Vocational evaluation and work adjustment services in vocational rehabilitation*. Washington, D.C.: HEW, 1972.

Deyoe, F. S., Jr. Spinal cord injury: Long-term follow-up of veterans. *Archives of Physical Medicine and Rehabilitation*, 1972, *53*, 523–529.

Dohrenwend, B., & Dohrenwend, B. (Eds.). *Stress life events: Their nature and effects*. New York: John Wiley & Sons, 1974.

Dolan, E., & Dolan, F. How we made our home accessible! *Accent on Living*, 1977, *22*, 24–30.

Donnie R. v. Wood, et al. *Amicus*, November 1977, *2*, 6.

Dowd, E., & Emener, W. Lifeboat counseling: The issue of survival decisions. *Journal of Rehabilitation*, 1978, *44*, 34–36.

Drennon v. Philadelphia General Hospital. *Amicus*, September 1976, *1*, 6.

Duff, R., & Campbell, A. Moral and ethical dilemmas in the special-care nursery. *New England Journal of Medicine*, 1973, *289*, 890–894.

Dunham, J. Blindness and visual impairment. In R. M. Goldenson, J. Dunham, & C. Dunham (Eds.), *Disability and rehabilitation handbook*. New York: McGraw-Hill, 1978.

————. Transportation. In R. M. Goldenson, J. Dunham, & C. Dunham (Eds.), *Disability and rehabilitation handbook*. New York: McGraw-Hill, 1978.

————, & Dunham, C. Hearing disorders. In R. M. Goldenson, J. Dunham, & C. Dunham (Eds.), *Disability and rehabilitation handbook*. New York: McGraw-Hill, 1978.

Dunn, L. M. (Ed.). *Exceptional children in the schools*. (2nd Ed.). New York: Holt, 1973.

Dunn, M. Satisfactions with social relationships of college students who are physically disabled. Unpublished dissertation, University of Illinois, 1967.

Duran v. City of Tampa. *Amicus*, September/October 1978, *3*, 5.

Eareckson, J., & Musser, J. *Joni*. Minneapolis, Minn.: World Wide Publications, 1976.

Eastern PVA position paper: access to mass transit buses for the wheelchair bound disabled. *Paraplegia News*, 1977, *30*, 24–25.

Ekman, P., & Friesen, W. *Unmasking the face*. Englewood Cliffs, N.J.: Prentice-Hall, 1975.

El Ghatit, A. E., & Hanson, R. W. Marriage and divorce after spinal cord injury. *Archives of Physical Medicine and Rehabilitation*, 1976, *57*, 470–472.

Emner, W. G. Professional burnout: Rehabilitation's hidden handicap. *Journal of Rehabilitation*, 1979, *45*, 1.

English, R. W. Combating stigma towards physically disabled persons. *Rehabilitation Research and Practice Review*, 1971, *2*, 19–27.

English, W. The application of personality theory to explain psychological reactions to disability. *Rehabilitation Research and Practice Review*, 1971, *3*, 35–47.

Farb, P. *Word play: What happens when people talk*. New York: Bantam, 1975.

Fareed, H. On intermarriage among the blind. *The New Outlook for the Blind*, 1967, 137–141.

Fast, J. *Body language*. New York: Pocket Books, 1971.

Fast v. Ross. *Amicus*, January/February 1979, *4*, 1.

Fay, F. Problems of the severely and multiply handicapped. In *White House Conference on Handicapped Individuals, vol. one: Awareness papers*. Washington, D.C.: U.S. Government Printing Office, 1977.

Felton, J. S., Perkins, D. C., & Levin, M. *A survey of medicine and medical practice for the rehabilitation counselor*. Washington, D.C.: U.S. Department of Health, Education, and Welfare, 1966.

Fenoglio, J. A. The severely disabled—a rehabilitation challenge. In B. Cobb (Ed.), *Special problems in rehabilitation*. Springfield, Ill.: Charles C Thomas, 1974.

Fiedler, L. *Freaks: Myths and images of the secret self*. New York: Simon & Schuster, 1978.

Fink, S., Skipper, J., & Hallenbeck, P. Physical disability and problems in marriage. *Journal of Marriage and the Family*, 1968, 64–73.

Fisher, S., & Cleveland, S. E. *Body image and personality*. New York: Van Nostrand, 1958.

Fitts, W. *Interpersonal competence: The wheel model*. Nashville, Tenn.: Dede Wallace Center, 1970.

————. *The Tennessee self-concept scale*. Nashville, Tenn.: Counselor Recordings and Tests, 1965.

Freed, M. M. The central nervous system; disorders of the spinal cord. In J. S. Meyers (Ed.), *An orientation to chronic disease and disability*. New York: Macmillan, 1965.

Freeman, J. M. *The practical management of meningomyelocele*. Baltimore: University Park Press, 1974.

Frieden, L. Community and residential based housing. In *White House Conference on Handicapped Individuals, vol. one: Awareness papers*. Washington, D.C.: U.S. Government Printing Office, 1977.

Fromm, E. *The art of loving*. New York: Harper, 1956.

Funk and Wagnalls standard college dictionary. New York: Harper & Row, 1977.

Funk, W. *Word origins and their romantic stories.* New York: Wilfred Funk Publishing, 1950.

Gardner, S. An open letter to single women wheel pushers. *Paraplegia News*, 1978, *31*, 26.

Garshwiler, et al. v. Marion County school district. *Amicus*, March 1976, *1*, 3.

Gee, H. H. Learning the physician-patient relationship. *Journal of the American Medical Association*, 1960, *173*, 1301–1304.

Gellman, W. Roots of prejudice against the handicapped. *Journal of Rehabilitation*, 1959, *25*, 4–6.

Gibson, G. & Ludwig, E. Family structure in a disabled population. *Journal of Marriage and the Family*, 1968, *30*, 54–63.

Gibson v. U. S. Postal Service. *Amicus*, July/August 1978, *3*, 4.

Gilbert, A. E. *You can do it from a wheelchair.* New Rochelle, N.Y.: Arlington House Publishers, 1973.

Glasser, W. *Reality therapy.* New York: Harper & Row, 1965.

Goffman, E. *Asylums: Essays on the social situation of mental patients and other inmates.* Garden City, N.Y.: Anchor Books, 1961.

————. *The presentation of self in everyday life.* Garden City, N.Y.: Doubleday, 1959.

————. *Stigma: Notes on the management of spoiled identity.* Englewood Cliffs, N.J.: Prentice-Hall, 1963.

Goldenson, R.M. Cerebral palsy. In R.M. Goldenson, J. Dunham, and C. Dunham (Eds.), *Disability and rehabilitation handbook.* New York: McGraw-Hill, 1978.

Goodkin, H. F. Transportation accessibility. In *White House Conference on Handicapped Individuals, vol. one: Awareness papers.* Washington, D.C.: U.S. Government Printing Office, 1977.

Goodyear, D. L., & Stude, E. W. Work performance: A comparison of severely disabled and non-disabled employees. *Journal of Applied Rehabilitation Counseling*, 1975, *6*, (4), 210–216.

Graves, W. Legislation. *Journal of Applied Rehabilitation Counseling*, Fall 1979, pp. 19–24.

Greenberg, J. *In this sign.* New York: Avon Books, 1970.

Grynbaum, B. B., Kaplin, L. I., Lloyd, et al. Methodology and initial findings in follow-up study of spinal cord dysfunction. *Archives of Physical Medicine and Rehabilitation*, 1963, *44*, 208–215.

Guilford, J. P. *Personality.* New York: McGraw-Hill, 1959.

Gurmankin v. Costanzo. *Amicus*, June 1977, *2*, 4.

Guttmann, L. Married life of paraplegics and tetraplegics. *Paraplegia*, 1964, *2*, 182–188.

Hairston v. Drosick. *Amicus*, March 1976, *1*, 3.

Hale, G. (Ed.) *The sourcebook for the disabled.* New York: Paddington Press, 1979.

Hall, E. & Cameron, P. Our failing reverence for life. *Psychology Today*, 1976, *9*, 104–108.

Hall, E. T. *The hidden dimension.* New York: Doubleday, 1972.

Halstead. L., & Hartley, R. Time care profile: an evaluation of a new method of assessing ADL dependence. *Archives of Physical Medicine and Rehabilitation*, 1975, *56*, 110–115.

Handicapped Americans Report, 1978, *1*, 1.

Hardin, G. The case against helping the poor. *Psychology Today*, 1974, *8*, 38, 126.

Haring, N. Perspectives in special education. In N. Haring (Ed.), *Behavior of exceptional children: An introduction to special education.* Columbus, Ohio: Charles E. Merrill, 1979.

Harris, et al. v. Kean, et al. *Amicus*, June 1977, *2*, 4.

Hayakawa, S. I. *Commercial Appeal,* Memphis, Tennessee, May 17, 1976.

Henley, N. *Body politics: Power, sex and nonverbal communications.* Englewood Cliffs, N.J.: Prentice-Hall, 1977.

Heslinga, K., et al. *Not made of stone.* Springfield, Ill.: Charles C Thomas, 1974.

Hiatt, H. Protecting the medical commons: Who is responsible? *The New England Journal of Medicine,* 1975, *293,* 235–241.

High court declines to review employment discrimination case. *Handicapped Americans Report,* June 22, 1979, *2,* 12.

Hirschberg, G. G., Lewis, L., & Vaughn, P. *Rehabilitation: A manual for the care of the disabled and elderly.* Philadelphia: J. B. Lippincott, 1976.

Hoch, Z. Sex therapy and marital counseling for the disabled. *Archives of Physical Medicine and Rehabilitation,* 1977, *58,* 413–415.

Hogue, E. Equal access to medical services. In R. Burgdorf (Ed.), *The legal rights of handicapped persons: Cases, materials, and text.* Baltimore: Brooks, 1980.

Hohmann, G. W. Considerations in management of psychosexual readjustment in the cord injured male. *Rehabilitation Psychology,* 1972, *19,* 50–58.

———. Psychological intervention in the spinal cord injury center: some cautions. *Rehabilitation Psychology,* 1975, *22,* 194–196.

———. Sex and the spinal cord injured male. *Accent on Living,* Spring 1973, 15–17.

Holland v. Boeing Company. *Amicus,* January/February, 1979, *4,* 1.

Hopkins, M. Patterns of self-destruction among the orthopedically disabled. *Rehabilitation Research and Practice Review,* 1971, *3,* 5–16.

Horn, J. Reactions to the handicapped—sweaty palms and saccharine words. *Psychology Today,* 1975, *9,* 122, 124.

Horn, J. Unpopularity contest. *Psychology Today,* 1975, *9,* 124.

Howard S. v. Friendswood Independent School District. *Amicus,* July/August 1978, *3,* 4.

Howell, L. Spina bifida. In R. M. Goldenson, J. Dunham, and C. Dunham (Eds.), *Disability and Rehabilitation Handbook.* New York: McGraw-Hill, 1978a.

———. Spinal cord injury. In R. M. Goldenson, J. Dunham, & C. Dunham (Eds.), *Disability and rehabilitation handbook.* New York: McGraw-Hill, 1978b.

Hugo, V. *The hunchback of Notre-Dame.* New York: Dodd, Mead, 1947.

Hull, O. B. Medical aspects of heart disease. In A. B. Cobb (Ed.), *Medical and psychological aspects of disability.* Springfield, Ill.: Charles C Thomas, 1973.

Hylbert, K., Sr., & Hylbert, K., Jr. *Medical information for human service workers.* State College, Penn.: Counselor Education Press, 1979.

Illustrated handbook of the handicapped section of the North Carolina state building code. North Carolina Department of Insurance, P.O. Box 26387, Raleigh, N.C. 27611.

Johnson, J. T. Gait training via videotaping procedures with selected psychiatric patients. Unpublished research, Memphis State University, 1977.

Johnson, W. R. Mental retardation and masturbation. Unpublished manuscript.

Jury, M., & Jury, D. Gramp. *Psychology Today,* 1976, *9,* 57–63.

Kampmeier, et al. v. Nyquist, et al. *Amicus,* June 1977, *2,* 4; March/April 1978, *3,* 2.

Kaufman, B. N. *Son rise.* New York: Harper & Row, 1976.

Kelly, L., & Verguson, G. *A dictionary of special education and rehabilitation.* Denver, Colo.: Love Publishing, 1978.

Kerr, N. Staff expectations for disabled persons: Helpful or harmful. *The Rehabilitation Counseling Bulletin,* 1970, *14,* 85–94.

Killilea, M. *Karen.* Englewood Cliffs, N.J.: Prentice-Hall, 1952.

Kirk, S. *Educating exceptional children.* 2d ed. Boston: Houghton Mifflin, 1972.

Kiser, B. *New light of hope.* New Canaan, Conn.: Keats Publishing, Inc., 1974.

Kleck, R. Emotional arousal in interactions with stigmatized persons. *Psychological Report,* 1966, *19,* 1226.

———. Physical stigma and non-verbal cues emitted in face-to-face interaction. *Human Relations,* 1968, *21,* 19–28.

———. Physical stigma and task oriented interaction. *Human Relations,* 1969, *22,* 51–60.

———, Ono, H., & Hastorf, A. H. Effects of physical deviancy upon face-to-face interactions. *Human Relations,* 1966, *19,* 425–436.

Kleinke, C. *First impressions.* Englewood Cliffs, N.J.: Prentice-Hall, 1973.

Knapp, M. *Non-verbal communications and human interaction.* New York: Holt, 1972.

Kovic, R. *Born on the Fourth of July.* New York: McGraw-Hill, 1976.

Kruse v. Campbell. *Amicus,* September/October 1978, *3,* 5.

Kutner, B. Rehabilitation: Whose goals? Whose priorities? *Archives of Physical Medicine and Rehabilitation,* 1971, *52,* 284–287.

Lancaster, J. Testimony before the Senate Subcommittee on the Handicapped of the Committee on Labor and Public Welfare. *Paraplegia News,* 1976, *29,* 32–34.

Landiss, C., & Bolles, M. M. *Personality and sexuality of the physically handicapped woman.* New York: Paul B. Hoeber, 1942.

Laurie, G. A compendium of employment experiences of 101 quadriplegics. *Rehabilitation Gazette,* 1975, *18,* 2–26.

———. A compendium of employment experiences of 25 disabled women. *Rehabilitation Gazette,* 1977, *20,* 3–17.

———. Housing and home services. In R. M. Goldenson, J. Dunham, & C. Dunham (Eds), *Disability and rehabilitation handbook.* New York: McGraw-Hill, 1978.

———. *Housing and home services for the disabled.* Hagerstown, Md.: Harper & Row, 1976.

———, & Laurie, J. (Eds.). A compendium of employment experiences of 21 more quadriplegics. *Rehabilitation Gazette,* 1976, *24,* 15–20.

———, & ——— (Eds.). Education/employment. *Rehabilitation Gazette,* 1974, *17,* 21–31.

Lavore, M. Legislation: A history. In F. Weintraub et al. (Eds.), *Public policy and the education of exceptional children.* Reston, Va.: Council for Exceptional Children, 1976.

———, & Duncan, J. Vocational rehabilitation: The new law and its implications for the future. *Journal of Rehabilitation,* 1976, *46,* 20–30.

Lawrence, D. H. *Lady Chatterley's lover.* London: Heinemann, 1961.

Lederer, W. *The mirages of marriage.* New York: Norton, 1968.

Legislation: New rehabilitation/developmental disabilities act amendments become law. *Amicus,* November/December 1978, *3,* 6, 8–13.

Lenihan, J. Disabled Americans: A history. *Performance,* 1977, *27,* 5–7.

Lewis, Royce L. Amputations and Amputees. In A. B. Cobb (Ed.), *Medical and psychological aspects of disability.* Springfield, Ill.: Charles C Thomas, 1965.

Long, C. Congenital and traumatic lesions of the spinal cord. In Kotke & Elwood (Eds.), *Handbook of physical medicine and rehabilitation.* Philadelphia: W. B. Saunders, 1971.

Lorber, J. Results of treatment of myelomeningocele: An analysis of 524 unselected cases with special reference to possible selection for treatment. *Developmental Medicine and Child Neurology,* 1971, *13,* 279–303.

Mace, R. L. Architectural accessibility. In *White House Conference on Handicapped Individuals, vol. one: Awareness papers.* Washington, D.C.: U.S. Government Printing Office, 1977.

Maguire, D. *Death by choice.* Garden City, N.Y.: Doubleday, 1974.

Maisel, E. *Meet a body.* New York: Institute for the Crippled and Disabled, 1953.

Malikin, M., & Rusalem, H. *Contemporary issues in vocational rehabilitation.* New York University Press, 1975.

———, & ———. *Vocational rehabilitation of the disabled.* New York University Press, 1969.

Mallik, K., & Mueller, J. Vocational aids and enhanced productivity of the severely disabled. In *Devices and systems for the disabled.* Philadelphia: Krusen Center for Research and Engineering at Moss Rehabilitation Hospital, 1975.

———, & Sablowsky, R. Model for placement: Job laboratory approach. *Journal of Rehabilitation,* 1975, *41*, 14–20.

———, & Yuspeh, S. *Bio-engineering services to the developmentally disabled adolescent.* Washington, D.C.: George Washington University Medical Center, Job Development Laboratory, 1975.

Margolin, R. J. Motivational problems and resolutions in the rehabilitation of paraplegics and quadriplegics. *American Archives of Rehabilitation Therapy,* 1971, *20*, 95–103.

Maslow, A. *Motivation and personality.* 2d Ed. New York: Harper & Row, 1970.

Mason, L., & Muhlenkamp, A. Patients' self-reported affective states following loss and caregivers' expectations of patients' affective loss. *Rehabilitation Psychology,* 1976, *23*, 72–76.

Mattie T. v. Holladay. *Amicus,* April 1977, *2*, 3; September 1977, *2*, 5; May/June 1979, *4*, 3.

McDaniel, J. W. *Physical disability and human behavior.* New York: Pergamon Press, 1969.

———. *Physical disability and human behavior.* 2d Ed. New York: Pergamon Press, 1976.

McKinlay, J. B. Who is really ignorant—physician or patient? *Journal of Health and Social Behavior,* 1975, *16*, 3–11.

McNutt v. Hills, et al. *Amicus,* September 1977, *2*, 5.

Memphis Press-Scimitar. Editorial, July 4, 1979, p. 6.

Merriam-Webster book of word histories. Springfield, Mass.: G & C Merriam Co., 1976.

Mesch, J. C. Content analysis of verbal communication between spinal cord injured and non-disabled male college students. *Archives of Physical Medicine and Rehabilitation,* 1976, *57*, 25–30.

Mitchell, J. C. Disabled counselors: Perception of their effectiveness in a therapeutic relationship. *Archives of Physical Medicine and Rehabilitation,* 1976, *57*, 348–352.

Mitchell, P. *Act of love: The killing of George Zygmanik.* New York: Alfred A. Knopf, Inc., 1976.

Mogetz v. Coppage. *Amicus,* November 1977, *2*, 6.

Montagu, A. *Touching: The human significance of the skin.* New York: Columbia University Press, 1971.

Mooney, T. O., Cole, T. M., & Chilgran, R. A. *Sexual options for paraplegics and quadriplegics.* New York: Little, Brown, 1975.

Morris, D. *Manwatching: A field guide to human behavior.* New York: Abrams, 1978.

Moses, H. A. I want to help. In C. Patterson & H. A. Moses (Eds.), *Readings in rehabilitation counseling.* Champaign, Ill.: Stipes, 1971.

Mosher, J. Employment and job placement. In R. M. Goldenson, J. Dunham, & C. Dunham (Eds.), *Disability and rehabilitation handbook.* New York: McGraw-Hill, 1978.

Mueller, A. Psychological factors in rehabilitation of paraplegic patients. *Archives of Physical Medicine and Rehabilitation,* 1962, *43*, 151–159.

Narot, J. R. The moral and ethical implications of human sexuality as they relate to the retarded. In F. De La Cruz & G. La Veck (Eds.). *Human sexuality and the mentally retarded.* Hot Springs, Ark.: Conference on Human Sexuality and the Mentally Retarded, 1971.

National Catholic Register, June 3, 1979, *1*, 9.

National Center for Law and the Handicapped. *Amicus*, 1977, *2*.

Neisworth, J., & Smith, R. *Retardation: Issues, assessment and intervention.* New York: McGraw-Hill, 1978.

Newland, T. E. Psychological assessment of exceptional children and youth. In W. Cruickshank (Ed.), *Psychology of exceptional children and youth*, 2d Ed. Englewood Cliffs, N.J.: Prentice-Hall, 1963.

Newsweek, The next minority. December 21, 1976.

New York City Transit Authority, et al. v. Beazer, et al. *Handicapped Americans Report*, March 30, 1979, *2*, 6.

New York State Association for Retarded Children and Parisi v. Carey. *Amicus*, January/February 1979, *4*, 1.

Nierenberg, G., & Callero, H. *How to read a person like a book.* New York: Hawthorn, 1971.

Obermann, C. E. *A history of the vocational rehabilitation program in America.* Minneapolis: The Dennison Co., 1965.

Office of Handicapped Individuals. *Programs for the handicapped, I*, January/February, 1979.

Omenn, G. S. Prevention through genetic counseling. In R.M. Goldenson, J. Dunham, & C. Dunham (Eds.), *Disability and rehabilitation handbook.* New York: McGraw-Hill, 1978.

Ort, R. S., Ford, A. B., & Liske, R. E. The doctor-patient relationship as described by physicians and medical students. *Journal of Health and Human Behavior*, 1964, *5*, 25–34.

———, ———, ———, & Pattishall, E. Expectation and experience in the reactions of medical students to patients with chronic illness. *Journal of Medical Education*, 1965, *40*, 840–849.

Overs, R. P., & Healy, J. Educating stroke patient families. *Milwaukee Media for Rehabilitation Research Reports*, No. 12, 1971.

Oxford English Dictionary. Oxford, England: At the Clarendon Press, 1933.

Paraplegia News, May, 1977.

Patrick, J. G. Little murders. *New Times*, April 1978, 32–37.

Perry, B. *Care without care.* New York: Avon, 1972.

Pratt, L., Seligmann, A., & Reader, G. Physicians' views on the level of medical information among patients. In E. G. Jace (Ed.), *Patients, physicians and illness.* Glencoe, Ill.: Free Press, 1958.

Pringle, M. The emotional and social readjustment of physically handicapped children: A review of the literature between 1928 and 1962. *Educational Research*, 1964, *6*, 207–215.

Pruet, R., & Pruet, M. S. *Run from the pale pony.* Grand Rapids, Mich.: Baker Book House, 1976.

Quick, A., Little, T., & Campbell, A. *Project MEMPHIS: Developmental progress in preschool exceptional children.* Belmont, Calif.: Fearon, 1974.

Ramsey, P. *Ethics at the edge of life.* New Haven, Conn.: Yale University Press, 1978.

Randall, G. C., Ewalt, J. R., & Blair, H. Psychiatric reaction to amputation. *Journal of the American Medical Association*, 1945, *128*, 645–652.

Richardson, S. A. People with cerebral palsy talk for themselves. *Developmental Medicine and Child Neurology*, 1972, *14*, 524–535.

Riel, D. The neglected minority. *Journal of Applied Rehabilitation Counseling*, 1977, *8*, 171–180.

Roessler, R., & Bolton, B. *Psychosocial adjustment to disability*. Baltimore, Md.: University Park Press, 1978.

Royal College of Physicians. *Report of the Royal Commission on the Care and Control of the Feebleminded*, vol. 3. London: H. M. Stationery Office, 1908.

Rubin, S., & Roessler, R. *Foundations of the vocational rehabilitation process*. Baltimore: University Park Press, 1978.

Rusk, H. A. *Rehabilitation medicine*. 4th Ed. St. Louis: C. V. Mosby, 1977.

———. *A world to care for: The autobiography of Howard A. Rusk*. New York: Random House, 1972.

Sadlick, M., & Penta, F. B. Changing nurse attitudes toward quadriplegics through the use of T.V. *Rehabilitation Literature*, 1975, *36*, 274–278.

Safilios-Rothschild, C. *The sociology and social psychology of disability and rehabilitation*. New York: Random House, 1970.

Salvia, J., & Ysseldyke, J. E. *Assessment in special education and remedial education*. Boston: Houghton Mifflin, 1978.

Scheflen, A. *Body language and the social order*. Englewood Cliffs, N.J.: Prentice-Hall, 1972.

Schilder, P. *The image and appearance of the human body*. New York: International Universities Press, 1950.

Sells, J. A., & Taranto, K. F. Health care utilization by persons with chronic disabilities who have been vocationally rehabilitated. *Archives of Physical Medicine and Rehabilitation*, 1976, *57*, 282–290.

Selye, H. *The stress of life*. 2nd Ed. New York: McGraw-Hill, 1976.

Sherer v. Maier, North Kansas City School District, et al. *Amicus*, January/February 1978, *3*, 1.

Shontz, F. Physical disability and personality: Theory and recent research. *Psychological Aspects of Disability*, 1970, *17*, 51–70.

———. Psychological adjustment to physical disability: Trends in theories. *Archives of Physical Medicine and Rehabilitation*, 1978, *59*, 251–254.

———. *The psychological aspects of physical illness and disability*. New York: Macmillan, 1975.

Siller, J. Attitudes toward disability. In H. Rusalem & M. Malikin (Eds.), *Contemporary vocational rehabilitation*. New York University Press, 1976.

———. Psychological situation of the disabled with spinal cord injuries. In N. Little et al. (Eds.), *Rehabilitation of the spinal cord injured*. Fayetteville, Ark.: Arkansas Rehabilitation Research and Training Center, 1974.

Sinick, D. Educating the community. *Journal of Rehabilitation*, 1968, *34* (3), 25–27, 40.

Sites v. Mckenzie. *Amicus*, February 1977, *2*, 2.

Smith v. Fletcher. *Amicus*, November 1977, *2*, 6.

Sokolow, J., Silson, J., Taylor, E., Anderson, E., & Rusk, H. A method for the functional evaluation of disability. *Archives of Physical Medicine and Rehabilitation*, 1959, *40*, 421–427.

———, & Taylor, E. Report of a national field trial of a method for functional disability evaluation. *Journal of Chronic Diseases*, 1967, *20*, 897–909.

Sontag, S. *Illness as metaphor*. New York: Farrar, Straus & Giroux, 1978.

A source book/Rehabilitating the person with spinal cord injury. Washington, D.C.: Veterans Administration, 1972.

Southeastern Community College v. Francis B. Davis. No. 78–711 (U.S. Sup. Ct.).

Southeastern Community College v. Francis B. Davis. U.S. Law Week, June 12, 1979, *47*, 4689–4693.

Special report: Accessible transportation: Will we get there from here? *Amicus*, January 1976, *1*, 8–11.

Special report: A history of section 504. *Amicus*, July 1976, *1*, 3, 12–14.

Stanton, E. *Clients come last.* Beverly Hills, Calif.: Sage Publications, 1970.

Stein, J. *Making medical choices: Who is responsible?* Boston: Houghton Mifflin, 1978.

Stewart, T. D., & Rossier, A. B. Psychological considerations in the adjustment to spinal cord injury. *Rehabilitation Literature*, 1978, *39*, 75–80.

Stoler, W. Letters to the editor. *Archives of Physical Medicine and Rehabilitation*, 1971, *52*, 393–395.

Strauss, A. L. *Chronic illness and the quality of life.* St. Louis: C. V. Mosby, 1975.

Sullivan, T., & Sill, D. *If you could see what I hear.* New York: New American Library, Inc., 1975.

Supreme court decides to hear first case on section 504. *Handicapped Americans Report*, January 19, 1979, *2*, 1.

Suran, B., & Rizzo, J. *Special children: An integrative approach.* Glenview, Ill.: Scott, Foresman, 1979.

Symington, S., & Shanks, G. Functional achievement in a patient with C-5 spared quadriparesis. *Archives of Physical Medicine and Rehabilitation*, 1970, *51*, 427–431.

Task Force on Concerns of Physically Disabled Women. *Toward intimacy: Family planning and sexuality concerns of disabled women.* New York: Human Sciences Press, 1978.

———. *Within reach: Providing family planning services to physically disabled women.* 2nd Ed. New York: Human Sciences Press, 1978.

Thorenson, R., Smits, S., Butler, A., & Wright, G. Counselor problems associated with client characteristics. *Wisconsin Studies in Vocational Rehabilitation*, Monograph No. 3. Madison, Wis.: Regional Rehabilitation Research Institute, 1968.

Time, August 11, 1975. (Kinmont).

Toffler, A. *Future shock.* New York: Bantam Books, 1971.

Trageser v. Libbie Rehabilitation Center. Amicus, January/February 1979, *4*, 1.

Trieschmann, R. Coping with disability, sliding scale of goals. *Archives of Physical Medicine and Rehabilitation*, 1974, *55*, 556–559.

———. Sex, sex acts and sexuality. *Archives of Physical Medicine and Rehabilitation*, 1975, *56*, 8–9.

Trigiano, L. L. Move that cardiac early. In Christopherson, V., Coulter, P., & Wolanin, M. (Eds.), *Rehabilitation nursing: Perspectives and applications.* New York: McGraw-Hill, 1974.

Trigiano, L. L., & Mitchell, J. Physical rehabilitation of quadriplegic patients. *Archives of Physical Medicine and Rehabilitation*, 1970, *51*, 592–594, 613.

Unified School District No. 1 v. Thompson. Amicus, November 1977, *1*, 6.

U. S. Congress. *Public Law 93-112, The Rehabilitation Act of 1973.*

———. *Public Law 93-516, The Rehabilitation Amendments of 1974.*

———. *Public Law 94-142, The Education of All Handicapped Children Act of 1975.*

Valens, E. *The other side of the mountain.* New York: Warner Books, Inc., 1975.

Vanderheiden, G. C., & Grilley, K. (Eds.). *Non-vocal communication techniques and aids for the severely physically handicapped.* Baltimore: University Park Press, 1977.

Vander Kolk, C. Physiological and self-reported reactions to the disabled and deviant. *Rehabilitation Psychology*, 1976, *23*, 77–83.

VEWAA. *Vocational evaluation project: Final report.* Menomonie, Wis.: Materials Development Center, Stout State University, 1975.

Vineberg, S., & Willems, E. Observation and analysis of patient behavior in the rehabilitation hospital. *Archives of Physical Medicine and Rehabilitation*, 1971, *52*, 8–14.

Viscardi, H., Jr. *A man's stature*. New York: John Day, 1952.

Warkany, J. *Congenital malformations*. New York: Yearbook Medical Publishers, 1971.

Weekley, E. *An etymological dictionary of modern English*, völs. 1 and 2. New York: Dover, 1967.

Weinberg, N., and Williams, Jr. How the physically disabled perceive their disabilities. *Journal of Rehabilitation*, 1978, *44*, 31–33.

Weiss, A. J., & Diamond, M. D. Sexual adjustment, identification, and attitudes of patients with myelopathy. *Archives of Physical Medicine and Rehabilitation*, 1966, *47*, 245–250.

Weiss, H. D. The physiology of human penile erection. *Annals of Internal Medicine*, 1972, *76*, 793–799.

Whitaker v. City University of New York. *Amicus*, January/February 1979, *4*, 1.

White, R. *The abnormal personality*. New York: Ronald Press, 1956.

Winkler, H. *Psychische Entwicklung und Krüppetum*. Leipzig: Leopold Voss, 1931.

Wolfensberger, W. The ideal human service for a societally devalued group. *Rehabilitation Literature*, 1978, *39*, 15–17.

———. *Normalization: The principle of normalization in human services*. Toronto: National Institute on Mental Retardation, 1972.

Woods, J. E. Drug effects on human sexual behavior. In N. Woods, *Human sexuality in health and illness*. St. Louis: C. V. Mosby, 1975.

Woods, N. F. *Human sexuality in health and illness*. St. Louis: C. V. Mosby, 1975.

Wright, B. A. *Physical disability: A psychological approach*. New York: Harper & Row, 1960.

Zunin, L., & Zunin, N. *Contact: The first four minutes*. New York: Ballantine, 1974.

Glossary

As mentioned in Chapter 2, the study of the psychosocial aspects of severe physical disability has a language all its own, consisting of conventional terms as well as a unique code system of abbreviations. The following is a glossary of some of the more commonly used abbreviations and terms.

ABBREVIATIONS

A-B, or A.B.—able-bodied An "in" abbreviation used by certain disabled individuals to refer to individuals who are nondisabled. The reference may or may not be derogatory in connotation, depending on the context: "We can't wheel around quickly like A.B.'s" versus "That's typical thinking for a dumb A.B.!"

ACCD—American Coalition of Citizens with Disabilities An umbrella consumer advocate organization formed in 1974 to work for the betterment of opportunities for the disabled (Carty, 1978). Its formation and efforts are explored in Chapter 8.

ADL—activities of daily living This refers to all tasks related to self-care, maintenance of one's immediate environment, meal preparation, feeding, and other related tasks. Mastery of ADL marks the beginning level of skill acquisition designed for independent living (Howell, 1978b).

AFB—American Foundation for the Blind A consumer advocate group designed to protect and promote the welfare of individuals with severe visual limitations. This organization also funds and prints materials for sightless individuals (Dunham, 1978).

A-K, B-K—above-knee, below-knee   Abbreviations describing amputations of the leg. Since the knee joint is critical to the full functioning of the leg, whether or not an amputation is above or below the knee becomes strategic. Training in the use of a prosthetic leg for an A-K amputation is usually much more complex than training in the use of B-K devices (Lewis, 1965).

ANSI—American National Standards Institute   A federal organization whose main responsibility is the establishment of standards for weight, measure, and other areas. It has the primary responsibility for establishing building standards for barrier-free architectural environments.

A&TBCB—Architectural and Transportation Barriers Compliance Board   The federal agency having primary responsibility for enforcement of federal regulations regarding architectural and transportation barriers. This board must "pull together" all federal laws and regulations regarding such barriers and oversee their implementation.

CP—cerebral palsy or cerebral-palsied   A term referring to a group of neuromotor conditions resulting in jerky, spastic, or involuntary movement and/or to an individual having such a condition. The common denominator of these conditions is a neuromotor disability, but frequently other severely handicapping conditions such as mental retardation and severe speech problems are involved.

DVR—Division of Vocational Rehabilitation   As used in this book, DVR refers usually to a local office of the Division of Vocational Rehabilitation. When reference is made to "the DVR counselor," this usually means a counselor assigned to a local office who works with clients. Other references, such as "DVR personnel," usually refer to the global aggregate of professionals in the field of vocational rehabilitation.

MR—mental retardation or mentally retarded   This denotes a condition of cognition limitations and/or an individual who has such a condition. It is generally agreed that there are three levels of mental retardation: mild, moderate, and severe. Such classifications are based on levels of functioning on a standardized intelligence test (Kelly and Verguson, 1978).

NPF—National Paraplegia Foundation   The civilian counterpart of the Paralyzed Veterans of America. It is a consumer advocate group for spinal-cord-injured individuals (Howell, 1978b).

OT—occupational therapy or occupational therapist   These terms refer either to a specialty area or to a professional working in that area. The primary responsibility of occupational therapy is the provision of services to enhance an individual's functioning in the area of fine motor movement. Such movements involve reach and grasp, eye-hand coordination activities, and other such functions involved in many ADL as well as other kinds of activities, such as work-related activities.

PHC—poor helpless cripple   This is one of the "in" abbreviations used by the disabled. It is usually a derogatory put-down of a nondisabled individual who treats the disabled in a stereotypic, patronizing manner: "He/she treated me like a PHC!"

PT—physical therapy or physical therapist   A field of therapy or a professional working in this field. The primary responsibility of physical therapy is to enhance an individual's use of large muscle groups (gross motor movement). Gross motor movement is involved in basic posture, walking, gross movement of the shoulder-arm area, etc.

PVA—Paralyzed Veterans of America   A relatively old, well-established organization designed to lobby for the interests of veterans with spinal cord injuries. It is one of the most viable and active consumer groups among the severely disabled (Howell, 1978b). Its nature and work are detailed in Chapter 8.

SCI—spinal cord injury or spinal-cord-injured A group of disabilities whose origin was some traumatic injury involving the spinal cord, or a person having such disabilities. Such injuries usually result in paralysis or the loss of function of certain body parts, particularly the limbs. In connection with SCI, the degree of body impairment is largely determined by the site of the injury, i.e., how high or low the injury occurs. In this book, frequent reference is made to a C4 injury, a T2 injury, etc. What do these mean? The spinal cord is divided anatomically into four major areas or *segments*. These segments are named according to the vertebrae they include, but can also refer to the spinal nerves coming out of the vertebral column. The four main segments are the cervical (C), thoracic (T), lumbar (L), and sacral (S). (There is also a fifth segment, the coccygeal, or tail-bone). There are seven cervical (neck) vertebrae. Emerging from between these seven neck vertebrae are eight spinal nerves. From the thoracic area on down, the spinal nerves directly correspond to the segmental vertebrae, i.e., there are twelve thoracic (chest) vertebrae and twelve thoracic nerves, five lumbar vertebrae and five lumbar (lower back) nerves, and finally, five sacral vertebrae and five sacral nerves. There is also one coccygeal spinal nerve. Designations such as C5, T2, S1, then, are ways of indicating the site of a spinal cord injury. Except for the cervical area, such designations are rather clear-cut. A T2 spinal cord injury involves some damage, trauma, etc., to the second thoracic vertebra. In regard to the cervical area specifically, damage to a cervical vertebra usually entails damage to the spinal nerve directly below it, i.e., damage to the seventh cervical vertebra will involve the eighth cervical nerve. As a general rule, the higher the level of injury, the greater the loss of function. Damage in the cervical area, then, involves all four limbs plus other functions. Therefore a C5 injury is usually more debilitating than a T2, for example (Freed, 1965). When reference is made in the text to a C, T, L, or S followed by a number, such a reference is to the exact location of an SCI. It is important to remember the following principles:

C1–C8:   most severe or debilitating
T1–T12:   less severe than Cs, more severe than Ls
L1–L5:   less severe than Ts, more severe than Ss
S1–S5:   least severe

Severity is used here in the sense of remaining general function. As is alluded to in the chapter on sex, however, S2–S4 and L1 and L3 have a critical role, particularly in male sexual functioning.

ST—speech therapy or speech therapist Terms referring to a specialized field and to professionals working in the field. The primary responsibility of this field is to enhance the individual's abilities in the general area of communication skills.

TTY—teletypewriter This is a device enabling nonhearing individuals to type or receive a message by telephone. The devices are usually installed in critical offices and agencies, such as fire and police departments. Through specialized techniques, the deaf can transmit and receive displayed messages over telephone lines (Dunham, 1978).

VA—Veterans Administration In this book, a term referring specifically to hospitals operated by the Veterans Administration. In some contexts, VA refers to the general organization, which provides a number of services to veterans other than hospitalization and medical care.

CONVENTIONAL TERMS

In this section, "conventional terms" refers to words, phrases, and other concepts used routinely in discussing the psychosocial aspects of physically disabling conditions. The definitions offered in this section will orient the reader to the usage of terms in this text. We have strived to make these definitions simple, since our purpose is to give the reader a general idea of what is meant by such terms.

Accessibility   A concept dealing with architectural and other barriers. Specifically, it refers to whether or not a disabled individual on crutches or in a wheelchair is able to move in and out of a building or other facility easily. "Intangible" accessibility concerns attitudinal and prejudicial barriers which stem from individuals' thinking and beliefs. Generally, accessibility relates to the degree of freedom disabled individuals have to come and go as they please.

Curb cut   A phrase used in discussing architectural barriers and accessibility. Specifically, it refers to the process of beveling out a portion of a concrete curb, usually along a sidewalk. Such beveling creates a gradual slope toward the street in lieu of the usual drop-off at the curb. In appearance, curb cuts resemble small, narrow driveways. They make it possible for individuals in wheelchairs to descend from the sidewalk to the street gradually. Curb cuts are superior to temporary, wedge-shaped ramps, which fit against a curb but which can be moved, crushed, or otherwise damaged.

Deinstitutionalization   This is one of the administrative implications of the concept of normalization. It is a process by which an individual is moved from a residential institution setting to a more "normative" community setting. The operating principle of this process is that "normal" behavior is fostered mainly within "normal" community settings. Deinstitutionalization, then, is the process of integrating an individual into a community setting to foster better adjustment.

504   This refers to a section of the Rehabilitation Act of 1973 prohibiting discrimination on the basis of handicap. As is elaborated upon in Chapter 9, there has been much controversy and debate concerning the application of this section. In general, 504 refers to civil rights for the handicapped in reference to services, employment, accessibility, etc.

Freak   Although this term has other meanings as commonly used in the vernacular, it is here used to designate persons with unusual and rare deformities of the body. In this sense, it pertains mainly to those individuals who can often be found in circus sideshows.

Hand controls   This phrase refers to a set of devices which permit an individual without the use of his legs to operate an automobile. Through the installation of certain instruments on or around the steering wheel of a car, a driver can operate by hand the accelerator, brake, clutch (if any), and other automotive controls otherwise operated with the feet.

Independent living   A phrase that may refer either to a goal or to a state. As a goal, this phrase refers to the rehabilitation of an individual to the point of being able to live and maintain himself or herself without outside assistance. As a state, this phrase refers to the level of skill in self-management enabling an individual to maintain himself or herself without outside assistance.

Level (of injury)   "Level" refers to the site of an injury to the spinal cord. The higher the injury (meaning the nearer to the shoulder, neck, or head), the more pervasive the loss of function. Understood with this term, then, is the phrase "of injury." Lower-level injuries refer to the lower chest, back, or pelvic region sites.

Mainstreaming   As discussed in Chapter 10, "mainstreaming" can be used to denote both a goal of special education and the process by which this goal is attained. In general, this term refers to the disabled's entering into daily activities with nondisabled individuals, particularly, in this sense, in an educational situation. In legislative terminology, this refers to educating a child in "the least restrictive environment." As a goal, mainstreaming refers to an educational process in which individuals attain not only basic academic skills but also those social interaction skills assumed essential to allow them to take their place in the mainstream of society. As a process, mainstreaming is an educational administrative plan in which "special" students are afforded the opportunity, to the maximum of their ability, to be educated in the "least restrictive (special) environment."

Medical specialties   Throughout this book, reference is made to certain medical specialists involved in the physical aspects of rehabilitation. Such specialists all possess an M.D. degree and specialize in rehabilitation-related areas of medicine. A *physiatrist* is a physician who specializes in the area of physical medicine, an area whose purpose is the medical treatment of physical debilitating conditions such as spinal cord injury, cerebral palsy, muscular dystrophy, cerebrovascular accidents (strokes), etc. Physiatrists are trained in the rehabilitative management of these conditions. This specialty is a rather rare one, and physiatrists are usually found only in communities with large rehabilitation centers. A *urologist* is a physician specializing in conditions affecting the urinary-genital system. This specialty concentrates on conditions involving the kidneys, bladder, and male genitals, with the urologist often functioning as a male's counterpart of the female's gynecologist. A *neurologist* is a specialist in diseases and conditions of the nervous system. As opposed to a neurosurgeon, the neurologist specializes in the nonsurgical treatment and management of nervous system disorders. Other medical specialties are mentioned throughout this text; however, other specialties may be more familiar to the reader than the three defined here.

Modified van   A van-model vehicle which is designed to allow persons in wheelchairs to drive. A van-type vehicle is more suitable for necessary modifications than a sedan automobile.

Normal   In this text, referring to an individual not possessing a physical disability or handicap. The term may also, in some contexts, refer to activities engaged in as part of the routine of most individuals' lives, i.e., shopping, employment, sexual relations, social activities, etc.

Normalization   Neisworth and Smith (1978) define "normalization" as ". . . the doctrine or conceptualization that goals for the mentally retarded should be as culturally normative as possible achieved through as culturally normative means as possible" (p. 545). This principle has also been applied to populations other than the retarded. In essence, this concept has been developed to promote the reintegration of special populations, such as the mentally retarded or the mentally ill, into the community from institutional settings.

Paralyze, paralysis   The process (paralyze) or the state (paralysis) involving the loss of function of a particular portion of the body. Such a process or state is usually brought about by some type of neurological damage and/or disease resulting in the loss of voluntary and/or involuntary control of the muscular function of the affected body parts. Paralysis can involve a large portion of the body or may be quite limited, affecting only one area of a limb or other body part. As a state or process, paralysis does not imply any degree of permanency.

Paraplegia   Technically, a term referring to the paralaysis and/or total loss of function of both lower limbs (legs). Such an impairment or loss may result from a number of causes. For example, a person whose cerebral palsy affected only the legs could be described as functioning as a paraplegic, as could an individual with both legs affected from rheumatoid arthritis. However, paraplegia usually describes loss of function in the legs due to some type of neurological condition, particularly spinal cord injury.

Quadriplegia   A term technically referring to the paralysis and/or the loss of functioning of both arms and both legs. Therefore, this term could apply equally to an individual with cerebral palsy which affects all four limbs or to an individual who has lost his arms and legs through amputation. Throughout this text, however, except when otherwise indicated, this term refers to the partial or total loss of function of the four limbs due to spinal cord injury. Frequently, this term is shortened to *quad*. It should always be remembered, however, that in actuality this term merely refers to the number of limbs affected by a condition and not to a specific condition.

Ramps   This term refers to sloping grades which replace steps in architectural function. A ramp makes it possible for an individual on crutches or in a wheelchair to ascend or descend from a building entrance above ground level, through a gradual sloping grade. Ramps may be permanent or temporary in structure.

Respite care   Respite care is a term denoting temporary, round-the-clock care for severely disabled individuals. As the name implies, the reason for such care is to grant temporary respite (rest) to those individuals normally responsible for the provision of care to the disabled. For example, parents of a severely disabled child or the family of a severely disabled adult, both of whom require constant care and attention, can place such a disabled individual in a respite facility for a weekend.

Return (of neurological function)   When people ask, "How much 'return' can we expect?" they are referring to the reacquisition of neurological functions after some type of traumatic injury to the nervous system. Most of these injuries are the result of cardiovascular accidents (strokes) or spinal cord injuries. In this book, return will generally be used to designate the regaining of lost neurological functions, whatever the reason for their reappearance.

Severely disabled   The definition for this phrase that will be followed in this book comes from the Rehabilitation Act of 1973, Pub. L. 93-112. In this act, the term defined is "severe handicap," which is defined as a ". . . disability which requires multiple services over an extended period of time and results from amputation, blindness, cancer, cerebral palsy, cystic fibrosis, deafness, heart disease, hemiplegia, mental retardation, mental illness, multiple sclerosis, muscular dystrophy, neurological disorders (including strokes and epilepsy), paraplegia, quadriplegia, and spinal cord conditions, renal failure, respiratory or pulmonary dysfunction . . ." (p. 7). Therefore, any conditions resulting from the impairments listed above will constitute "severe disability" in this book.

Severe physical disability   Severe physical disability is here defined as any severe disability resulting from a physical disease or condition. Therefore, this will include all conditions listed in the definition referred to in Pub. L. 93-112, except those resulting *primarily* from mental retardation or mental illness. In the current text, this term refers primarily, but not exclusively, to multiple amputation, cerebral palsy, blindness, deafness, or any neurological condition, as well as spinal cord injury.

Sheltered workshop, sheltered employment   A sheltered workshop is a facility designed primarily to employ disabled workers. Such workshops must be certified by the Department of Labor in order to pay subminimal wages. Although such facilities are optimally designed to afford an individual the opportunity to prepare for employment in the competitive labor market, many such facilities provide long-term, terminal employment for those who will never be capable of competing in the outside labor market. Employment in such a facility is termed sheltered employment. "Sheltered" in this sense means protected from the competition normally found in the competitive labor market (Kelly and Verguson, 1978).

Tranbus   A model mass transit vehicle specially designed for transporting the disabled, developed under the auspices of the U.S. Department of Transportation. A unique feature of this vehicle is its pneumatic shock absorbers on the front axle which will deflate, thus lowering the front of the vehicle to near ground level. A ramp also lowers to allow wheelchair passengers as well as the elderly, etc., to enter with minimal effort on their part. Due to the pneumatic (air) type of design, this vehicle is much quieter and more comfortable to ride than other buses.

Visually limited   A general term referring to persons having a visual defect that constitutes a substantial handicap to their general adjustment. Generally, this category is divided into two groups, based on the severity of visual limitation: the partially sighted and the blind (i.e., legally blind). The *partially sighted* have 20/70 to 20/200 central visual acuity in the better eye after correction, while *legal blindness* is defined as 20/200 or less central visual acuity and/or a restriction of visual range to less than 20°. It should be noted that, contrary to some persons' opinions, legal blindness does not imply total lack of sight (Dunham, 1978).

White House Conference (on Handicapped Individuals)   A nationwide conference held in Washington, D.C., in May 1977. This conference was attended by handicapped citizens, professionals in the field of rehabilitation, and other personnel concerned with the affairs of the nation's handicapped. The conferees grouped themselves into special interest groups, which produced position papers on what they felt to be the state of affairs in their interest area as well as recommendations for future trends and services. Three sets of documents—preconference working papers, a final report, and an implementation plan—were the products of this conference.

Personal Narratives of Disabled Individuals: An Annotated Bibliography

These references represent a partial, but by no means exhaustive, listing of books written by professionals, parents of disabled individuals, and disabled individuals themselves. Each reference has been rated according to the following system:

    * Poor
   ** Average
  *** Excellent

The ratings were assigned primarily on the basis of each book's usefulness as a resource tool for disabled individuals, parents of the disabled, and professionals.

** Armes, J. J. (as told to F. Nolan). *Jay J. Armes, Investigator*. New York: Avon, 1976. Paperback. 280 pp.
The fascinating autobiography of one of the greatest (and wealthiest) private detectives in the world—Jay J. Armes of El Paso, Texas. Armes tells the truly amazing story of how he lost both hands in an explosion when he was 12 years old, and how he accomplishes near miracles with two prosthetic devices.

** Bodenheimer, A. R. *Doris: The Story of a Disfigured Deaf Child*. Detroit: Wayne State University Press, 1974. 124 pp.

A psychotherapist's case study of a child in Germany, born deaf and with a severely disfigured face, who at puberty became psychotic. Through intensive psychotherapy, Doris gained a positive self-image and successfully overcame her serious emotional problems.

*** Blank, J. P. *19 Steps Up the Mountain: The Story of the DeBolt Family*. Philadelphia: Lippincott, 1976. 234 pp.
The heartwarming story of the DeBolts—a couple who had six biological children and adopted, in addition, many others, including Vietnamese and Korean refugees. Most of these adopted children were physically disabled—blind, paraplegic, or quadriplegic. A truly inspiring story.

** Breisky, W. *I Think I Can*. Garden City, N.Y.: Doubleday, 1974. 232 pp.
A father's account of his daughter's recovery, at the age of 25 months, from epiglottitis (a form of croup), which left her with massive brain damage—unable to talk, see, or move. After five years of intensive therapy and patterning, Karen recovered much of her sight and mobility.

** Brown, C. *Down All the Days*. Greenwich, Conn.: Fawcett, 1970. Paperback. 223 pp.
A well-written novel by a severely cerebral-palsied man (who types with the little toe of his left foot) about his boyhood in Ireland.

* Browning, E. *I Can't See What You're Saying*. New York: Coward-McCann & Geoghegan, 1973. 196 pp.
An English mother tells of her trials in attempting to obtain appropriate schooling for her partially deaf, aphasic son.

*** Buck, P. S. *The Child Who Never Grew*. New York: John Day, 1950. 62 pp.
A touching story by Pearl S. Buck about her mentally retarded daughter, and the difficult decision she had to make about placing her in an institution.

** Calkins, E. E. *"Louder, Please!"* Boston: Atlantic Monthly, 1924. 260 pp.
A deaf man's autobiography from his early school years to the age of 54. Geared especially to the deaf and hearing-impaired.

** Cameron, C. C. *A Different Drum*. Englewood Cliffs, N.J.: Prentice-Hall, 1973. 241 pp.
This book deals primarily with the way in which a mother, through constant effort and patience, taught her 3-year-old son basic language and number concepts after learning that he suffered from a severe form of expressive and receptive aphasia.

** Campanella, R. *It's Good To Be Alive*. Boston: Little, Brown, 1959. Paperback. 288 pp.
A play-by-play review of Roy Campanella's life before and after the automobile accident which left him almost totally paralyzed from the neck down.

** Carson, M. *Ginny*. Garden City, N.Y.: Doubleday, 1971. 211 pp.
A mother's poignant story of her 5-year-old child's recovery from serious, almost fatal, brain damage as the result of being hit by a truck.

* de Vries-Kruyt, T. *A Special Gift: The Story of Jan*. New York: Peter H. Wyden, 1966. 115 pp.
The story of an unusual Down's-syndrome child who learned to read, write, and play musical instruments, and who lived to be 25 years of age.

** Eareckson, J. *Joni*. Minneapolis: World Wide Publications, 1976. 190 pp.
The story of a 17-year-old girl who broke her neck in a diving accident and became

a quadriplegic confined to a wheelchair. Joni tells how her strong religious faith helped her overcome depression and become a successful artist who paints with a brush held in her teeth.

*** Greenberg, J. *In This Sign*. New York: Avon, 1970. Paperback. 289 pp.
The author of *I Never Promised You a Rose Garden* tells the fascinating and utterly believable story of a young deaf-mute couple and their struggle to survive, keep their jobs, and raise a family in the "World of the Hearing."

*** Greenfeld, J. *A Child Called Noah: A Family Journey*. New York: Holt, 1970. 191 pp.
This book is an excellent chronicle of a young autistic boy named Noah, written by his father. Noah's slow motor development and his gradual loss of speech are described; the despair of his family and the difficulties imposed upon them by his emotional disturbance are portrayed in graphic detail.

*** Greenfeld, J. *A Place for Noah*. New York: Holt, 1978. 310 pp.
This sequel to *A Child Called Noah*, covering Noah's fifth to eleventh years, reflects the pain and traumas involved for brain-injured (or autistic) children and their families. The author, Noah's father, describes the parents' growing realization that Noah will eventually have to be institutionalized, and their search for a humane, caring atmosphere for their son.

** Johnson, E. L., and M. Miller. *Shannon: A Book for Parents of Children with Leukemia*. New York: Hawthorn, 1975. 127 pp.
A small child's three-year battle with leukemia (currently still in remission) is well told in alternating chapters by her pediatrician and her grandmother.

*** Kaufman, B. N. *Son-Rise*. New York: Warner Books, 1977. Paperback. 221 pp.
The story of a young couple who, against all odds and professional advice, transformed their autistic son from a mute, lost child to a loving, aware, articulate young boy.

*** Keller, H. *The Story of My Life*. New York: Dell, 1954. Paperback. 406 pp.
Helen Keller's own story of her rescue from the prison of blindness and deafness by Miss Annie Sullivan, her devoted teacher. The book contains a brief autobiography written by Miss Keller as a sophomore in college, letters of Annie Sullivan, and editors' comments.

*** Killilea, M. *Karen*. New York: Dell, 1952. Paperback. 286 pp.
A warm and humorous biography of Karen Killilea, who was born with severe cerebral palsy and overcame many obstacles in her efforts to walk and talk like other children.

*** Kirkendall, D., and M. P. Warren. *Bottom High to the Crowd*. New York: Walker & Co., 1973. 222 pp.
An excellent and realistic autobiography of a man who lost the use of both legs and one arm and was confined to a wheelchair as a result of polio contracted at the age of 4. With a great deal of spirit, he tells of the personal and business failures he endured before ultimately achieving a successful business, a happy marriage, and three healthy children.

** Kiser, B. *New Light of Hope*. New Canaan, Conn.: Keats, 1974. 223 pp.
The story of a severely cerebral-palsied individual who, after an ill-fated laser beam operation which significantly increases the severity of his disability, ultimately succeeds in his struggle to live semi-independently.

*** Kovic, R. *Born on the Fourth of July*. New York: McGraw-Hill, 1976. Paperback. 224 pp.
A compelling biography of a Vietnam veteran's disillusionment after returning from the war as a paraplegic.

*** Krents, H. *To Race the Wind*. New York: Putnam, 1972. 282 pp.
An autobiography written by the blind man, Harold Krents, who inspired the Broadway play *Butterflies Are Free*. The author relates the story of his progress from total blindness at the age of 8 to graduation from Harvard Law School.

*** Landvater, D. *David*. Englewood Cliffs, N.J.: Prentice-Hall, 1976. 157 pp.
A mother's story of her 17-year-old son's near-fatal automobile accident and the resulting brain damage. Although at first David could not move, speak, hear, or see, he progressed in 3½ years to almost total recovery.

*** Lund, D. *Eric*. New York: Dell, 1974. Paperback. 267 pp.
A well-written biography of a 17-year-old boy who suddenly became a man when faced with the fact that he was dying of leukemia.

** Luria, A. R. *The Man with a Shattered World*. New York: Basic Books, 1972. 160 pp.
Renowned Russian psychologist A. R. Luria tells the story of a young soldier's severe brain injury (in the left hemisphere) that resulted in impaired vision, loss of memory, and aphasia. Much is drawn from the patient's own diary written over a period of 25 years, during which some, but not all, of his abilities were recovered.

* Marx, J. L. *Keep Trying*. New York: Harper & Row, 1974. 193 pp.
An autobiography of a man who was stricken with polio at the age of 3. Now in his sixties, he is a professional writer and author of several books and many articles.

*** Massie, R., and S. Massie. *Journey*. New York: Warner Books, 1976. Paperback. 459 pp.
An exceptionally well written biography of a young boy's battle with hemophilia, written by his parents, who are both authors. Of special interest are the Massies' experiences in attempting to obtain blood in various parts of the United States for transfusions for their son.

** Napear, P. *Brain Child: A Mother's Diary*. New York: Harper & Row, 1974. 432 pp.
A blow-by-blow chronicle of a mother's experiences in using the Doman-Delacatto method of patterning for her three children. The youngest is brain-injured, spastic, functionally deaf and blind, cross-eyed, and hyperactive; another suffers from a severe stuttering problem; and a third has a mild learning disability.

*** Nasaw, J. L. *Easy Walking*. Philadelphia: Lippincott, 1975. 224 pp.
A humorous, salty, and starkly realistic account of a young man's experiences in being "rehabilitated" after an automobile accident at the age of 21 left him paralyzed from the waist down.

** Nason, M., and D. Nason. *Tara*. New York: Hawthorn Books, Inc., 1974. 160 pp.
The authors' story of their 2-year-old daughter's skull fracture which resulted in severe brain damage. Through intensive patterning therapy, she progressed in 3 years from a comatose state to normal functioning in every area except mobility and hand functioning.

* Pruet, R., and M. S. Pruet. *Run from the Pale Pony*. Grand Rapids, Mich.: Baker Book House, 1976. 159 pp.

The story of a man who developed MS (multiple sclerosis) in the prime of life, told by the "victim" and his wife. The book centers around the Pruets' strong religious faith and how it has helped them meet many challenges and adversities.

** Resnick, R. *Sun and Shadow*. New York: Atheneum, 1975. 274 pp.
The autobiography of a talented and creative woman who, blinded at the age of 2, obtained several college degrees and was instrumental in establishing camps and recreational services for blind children and adults.

** Sanderlin, O. *Johnny*. New York: Pyramid Publications, 1968. Paperback. 144 pp.
Notes taken from the diary of a 15-year-old boy whose parents were told when he was 11 years old that he would not live more than fifteen months. He survived in spite of his leukemia for almost four years, even winning the National Doubles Championship in tennis.

*** Spradley, T. S., and J. P. Spradley. *Deaf Like Me*. New York: Random House, 1978. 280 pp.
An excellent story of a "rubella baby," Lynn Spradley, who was born profoundly deaf. Written by her father, the book chronicles the struggle of Lynn and her parents to communicate with each other, and tells of the dramatic breakthrough they achieved when Lynn began to use sign language.

*** Tidyman, E. *Dummy*. New York: Little, Brown, 1974. Paperback. 241 pp.
The true story of an illiterate deaf-mute who cannot defend himself against the charges of murdering two young women.

** Ulrich, S. *Elizabeth*. Ann Arbor: University of Michigan Press, 1972. 122 pp.
A mother's story of how her 5-year-old daughter, blind from birth, learned to compensate for her lack of vision and became eligible for a "normal" preschool at a young age.

** Viscardi, H., Jr. *The Phoenix Child: A Story of Love*. New York: Paul S. Eriksson, Inc., 1975. 208 pp.
A well-known educator, himself handicapped (legless), tells the story of a small black boy named Warren who was born missing one eye and one ear, and with a cleft palate and a harelip. His experiences in a warm, loving foster family give him the chance to become healthy, active, and well adjusted.

*** White, R. *Be Not Afraid*. New York: Dial, 1972. 235 pp.
A father's story about his son Checkers' life as a normal child until the age of 8, when severe epileptic seizures began. The book centers around Checkers' emotional and mental difficulties as the result of the medication he was forced to take, and his family's alternating courage and despair in dealing with his behavior.

*** Willis, J., and M. Willis. *"But There Are Always Miracles."* Greenwich, Conn.: Fawcett, 1974. Paperback. 238 pp.
An excellent account of a young man's almost complete recovery from a broken neck caused by a surfing accident, written by himself and his fiancee (now his wife).

*** Wilson, D. C. *Hilary: The Brave World of Hilary Pole*. New York: McGraw-Hill, 1972. 259 pp.
The story of a 21-year-old woman whose bout with myasthenia gravis left her with no physical functions except a slight movement of her toes. With the aid of an environmental control unit, she became able to communicate because of her unflagging desire to reach the outside world.

** Valens, E. G. *The Other Side of the Mountain*. New York: Warner Books, 1975. Paperback. 301 pp.

The true story of Jill Kinmont, the world-famous skier who became a quadriplegic at the age of 18 due to a skiing accident. The book relates Jill's story of her life as a disabled young adult and her decision to become an elementary school teacher.

** Valens, E. G. *The Other Side of the Mountain II*. New York: Warner Books, 1978. Paperback. 270 pp.

The sequel to *The Other Side of the Mountain*, this book is based on the motion picture by the same name. It follows Jill Kinmont's life as she becomes a successful teacher and marries a young man in her home town, John Boothe.

Addresses for Action

ADDRESSES

Addresses of agencies and procedures for seeking other relevant action or information can be found in *Access*, by Lilly Bruck (New York: Random House, 1978). $12.95 cloth, $5.95 paper.

BARRIERS

To file a complaint about an inaccessible federal building or a building built with some federal funds, write to:

> Executive Director
> Architectural and Transportation Barriers Compliance Board
> Washington, DC   20201

Include as much of the following information as possible:

1 Description of why the building is inaccessible
2 Description of the location of the barriers within or preventing entrance to the building
3 Name and telephone number of the person responsible for the building
4 Name of the building's owner
5 Name of the building's tenant

6 Name of the federal agency involved
7 Any suggestions you have for eliminating the problem

EMPLOYMENT

To file a complaint on behalf of a client who you believe has been discriminated against under Section 503 or Section 504 of the 1973 Rehabilitation Act, write:

1 *Under Section 503 (affirmative action)*
   Office of Federal Contract Compliance Programs
   U.S. Department of Labor
   Washington, DC   20210
2 *Under Section 504 (nondiscrimination)*
   Office for Civil Rights
   U.S. Department of Health, Education, and Welfare
   Washington, DC   20201

Include the following:

1 Name, address, and telephone number
2 Nature of disability
3 Name and address of organization which discriminated
4 Nature of discriminatory action
5 The date of such action. (Complaints must be filed within 180 days.)
6 Any additional background information
7 How the discriminatory action was harmful to the complainant
8 escription of previous efforts made to resolve complaints
9 Name and address of person involved in taking discriminatory action
10 Copies of correspondence or papers substantiating the complaint
11 Signature of person who has been discriminated against

FUNDING

Architectural Barriers Removal, A HEW Pub. No. (OHDS) 79-22006.
   Department of Health, Education, and Welfare
   Washington, DC   20201
   A free guide to resources, funding, and federal publications.

Public Interest Law Center of Philadelphia
1315 Walnut Street, 16th Floor
Philadelphia, PA   19107
   Will provide the information needed to apply for and obtain federal funding for accessible buses.

Films for Professionals in Training

FILMS ON ACCESSIBILITY

1 *Access*
> Social Planning and Review Council of British Columbia
> 2210 West 12th Avenue
> Vancouver, B.C.
> V6K 2N6 Canada

2 *Accessibility Barriers: Problems, Solutions and Code Requirements*
> Special Office for the Handicapped
> P.O. Box 26387
> Raleigh, NC   27611

3 *Beating the Averages*   (27 minutes)
Depicts difficulties of persons using wheelchairs when they attempt to move around in inaccessible homes, offices, and factories. USNAC. LC No. 71-708584.
> United States National Audiovisual Center
> General Services Administration
> Washington, DC   20409

4 *Walk Awhile in My Shoes*
Underlines problems that inaccessible transportation systems, inaccessible buildings, and public attitudes create for disabled persons in our society.

> The Stanfield House
> P.O. Box 3208
> Santa Monica, CA   90403

FILMS ON ACTIVITIES OF DAILY LIVING

1 *Ability—Not Disability*
Series of twelve 15-minute films on housekeeping with a variety of disabilities.

> Visual Aids Library of the Architectural Extension Service
> University of Minnesota
> St. Paul, MI   55108

2 *A Blind Teacher in a Public School*   (23½ minutes)
A teacher, legally blind from birth, shows how he carries out his daily responsibilities as a full-time teacher of seventh-grade English. His teaching methods are explained, and the advantages a blind teacher may bring to a classroom are explored. 31FB689. $17.50 rental.

> International Film Bureau
> 332 South Michigan Avenue
> Chicago, IL   60604

3 *Blindness Is*
Shows blind children engaging in everyday activities as they develop the confidence to lead a normal life. UIOWA.

> University of Iowa
> Audio-Visual Center
> C-5 East Hall
> Iowa City, IA   52240

4 *A Day in the Life of Bonnie Consolo*   (17 minutes)
Follows a housewife who was born without arms and who uses no prosthetic devices as she cooks, barbers her children's hair, drives an unmodified car, and does her grocery shopping. As she goes about her daily routine, she discusses both her reactions and the reactions of others to her disability. BARR.

> Barr Films
> 3490 E. Foothill Blvd.
> Pasadena, CA   91107

5 *A Different Approach*
A humorous, exceptionally effective approach to promoting the employment of persons with all types of disabilities.

> Modern Talking Pictures
> 4705-F Bakers Ferry Road
> Atlanta, GA   30336

6 *A Matter of Inconvenience*   (10 minutes)
Film of blind and amputee skiers which demonstrates that a disability does not have to be a handicap.

The Stanfield House
P.O. Box 3208
Santa Monica, CA   90403

7   *One Step at a Time*   (16 minutes)
Shows the most recent techniques in the design and fitting of artificial limbs.
International Film Bureau
332 South Michigan Avenue
Chicago, IL   60604

8   *Out of Silence*   (38 minutes)
Shows how the Montreal Oral School for the Deaf teaches deaf children to communicate.
The Stanfield House
P.O. Box 3208
Santa Monica, CA   90403

9   a   *Quadriplegic Functional Skills: Dressing*   (17 minutes)
    b   *Quadriplegic Functional Skills: Bowel and Bladder Techniques*   (14 minutes)
    c   *Quadriplegic Functional Skills: Showering and Grooming*   (14 minutes)
    d   *Quadriplegic Functional Skills: Driving*   (18 minutes)
Media Resources Branch
National Medical Audiovisual Center (Annex)
Station K
Atlanta, GA   30324

10   *The Triumph of Christy Brown*   (60 minutes)
Traces the life of author and painter Christy Brown, who has cerebral palsy which allows him control over only his left foot. IU. LC No. 71-711458.
Indiana University
Audio-Visual Center
Bloomington, IN   47401

11   *Where There's a Will*   (29 minutes)
Shows (1) a man with artificial hands demonstrating his hobby of cooking, and (2) two disabled housewives who demonstrate how disabled persons can manage a home. VRA. LC No. 74-705950.
Vocational Rehabilitation Administration
U.S. Department of Health, Education, and Welfare
Washington, DC   20420

FILMS ON PSYCHOSOCIAL ASPECTS OF DISABILITY

1   *Access*   (23 minutes)
A portrayal of the struggles of two totally disabled persons to overcome the physical and emotional barriers between them and a satisfying, productive life.
Polymorph Films
331 Newbury Street
Boston, MA   02115

2 *Blindness*   (28 minutes)
Traces the process of adjustment to blindness which develops in adulthood. Shows how the central character learns to cope with blindness and resume his responsibilities as a wage earner, husband, and father. EBEC.
 Encyclopaedia Britannica Educational Corp.
 425 N. Michigan Avenue
 Chicago, IL   60611

3 *Della*   (12 minutes)
Shows the deterioration of a deaf paraplegic prior to her rehabilitation. After learning to live with her handicaps, she demonstrates her ability to live independently and to help the deaf children who live in her community.
 Sister Kenny Institute
 Chicago Avenue at 27th Street
 Minneapolis, MN   55404

4 *A Family of Friends*
Explains the everyday lives of mentally retarded young adults who live in a group home.
 Richfield Production Services, Inc.
 8006 Takoma Ave.
 Silver Spring, MD   20910

5 *I Am Not What You See*
A psychologist who is a quadriplegic from cerebral palsy tells of her fight for social and professional acceptance.
 CBC Educational Films
 P.O. Box 500, Terminal "A"
 Toronto, Ont.
 M5W 1E6 Canada

6 *Like Other People*   (37 minutes)
An outstanding film which deals with the sexual, emotional, and social needs of severely physically disabled persons. Centering on the relationship between a man and a woman with severe cerebral palsy, this film touches on many issues of concern to professionals, e.g., the need to work, the right to marry, the quality of life in residential homes and institutions. Although the central characters have speech impediments, the film contains few subtitles. Because one of the major problems facing persons with severe cerebral palsy is communication, the assumption of the film is that struggling to understand the speech of the main characters is an important learning experience. Most persons should be able to understand the palsied speech fully in 8 minutes. Film scripts, however, are available upon request.
 Perennial Education, Inc.
 1825 Willow Road
 Northfield, IL   60093

7 *Meeting the Challenge of Blindness*   (26 minutes)
Four persons from diverse backgrounds—a career woman, a homemaker, a working husband, and a retired businessman—demonstrate how they cope with their blindness.

Seeing Eye Inc.
Office of Public Information
9 Rockefeller Plaza
New York, NY   10020

8   *Mimi*   (12 minutes)
A young woman, paralyzed from birth, talks about her life and how the nondisabled
relate to her.
Billy Budd Films, Inc.
235 East 57th Street
New York, NY   10022

9   *No Whistles, No Bells, No Bedlam*   (20 minutes)
Exploration of the myths concerning the employment of deaf persons.
National Technical Institute of the Deaf
Rochester Institute of Technology
1 Lomb Memorial Drive
Rochester, NY   14623

10   *A Talk with Irene*   (30 minutes)
A teenage epileptic discusses her fears and problems relating to other persons. GROVE.
Grove Press–Cinema 16 Film Library
196 West Houston Street
New York, NY   10014

11   *Views of Impaired Vision*   (43 minutes)
Explains the psychological impact of visual impairments.
Film Distributors Supervisor
Ohio State University
Dept. of Photographs and Cinema
156 West 19th Avenue
Columbus, OH   43210

12   *What Do You Do When You See a Blind Person?*
Humorous treatment of the correct and incorrect ways of interacting with and offer-
ing help to blind persons.
Public Education Division
American Foundation for the Blind
15 West 16th Street
New York, NY   10011

FILMS ON SEXUALITY

1   *Don't Tell the Cripples About Sex*
Multi Media Resource Center
340 Jones Street #439F
San Francisco, CA   94102

2 *Just What Can You Do?* (23 minutes)
A group discussion in which spinal-cord-injured persons and their spouses discuss the sexuality of the disabled and how the nondisabled view the sexual attraction and opportunities for sexual fulfillment of disabled persons.

    Multi Media Resource Center
    340 Jones Street #439F
    San Francisco, CA   94102

3 *Sexuality and the Spinal Cord Injured Person*
    Multi Media Resource Center
    340 Jones Street #439F
    San Francisco, CA   94102

4 *Touching* (17 minutes)
A husband who acquired a C6 spinal cord injury seven years ago and his wife of three years demonstrate the sexual activities which allow them to gratify each other.

    Multi Media Resource Center
    340 Jones Street #439F
    San Francisco, CA   94102

OTHER FILM SOURCES

The following organizations publish directories of films which are especially relevant to rehabilitation educators:

1 *Educator's Guide to Free Films*
    Educators Progress Service
    Randolph, WI   53956

2 *Rehabilitation Film Library Catalogue*
    International Rehabilitation Film Review Catalogue
    20 West 49th Street
    New York, NY   10018

Selected Sources for Professionals

Accent on Living
P.O. Box 700
Bloomington, IL   61701
$5.00 per year

Published four times a year, this magazine is a unique combination of product information, legislative updates, independent living advice (such as how to care for a baby from a wheelchair), leisure-time activities (such as amputee skiing), and other matters of vital importance to the severely physically disabled and those professionals who work with them.

Accent on Living Buyer's Guide
Accent Special Publications
Box 700
Bloomington, IL   61701

A compilation of products and sources of products needed to enhance the living skills of severely disabled persons. This book attempts to bring together in one handy volume sources of aids and information which would otherwise have to be tracked down individually. 70 pp. $10.00

Access: The Guide to a Better Life for Disabled Americans. Bruck, Lillian. New York: Random House, 1978.

A consumer's guide for the disabled and those who teach the disabled practical living skills.

Amicus
>   National Center for Law and the Handicapped, Inc.
>   1235 N. Eddy Street
>   South Bend, IN   46617
>   Bimonthly. $10 for individuals, $12 for organizations

Monitors developments in the law, specifically court cases and legislation, as they relate to the rights of handicapped individuals. Frequently publishes articles on topical issues of interest to handicapped persons, with reports on federal and state legislation, litigation, problem areas, and forecasts of future developments.

Closer Look
>   National Information Center for the Handicapped
>   Box 1492
>   Washington, DC   20013

A free informational pamphlet published by the Bureau of Education for the Handicapped. The center itself offers an information service designed for parents but available to professionals on a limited basis. The service includes referral to publications on specific disabilities and helping organizations, suggestions as how to locate needed services, and provision of facts about legislation affecting the disabled. *Closer Look* also provides technical assistance to groups of disabled persons and to parents who are attempting to organize effective groups of their own.

Handicapped Americans Report
>   2626 Pennsylvania Ave., N.W.
>   Washington, DC   20037
>   Biweekly. $111 per year

Comprehensive survey of federal laws, regulations, and policy of interest to handicapped individuals. Details agency activities, including funding, programs, and compliance with important regulations. Reports on significant court rulings and compliance efforts of organizations affected by federal regulations.

Housing and Home Services for the Disabled. Laurie, G. Hagerstown, Maryland: Harper & Row, 1977.

A comprehensive work which should be included in every rehabilitation professional's library. In addition to various plans for home modifications or designs, Laurie's book covers such topics as attendant care, alternate living arrangements, housing projects which have succeeded and those which have failed, legislation, and self-care devices. 432 pp. $20.00.

A List of Guidebooks for Handicapped Travelers
>   President's Committee on Employment of the Handicapped
>   Washington, DC   20210

A listing of eighty cities in the United States, Canada, and some European countries, with addresses of organizations which publish guidebooks for these cities.

Paraplegia News
>   935 Coastline Dr.
>   Seal Beach, CA
> $4.50, published monthly

Contains texts of testimony in Congressional hearings, the latest in assistive devices and products for the severely disabled with mobility limitations, and a miscellany of useful information and survival tips.

Planning for Accessibility: A Guide to Developing and Implementing Campus Transition Plans
Association of Physical Plant Administrators of Universities and Colleges
Suite 250, Eleven Dupont Circle
Washington, DC   20036
An 88-page illustrated manual for implementing HEW regulations for Section 504 of the Rehabilitation Act of 1973.

Programs for the Handicapped
Office for Handicapped Individuals
3380 Hubert H. Humphrey Building
200 Independence Ave., S.W.
Washington, DC   20201
A general newsletter booklet giving information regarding recently enacted legislation, information sources, and general news in regard to the handicapped.

Rehabilitation Gazette
4502 Maryland Ave.
St. Louis, MO   63108
Published yearly. $3 disabled, $5 nondisabled
An international journal which contains up-to-date consumer surveys of assistive aids and devices. The section titled "Potpourri" is an especially useful source of new publications and otherwise hard-to-obtain information for any rehabilitation professional.

Sexuality and Disability
Purdue University
Human Sciences Press
72 Fifth Ave.
New York, NY   10011
$15 individuals, $35 institutions
A new journal dealing with the sexuality of mentally and physically disabled persons.

The Source Book for the Disabled. Hale, G. (ed.). New York: Paddington Press, 1979.
An illustrated guide to easier, more independent living for physically disabled persons. Comprehensive in nature, it has sections on housing design, adaptive aids, and disability management that will be particularly useful to the special educator or those who work with disabled persons in medical or vocational rehabilitation settings.

The Wheelchair Traveler. Annand, Douglass.
Bay Hill Road
Milford, NH   03055
Over 3500 listings from the United States and some foreign countries of hotels, motels, restaurants, and tourist attractions that are accessible to those with some mobility impairment, i.e., those who are ambulatory but have heart or pulmonary disorders; amputees; arthritics; and those who use wheelchairs.

Word from Washington
Suite 141, Chester Arthur Building
425 I Street, N.W.
Washington, DC   20001
Sponsored by the United Cerebral Palsy Association, the Epilepsy Foundation of America, and the National Society for Autistic Children, this monthly newsletter discusses recent and proposed legislation and the implications of that legislation.

You Can Do It From a Wheelchair. Gilbert, Arlene E. New Rochelle, N.Y.: Arlington
    House, 1973. $6.95.
A wife and mother shares her experiences and techniques for cooking, cleaning, and caring
for her children from a wheelchair.

Index

Name Index

Subject Index